LAW & THE MODERN MIND

Law & the Modern Mind

Jerome Frank

With a new introduction by
Brian H. Bix

Transaction Publishers
New Brunswick (U.S.A.) and London (U.K.)

New material this edition copyright © 2009 by Transaction Publishers, New Brunswick, N. J.
Copyright © 1930 originally published by Brentano's, Inc.

Library of Congress Catalog Number: 2008027423
ISBN: 978-1-4128-0830-9
Printed in the United States of America

Library of Congress Cataloging-in-Publication

Frank, Jerome, 1889-1957.
  Law and the modern mind / Jerome Frank.
    p. cm.
  Originally published: New York : Brentano's, c1930. With a new introd. by Brian H. Bix.
  Includes bibliographical references and index.
  ISBN 978-1-4128-0830-9 (alk. paper)
    1. Law—Psychological aspects. 2. Jurisprudence. I. Title.

K346.F73 2008
340'.19--dc22

2008027423

To
Florence Kiper Frank
and
Clara Frank

CONTENTS

INTRODUCTION TO THE
TRANSACTION EDITION

Jerome Frank (1889-1957) was the most distinctive voice among the American legal realists, and his prominence in that movement was second only to his sometime co-author Karl Llewellyn,[1] though today he is probably less well known (and less frequently read) than Llewellyn.[2] *Law and the Modern Mind* (1930, preface to sixth printing written in 1948[3] for the 1949 revised edition), along with *Courts on Trial* (1949a), are the works for which he is best known.[4] Frank's works are consistently provocative, accessible, and refreshing; readers may not always agree with his conclusions but (unlike most legal scholars, of both his time and our own) one never leaves his work either bored or mystified.

The contrast between Frank and Llewellyn is telling. Llewellyn's name is associated with the Uniform Commercial Code, the uniform law that (with revisions and amendments) continues to govern American commercial transactions, and Llewellyn is also associated with terms like "situation sense" and "the Grand Style" of judging. The mention of Jerome Frank's name will not bring up any comparable list from legal practitioners, or even from most legal academics. On the whole, if he is remembered at all it is usually a half-formed memory of caricatured strange views about judges and judging.[5] Yet, in many ways, Frank was both more of a mainstream figure in his life and a more radical figure in his ideas than Llewellyn (and, for that matter, than most of his realist colleagues), as will be discussed further below. Frank's "mainstream" life included many years in a conventional corporate/business law practice in Chicago and New York, government work as the head of a federal governmental agency (chair of the Securities and Exchange Commission), and a position as a federal appellate judge (U.S.

Court of Appeals for the Second Circuit, 1941-1957) (Glennon 1985: 15-37; Duxbury 1991: 176-77).

It is worth a moment to pause to think about how many of the radical critics of an earlier generation of legal theorists, like Frank, held positions deep within the establishment. Other examples include, of course, Justice Oliver Wendell Holmes, Jr., Judge (and later Justice) Benjamin Cardozo, and Judge Joseph Hutcheson, Jr. And many followers of the realist movement went on to positions in the administration of President Franklin D. Roosevelt's New Deal. One can barely imagine theoretical adherents of critical legal studies, critical race theory, or radical feminist theory on the bench, or at the heart of government. (The closest comparison we have is law and economics scholars like Richard Posner, Frank Easterbrook, and Robert Bork, serving as federal appellate judges and in high positions of governmental agencies. However, the politically conservative nature of the law and economics movement makes their presence in government less surprising and discordant.)

If Frank's work is not especially well known today, it is likely because many of his views (as is the case with many of the views of the American legal realists), novel or heavily contested at the time they were made, have become part of received wisdom.[6] What was relatively distinctive in Frank's work was his insistence on focusing on the trial courts, not the appellate courts, and on jury and judicial fact-finding along with (and to some extent, instead of) the judicial declaration of legal rules. Frank famously divided the American legal realists into "rule skeptics" and "fact skeptics," and counted himself among the latter; this distinction appears, perhaps for the first time, in the 1948 preface to the sixth printing of *Law and Modern Mind* (included in this edition).

It is important to remember that when *Law and the Modern Mind* was first published, the author was a Wall Street lawyer unknown to academia, but this work instantly pushed him to the forefront of the realist movement. The book was praised (at the time of its 1949 reprinting), in the following terms: "Few if any works on legal theory have had a more stimulating effect on our generation," and "it remains the best statement of what has been called the 'new realism' " (Chorley 1950: 392).

Frank's Views

In *Law and the Modern Mind*, Frank properly ridicules writers who prefer to talk about "law" distracted from actual court decisions. Under the view Frank criticizes, stating that "the law is X," without regard to whether that is the rule that has been applied, or would be applied, to the facts of a relevant case. Also, according to Frank, those who hold the criticized view refuse to speak of "the law" changing or being changed, even when courts give radically different outcomes, or when the Supreme Court reverses course on some issue (often due to a change in Court personnel). However, to criticize an indifference to judicial decisions may not be sufficient to ground Frank's favored position. Frank's position, as summarized towards the end of *Law and the Modern Mind* (criticizing what he calls "rule-fetichism" [sic] even among other legal realists), "law is what has happened or what will happen in concrete cases" (p. 297).[7] Frank thus follows Holmes (1897: 460-62) in equating the law with the decisions in actual cases, and predictions of decisions, rather than the rules promulgated by judges (or by scholars purporting to summarize what judges have decided).

Frank does not wrestle sufficiently with potential alternatives to a decision-based, judge-centered, and predictive theory of law. One problem with a theory of law that focuses on actual official actions (especially actual judicial decisions) is that it does not have the resources to explain the idea of "legal mistake[1]" (cf. Bix 1991: 84-88). Under the Frank/Holmes approach, the law *simply is* whatever the judges decide, and a later discussion (by a commentator or a later court) stating that the prior decision was mistaken, under this approach, simply misunderstands law. Equating law this closely with actual decisions, and leaving no conceptual room for "the law" diverging from those decisions, is a more radical conclusion than most judges, lawyers, and legal scholars are willing to swallow. Perhaps it may yet turn out to be the correct answer, but I do not think that either Frank or

Holmes produce the work necessary to ground conclusions that are so counterintuitive.

Also, an approach which equates "the law" with actual decisions, or the predictions of actual decisions, will have trouble explaining what it is that judges do when they decide cases, citing legal rules as the basis for their decisions. One might take lower-court judges to be predicting how higher-court judges treat a decision on appeal, with law for lower-court judges thus being just an effort to minimize the chance of reversal, but this still leaves the question of how to understand the actions of judges on the highest court who need not fear reversal.

Some skeptics might say (and at times Frank seems to say) that though judges may talk about basing their decisions on "the law" (statutes, precedent, etc.), that is only "window dressing" for decisions actually being based on the judge's biases and policy preferences. It is true that sometimes what courts do is best explained in terms of the judges' policy preferences, judicial biases, or the politics of judicial appointments, but is there nothing further to say beyond that? Judges may be fooling others, or themselves, when they claim, for example, that the law has been constant when the results actually directly contradict earlier decisions. However, is it *always* rationalization and mythology when a judge (or lawyer) claims that a prior decision was mistaken? Most of us believe (or at least hope) otherwise.

H. L. A. Hart (1994) argued that a legal theory should be able to account for those who take an "internal point of view" towards the law, viewing the law as giving them reasons for action. It is not enough to say that lawyers may be well advised, in counseling clients, to offer the best guess of what a judge will eventually decide (as Holmes discussed in terms of what a "bad man" wants to know about the law (Holmes 1897). Along with judges on the highest court obviously not simply predicting what they themselves will decide, in most societies there will be many people who act at least sometimes because of what they perceive the law to require (and not just because they fear sanctions). A theory about the nature of law should, presumptively, take into account such people who take an internal point of view on the law, and should not too quickly dismiss them as deluded fools.

On a related topic, Frank, like many legal realists, attacks the conceptualism or philosophical realism (Platonism) he finds in some commentators and judges. However, he may at times verge on the opposite danger, pointed out by Lon L. Fuller in his insightful discussion of American legal realism: an extreme nominalism (Fuller 1934: 443-47).

What was—and is—most distinctive about *Law and the Modern Mind* is also what now seems both strangest and least persuasive: the attempt to incorporate psychoanalytic theory into a legal realist jurisprudence. Frank's initial general point is that "[t]he demand for excessive legal certainty produces...a violent prejudice against a recognition of the practical need for flexible adaption and individuation of law based upon the unique facts of particular cases" (p. 183). He adds:

> Is it not absurd to keep alive the artificial, orthodox tradition of the "ideal judge?" The rational alternative is to recognize that judges are fallible human beings. We need to see that biases and prejudices and conditions of attention affect the judge's reasoning as they do the reasoning of ordinary men. (p. 156)

The more controversial part of Frank's analysis is his ascription of the desire for certainty to "an infantile longing to find a father-substitute in the law" (p. 192). While Frank regularly repeats that this psychoanalytic theory is offered only as a "partial explanation" (e.g., xxiv, 20-22, 251 n.2, 281-82, 391), and Frank himself summarizes a long list of potential alternative explanations (pp. 281-82), it is the psychoanalytic explanation to which the text regularly returns.

On one hand, I agree with Frank that the persistent and pervasive quest for certainty in the law—or assumption that there already is great certainty in the law—is a mystery that calls for explanation. On the other hand, I must agree with Llewellyn, in the end, that Frank's psychoanalytic approach is more distracting than helpful (p. xxv).

Conclusion

Law and the Modern Mind is a fascinating book, one that continues to raise important questions about law, judicial decision-making, and legal scholarship, over seventy-five years after it was originally written. Perhaps it is too much to demand of theorists that they both demolish the way of thinking dominant in their times, and that they find something adequate to put in its place. Bruce Ackerman, discussing *Law and the Modern Mind*, refers to the "extraordinary optimism" at the core of American legal realism, "a belief that once men were free from all the damaging myths of the past, they would have little difficulty understanding the proper shape of a just society" (Ackerman 1974: 122). One might well be more confident of the criticisms Frank offers in *Law and the Modern Mind* of earlier approaches, than with the sketches of a new approach that he puts forward. That leaves work for the rest of us, and perhaps for generations to come. In the meantime, we still have much to learn from Jerome Frank, and from *Law and the Modern Mind*.

Brian H. Bix
December 2007
Minneapolis, Minnesota

Notes

1. Llewellyn indicates that Frank had been a co-author with him of one of the best-known works of, and about, American legal realism, but that Frank had, in the end, refused to have his name on the article (Llewellyn 1931b: 1222 n.*). While the views of the two converged at many points, there were also prominent points of difference: see, e.g., Frank on Llewellyn in the 1948 Preface to the present book (xxiv-xxviii), and Llewellyn on Frank in a 1931 review of *Law and the Modern Mind* (Llewellyn 1931a).

2. Boris Bittker writes: "Legal reputations fade fast. Is Jerome N. Frank's name known to anyone under the age of fifty?" (Bittker 1986:1555). I think this definitely overstates matters, even for today, over twenty years later: anyone with interest in American legal realism, and this is a large group, knows of Jerome Frank.

3. That preface was also separately published in an American law journal (Frank 1949b).

4. His most important articles are probably Frank (1931, 1932). For a bibliography of Frank's (non-judicial) publications, see University of Chicago Law Review (1957).

5. In the course of a sympathetic discussion of Frank, Sanford Levinson wrote: "I think it fair to say that Jerome Frank has no discernible impact on contemporary discussions of American law" (Levinson 1985: 899). Again, I think this is at least a partial overstatement: if Frank has little distinct impact, it is because his views converge with those of others, which collectively contribute to the legal realists' *quite significant* impact on American legal scholarship and practice.

6. The cliché among American law professors is that "we are all realists now."

7. Where the reference is a number within parentheses, without an author being named, the reference is to a page number from *Law and the Modern Mind*.

References

Ackerman, Bruce A. 1974. "*Law and the Modern Mind* by Jerome Frank." *Daedalus* 103: 119-27.

Bittker, Boris I. 1986. "Book Review." *Wayne Law Review* 32: 1555-63.

Bix, Brian.1991. *Law, Language, and Legal Determinacy*. Oxford: Clarendon Press.

Chorley, Theo. 1950. "Book Review." *Modern Law Review* 13: 392-95.

Duxbury, Neil. 1991. "Jerome Frank and the Legacy of Legal Realism." *Journal of Law and Society* 18, pp. 175-205.

Frank, Jerome. 1930. *Law and the Modern Mind*. New York: Brentano's. (rev. ed., with a new preface, New York: Coward-McCann, 1949).

_____. 1931. "Are Judges Human?" parts I & II, *University of Pennsylvania Law Review* 80: 17-53, 233-67.

_____. 1932. "What Courts Do In Fact." parts I and II, *Illinois Law Review* 26: 645-66, 761-84.

_____. 1949a. *Courts on Trial: Myth and Reality in American Justice*. Princeton, NJ: Princeton University Press.

_____. 1949b. "Legal Thinking in Three Dimensions." *Syracuse Law Review* 1: 9-25.

Fuller, Lon L. 1934. "American Legal Realism." *University of Pennsylvania Law Review* 82: 429-62.

Glennon, Robert Jerome. 1985. *The Iconoclast as Reformer: Jerome Frank's Impact on American Law*. Ithaca, NY: Cornell University Press.

Hart, H. L. A. (1994), *The Concept of Law*, rev. ed. Oxford: Clarendon Press.

Holmes, Oliver Wendell, Jr. 1897. "The Path of the Law." *Harvard Law Review* 10: 457-78.

Levinson, Sanford. 1985. "Writing About Realism." *American Bar Foundation Research Journal* 1985: 899-908.

Llewellyn, Karl N. 1931a. "Legal Illusion." *Columbia Law Review* 31: 82-90.

_____. 1931b. "Some Realism about Realism—Responding to Dean Pound." *Harvard Law Review* 44: 1222-64.

University of Chicago Law Review. 1957. "A Bibliography of the Non-Judicial

Writings of Judge Frank." *University of Chicago Law Review* 24: 706-708.

PREFACE

Some of our ablest teachers of law have spoken of a blighting prepossession deep-rooted in the minds, of lawyers. For years in my own thinking and in that of my betters at the bar I have encountered certain baffling characteristics. I have here attempted a *partial* explanation of those characteristics. I hope that this explanation may help to make the nature of the law somewhat less puzzling both to lawyers and laymen.

The notes in the text to which reference is made by numbers will be found in Appendix IX, beginning at page 353. These notes contain some bibliographical material and qualifying statements which the more casual reader may not care to consider. The italics in most of the quotations are mine,

For encouragement in undertaking and finishing this book I owe thanks to many of my friends and especially Dr. Bernard Glueck, Randolph E. Paul, Frederick Hier and Dr. David M, Levy. Thanks are also due Lee Pressman for assistance in preparing the index.

June, 1930   *Jerome Frank*

PREFACE TO SIXTH PRINTING

Said Bernard Shaw in his 1913 preface to his book, "The Quintessence of Ibsenism," originally published in 1891: "In the pages which follow I have made no attempt to tamper with the work of the bygone man of thirty-five who wrote them. I have never admitted the right of an elderly author to alter the work of a young author, even when the young author happens to be himself." I am no Shaw, but, in penning this preface to a new printing of a book I published in 1930, I echo his sentiments.

I confess, however, that I would not today write that book precisely as I wrote it eighteen years ago. For one thing, I seriously blundered when I offered my own definition of the word Law. Since that word drips with ambiguity, there were already at least a dozen defensible definitions. To add one more was vanity. Worse, I found myself promptly assailed by other Law-definers who, in turn, differed with one another. A more futile, time-consuming contest is scarcely imaginable. Accordingly, I promptly backed out of that silly word battle. In 1931, I published an article in which I said that, in any future writing on the subject-matter of this book, I would, when possible, shun the use of the word Law; instead I would state directly—without an intervening definition of that term—what I was writing about, namely (1) specific court decisions, (2) how little they are predictable and uniform, (3) the process by which they are made, and (4) how far, in the interest of justice to citizens, that process can and should be improved. I wish I had followed that procedure in this book. I trust that the reader, whenever he comes upon "Law," will understand that (as I said at the end of Chapter V in Part One) I meant merely to talk of actual past decisions, or guesses about future decisions, of specific lawsuits.

I made another blunder, leading to misunderstandings,

when I employed the phrase "legal realism" to label the position, concerning the work of the courts, which I took in this book. That phrase I had enthusiastically borrowed from my friend Karl Llewellyn. He had used it to designate the views of a number of American lawyers who, each in his own way, during the first two decades of this century had in their writings expressed doubts about one or another of the traditional notions of matters legal. But, in 1931, less than a year after this book appeared, I published an article stating regrets at the use of this label, because, among other things, "realism," in philosophic discourse, has an accepted meaning wholly unrelated to the views of the so-called "legal realists." I then suggested that the legal realists be called "constructive skeptics," and their attitude, "constructive skepticism."[1]

There was a more cogent reason for regretting the use of "realists" as a method of ticketing these legal skeptics. The label enabled some of their critics to bracket the realists as a homogeneous "school," in virtual accord with one another on all or most subjects. This misconception—not certainly the result of any careful reading of their works —led to the specious charge that the "realistic school" embraced fantastically inconsistent ideas. Actually no such "school" existed. In the article mentioned above, I referred to one critic's use of this lumping-together method as follows: "It may be roughly described thus: (1) Jones disagrees with Smith about the tariff. (2) Robinson disagrees with Smith about the virtues of sauerkraut juice. (3) Since both Jones and Robinson disagree with Smith about something, it follows that (a) each disagrees with Smith about everything, and that (b) Jones and Robinson agree with one another about the tariff, the virtues of sauerkraut juice, the League of Nations, the quantity theory of money, vitalism, Bernard Shaw, Proust, Lucky Strikes, Communism, Will Rogers—and everything else. Llewellyn, Green, Cook, Yntema, Oliphant, Hutcheson, Bingham, and Frank

---

[1] In an article published in 1933, I suggested that the "realists" might be named "experimentalists."

in their several ways have expressed disagreement with conventional legal theory. Dickinson therefore assumes (a) that they disagree with that theory for identical reasons; and (b) that they agree with one another on their proposed substitutes for that theory. It is as if he were to assume that all men leaving Chicago at a given instant were going north and were bound for the same town. Dickinson has produced a composite photograph of the writers he is discussing. One sees, so to speak, the hair of Green, the eyebrows of Yntema, the teeth of Cook, the neck of Oliphant, the lips of Llewellyn. . . . The picture is the image of an unreal imaginary creature, of a strange, misshapen, infertile, hybrid."

Actually, these so-called realists have but one common bond, a negative characteristic already noted: skepticism as to some of the conventional legal theories, a skepticism stimulated by a zeal to reform, in the interest of justice, some court-house ways. Despite the lack of any homogeneity in their positive views, these "constructive skeptics," roughly speaking, do divide into two groups; however, there are marked differences, ignored by the critics, between the two groups.

The first group, of whom Llewellyn is perhaps the outstanding representative, I would call "rule skeptics." They aim at greater legal certainty. That is, they consider it socially desirable that lawyers should be able to predict to their clients the decisions in most lawsuits not yet commenced. They feel that, in too many instances, the layman cannot act with assurance as to how, if his acts become involved in a suit, the court will decide. As these skeptics see it, the trouble is that the formal legal rules enunciated in courts' opinions—sometimes called "paper rules"—too often prove unreliable as guides in the prediction of decisions. They believe that they can discover, behind the "paper rules," some "real rules" descriptive of uniformities or regularities in actual judicial behavior, and that those "real rules" will serve as more reliable prediction-instruments, yielding a large measure of workable predictability of the outcome of future suits. In this undertaking, the rule skeptics concentrate almost exclusively on upper-court opinions. They do not ask themselves whether their own or any other prediction-device will render it possible for a lawyer or layman to prophesy, before an ordinary suit is instituted or comes to trial in a trial court, how it will be decided. In other words, these rule skeptics seek means for making accurate guesses, not about decisions of trial courts, but about decisions of upper courts when trial-court decisions are appealed. These skeptics cold-shoulder the trial courts. Yet, in most instances, these skeptics do not inform their readers that they are writing chiefly of upper courts.

The second group I would call "fact skeptics." They, too, engaging in "rule skepticism," peer behind the "paper rules." Together with the rule skeptics, they have stimulated interest in factors, influencing upper-court decisions, of which, often, the opinions of those courts give no hint. But the fact skeptics go much further. Their primary interest is in the trial courts. No matter how precise or definite may be the formal legal rules, say these fact skeptics, no matter what the discoverable uniformities behind these formal rules, nevertheless it is impossible, and will always be impossible, because of the elusiveness of the facts on which decisions turn, to predict future decisions in most (not all) lawsuits, not yet begun or not yet tried. The fact skeptics, thinking that therefore the pursuit of greatly increased legal certainty is, for the most part, futile—and that its pursuit, indeed, may well work injustice—aim rather at increased judicial justice. This group of fact skeptics includes, among others, Dean Leon Green, Max Radin, Thurman Arnold, William O. Douglas (now Mr. Justice Douglas), and perhaps E. M. Morgan.

Within each of these groups there is diversity of opinion as to many ideas. But I think it can be said that, generally, most of the rule skeptics, restricting themselves to the upper-court level, live in an artificial two-dimensional legal world, while the legal world of the fact skeptics is three-dimensional. Obviously, many events occurring in the fact skeptics' three-dimensional cosmos are out of sight, and therefore out of mind, in the rule skeptics' cosmos.

The critical anti-skeptics also live in the artificial upper-court world. Naturally, they have found less fault with the rule skeptics than with the fact skeptics. The critics, for instance, said that Llewellyn was a bit wild, yet not wholly unsound, but that men like Dean Green grossly exaggerated the extent of legal uncertainty (*i.e.,* the unpredictability of decisions). To my mind, the critics shoe the wrong foot: Both the rule skeptics and the critics grossly exaggerate the extent of legal certainty, because their own writings deal only with the prediction of upper-court decisions. The rule skeptics are, indeed, but the left-wing adherents of a tradition. It is from the tradition itself that the fact skeptics revolted.

As a reading of this book will disclose, I am one of the fact skeptics. See especially Part One, Chapters XII–XVI, Appendix II, note 7, and Appendix V, which relate to trial-court doings. The point there made may be summarized thus: If one accepts as correct the conventional description of how courts reach their decisions, then a decision of any lawsuit results from the application of a legal rule or rules to the facts of the suit. That sounds rather simple, and apparently renders it fairly easy to prophesy the decision, even of a case not yet commenced or tried, especially when, as often happens, the applicable rule is definite and precise (for instance, the rule about driving on the right side of the road). But, particularly when pivotal testimony at the trial is oral and conflicting, as it is in most lawsuits, the trial court's "finding" of the facts involves a multitude of elusive factors: First, the trial judge in a non-jury trial or the jury in a jury trial must learn about the facts from the witnesses; and witnesses, being humanly fallible, frequently make mistakes in observation of what they saw and heard, or in their recollections of what they observed, or in their court-room reports of those recollections. Second, the trial judges or juries, also human,

may have prejudices—often unconscious, unknown even to
themselves—for or against some of the witnesses, or the
parties to the suit, or the lawyers.

Those prejudices, when they are racial, religious, political, or economic, may sometimes be surmised by others.
But there are some hidden, unconscious biases of trial
judges or jurors—such as, for example, plus or minus reactions to women, or unmarried women, or red-haired
women, or brunettes, or men with deep voices or high-
pitched voices, or fidgety men, or men who wear thick eye-
glasses, or those who have pronounced gestures or nervous
tics—biases of which no one can be aware. Concealed and
highly idiosyncratic, such biases—peculiar to each individual judge or juror—cannot be formulated as uniformities
or squeezed into regularized "behavior patterns." In that
respect, neither judges nor jurors are standardized.

The chief obstacle to prophesying a trial-court decision
is, then, the inability, thanks to these inscrutable factors,
to foresee what a particular trial judge or jury will believe
to be the facts. Consider, particularly, the perplexity of a
lawyer asked to guess the outcome of a suit not yet commenced: He must guess whether some of the witnesses will
persuasively lie, or will honestly but persuasively give inaccurate testimony; as, usually, he does not even know
the trial judge or jury who will try the case, he must also
guess the reactions—to the witnesses, the parties and the
lawyers—of an unknown trial judge or jury.

These difficulties have been overlooked by most of those
(the rule skeptics included) who write on the subject of
legal certainty or the prediction of decisions. They often
call their writings "jurisprudence"; but, as they almost
never consider juries and jury trials, one might chide them
for forgetting "juriesprudence."

Moreover, most of them overlook another feature, not
revealed in the conventional description of how courts decide cases, a feature unusually baffling: According to the
conventional description, judging in a trial court is made
up of two components which, initially distinct, are logically

combined to produce a decision. Those components, it is said, are (1) the determination of the facts and (2) the determination of what rules should be applied to those facts. In reality, however, those components often are not distinct but intertwine in the thought processes of the trial judge or jury. The decision is frequently an undifferentiated composite which precedes any analysis or breakdown into facts and rules. Many a time, for all anyone can tell, a trial judge makes no such analysis or breakdown when rendering his decision unaccompanied by an explanation. But even when he publishes an explanation, it may be misdescriptive of the way in which the decision was reached. This baffling aspect of the decisional process, as it relates to the trial judge, is discussed in Part One, Chapters XII and XIII. The impenetrability of the composite shows up strikingly in jury cases, discussed in Part One, Chapter XVI and Appendix V. The interested reader will find this subject of the composite more extensively considered in my recently published article, "Say It With Music," 61 Harvard Law Review 921; there I refer to the composite as a sort of *gestalt*.

Shutting their eyes to the actualities of trials, most of the lawyers who write for other lawyers or for laymen about the courts are victims of the Upper-Court Myth. They have deluded themselves and, alas, many non-lawyers, with two correlated false beliefs: (1) They believe that the major cause of legal uncertainty is uncertainty in the rules, so that if the legal rules—or the "real rules" behind the "paper rules"—are entirely clear and crisp, the doubts about future decisions largely vanish. (2) They believe that, on appeals, most mistakes made by trial courts can be rectified by the upper courts. In truth, as noted above, the major cause of legal uncertainty is fact-uncertainty—the unknowability, before the decision, of what the trial court will "find" as the facts, and the unknowability after the decision of the way in which it "found" those facts. If a trial court mistakenly takes as true the oral testimony of an honest but inaccurate witness or a lying witness, seldom can an upper court detect this mistake; it therefore usually adopts the facts as found by the trial court. It does so because the trial court saw and heard the witnesses testify, while the upper court has before it only a lifeless printed report of the testimony, a report that does not contain the witnesses' demeanor, which is often significantly revealing.

When a trial court, relying on inaccurate testimony, misapprehends the real facts, it decides an unreal, hypothetical case. An upper court is still more likely to do so; for, further removed from the real facts, it usually uses, perforce, the trial court's version of the facts as something "given." As the trial courts in most cases have an uncontrollable power ("discretion") to choose the facts—that is, to choose to believe one witness rather than another—those courts, not the upper courts, play the chief role in court-house government. All of which goes to expose the fallacy of the Upper-Court Myth.

With this perspective, we get new light on the doctrine of following the precedents. This doctrine demands that, when a court has laid down—expressly or by implication —a rule in one case, the court should, except in unusual circumstances, apply that rule to later cases presenting substantially similar facts. That doctrine—as Gray showed in his comments quoted on page 39—may have less practical importance to the ordinary man than its more ardent advocates accord it. Yet no sane informed person will deny that, within appropriate limits, judicial adherence to precedents possesses such great value that to abandon it would be unthinkable. (What I regard as the virtue and the appropriate limits of the doctrine, I stated in 1942 in my opinion in Aero Spark Plug v. B. G. Corp., 130 F. (2d) 290, 294–299; as I there said, "courts should be exceedingly cautious in disturbing—at least retrospectively—precedents in reliance on which men may have importantly changed their positions." See also "Words and Music," 47 Columbia Law Review 1259.)

However, even when properly and conscientiously utilized, the practice of following the precedents cannot guarantee the stability and certainty it seems to promise to some of those who confine their scrutiny to upper-court decisions. For, in an upper court, ordinarily no fact-finding problem exists, as the facts are beyond dispute, having already been found by the trial court. The usual questions for the upper court are, then, these: Do the facts of the case now before the court sufficiently resemble those of an earlier case so that the rule of that case is applicable? If there is such a resemblance, should that rule now be applied or should it be modified or abandoned? Although able lawyers cannot always guess how an upper court will answer those questions, the educated guesses of those lawyers are good in the majority of instances. When, in a trial court, the parties to a suit agree on the facts, so that the facts are undisputed, that court faces only those same questions; and again, usually, able lawyers can guess the answers.

But, to repeat, in most cases in the trial courts the parties do dispute about the facts, and the testimony concerning the facts is oral and conflicting. In any such case, what does it mean to say that the facts of a case are substantially similar to those of an earlier case? It means, at most, merely that the trial court regards the facts of the two cases as about the same. Since, however, no one knows what the trial court will find as the facts, no one can guess what precedent ought to be or will be followed either by the trial court or, if an appeal occurs, by the upper court. This weakness of the precedent doctrine becomes more obvious when one takes into account the "composite" factor, the intertwining of rules and facts in the trial court's decision.

This weakness will also infect any substitute precedent system, based on "real rules" which the rule skeptics may discover, by way of anthropology—*i.e.*, the mores, customs, folkways—or psychology, or statistics, or studies of the political, economic, and social backgrounds of judges, or otherwise. For no rule can be hermetically sealed against the intrusion of false or inaccurate oral testimony which the trial judge or jury may believe.[2]

This weakness of the precedent doctrine is a recurrent theme of Part One, Chapters XII, XIII, and XIV. As shown by many passages, those chapters deal with trial-court decisions, particularly in cases involving oral testimony. Since the thesis was novel, maybe I was at fault in not so stating with greater emphasis. Had I done so, I might perhaps have forestalled the criticism made by some critics that, in my view, any court—even when the facts are undisputed or, as in many cases on appeal, indisputable—is and should be untrammeled by precedents or by the language of statutes. Of course, that was not my position.

Because, in almost any lawsuit, one side can raise an issue of fact, so that the decision will turn on the unforeseeable belief or disbelief of a trial judge or jury in some part of the conflicting oral testimony, it is astonishing that so sagacious a thinker as Roscoe Pound could say, and persuade many others to agree, that, when a case relates to "property" or "commercial or business transactions," the decision will usually be easily foretellable because it will result from a precise legal rule "authoritatively prescribed in advance and mechanically applied." This Poundian thesis (discussed in Part Two, Chapter I) has plausibility only as long as one refuses to look at daily happenings in trial courts. As I put it in 1931, "In cases involving . . . promissory notes . . . , it is always possible to introduce some question of fact relating to fraud, negligence, mistake, alteration, or estoppel. In most contested cases,[3] one side or the other usually injects such a question. Suppose such a case is tried before a jury and, on the question of fact, 'goes to the jury.' Is it not absurd to say that the rules will then be mechanically applied?

---

[2] If anyone has doubts on that score, let him read Corbin's masterful article in 53 Yale L.J. 603.

[3] "Contested" here was said to mean a case where conflicting oral testimony is introduced with regard to relevant and disputed questions of fact.

Anyone who has ever watched a jury trial knows the rules often become a mere subsidiary detail, part of a meaningless but dignified liturgy recited by the judge in the physical presence of the jury and to which the jury pays scant heed. To say that fixed rules invariably govern property and commercial cases when the jury sits and decides is to deny the plain truth. The pulchritude of the plaintiff or his religion or his economic status or the manners of the respective attorneys, or the like, may well be the determining factor inducing the decision. And if a judge sits and decides without a jury and similar questions of fact are raised, will the crystallized unalterable rules, about identical . . . promissory notes, mechanically produce the decision? Surely not. Of course, if the judge writes an opinion, the stereotyped rules will appear in the opinion. But the judge will decide one way or the other on the 'facts,' and those 'facts' vary with the particular case and with the judge's impressions of those 'facts'—although the instrument in suit is a promissory note precisely like every other promissory note. The truth is that the talk about mechanical operation of rules in property, or commercial, or other cases is not at all a description of what really happens in courts in contested cases. It is a dogma based upon inadequate observation. For it fails to take into account the important circumstance that any future law suit about a piece of property or a commercial contract can be contested, and that, if it is contested, questions of fact can be raised involving the introduction of conflicting testimony.
. . . The 'facts,' as we have seen, may be crucial when, as is often the case, a question of 'fact' is injected into litigation. . . . And those facts are, *inter alia,* a function of the attention of the judge. Certain kinds of witnesses may arouse his attention more than others. Or may arouse his antipathies or win his sympathy. The 'facts,' it must never be overlooked, are not objective. They are what the judge thinks they are. And what he thinks they are depends on what he hears and sees as the witnesses testify—which may not be, and often is not, what another judge would

hear and see. Assume ('fictionally') the most complete rigidity of the rules relating to commercial transactions. . . . Still, since the 'facts' are only what the judge thinks they are, the decision will vary with the judge's apprehension of the facts. The rules, that is, do not produce uniformity of decisions in what we have called 'contested' cases, but only uniformity of that portion of opinions containing the rules. Judge Alpha may try a 'contested' case relating to a promissory note and decide for the holder. If Judge Beta tried the same case he might decide for the maker. The opinion of Judges Alpha and Beta would contain identical rules. That, and little more, is what truth there is in the dogma about the non-uniqueness of promissory notes in 'contested' cases."

The reader will probably recognize the cause of the misunderstanding of this book by some legal pundits: The traditionalists—right-wing and left-wing alike—assumed that most uncertainty in the legal realm stems from rule-uncertainty. They therefore concluded that, when a fact skeptic spoke of legal uncertainty, he, too, must have meant merely rule-uncertainty. Consequently, the traditionalists condemned, as hyperbolic distortions, my statements as to the large proportion of decisions which are unpredictable before suits are brought or tried.

The legal traditionalists' viewpoint has carried over to many educated non-lawyers, giving them a false and generally soothing impression of the operations of our court-house government. In this book, I tried—I hope in a manner understandable to intelligent laymen—to dissipate that false impression, because I felt that, in a democracy, the citizens have the right to know the truth about all parts of their government, and because, without public knowledge of the realities of court-house doings, essential reforms of those doings will not soon arrive.

This book contains no mention of Natural Law. But, as some Roman Catholics have read into it an implied

criticism of the Scholastic (Thomistic) version of Natural
Law, I want now to say this:[4] I do not understand how
any decent man today can refuse to adopt, as the basis
of modern civilization, the fundamental principles of Natural Law, relative to human conduct, as stated by Thomas
Aquinas. There are, he said, some primary principles, such
as seek the common good, avoid harm to others, render
to each his own; there are also a few secondary principles,
such as not to kill, not to steal, to return goods held in trust.
Now the Thomists freely acknowledge that the applications
of those highly general and flexible principles—applications
which necessarily take the form of man-made rules—must
vary with time, place, and circumstances. Indeed, Brendan
Brown, a Thomist, recently advocated a "scholastic pragmatism." More important, Natural Law, Catholic or non-
Catholic, yields, at best, a standard of justice and morality
for critically evaluating the man-made rules, and, perhaps,
for ensuring a moderate amount of certainty in those rules;
but it furnishes no helpful standard for evaluating the fact-
determinations of trial courts in most lawsuits, and no assistance in ensuring uniformity, certainty, or predictability
in such determinations. Natural Law aims at justice, and
at moderate certainty, in the man-made rules, that is, in
the more or less abstract, generalized, human formulations
of what men may or may not lawfully do. To be practically
meaningful, however, judicial justice must be justice not
merely in the abstract but in the concrete—in the courts'
decisions of the numerous particular individual cases. A
general rule against forgery, or a general rule against
breaking contracts, is eminently just and fairly certain. But
a court decision that a particular man, Campbell, committed forgery, or a court decision that a particular man,
Wilcox, broke a contract, is surely unjust if in truth he did
not so act, yet a trial court mistakenly believes he did, because of its belief in the reliability of oral testimony which

[4] See Frank, "A Sketch of An Influence," in the volume, "Interpretations of Modern Legal Philosophies," (1947) 189, 222–230,
234–237; Frank, "Fate and Freedom," (1945) 115–142, 294–297.

does not match the actual facts. Thence arises the problem
of achieving justice, certainty, and uniformity, in trial-
court ascertainments of facts in divers individual lawsuits,
a problem which can be solved, via Natural Law, only to
the extent that Natural Law principles operate on and
control the subjective, un-get-at-able, often unconscious,
and unstandardized ingredients of trial-court fact-findings,
when oral testimony is in conflict as to crucial issues of
fact. I see no signs that those principles do so operate and
control. So far as I know, Natural Law adherents—whether
or not Catholics—have considered neither that problem nor
the one of coping with the "composite" in trial-court decisions.

I should add that my references in this book to "scholasticism" were superficial and unfair. I have since apolo-
gized; see my opinion in Aero Spark Plug Co. v. B. G.
Corporation, 130 F. (2d) 290, 298, and my book "Fate
and Freedom" (1945), 98–99, 259–260.[5] I was also glib
and unfair in some of my comments on Aristotle; I trust
I have made amends in my books, "If Men Were Angels"
(1942), and "Fate and Freedom." What, in the present
book, I said of logic I have supplemented in two articles,
"Mr. Justice Holmes and Non-Euclidean Legal Thinking,"
17 Cornell Law Quarterly (1932) 568, and "Say It With
Music," 61 Harvard Law Review (1948) 921, 928–933,
950–952.

Much of the mood which permeates this book I later
articulated, after I became a judge, in a judicial opinion
relative to trial judges, delivered in 1943:[6]

"Democracy must, indeed, fail unless our courts try cases
fairly, and there can be no fair trial before a judge lacking in
impartiality and disinterestedness. If, however, 'bias' and
'partiality' be defined to mean the total absence of preconcep-

[5] I invite the reader to read "Fate and Freedom" (pp. 168–169,
206–220) if perchance he views Chapter XVIII of the present volume as expressive of irreligious sentiments.
[6] In re J. P. Linahan, 138 F. (2d) 650, 652–654.

tions in the mind of the judge, then no one has ever had a fair trial and no one ever will. The human mind, even at infancy, is no blank piece of paper. We are born with predispositions; and the process of education, formal and informal, creates attitudes in all men which affect them in judging situations, attitudes which precede reasoning in particular instances and which, therefore, by definition, are pre-judices. Without acquired 'slants,' pre-conceptions, life could not go on. Every habit constitutes a pre-judgment; were those pre-judgments which we call habits absent in any person, were he obliged to treat every event as an unprecedented crisis presenting a wholly new problem he would go mad. Interests, points of view, preferences, are the essence of living. Only death yields complete dispassionateness, for such dispassionateness signifies utter indifference. 'To live is to have a vocation, and to have a vocation is to have an ethics or scheme of values, and to have a scheme of values is to have a point of view, and to have a point of view is have a prejudice or bias. . . .'[7] An 'open mind,' in the sense of a mind containing no preconceptions whatever, would be a mind incapable of learning anything, would be that of an utterly emotionless human being, corresponding roughly to the psychiatrist's descriptions of the feeble-minded. More directly to the point, every human society has a multitude of established attitudes, unquestioned postulates. Cosmically, they may seem parochial prejudices, but many of them represent the community's most cherished values and ideals. Such social pre-conceptions, the 'value judgments' which members of any given society take for granted and use as the unspoken axioms of thinking, find their way into that society's legal system, become what has been termed 'the valuation system of the law.' The judge in our society owes a duty to act in accordance with those basic predilections inhering in our legal system (although, of course, he has the right, at times, to urge that some of them be modified or abandoned). The standard of dispassionateness obviously does not require the judge to rid himself of the unconscious influence of such social attitudes.

"In addition to those acquired social value judgments, every judge, however, unavoidably has many idiosyncratic 'leanings

[7] Kenneth Burke, "Permanence and Change" (1936), 329.

of the mind,' uniquely personal prejudices, which may interfere with his fairness at a trial. He may be stimulated by unconscious sympathies for, or antipathies to, some of the witnesses, lawyers or parties in a case before him. As Josiah
Royce observed, 'Oddities of feature or of complexion, slight
physical variations from the customary, a strange dress, a scar,
a too-steady look, a limp, a loud or deep voice, any of these
peculiarities . . . may be to one, an object of fascinated
curiosity; to another . . . , an intense irritation, an object of
violent antipathy.' . . . Frankly to recognize the existence of
such prejudices is the part of wisdom. The conscientious judge
will, as far as possible, make himself aware of his biases of
this character, and, by that very self-knowledge, nullify their
effect. Much harm is done by the myth that, merely by putting
on a black robe and taking the oath of office as a judge, a
man ceases to be human and strips himself of all predilections,
becomes a passionless thinking machine. The concealment of
the human element in the judicial process allows that element
to operate in an exaggerated manner; the sunlight of awareness has an antiseptic effect on prejudices. Freely avowing that
he is a human being, the judge can and should, through self-
scrutiny, prevent the operation of this class of biases. This
self-knowledge is needed in a judge because he is peculiarly
exposed to emotional influences; the 'court room is a place of
surging emotions . . . ; the parties are keyed up to the contest; often in open defiance; and the topics at issue are often
calculated to stir up the sympathy, prejudice, or ridicule of
the tribunal.' The judge's decision turns, often, on what he
believes to be the facts of the case. As a fact-finder, he is himself a witness—a witness of the witnesses; he should, therefore,
learn to avoid the errors which, because of prejudice, often
affect those witnesses.

"But, just because his fact-finding is based on his estimates
of the witnesses, of their reliability as reporters of what they
saw and heard, it is his duty, while listening to and watching
them, to form attitudes towards them. He must do his best to
ascertain their motives, their biases, their dominating passions and interests, for only so can he judge of the accuracy
of their narrations. He must also shrewdly observe the stratagems of the opposing lawyers, perceive their efforts to sway
him by appeals to his predilections. He must cannily penetrate
through the surface of their remarks to their real purposes and

motives. He has an official obligation to become prejudiced in that sense. Impartiality is not gullibility. Disinterestedness does not mean child-like innocence. If the judge did not form judgments of the actors in those court-house dramas called trials, he could never render decisions. His findings of fact may be erroneous, for, being human, he is not infallible; indeed, a judge who purports to be super-human is likely to be dominated by improper prejudices."

In "If Men Were Angels," pages 226–315, I have attempted to reply in some detail to most of the criticisms of "Law and the Modern Mind." I shall here briefly consider a few of those criticisms.[8]

The opening chapters pose this problem: Why do many lawyers and non-lawyers insist that legal certainty now does or can be made to exist to a far greater extent than it does or ever possibly could? Why this persistent longing for a patently unachievable legal stability? I put forward but one explanation, stating again and again that it was but partial. I enumerated fourteen other partial explanations (Appendix I). Some critics, nevertheless, maintained that I put mine forward as the sole explanation.

Kennedy (echoing Pound) said that I tried to explain "the uncertainty in law in terms of Freudian complexes." Of course I did nothing of the kind. I sought to uncover one of the roots of a yearning for an unattainable legal certainty. In doing so, I drew on some of the works on child psychology of Freud and Piaget, especially with reference to the young child's father-dependence and the grown-up's resultant tendency to hanker after father-substitutes. Some critics failed to note that I observed (Appendix IX ["Reference Notes"] Part One, Chapter II, note 5) that my thesis related to our "quasi-patriarchal society," but would not hold as to one where the father is assigned a less disciplinary role vis-a-vis the young child. The suggestion that I spoke of "the child," as if that word

[8] It might be well for the reader to skip the next seven paragraphs until he has completed a reading of the book.

indicated a constant, is answered in Part One, Chapter VIII, note 2. Although I repeatedly said (pages 22 note, 175, 395–397) that I considered psychology not a science but an art, and still in its infancy, some critics charged me with abject devotion to psychology as an "authoritative science." Llewellyn regarded my psychological discussion as distractingly superfluous. To some present-day readers, however, it may seem almost too obvious, now that Freud's disciples write articles for the popular magazines. But in 1930, there was novelty in the notions, particularly as applied to legal subjects, of "sublimation" and the reaction of the adult to his childhood problems concerning his father. Even now, such notions have not much influence on legal thinkers: As late as 1946, Simpson and Field wrote that the psychological approach to the judging process, suggested by me among others, was just a beginning and should be further developed. Two non-lawyers have recently deemed my psychological thesis still suggestive in non-legal fields; see Stevenson, "Ethics and Language" (1944), and de Grazia, "The Political Community" (1948).

Kennedy and others have asserted that I was a devotee of "behavioristic" psychology. But in this book (pages 174–176), I criticized a basic tenet of behaviorism and (page 162) the efforts of the rule skeptic Oliphant to apply that veterinary's psychology to matters legal; the next year (1931) I published an article criticizing behaviorism in some detail. Pound has pigeon-holed me as a psychological determinist; nothing in this book, however, faintly intimates a belief in determinism. The discussion of science (Appendix III), is patently anti-determinist; and in two subsequent books, I elaborately attacked determinism, Freudian, Marxist, and every other kind; see "Save America First" (1938) and "Fate and Freedom" (1945).

Many rule skeptics have urged the desirability and possibility of creating a legal "science" built on the model of the natural sciences. Some critics have ascribed that fatuous notion to me. The reader will see for himself how groundless is that suggestion. I have been at pains in later writings to point out, more in detail, what I consider the folly, and the undesirability, of striving to create either a legal science or "social sciences." Several critics have said that I depicted natural science as if it and its "laws" can give men a finality and certainty not achievable in the legal realm; those critics could not have read Part One, Chapter XI; Part Three, Chapter I, and Appendix III. The distinction there made between science and the "scientific spirit," I developed in "Are Judges Human?" 80 University of Pennsylvania Law Review (1931) 254–258, and also in "Fate and Freedom" (1945) 40–41.

My reference to a "government of laws and not of men" evoked some objections; my answer is contained in my more detailed consideration of that phrase in "If Men Were Angels" (Chapter 12). In the present volume, I welcomed the attack of the semanticists on word-magic and on the diseases of language; but I also stated at some length my reasons for believing that the prescriptions of the word-doctors are no cure-all for popular misconceptions of matters legal. One critic, however, called me a dogmatic semanticist, and said, too, preposterously, that I believed language the inveterate enemy of clear thinking. Anyone disposed to agree with critics who claim that I delighted in chaos, legal or otherwise, or in incessant change, should read Part Three, Chapter I and Appendix X, Section 3.

It has been said by Llewellyn, Pound, and others that I underestimated the judicial uniformities resulting from the pressure of (1) the likeness in the legal education and in the professional experiences of lawyers who become judges plus (2) the common judicial tradition. But these pressures do not penetrate deep enough to produce similarities in those unique, idiosyncratic, sub-threshold biases and pre-dilections, of the divers individual trial judges, which affect their reactions to witnesses, parties, and lawyers, and which terminate in fact-findings; and, of course, those pressures do not operate on jurors.[9]

Some critics have said that all the so-called "realists," including me, centered on the interests of the lawyer and did not consider the judge's point of view; other critics have made exactly the opposite criticism. I think it clear that this book tries, however inadequately, to envision how judging looks both to lawyers and to judges.

Because, in common with the other fact skeptics, I stressed the effects of many non-rule ingredients in the making of court decisions, several critics complained that I cynically sneered at legal rules, considered them unreal or useless. That criticism, I submit, is absurd. If a man says that there is hydrogen as well as oxygen in water, discussing both, surely he cannot be charged with denigrating the oxygen or with saying that it is unreal or useless. I have always heartily endorsed the aim of those who, following Holmes, point out that the rules (whether made by legislatures or judge-made) are embodiments of social policies, values, ideals, and who urge that, for that reason, the rules should be recurrently and informedly re-examined. I may add that, since, for the past seven years, I have sat on an upper court which concerns itself primarily with the rules and which has little to do with fact-finding, it should be plain that I regard the rules as significant.

But the rules, statutory or judge-made, are not self-operative. They are frustrated, inoperative, whenever, due to faulty fact-finding in trial courts, they are applied to non-existent facts. Is the highly moral rule against murder actually enforced when a court goes wrong on the facts and convicts an innocent man? What of the rule against

[9] This should serve to answer the economic determinists, with their sweeping, dogmatic, class-bias thesis. To a limited extent, this thesis sometimes has some partial validity. But, all else aside, it is useless as even a partial explanation of decisions in that vast multitude of lawsuits in which class-bias is wholly absent, e.g., suits between two economically equal "small" businessmen, or between two giant corporations, or between two members of the "proletarian class."

fraud when a court, through a mistake of fact, decides that a fraud-doer was guiltless of fraud? To see to it that the legal rules express moral values is no mean task. But our judicial system does not fulfill its function in merely contriving or interpreting rules. In so far as, in individual lawsuits, the rules are not applied to actual facts, the system is imperfect.

Perfection is a fool's dream. With the best possible court-system men could invent, there would be no assurance that the actual facts would always be ascertained or approximated; since trial courts must be conducted by fallible human beings who must learn what they can of the facts from witnesses, likewise humanly fallible, many unavoidable mistakes would still occur. But *avoidable* court-room mistakes about the facts ought to distress all men who believe in justice; and such mistakes—due not to the rules but to needless deficiencies in trial-court fact-finding—cause needless tragedies every day.

When I call them "needless," I am not even intimating that most trial judges have less ability and integrity than upper-court judges. My point is (1) that the job of trial judges is far more difficult and perplexing, calls for a much wider range of talents than does upper-court judging, and (2) that our trial methods, which trial judges are now obliged to condone, are hopelessly antiquated. If our judicial system is to move as near as is humanly practicable to adequacy in dispensing justice, I think we must, at least, overhaul our methods of trial, and provide special training for future trial judges.

The complacency of those who think such reforms unnecessary, who think that our courts now rather competently protect legal rights, should be deflated by the following comment, made in 1926 by our greatest judge, Learned Hand, after a long period of service on the trial bench: "I must say that as a litigant I should dread a law suit beyond almost anything else short of sickness and death." That succinct revelation of the chanciness of litigation should destroy the satisfaction with our courts likely to be engendered by Cardozo's relatively placid picture of the judicial process.[10] Unfortunately, Cardozo omitted the chancy character of trials from his description. That description, superlative in respect of upper courts, is bizarre if deemed to include an account of trial-court ways—as bizarre as would be an account of manners at Buckingham Palace if taken as also a true portrayal of rush-hour behavior in the New York subways. Cardozo, most of his days an appellate court lawyer or appellate court judge, suffered from a sort of occupational disease, appellate-court-itis. In the kind of courtroom where he spent his professional life, the atmosphere is serene, stratospheric. There, no witnesses intrude; lawyers alone address the court, and they must do so with decorum, in an orderly, dignified manner. Not so in the trial courtroom. Absent there the stratospheric hush. Such a courtroom is, as Wigmore notes, "a place of . . . distracting episodes, and sensational surprises." The drama there, full of interruptions, is turbulently conducted, punctuated by constant clashes between counsel and witnesses or between counsel. But in the upper court those clashes appear only in reposeful, silent, printed pages. Cardozo, an upper-court dweller, wrote nothing of that unserenity which characterizes trials. His books, invaluable to students of appeal courts, have thus unfortunately helped to distract public attention from our tragically backward trial practices.

In the light of the foregoing, the reader will understand why I was surprised at the comments of some critics that in this book I encouraged "anti-rationalism" and "anti-idealism"; devoted myself solely to what happens in courts; and ignored not only the rational and moral elements now operative in judicial decisions but also the possibility of

---

[10] See "Selected Writings of Benjamin N. Cardozo" (1947) which includes "The Nature of The Judicial Process," (1921) and "The Growth of The Law" (1924). See also Frank, "Cardozo and The Upper-Court Myth," 13 Law and Contemporary Problems (1948) 369.

bringing still closer together the ideal and the actual in courtroom performances. The truth is that, like most of the "constructive skeptics," I was motivated by an eager —perhaps too eager—desire to reform our judicial system, to inject, so far as feasible, more reason and more justice into its daily workings. To accomplish such reform, however, one needs to look at, not away from, the non-rational and non-idealistic elements at play now in court-house government. Some of those elements are disturbing. But one who calls attention to defects should not be presumed to be delighting in defects. The physician who publicizes the prevalence of a dangerous and preventable disease does not desire its perpetuation but its cure. There can be no greater hindrance to the growth of rationality than the illusion that one is rational when one is the dupe of illusions. Man can invent no better way to balk any of his ideals than the delusion that they have already been achieved. If we really cherish our ideals of democratic justice, we must not be content with merely mouthing them.

Whatever the faults of the rule-skepticism sponsored by both rule skeptics and fact skeptics, I think it had some markedly desirable consequences. Provoking controversy and sometimes unfair retorts, nonetheless it has subtly invaded much judicial thinking. It has contributed, in part, to the liberation of many judges—including some who decried that skepticism—from enslavement by unduly rigid legal concepts, caused those judges to ground their reasoning on broader and more human rule-premises. I perceive, however, little improvement in court-house fact-finding, and none that may be attributed to the fact-skepticism of the fact skeptics. But perhaps here, too, controversy may, in time, translate itself into new thought-habits. Perhaps the stirring of doubts concerning our present unjust fact-finding methods will some day, before long, issue in much needed improvements.

NOTE: If the reader has some questions about the notions expressed in this book, he will perhaps find some of his questions answered in the following articles and books I published after 1930:

"Are Judges Human?" 80 University of Pennsylvania Law Review (1931) 17, 233

"What Courts Do In Fact," 26 Illinois Law Review (1932) 645, 761

"Mr. Justice Holmes and Non-Euclidean Legal Thinking," 17 Cornell Law Quarterly (1932) 568

"Why Not a Clinical Lawyers' School?" 81 University of Pennsylvania Law Review (1933) 907

"What Constitutes a Good Legal Education?" 19 American Bar Association Journal (1933) 723

"Save America First" (1938)

"If Men Were Angels" (1942)

Book Review, 54 Harvard Law Review (1941) 905

"White Collar Justice," Saturday Evening Post, July 17, 1943

Book Review, 52 Yale Law Journal (1943) 935

Book Review, 57 Harvard Law Review (1944) 1120

"The Cult of the Robe," 28 Saturday Review of Literature (1945) 12

"Fate and Freedom" (1945)

Book Review, 59 Harvard Law Review (1946) 1004

Book Review, 56 Yale Law Journal (1947) 549

"A Plea For Lawyer-Schools," 56 Yale Law Journal (1947) 1303

"A Sketch of An Influence," in the volume "Interpretations of Modern Legal Philosophies" (1947) 189

"Words and Music," 47 Columbia Law Journal (1947) 1259

"Say It With Music," 61 Harvard Law Review (1948) 921

Book Review, 15 University of Chicago Law Review (1948) 462

"Cardozo and the Upper-Court Myth," 13 Law and Contemporary Problems (1948) 369

November 21, 1948   *Jerome Frank*

Part One

THE BASIC LEGAL MYTH, AND
SOME OF ITS CONSEQUENCES

CHAPTER I

THE BASIC MYTH

The lay attitude towards lawyers is a compound of contradictions, a mingling of respect and derision. Although lawyers occupy leading positions in government and industry, although the public looks to them for guidance in meeting its most vital problems, yet concurrently it sneers at them as tricksters and quibblers.

Respect for the bar is not difficult to explain. Justice, the protection of life, the sanctity of property, the direction of social control—these fundamentals are the business of the law and of its ministers, the lawyers. Inevitably the importance of such functions invests the legal profession with dignity.

But coupled with a deference towards their function there is cynical disdain of the lawyers themselves. "Good jurist, bad Christian," preached Martin Luther in the sixteenth century. Frederick the Great and Herbert Hoover, Rabelais and H. G. Wells have echoed that sentiment. In varying forms it is repeated daily. The layman, despite the fact that he constantly calls upon lawyers for advice on innumerous questions, public and domestic, regards lawyers as equivocators, artists in double-dealing, masters of chicane.

The stage comedian can always earn a laugh with the pun on lawyers and liars. Still popular are Gay's couplets,

> "I know you lawyers can, with ease,
> Twist words and meanings as you please;
> That language, by your skill made pliant,
> Will bend to favor every client."

Not all the criticism is as gentle: "Going tew law," said Josh Billings, "is like skinning a new milch cow for the hide and giving the meat tew the lawyers." Butler in "Hudibras" was of like mind:

> "He that with injury is grieved
> And goes to law to be relieved,
> Is sillier than a Scottish chouse
> Who, when a thief has robbed his house,
> Applies himself to cunning men
> To help him to his goods again."

Arnold Bennett denounces the "lawyers as the most vicious opponents of social progress today." Ambassador Page wrote, "I sometimes wish that there were not a lawyer in the world."

Diatribes against lawyers contain such words and phrases as "duplicity," "equivocation," "evasions," "a vast system of deception," "juggling," "sleight of hand," "craft and circumvention," "the art of puzzling and confounding," "darken by elucidation," "the pettifoging, hypocritical, brigandage rampant under forms of law." Kipling expresses the feeling of many in his fling at the "tribe who describe with a gibe the perversions of Justice."

What is the source of these doubts of the lawyer's honesty and sincerity?

A false tradition "invented by twelfth-century priests and monks," replies Dean Roscoe Pound.[1], [1] "For the most part clerical jealousy of the rising profession of non-clerical lawyers was the determining element. . . . Naturally, the clergy did not relinquish the practice of law without a protest." What those priests began, says Pound, Luther developed, and since Luther's day the other learned professions have taken over. "Unless one perceives that a struggle of professions for leadership is involved," one cannot understand the distrust of the legal profession. The

---

[1] The numbers in brackets [] refer to notes found in Appendix IX, "Reference Notes, by chapter."

lawyer is today, as he was in the twelfth century, in a marked position of advantage. This irks the other learned men. "Their minds are fertile soil for the time-worn tradition."

An ingenious explanation, but patently superficial.[2] Surely twentieth-century mistrust of lawyers is based on something more than a twelfth-century monkish invention embodied in a tradition kept alive principally because the physicians, the engineers, and the journalists have been jealous of the lawyers' prestige. Modern dispraise of the Bar is not to be explained as merely an outcropping of angry rivalry; obviously it is not confined to members of competing professions. That lawyers are scheming hair-splitters is a popular commonplace.

What lies back of this popular criticism? It appears to be founded on a belief that the lawyers complicate the law, and complicate it wantonly and unnecessarily, that, if the legal profession did not interpose its craftiness and guile, the law could be clear, exact and certain. The layman thinks that it would be possible so to revise the law books that they would become something like logarithm tables, that the lawyers could, if only they would, contrive some kind of legal slide-rule for finding exact legal answers. Public opinion agrees with Napoleon who was sure that "it would be possible to reduce laws to simple geometrical demonstrations, so that whoever could read and tie two ideas together would be capable of pronouncing on them."[2]

But the law as we have it is uncertain, indefinite, subject to incalculable changes. This condition the public ascribes to the men of law; the average person considers either that lawyers are grossly negligent or that they are guilty of malpractice, venally obscuring simple legal truths in order to foment needless litigation, engaging in a guild

2 Pound's other writings indicate that he would admit as much. The explanation quoted in the text is perhaps what Llewellyn calls one of Pound's "bed-time stories for the tired bar."

conspiracy of distortion and obfuscation in the interest of larger fees.[3]

Now it must be conceded that, if the law can be made certain and invariable, the lawyers are grievously at fault. For the layman is justified in his opinion that the coefficient of legal uncertainty is unquestionably large, that to predict the decisions of the courts on many a point is impossible. Any competent lawyer, during any rainy Sunday afternoon, could prepare a list of hundreds of comparatively simple legal questions to which any other equally competent lawyer would scarcely venture to give unequivocal answers.

Yet the layman errs in his belief that this lack of precision and finality is to be ascribed to the lawyers. The truth of the matter is that the popular notion of the possibilities of legal exactness is based upon a misconception. The law always has been, is now, and will ever continue to be, largely vague and variable. And how could this well be otherwise? The law deals with human relations in their most complicated aspects. The whole confused, shifting helter-skelter of life parades before it—more confused than ever, in our kaleidoscopic age.

Even in a relatively static society, men have never been able to construct a comprehensive, eternized set of rules anticipating all possible legal disputes and settling them in advance. Even in such a social order no one can foresee all the future permutations and combinations of events; situations are bound to occur which were never contemplated when the original rules were made. How much less is such a frozen legal system possible in modern times. New instruments of production, new modes of travel and of dwelling, new credit and ownership devices, new concentrations of capital, new social customs, habits, aims and ideals—all these factors of innovation make vain the hope that definitive legal rules can be drafted that will forever after solve all legal problems. When human relationships are transforming daily, legal relationships cannot be expressed in enduring form. The constant development of unprecedented problems requires a legal system capable of fluidity and pliancy.[3] Our society would be strait-jacketed were not the courts, with the able assistance of the lawyers, constantly overhauling the law and adapting it to the realities of ever-changing social, industrial and political conditions; although changes cannot be made lightly, yet law must be more or less impermanent, experimental and therefore not nicely calculable. *Much of the uncertainty of law is not an unfortunate accident: it is of immense social value.*[4]

In fields other than the law there is today a willingness to accept probabilities and to forego the hope of finding the absolutely certain.[5] Even in physics and chemistry, where a high degree of quantitative exactness is possible, modern leaders of thought are recognizing that finality and ultimate precision are not to be attained.[4] The physicists, indeed, have just announced the Principle of Uncertainty or Indeterminacy. If there can be nothing like complete definiteness in the natural sciences, it is surely absurd

[3] Unheeded by most members of the Bar, a minority group of brilliant critics of our legal system have demonstrated that anything like complete legal certainty cannot be realized. They have made clear that, in the very nature of things, not nearly as much rigidity in law exists or can be procured as laymen or most lawyers suppose. The law, they point out, can make only relative and temporary compromises between stability and indispensable adjustment to the constantly shifting factors of social life. "All thinking about law has struggled to reconcile the conflicting demands of the need of stability and the need of change." And this struggle has been incessant. Law, in attempting a harmony of these conflicting demands, is at best governed by "the logic of probabilities." This point the reader will find expounded by such writers as Maine, Holmes, Pound, Cohen, Cardozo, Cook, Demogue, Geny, Gmelin, Gray, Green, Coudert, Bingham, Yntema, Hutcheson, Radin, Llewellyn and Lehman.

Evidence of the uncertain character of the law will appear in the following chapters.

[4] No approbation of *mere change* is intended; see Part Three, Chapter I, last three pages.

[5] See Appendix III on "Science and Certainty: an Unscientific Conception of Science."

to expect to realize even approximate certainty and predictability in law, dealing as it does with the vagaries of complicated human adjustments.

Since legal tentativeness is inevitable and often socially desirable, it should not be considered an avoidable evil. But the public learns little or nothing of this desirability of legal tentativeness from the learned gentlemen of the law. Why this concealment? Have the lawyers a sinister purpose in concealing the inherent uncertainty of law? Why, it may fairly be asked, do they keep alive the popular belief that legal rules can be made predictable? If lawyers are not responsible for legal indefiniteness, are they not guilty, at any rate, of duping the public as to the essential character of law? Are they not a profession of clever hypocrites?

There is no denying that the bar appears to employ elaborate pretenses to foster the misguided notions of the populace. Lawyers do not merely sustain the vulgar notion that law is capable of being made entirely stable and unvarying; they seem bent on creating the impression that, on the whole, it is already established and certain. When a client indignantly exclaims, "A pretty state of affairs when I can't learn exactly what my rights are!" how does the lawyer usually respond? With assurances that the situation is exceptional, that generally speaking the law is clear enough, but that in this particular instance, for some reason or other the applicable rules cannot be definitely ascertained. Often the facts are the scape-goat: "If," says the lawyer, "the facts of your case were established and undisputed, the law could be categorically stated." When this explanation won't wash, because the pertinent facts do not happen to be in doubt, the client is told that the rules affecting his problem have become but temporarily unsettled: "Congress has just passed a badly worded statute," or "The judges who have recently tampered with the law of the subject are exceptionally stupid, or thoughtless, or weak, or radical, or what not." Implicit in these rejoinders is the view that, for the most part, legal rights and obligations are clear and indubitable, and that such small portion of the law as is not already certain can easily be made so.

Of course, such assurances are unwarranted. Each week the courts decide hundreds of cases which purport to turn not on disputed "questions of fact" but solely on "points of law."[5] If the law is unambiguous and predictable, what excuses can be made by the lawyers who lose these cases? They should know in advance of the decisions that the rules of law are adverse to their contentions. Why, then, are these suits brought or defended? In some few instances, doubtless, because of ignorance or cupidity or an effort to procure delay, or because a stubbornly litigious client insists. But in many cases, honest and intelligent counsel on both sides of such controversies can conscientiously advise their respective clients to engage in the contest; they can do so because, prior to the decision, the law is sufficiently in doubt to justify such advice.

It would seem, then, that the legal practitioners must be aware of the unsettled condition of the law. Yet observe the arguments of counsel in addressing the courts, or the very opinions of the courts themselves: they are worded as if correct decisions were arrived at by logical deduction from a precise and pre-existing body of legal rules. Seldom do judges disclose any contingent elements in their reasoning, any doubts or lack of whole-hearted conviction. The judicial vocabulary contains few phrases expressive of uncertainty. As Sir Henry Maine put it—

When a group of facts comes before a court for adjudication, "the whole course of the discussion between the judge and the advocate assumes that no question is, or can be, raised which will call for the application of any principles but old ones, or of any distinctions but such as have long since been allowed. It is taken absolutely for granted that there is somewhere a rule of known law which will cover the facts of the dispute now litigated, and that, if such a rule be not discovered, it is only that the necessary patience, knowledge or acumen, is not forthcoming to detect it. The uninformed listener would conclude that court and counsel unhesitatingly accept a doctrine that somewhere, *in nubibus,* or *in gremio magistratum,* there existed a complete, coherent, symmetrical body of . . . law, of an amplitude sufficient to furnish principles which would apply to any conceivable combination of circumstances."

Why these pretenses, why this professional hypocrisy? The answer is an arresting one: There is no hypocrisy. The lawyers' pretenses are not *consciously* deceptive. The lawyers, themselves, like the laymen, fail to recognize fully the essentially plastic and mutable character of law.[6] Although it is the chiefest function of lawyers to make the legal rules viable and pliable, a large part of the profession believes, and therefore encourages the laity to believe, that those rules either are or can be made essentially immutable. And so you will find lawyers saying that "The judicial process in ascertaining or applying the law is essentially similar to the process by which we acquire our knowledge of geometry. . . . In the great majority of cases the solution of them [legal problems] is as certain and exact as an answer to a problem in mathematics."[6]

Now the true art of the lawyer is the art of legal modification, an art highly useful to the layman. For the layman's interests, although he does not realize it, would be poorly served by an immobile system of law. Especially is this so in the twentieth century. The emphasis of our era is on change. The present trend in law is, accordingly, away from static security—the preservation of old established rights—and towards dynamic security—the protection of

[6] Except, that is, an astonishingly small minority who have heeded the critical writings noted above. The great majority of lawyers ignore these writings and accept views such as those expressed by Professor Beale that "Wherever there is a political society, there must be a complete body of law, which shall cover every event there happening."

Of course, even among the majority, there are varying degrees of awareness of the inherent uncertainty of law. Indeed, any one lawyer may vary from time to time in his apprehension of this truth.

men engaged in new enterprises.[7] Which means that the
layman's ordinary practical needs would be seriously
thwarted by an inelastic legal arrangement. A body of undeviating legal principles he would find unbearably procrustean. Yet paradoxically he and his lawyers, when they
express their notions of a desirable legal system, usually
state that they want the law to be everlastingly settled.

Here we arrive at a curious problem: Why do men crave
an undesirable and indeed unrealizable permanence and
fixity in law? Why in a modern world does the ancient
dream persist of a comprehensive and unchanging body of
law? Why do the generality of lawyers insist that law
should and can be clearly knowable and precisely predictable although, by doing so, they justify a popular belief in
an absurd standard of legal exactness? Why do lawyers,
indeed, themselves recognize such an absurd standard,
which makes their admirable and socially valuable
achievement—keeping the law supple and flexible—seem
bungling and harmful?[7] Why do men of our time repeat
the complaint made by Francis Bacon several hundred
years since, that "our laws, as they now stand, are subject
to great incertainties" and adhere to his conviction that
such "incertainties" are pernicious and altogether avoidable?

Why this unceasing quest of what is unobtainable and
would often be undesirable?

One keen thinker, Wurzel,[8] has directed his attention
to this question. He, too, questions why there exists a longing for complete certainty in law and why a pretense that
it can be attained. He finds the answer in what he terms a

---

7 At the very moment when they are doing their best work, when
they are engaged in the indispensable task of skillfully renovating
the law and adjusting it to meet new problems, the men of law seem
to the public, and often to themselves, to be desecrating the ideals
to which they have vowed allegiance. Inevitably, as a result, lawyers are attacked as incompetent or dishonest. Inevitably, too, the
lawyers are baffled by their own apparently dual and inconsistent
obligations. See further on this point, Part One, Chapter III.

"social want" for a body of law which shall appear to be, what it can never be, an exhaustive list of commands, issued by the State, sufficient to settle every conceivable controversy which may arise. He maintains that the psychology of our administration of justice imperatively requires that this "social want" be satisfied by false appearances.

This is scarcely a sufficient answer.[8] It provokes the further questions, What is back of this "social want"? Why must law seem to be, what it is not, a virtually complete set of commands? Why do lawyers who seem to be keen-minded, hard-headed realists, use numerous devices, however unwittingly, to deceive themselves and the public? Why this desire to be fooled? What is the source of this curious "social want"?

We shall in this essay attempt a partial answer.

Let us first rephrase our problem. Only a limited degree of legal certainty can be attained. The current demand for exactness and predictability in law is incapable of satisfaction because a greater degree of legal finality is sought than is procurable, desirable or necessary. If it be true that greater legal certainty is sought than is practically required or attainable, then the demand for excessive legal stability does not arise from practical needs. It must have its roots not in reality but in a yearning for something unreal.[9]

[8] For the writer's indebtedness to Wurzel, see Part Two, Chapter IV, and Appendix IX, Part One, Chapter I, note 8.

[9] There is no denying that, in part, the demand for exactly predictable law arises from practical needs, has its roots in reality. But the practical aspect of the demand is usually exaggerated. (See below, Part One, Chapter III.) Moreover, it often happens that the same man who today wants law to be inflexible, tomorrow wants it pliable; yet, significantly, when he comes to articulate his notion of desirable law he usually remembers only his demand for legal fixity and forgets the occasions when his practical aims were best served by fluid law. (See below, page 239.)

Finally, it must not be overlooked that although a demand arises from practical needs, it may yet be incapable of satisfaction; such a demand any man, so far as he is objective-minded, therefore abandons. Jones may be in Tokio at the very moment when his

Which is to say that the widespread notion that law either is or can be made approximately stationary and certain is irrational and should be classed as an illusion or a myth.

What is the source of this basic legal myth?[10]

---

practical needs require him to be physically present in New York. A wishing-rug would be handy. But although practical needs prompt his desire for instantaneous transportation across the globe, it can scarcely be said that, if Jones insists upon procuring a wishing-rug, his demand is therefore practical in its nature. (See below, Part One, Chapter XIV and page 398.)

[10] This myth is an old one, although its form and expression have often changed. See pages 283–284 and 313–317.

CHAPTER II

A PARTIAL EXPLANATION

We are on the trail of a stubborn illusion. Where better, then, to look for clues than in the direction of childhood? For in children's problems, and in children's modes of meeting their problems, are to be found the sources of most of the confirmed illusions of later years.

It is indeed true, however platitudinous, that the child is father to the man. With more or less awareness, educators have always applied that truth; they have known—and not those in the Catholic Church alone—that attitudes formed in early years persist and play important rôles in the views and opinions of adult life. Yet it is but yesterday that psychiatrists began systematically to relate the bad habits of youth to the maladjustments of later life. And only today are psychologists noting that the behavior patterns of early childhood are the basis of many subsequent adaptations. At long last, they are using a genetic approach; the emotional handicaps of adult life, they now tell us, "represent almost invariably, if not always, the unsolved problems or the partially solved or badly solved problems of childhood."[1]

For our purpose, then, of finding the cause of a vigorous illusion of grown men, we shall probably not go astray in observing some phases of child development.

The child at birth is literally forced from a small world of almost complete and effortless security into a new environment which at once sets up a series of demands. Strange sensations of light, sound, touch and smell attack him. The nearly perfect pre-birth harmony and serenity are over. The infant now must breathe and eat. His struggle for existence has begun. But his wants, at first, are few and are satisfied with a minimum of strain on his own part. The parents do their best to meet, almost instantly, the infant's desires. In this sense, he approximates omnipotence, because, relative to his askings, he achieves nearly complete obedience. His handwavings and cries magically command responses on the part of the environment.

As infancy recedes his direct omnipotence diminishes. But that there is omnipotence somewhere the child does not doubt. Chance does not yet exist for him. Everything is explainable. All events can be accounted for. There is, he believes, no happening without a knowable reason. The contingent and the accidental are unthinkable. There must always be whys and wherefores. Chaos is beyond belief. Order and rule govern all.

As early childhood passes and consciousness grows keener, now and again the child becomes sharply aware of his incapacity for controlling the crushing, heedless, reluctant and uncertain facts of the outer world. Recurrently, confusion descends upon him. Sudden experiences surprise him, crash in on his childish scheme of things, and temporarily overwhelm him. Fears beset him—fear of the vague things that stalk the darkness, fear of the unruly, the unseen, the horrible bogies of the unknown.

Then he rushes to his parents for help. They stand between him and the multitudinous cruelties and vagaries of life. They are all-powerful, all-knowing. If the child can no longer believe himself capable of controlling the universe, he can still believe that his parents do so—and for him. They hold sway over the outer world, they run things, they are rulers and protectors. They know everything. They understand the strange ways of life which are at times oppressively baffling to him. Father and mother are unabashed by complications. They know what is right and what is wrong. They bring order out of what seems to be chaos.

The child still possesses omnipotence—but now, vicariously. Through his dependence upon his parents' omnipotence he finds relief from unbearable uncertainty. His overestimation of the parental powers is an essential of his development.

It must not be overlooked that a significant division of parental functions takes place early in the life of the child. In all communities where the father is head of the family, the mother comes to "represent the nearer and more familiar influence, domestic tenderness, the help, the rest and the solace to which the child can always turn," writes Malinowski in a recent anthropological study. But "the father has to adopt the position of the final arbiter in force and authority. He has gradually to cast off the rôle of tender and protective friend, and to adopt the position of strict judge, and hard executor of law." And so, in the childish appraisal of the parents, the mother tends to become the embodiment of all that is protectively tender while the father personifies all that is certain, secure, infallible, and embodies exact law-making, law-pronouncing and law-enforcing. The child, in his struggle for existence, makes vital use of his belief in an omniscient and omnipotent father, a father who lays down infallible and precise rules of conduct.

Then, slowly, repeated experiences erode this fictional overestimate. "Adam," said Mark Twain's Eve, "knows ever so many things, but, poor dear, most of them aren't so." To the child, parental wisdom now comes to seem like Adam's. There are many things father doesn't know, things he can't do. Other humans successfully oppose him. And there are forces loose in the world beyond his control. One's own father is at times helpless, deficient; he is all-too-human. The child's lofty conception of fatherly dignity and infallibility crumbles before the cumulative evidence of disappointing paternal weakness and ignorance.[1]

[1] Edmund Gosse in his autobiography, "Father and Son" relates the following: "I believed that my Father knew everything and saw everything. One morning in my sixth year, my Mother and I were alone in the morning-room, when my Father came in and announced some fact to us. I was standing on the rug, gazing at him,

But the average child cannot completely accept this disillusionment. He has formed an irresistible need for an omniscient and omnipotent father who shall stand between him and life's uncertainties. The child's own sense of power and control vanished in early infancy. Now life seems to demand that he shall take a next step and abandon his reliance on the conviction that someone close to him possesses consummate wisdom. His attitudes and adaptations had been built upon his relations to his idealized, his incomparable father. The child is disoriented. Again panic fear attacks him. He is unwilling and largely unable to accept as realities the ungovernable, the unorderable aspects of life. Surely, he feels, somewhere there must be Someone who can control events, make the dark spots light, make the uncertain clear. Chance and contingency he will not submit to as finalities; the apparently fortuitous must be susceptible of subjection to the rule of some person—a person, too, like his father, whom the child can propitiate.

Many are the persons who become substitutes for the deposed father: the priest or pastor, the rulers and leaders of the group. They, too, turn out to be disappointing. But the demand for fatherly authority does not die. To be sure, as the child grows into manhood, this demand grows less and less vocal, more and more unconscious.[2] The father-substitutes become less definite in form, more vague and

---

and when he made this statement, I remember turning quickly in embarrassment, and looking into the fire. The shock to me was as that of a thunderbolt, for what my Father had said *was not true.* My Mother and I, who had been present at the trifling incident, were aware that it had not happened exactly as it had been reported by him. My Mother gently told him so, and he accepted the correction. Nothing could possibly have been more trifling to my parents, but to me it meant an epoch. Here was the appalling discovery, never suspected before, that my Father was not as God, and did not know everything. The shock was not caused by any suspicion that he was not telling the truth, as it appeared to him, but by the awful proof that he was not, as I had supposed, omniscient."

[2] The reader who objects to the use of the term "unconscious," will find an alternative description, in somewhat more physiological terms, in Appendix VIII.

impersonal. But the relation to the father has become a paradigm, a prototype of later relations.[3] Concealed and submerged, there persists a longing to reproduce the father-child pattern, to escape uncertainty and confusion through the rediscovery of a father.

For although as we grow older we are compelled to some extent to acknowledge the existence of reasonless, limitless and indeterminate aspects of life, yet most of us strive to blind our eyes to them. And then, at moments when chaos becomes too evident to be denied, we rush, fear-ridden, as if we were children, to some protective father-like authority. Most men, childishly dreading the unknown, strive to find behind everyday experiences a Something resembling paternal control, a Something that can be relied upon to insure, somehow, against the apparent reality of the chanciness and disorder of events. Few are the persons able to relinquish the props of childhood and bravely admit that life is full of unavoidable hazards beyond the control, direct or indirect, of finite humans.

A book has been written with the witty title, "Were You Ever a Child?"[2] That is a question well worth asking. It prompts the further question: To what extent is a grown man still a child? To the extent perhaps that he cannot stand the idea of pure and avoidless chance.

William James' career is suggestive. As a young man "a sense of the insecurity of life," a consciousness of a "pit of insecurity beneath the surface of life," so obsessed him that he was seized with that morbid melancholy "which takes the form of panic fear" and reached the point of suicidal mania. He might, he reports, have gone insane, if he had not clung to scripture-texts such as "The Eternal God is my refuge." Suddenly he was "cured." And the cure consisted in a sudden shift to a positive delight in the hazardous, incalculable character of life. Life's very insecurity became its most inviting aspect. He came to enjoy

---

[3] "Not only," says Malinowski, "is the family the link between biological cohesion and social cohesion; it is the pattern on which all wider relations are based."

an attitude which "involves an element of active tension, of holding my own, as it were, and trusting outward things to perform their part so as to make it a full harmony, but without any *guaranty* that they will. Make it a guaranty —and the attitude immediately becomes to my consciousness stagnant and stingless. Take away the guaranty, and I feel . . . a sort of deep enthusiastic bliss, of utter willingness to do and suffer anything. . . ." This sudden shift from panic fear of insecurity to a deep enthusiastic bliss in the absence of security marked for James the advent of emotional adulthood. He then first began to play a man's part.[3]

But there are few who reach such adult stature. Most men do not achieve, as James did, the courage to tolerate, much less to enjoy, the idea of ultimate and irreducible contingency; they retain a yearning for Someone or Something, qualitatively resembling father, to aid them in dissipating the fear of chance and change.

That religion shows the effects of the childish desire to recapture a father-controlled world has been often observed.[4] But the effect on the law of this childish desire has escaped attention. And yet it is obvious enough: To the child the father is the Infallible Judge, the Maker of definite rules of conduct. He knows precisely what is right and what is wrong and, as head of the family, sits in judgment and punishes misdeeds. The Law—a body of rules apparently devised for infallibly determining what is right and what is wrong and for deciding who should be punished for misdeeds—inevitably becomes a partial substitute for the Father-as-Infallible-Judge. That is, the desire persists in grown men to recapture, through a rediscovery of a father, a childish, completely controllable universe, and that desire seeks satisfaction in a partial, unconscious, anthropomorphizing of Law, in ascribing to the Law some of the characteristics of the child's Father-Judge. That childish longing is an important element in the explanation of the absurdly unrealistic notion that law is, or can be made, entirely certain and definitely predictable.

This, then, is our partial explanation of the basic legal myth: The filial relation is clearly indicated as one important unconscious determinant of the ways of man in dealing with all his problems,[5] including the problem of his attitude towards the law. The several components of this explanation may be summarized thus:

(1) The infant strives to retain something like pre-birth serenity. Conversely, fear of the unknown, dread of chance and change, are vital factors in the life of the child.

(2) These factors manifest themselves in a childish appetite for complete peace, comfort, protection from the dangers of the unknown.[4] The child, "unrealistically," craves a steadfast world which will be steady and controllable.

(3) The child satisfies that craving, in large measure, through his confidence in and reliance on his incomparable, omnipotent, infallible father.

(4) Despite advancing years, most men are at times the victims of the childish desire for complete serenity and the childish fear of irreducible chance. They then will to believe that they live in a world in which chance is only an appearance and not a reality, in which they can be free of the indefinite, the arbitrary, the capricious. When they find life distracting, unsettling, fatiguing, they long to rise above the struggle for existence; to be rid of all upsetting shifts and changes and novelties; to discover an uninterrupted connection between apparently disjunctive events; to rest in an environment that is fundamentally stable. They revert, that is, to childish longings, which they attempt to satisfy through "the rediscovery of father," through father-substitutes. Even where the fear factor is absent, the desire for father-substitutes may persist; father-dependence, originally a means of adaptation, has become an end-in-itself.[5]

---

[4] There are opposing dynamic childish tendencies which will be discussed in later chapters.

[5] Father-dependence in adult years was once socially valuable —when the economic organization of society was patriarchal. The

(5) The Law can easily be made to play an important part in the attempted rediscovery of the father. For, functionally, the law apparently resembles the Father-as-Judge.[6]

(6) The child's Father-as-Judge was infallible. His judgments and commands appeared to bring order out of the chaos of conflicting views concerning right conduct. His law seemed absolutely certain and predictable. Grown men, when they strive to recapture the emotional satisfactions of the child's world, without being consciously aware of their motivation, seek in their legal systems the authoritativeness, certainty and predictability which the child believed that he had found in the law laid down by the father.

(7) Hence the basic legal myth that law is, or can be made, unwavering, fixed and settled.[7]

Other explanations of the legal-certainty myth there are, to be sure.[6] Some of them (such as the religious expla-

---

social code then reinforced that component of the individual's make-up which makes him seek to prolong his infantile dependence on his father. Floyd Dell (in a work, "Love in the Machine Age," published while this book was in preparation) maintains that we have but recently advanced beyond patriarchalism economically and are therefore still largely controlled psychologically by mores, no longer appropriate to our times, which favor excessive reliance on the father.

[6] Law and Religion are, of course, not the only activities affected by the search for fatherly authority. Science, too, suffers when it is made to bear the burden of being a complete guarantor of cosmic certainty. (See Appendix III.)

What is significant is that the law, which, as we have seen, inherently is one of the least certain of human enterprises, is looked to for an absurdly disproportionate degree of certainty; more certainty is demanded in law than in biology, for instance. The fact that, more obviously than most other departments of life, the law seems to resemble the child's conception of the Father-as-Judge, will serve as a partial explanation of this paradox. (See further, Part Three, Chapter I and Chapter II.)

[7] The description of childish thought processes is amplified below. *As to the validity of psychological explanations, see Appendix X, Section 2.*

nation)[7] are based on the supposed effects of tendencies no longer operative except as "survivals"[8] of past history. The particular cause we are isolating is no mere "survival"; it is as powerfully operative today as it was in the past. It could be said of any period of history as it can be said at this moment; society is made up of persons all of whom now are, or recently were, children. Our thesis rests on observations of current phenomena clear to the eye of any amateur anthropologist in any modern group.

We have used the phrases "one important determinant" and "an important element" in referring to the father-regarding attitude as an explanation of the basic illusion of complete legal predictability. For it is not pretended that we have isolated the sole cause of a reaction which, like most human reactions, is of course the product of a constellation of several forces. Yet, for the sake of emphasis, we shall in what follows treat a partial explanation as if it were the only one. We shall openly and avowedly take a part for the whole; we shall employ what has been aptly called a "neglective fiction."[9]

With such qualifications we may now state succinctly our answer to the puzzling question: Why do men seek unrealizable certainty in law? Because, we reply, they have not yet relinquished the childish need for an authoritative father and unconsciously have tried to find in the law a substitute for those attributes of firmness, sureness, certainty and infallibility ascribed in childhood to the father.[8]

---

[8] We do not intend to assert that lawyers are "childish" nor to deny that lawyers are far less prone than laymen to be controlled in their thinking by illusory aims with respect to law. See further, pp. 83, 90, 99.

We said a *partial* explanation. Others, of course, will occur to the reader. (Fourteen among many additional possible explanations are listed in Appendix I.) *The one "cause" singled out and treated as incessant is not the only cause, is often not the most important, is not unceasing, is largely unconscious. But it has been neglected. And to pretend, temporarily, that that "cause" is exclusive and unceasing is a useful "fiction" serving to bring it forcibly to attention.* Such "let's pretend" devices are explained in Appendix IX,

Part One, Chapter II, note 9, and in Appendix VII. The correct use of such an avowedly *partial analysis* produces a more informed synthesis. The "economic man," properly used, is illustrative. Or Beard's economic interpretation of our Constitution. Or Weber's explanation of the effect of Calvinism on capitalism. These are deliberately partial analyses. They are as "true" and as "false" as the hydrogen photograph of the sun; that photograph reveals the sun "as if" it were made up solely of hydrogen; once you have seen it you know far more about the sun than before, but it is not the sun's picture except in a "fictional" sense.

Another caution. *Psychology is still in its early youth; most of its concepts are "as ifs" or "let's pretends" and too little recognized as such by the psychologists.* But blunt instruments though these concepts still are, they are products of far more direct observation than the older (so-called) science of law has devoted to its material. They are the best instruments now available for the study of human nature. Among those concepts is the "father-substitute" notion. It has been found highly effective in dealing with actual behavior problems of many children and with the quirks in the ways of many adults. *It is not the only such concept.* But it seemed peculiarly helpful in vividly disclosing befuddled thinking about law.

As to all the foregoing see Appendix X.

This book, then, from now on, reads as if unconscious "father-substitution" were *the* explanation of the oddities it discusses. But, we repeat, we are consciously using a partial explanation. It is employed to further the chief aim of this book: the development of that "realistic" movement in law which seeks to overcome an astonishingly prevalent blindness to legal realities.

CHAPTER III

THE LANGUAGE OF THE LAW: LAWYERS AS A PROFESSION OF RATIONALIZERS

When the layman speaks derisively of lawyers' language he is usually met with a patronizing smile and is told that the practice of the law necessitates a special technique of speech which may seem to the uninitiate to be indirect but which lawyers have discovered to be vitally necessary to the effective handling of legal concepts. Perhaps both the lay criticism and the professional answer are, after their respective fashions, correct. Let us note one or two stock instances of the sort of judicial utterance that provokes public scorn:

In 1890 Congress passed the Sherman Act making illegal *"every* contract or combination . . . in restraint of trade or commerce." In a series of cases, heard during the years 1896 to 1904, the United States Supreme Court was urged to construe this statute as prohibiting merely those contracts which "unreasonably" restrained trade. But the Court repeatedly and steadfastly refused to apply this so-called "rule of reason." Congress, it held, had made unlawful *every* contract in restraint of trade and not merely those which created an unreasonable restraint. "The plain and ordinary meaning of such language," said the Supreme Court, "is not limited to that kind of restraint of trade, but all contracts are included in such language and no exception or limitation can be added without placing in the Act that which has been omitted by Congress."

These cases were decided by a divided Court, three to

four of the Judges dissenting in each instance. The minority opinions during these ten years were usually written by Mr. Justice White, who frequently reiterated the conviction that the majority of the Court was erroneously interpreting the meaning of Congress.

In 1911, however, the Court, in the *Standard Oil* and *Tobacco* cases, decided that the language of the Act meant and had always meant that only contracts *"unreasonably"* restraining trade were illegal. The majority opinions in these later cases were written by Mr. Justice White. He announced that ever since its enactment the Court had been interpreting the Sherman Act according to "the rule of reason." White's opinions developed this argument extensively and this despite the fact that the language of the earlier majority opinions had explicitly repudiated such an interpretation.

Now it is plain enough that the Court changed its mind. How can this about-face be explained? To the unbiased observer, the cause of this shift is simple. By 1911 several of the judges who had participated in the earlier cases had resigned or died, and new judges had been appointed in their places. The views of these new judges coincided with Mr. Justice White's. He now represented the majority of the Court where, theretofore, he had represented the minority. He could now speak for the majority, while before he had spoken only for the minority. What had been his dissenting opinions he could now file as the majority opinions with scarce the change of a syllable. The Court had, by process of death and disease, changed its membership and its mind. The "rule of reason," theretofore often rejected, was now the law of the land by a vote of five to four judges.

But Mr. Justice White in these later cases gives no such explanation. On the contrary, he maintains that the Court had in no wise changed its views, that the majority opinions in the 1911 cases are entirely consistent with the majority opinions in the 1896–1904 cases: the identical doctrine, supporting the "rule of reason," runs through all the majority opinions, he insists. To be sure, there are judicial expressions vehemently to the contrary in the majority views expressed in the earlier cases. A superficial reader might assume that, until the *Standard Oil* case, the Court had again and again flatly refused to apply the "rule of reason." But, says White, beneath the surface of the faulty verbiage lay the one unvarying principle that not all contracts in restraint of trade, but only the more limited group, were illegal; although the Court had apparently held otherwise—and although White, in his earlier dissents, had plainly expressed the opinion that the Court had held otherwise—in truth and in fact the Court had never deviated from the true rule which he was now applying.

White, that is, refused to admit the fact of change. He devoted many words to demonstrating that the abandonment of the former rule was merely apparent and not real. In so doing, White was true to the juridical conventions: he went to elaborate care to avoid admitting that the law could be modified by the courts and was therefore possibly inconstant and unpredictable. But so strained did his language seem to the public that the discrepancy between what the Supreme Court did, and what it said, became too glaringly obvious and provoked many a cynical comment on the tricky ways of the law and the disingenuousness of judges.[1] But, as we shall see, the popular references to Mr. Justice White's insincerity were entirely unjustified.

Yet another illustration of similar verbal habits:

Under our Federal constitution and statutes the Federal courts may hear only a limited class of cases. If the subject matter of a dispute is not within any of these classes, the parties cannot ordinarily seek relief in the Federal, as distinguished from the state courts. It is expressly provided, however, that, regardless of the nature of the subject-matter, suit may be brought in the Federal courts whenever the controversy is one "between citizens of different states."

---

[1] There were also economic and political reasons for the adverse comments on White's opinions. What we are stressing here is the false charge that White was a hypocrite.

In other words, whatever the nature of the dispute, Jones, a citizen of Massachusetts, can sue Smith, a citizen of Rhode Island, in the Federal courts.

Early in its career the United States Supreme Court was called on to consider whether, for the purpose of such suits, a corporation is a "citizen": If Jones of Massachusetts brings suit in the United States District Court against the Smith Corporation, organized in Rhode Island, can it be said that there exists a controversy "between *citizens of different states*"? No, said the Supreme Court. The controversy is between a citizen and a corporation. A corporation is obviously not a citizen. Therefore there is no controversy between citizens of different states and we cannot hear the case.

Subsequently other cases arose in which, in spite of the earlier ruling, the Court felt constrained, for practical reasons, to permit such suits. And gradually the Court evolved a rule that, while a corporation is not a citizen, yet in actual effect and for this special purpose, it will be treated exactly as if it were a citizen of the state in which it is incorporated. The Court, to all intents and purposes has abandoned its original doctrine. But, by the use of involved verbal processes (set forth in the footnote below) it still adheres to its original statement that a corporation is not a citizen.[2]

[2] A general outline of the course of reasoning pursued by the court is as follows:

(1) In the first case, the court held that a corporation was not a citizen.

(2) In a later case, where a Rhode Island corporation was sued by a Massachusetts citizen, it was shown that all the stockholders of the corporation were citizens of Rhode Island. The court held that it would peer behind the corporation to observe the real parties, the Rhode Island stockholders, who were being sued in the guise of a corporation. Thus viewing the facts, the opposing parties to the suit were seen to be citizens of different states and the suit was allowed to be maintained in the Federal court.

(3) Then the following type of case arose: A Rhode Island corporation was sued by a citizen of Massachusetts. It appeared that some of the stockholders of the Rhode Island corporation were also

To the layman this circumlocutory mode of speech seems at times unnecessarily strained, artificial and almost dishonest. Why did not the Court, when its first decisions came before it for reconsideration, bluntly state that its earlier decisions, to the effect that a corporation was not a citizen, had been shown to work an unfortunate result; that, therefore, the earlier decisions were being abandoned;

---

citizens of Massachusetts, *i.e.* of the same state as the plaintiff. The corporation argued that, pursuant to the rule laid down in case (2), the suit could not be maintained because the court should peer behind the corporation to the real parties; if it did so, then the suit would appear to be between citizens, to be sure, but citizens of the same state. The court refused to accept that "logically" correct position, but avoided it by creating a new rule, holding that in such a case it would be conclusively presumed, regardless of the actual facts, that all the stockholders of the Rhode Island corporation were citizens of Rhode Island. On the basis of such a presumption, the suit was one between a Massachusetts citizen on the one side and Rhode Island citizens on the other side and the suit could be maintained in the Federal court. In other words, the court was in truth abandoning the rule laid down in case (1) without so admitting.

(4) The following type of case arose: A Massachusetts citizen sued a Rhode Island corporation. This Massachusetts citizen was a stockholder of the Rhode Island corporation. The corporation argued that, under the rule laid down in case (3), the Massachusetts citizen must be conclusively presumed to be a citizen of Rhode Island. On the basis of this presumption, both parties to the suit would be citizens of Rhode Island, and hence the suit could not be maintained because there was no diversity of citizenship. The court ruled otherwise, escaping this logically correct contention by inventing a new special rule that in a case where a stockholder sued a corporation, it would be conclusively presumed that all the stockholders, other than the stockholder who brought the suit, were citizens of the state in which the corporation was organized, but that, as to the citizen who brought the suit, the actual facts as to his citizenship could be proved, and the suit then before the court was thereby sustained.

The net result is that today, for all purposes of Federal court jurisdiction, a corporation is treated as if it were a citizen of the state in which it is incorporated, although the Supreme Court still refuses to say that a corporation is a citizen within the meaning of the "diversity of citizenship" provisions of the constitution and statutes.

and that henceforth it would hold that a corporation was a citizen within the meaning of the "diversity of citizenship" provision? Because to have made such a bald statement would have been to make too painfully clear the fact of retroactive law-making by the court. Because thereby the fact of unpredictable changes in the law would have become too disagreeably obvious.

Such and related speech habits have led some distinguished observers, such as Sir Henry Maine, to comment that lawyers employ "a double language" by which they entertain "a double and inconsistent set of ideas," or that they constantly misdescribe—to themselves and to others —what they are about.[3] There is much evidence to bear out such a charge. If, for example, judges have to decide the effect of some statutory law on a given set of facts, they purport to carry out the "intention of the legislature" which enacted that law although the legislature passed the law many years before the kinds of facts in question could conceivably have been imagined. Many old statutes, enacted when only horse-driven vehicles were known, have been applied in this fashion to qualitatively new problems arising from the use of automobiles, just as the "intention" of those who drafted our Constitution in the eighteenth century is said to be carried out with reference to twentieth-century circumstances which no sane eighteenth-century law maker would have dreamed of. The purposes of the actual human beings who comprised the legislature are only to a very limited extent considered legally pertinent. The legislators whose will the courts purport to obey are unreal and undiscoverable persons.

---

[3] "We in England," wrote Sir Henry Maine, "are well accustomed to the extension, modification, and improvement of law by a machinery which, in theory, is incapable of altering one jot or one line of existing jurisprudence. The process by which this virtual legislation is effected is not so much sensible as unacknowledged. With respect to that great portion of our legal system which is enshrined in cases and recorded in law reports, *we habitually employ a double language* and entertain, as it would appear, *a double and inconsistent set of ideas.*"

Or, on occasion, the guide to a correct legal conclusion is said to be the "manifest intention" of the maker of an instrument. Someone has observed that whenever a lawyer says that something or other was the manifest intention of a man, "manifest" means that the man never really had such an intention. Lawyers use what the layman describes as "weasel words," so-called "safety-valve concepts,"[4] such as "prudent," "negligence," "freedom of contract," "good faith," "ought to know," "due care," "due process," —terms with the vaguest meaning—as if these vague words had a precise and clear definition; they thereby create an appearance of continuity, uniformity and definiteness which does not in fact exist.

A special legal style, says Wurzel, a special manner of legal expression, has been developed such as "we must assume as proved," "it appears to be without foundation," "we cannot justly doubt." It is the purpose of such phrases "to render the difference between the real degree of probability and the cogency of the inference drawn, as inconspicuous as possible." In place of direct assertion, lawyers' language asserts an obligation to believe, and this modifying factor is afterwards disregarded. "No small part of the training of practical lawyers consists in becoming accustomed to such forms of expression and processes of thought." Wurzel concludes that lawyers have a peculiar and distinctive verbiage which conceals the real nature of their reasoning processes.[5]

The correctness of such comments seems inescapable. We lawyers do use a double language and do entertain a double and inconsistent set of ideas. And yet, in a certain sense, Wurzel's conclusions are wrong. Legal locutions and thinking are not so distinctive as he supposes. Not only lawyers but all humans use verbal devices similar to those

[4] Wurzel, "Methods of Juridical Thinking."
[5] We shall discuss below, Part One, Chapter VII, what is in effect the reverse of this charge, viz., that lawyers' foibles are caused by their misuse of words.

to which he refers. One suspects that the difference between legal and non-legal usages is one of degree.

Since Wurzel wrote his treatise on legal thinking, the psychologists have been more painstakingly describing ordinary human thinking and have developed the important concept of "rationalization." Let us compare the process of "rationalization" with Wurzel's description of the lawyer's modes of speech.

The ideas and beliefs of all of us may be roughly classified as of two kinds: those that are based primarily on direct observation of objective data and those that are entirely or almost entirely a product of subjective factors —desires and aims which push and pull us about without regard to the objective situation.

These beliefs of the second kind are usually emotionally toned to a high degree. We are usually more or less unaware of their existence although they have marked effects upon our thinking.[6] For convenience we may refer to any such belief as a "bias."

I am, let us say, an ardent Republican. The Republican party is in office and puts through a new high protective tariff. An election campaign ensues in which the merits of this tariff are in controversy. I advance many reasons in support of the Republican tariff. Now, I have not carefully investigated the problem and my arguments have little reference to the actual facts. Yet in a short time I convince myself that the Democrats are unreasonably opposing my party's position. I am sure that my views are the result of my "reasons" whereas the real determinant of my views is my political "bias" and my "reasons" are more or less illusory and after the fact. But I would most reluctantly make such an admission. I have a stubborn pride in my rationality and cannot easily let myself know that my thoughts are responsive to non-rational aims and impulses.

Such a political bias is relatively superficial. Our most

[6] The personificatory language used above is, of course, a "fictional" convenience and is not to be taken literally. See Appendix VII.

npelling biases have deeper roots and are far better concealed from consciousness. They often grow out of childish aims which are not relevant to our adult status.[7] To admit their existence would be difficult and painful. Most of us are unwilling—and for the most part unable—to concede to what an extent we are controlled by such biases. We cherish the notion that we are grown-up and rational, that we know why we think and act as we do, that our thoughts and deeds have an objective reference, that our beliefs are not biases but are of the other kind—the result of direct observation of objective data. We are able thus to delude ourselves by giving "reasons" for our attitudes. When challenged by ourselves or others to justify our positions or our conduct, we manufacture *ex post facto* a host of "principles" which we induce ourselves to believe are conclusions reasoned out by logical processes from actual facts in the actual world. So we persuade ourselves that our lives are governed by Reason.

This practice of making ourselves appear, to ourselves and others, more rational than we are, has been termed "rationalization."[8]

Rationalization not only conceals the real foundations of our biased beliefs but also enables us to maintain, side by side as it were, beliefs which are inherently incompatible. For many of our biased beliefs are contradicted by other beliefs which are related more directly to clear reasoning from real knowledge of what is going on in the outside world. We seem to keep these antagonistic beliefs apart by putting them in "logic-tight compartments." They do, however, come into contact, but, as Bernard Hart de-

---

[7] Many of these powerful biases derive from childish attempts to solve childhood problems, that is, problems which properly concerned us as children and which, with the limited equipment of children, we could not then adequately solve. We do not as adults consciously confront these problems but the infantile efforts to solve them continue, buried and concealed, to affect our adult thought and behavior.

[8] Gates suggests that "irrationalization" would have been more descriptive.

scribes it, "only through a medium which so distorts the connecting processes that the real significance of the incompatible forces is concealed, and the mind fails to appreciate that any actual contradiction is present. This distorting medium is provided by the mechanism of rationalization." The incompatible beliefs or ideas are allowed to meet, but only by means of "a bridge of rationalizations." In this manner the logical significance of each of the antagonistic beliefs or ideas is so distorted that the conflict between them is concealed.

The unique qualities of legal diction and modes of expression portrayed by Wurzel we are now prepared to see as in large part due to something in the nature of "rationalization."[9] And if "rationalization" is the normal human way of avoiding recognition of the conflict of incompatible beliefs, then the lawyer's way of thinking and talking is not as distinctive as Wurzel indicates.[1]

But this much is true: There are more rationalizations discernible in reasoning about law than in reasoning about many other subjects. Why? Because lawyers, more than most men, are compelled to reconcile incompatibles. Their everyday task is expert practical adjustment. Their life work is based upon a logic of probability. Realistic recognition of novel circumstances, tentativeness, adaptation, are of the very essence of the lawyer's invaluable technique. And yet a powerful bias—an unconscious longing for the re-creation of a child's world stimulated in all men, lawyers and laymen, by the very nature of law—requires the lawyers to seek to achieve certainty, rigidity, security, uniformity. The two aims are contradictory. Seldom can the law serve efficiently its practical function and yet operate definitely, certainly, mechanically. Usually the practical and the "ideal" functions are at cross-purposes. But the conflict between the incompatibles is concealed. In the long run, practicality is served. But by means of rationali-

[9] Judicial use of rationalization will be further considered in Part One, Chapter XII.

zations it is made to appear that there has been little or no sacrifice of the desired rigid certainty.

Viewed thus, lawyers seem to be professional rationalizers, and not, as the layman often charges, professional hypocrites—or worse. It becomes more plain why the practice of law is often referred to as an "art," an art which cannot be taught rationally but must be grasped intuitively. Indeed the practice of law as now practiced is one of the major arts of rationalization. We can now understand the better why the young lawyer is baffled by the huge gap between what he has learned in school and what he observes in the office and the courtroom. It is clear, too, why older lawyers, regardless of their spoken creeds, often are more daring and creative than recent graduates. Experience has schooled the older men to deal flexibly with changing realities and yet, without hypocrisy, use locutions which enable them to pay tribute to an unconscious childish[10] insistence on the achievement of impossible legal certainty.[11]

[10] The reader will recall that we are using a *"partial* explanation." See Part One, Chapter II, note 8, and Appendix X.

[11] An insistence often more intense among the laity than among lawyers.

No doubt Mr. Justice White in the *Standard Oil* and *Tobacco* cases was using "a double language" in response to his own inner need to preserve the appearance of legal stability when he was, in fact, changing the law. But no less was he meeting a like nonrational demand from the public. The public, that is, makes inconsistent demands upon the judges, and then indulges in unpleasant comments when the judges use rationalizing verbiage in an effort to comply with these inconsistent demands.

CHAPTER IV

JUDICIAL LAW-MAKING

Have judges the right and power to make law and change law? Much good ink has been spilled in arguing that question. A brief survey of the controversy will illuminate our thesis.

The conventional view may be summarized thus:

Law is a complete body of rules existing from time immemorial and unchangeable except to the limited extent that legislatures have changed the rules by enacted statutes. Legislatures are expressly empowered thus to change the law. But the judges are not to make or change the law but to apply it. The law, ready-made, pre-exists the judicial decisions.

Judges are simply "living oracles" of law. They are merely "the speaking law." Their function is purely passive. They are "but the mouth which pronounces the law." They no more make or invent new law than Columbus made or invented America.[1] Judicial opinions are evidence of what the law is; the best evidence, but no more than that. When a former decision is overruled, we must not say that the rule announced in the earlier decision was once the law and has now been changed by the later decision. We must view the earlier decision as laying down an erroneous rule. It was a false map of the law just as a pre-Columbian map of the world was false. Emphatically,

---

[1] "Men do not make laws," writes Calvin Coolidge. "They do but discover them. . . . That state is most fortunate in its form of government which has the aptest instruments for the discovery of laws."

we must not refer to the new decision as making new law. It only seems to do so. It is merely a bit of revised legal cartography.

If a judge actually attempted to contrive a new rule, he would be guilty of usurpation of power, for the legislature alone has the authority to change the law. The judges, writes Blackstone, are "not delegated to pronounce a new law, but to maintain and expound the old law"; even when a former decision is abandoned because "most evidently contrary to reason," the "subsequent judges do not pretend to make new law, but to vindicate the old one from misrepresentation." The prior judge's eyesight had been defective and he made "a mistake" in finding the law, which mistake is now being rectified by his successors.

Such is the conventional notion. There is a contrary minority view, which any dispassionate observer must accept as obviously the correct view:[1]

"No intelligent lawyer would in this day pretend that the decisions of the courts do not add to and alter the law,"[2] says Pollock, a distinguished English jurist. "Judge-made law is real law," writes Dicey, another famous legal commentator, "though made under the form of, and often described by judges no less than jurists, as the mere interpretation of law. . . . The amount of such judge-made law is in England far more extensive than a student realizes. Nine-tenths, at least, of the law of contract, and the whole, or nearly the whole, of the law of torts are not to be discovered in any volume of the statutes. . . . Whole branches, not of ancient but of very modern law, have been built up, developed or created by action of the courts."[2]

Judges, then, do make and change law. The minority view is patently correct; the opposing arguments will not bear analysis. What, then, explains the belief so tenaciously held that the judiciary does not ever change the law or that, when it does, it is acting improperly? Why is

[2] Pollock is clearly in error: most lawyers deny the reality of judge-made law.

it that judges adhere to what Morris Cohen has happily called "the phonographic theory of the judicial function"? What explains the recent remark of an eminent member of the Bar: "The man who claims that under our system courts make law is asserting that the courts habitually act unconstitutionally"?[3] Why do the courts customarily deny that they have any law-making power and describe new law which they create to deal with essentially contemporary events, as mere explanations or interpretations of law which already exists and has existed from time immemorial? Why this obstinate denial of the juristic realities?

We revert to our thesis: The essence of the basic legal myth or illusion is that law can be entirely predictable. Back of this illusion is the childish desire to have a fixed father-controlled universe, free of chance and error due to human fallibility.[4]

In early stages of legal development this desire was more intense than now and there was what Sir Henry Maine has called "a superstitious disrelish of change" which went to the extent of making men oppose any modification of existing law even by statutory legislation. We have partially overcome the superstitious antipathy to legal change so far as the change results from the action of legislative bodies, and no little part of law is modified each year by statutes enacted by state legislatures and by Congress.

But such statutory legislation, while it may alter the law, does so, ordinarily, only prospectively. It is the usual practice—to some extent it is required by constitutional prohibitions—that changes embodied in statutes enacted by legislative bodies should not be retroactive but should apply only to future conduct. Which is to say that, generally speaking, a legal novelty brought about through statutory legislation can be known *before* men do any acts which may be affected by the innovation. In so far, a man can conduct himself in reliance upon the existing law, knowing, at the time he acts, that any changes thereafter made by a legislative body will not modify the law upon which he relied.

Consequently, absolute certainty and predictability are apparently not endangered by alterations of law made or adopted by legislatures.[5]

But if it is once recognized that a judge, in the course of deciding a case, can for the first time create the law applicable to that case, or can alter the rules which were supposed to exist before the case was decided, then it will also have to be recognized that the rights and obligations of the parties to that case may be decided retroactively. A change thus made by a judge, when passing upon a case, is a change in the law made with respect to past events,—events which occurred before the law came into existence. Legal predictability is plainly impossible, if, at the time I do an act, I do so with reference to law which, should a lawsuit thereafter arise with reference to my act, may be changed by the judge who tries the case. For then the result is that my case is decided according to law which was not in existence when I acted and which I, therefore, could not have known, predicted or relied on when I acted.

If, therefore, one has a powerful need to believe in the possibility of anything like exact legal predictability, he will find judicial law-making intolerable and seek to deny its existence.

Hence the myth that the judges have no power to change existing law or make new law: it is a direct outgrowth of a subjective need for believing in a stable, approximately unalterable legal world—in effect, a child's world.

This remark might be challenged on the ground that the desire to avoid legal retroactivity is not "subjective" but practical, because, it may be said, men cannot and will not engage in affairs without having in mind the pertinent law. Yet reflection reveals the fact that the supposed *practical* importance of avoiding legal retroactivity and uncertainty is much overrated, since most men act without regard to the legal consequences of their conduct, and, therefore, do not act in reliance upon any given pre-existing law:

"Practically," says John Chipman Gray, "in its application to actual affairs, for most of the laity, the law, except for a few crude notions of the equity involved in some of its general principles, is all *ex post facto*. When a man marries, or enters into a partnership, or buys a piece of land, or engages in any other transactions, he has the vaguest possible idea of the law governing the situation, and with our complicated system of Jurisprudence, it is impossible it should be otherwise. If he delayed to make a contract or do an act until he understood exactly all the legal consequences it involved, the contract would never be made or the act done. *Now the law of which a man has no knowledge is the same to him as if it did not exist.*"[6]

Which is to say that the factor of uncertainty in law has little bearing on practical affairs. Many men go on about their business with virtually no knowledge of, or attention paid to, the so-called legal rules, be those rules certain or uncertain.[7] If the law but slightly affects what a man does, it is seldom that he can honestly maintain that he was disadvantaged by lack of legal stability. Although, then, judges have made law, vast quantities of law, and judge-made innovations, retroactively applied, are devised yearly; although frequently a man must act with no certainty as to what legal consequences the courts will later attach to his acts; although complete legal predictability and with it safety from slippery change are therefore by no means possible,—yet retroactivity and the resulting unavoidable uncertainty are not as great practical evils as they are often assumed to be. The no judge-made law doctrine, it seems, is not, fundamentally, a response to practical needs.[8] It appears rather to be due to a hunger and a craving for a non-existent and unattainable legal finality—which, in turn, may be ascribed to a concealed but potent striving to recapture in the law the child's conception of the fatherly attributes.

But what of it? What harm in this myth? No harm, if

the denial of judicial law-making were a mere pleasantry, in the category of what Austin and Morris Cohen refer to as polite or euphemistic fictions; that is, statements contrary to fact, but known by all to be such and comparable to the fibs of daily social intercourse.

But the denial of the fact of judge-made law is no mere fib. At times, indeed, it seems to resemble an outright benevolent lie, a professional falsehood designed actually to deceive the laity for their own good; Gray suggests that the misrepresentation derives in part from a belief of the legal profession that it is "important that judges should say, *and that the people should believe,* that the rules according to which the judges decide these cases had a previous existence." The lay public, that is, are to be duped.

Now this dupery is not harmless. It leads, sooner or later, to a distrust of the judges, a disrespect for their opinions. For now and again the public becomes aware that in some actual cases the judges have made or changed the law. Then follow accusations of dishonesty, of corruption, of usurpation of authority, of revolutionary violation of the judicial oath of office, and the like. And it is difficult to reply to such accusations when the judges themselves deny that they have power to make law and yet go on (unavoidably and unmistakably) making it.

Why, then, do the judges deceive the public? Because they are themselves deceived. The doctrine of no judge-made law is not, generally speaking, a *"lie"*—for a lie is an affirmation of a fact contrary to the truth, made with knowledge of its falsity and with the intention of deceiving others. Nor is it a "fiction"[9]—a false affirmation made with knowledge of its falsity but with no intention of deceiving others.

It is rather a myth—a false affirmation made without complete knowledge of its falsity.[10] We are confronting a kind of deception which involves self-deception. The self-deception, of course, varies in degree; many judges and lawyers are half-aware that the denial of the existence

of judicial legislation is what Gray has called "a form of
words to hide the truth."[11] And yet most of the profession
insists that the judiciary cannot properly change the law,
and more or less believes that myth. When judges and
lawyers announce that judges can never validly make law,
they are not engaged in fooling the public; they have successfully fooled themselves.

And this self-delusion has led to many unfortunate results. With their thinking processes hampered by this myth,
the judges have been forced, as we have seen, to contrive
circumlocutions in order to conceal from themselves and
the laity the fact that the judiciary frequently changes the
old legal rules. Those evasive phrases are then dealt with
as if they were honest phrases, with consequent confusion
and befuddlement of thought. Legal fictions are mistaken
for objective legal truths and clear legal thinking becomes
an unnecessarily arduous task.

This is not the place to discuss at length the immense
importance of valid fictions.[12] Suffice it to say that valid
fictions, whether in mathematics, physics, medicine or law,
are invaluable. But the correct and effective use of a fiction
involves a constant recognition of its character. It is often
desirable to treat A "as if" it were B. Mathematics, for
instance, finds it useful to employ the fiction that a circle is
a polygon; *i.e.,* to be dealt with, for certain purposes, as
if it were a polygon. Medical thinking is aided by the fiction of the completely healthy man. So in law, it is helpful
at times to treat a corporation as if, for certain purposes,
it were a real citizen, distinct and apart from its flesh-and-
blood stockholders, directors, officers, and agents.[13]

But there are a vast number of so-called fictions which
are really bastard fictions or semi-myths, where the "as
if" or "let's pretend" factor has, in some measure, been
submerged. It is said, not that A is to be treated *for certain
purposes* "as if" it were B, but instead it is said and believed, incorrectly, that A *is* B. While thinking is often
advanced by a valid fiction, it is hindered when a fiction

becomes a myth or semi-myth; *i.e.*, when the artificial character of the fiction, its lack of literalness, its basically metaphorical significance, are in whole or in part over-looked.[3]

The law has suffered much from such bastard fictions or semi-myths. Thus we have such things as "contracts implied in law." Now the essence of a contract is that the parties to the contract consent to be bound. But the essence of a so-called "contract implied in law" is that there is no consent. To use the word "contract" in the latter case without constant awareness of the fact that one is speaking metaphorically is to blur and obfuscate. What is actually meant by the phrase is that under certain circumstances the courts will compel parties who have not made a contract to act "as if" they had made a contract. The courts have often been led astray through a failure to keep in mind the "as if" in that verbal construct.

In like manner, we have unfortunate consequences flowing from the careless use of such phrases as "constructive fraud," where all fraud is absent, and "malice in law" where there is no malice whatsoever.

Because of these semi-myths and a host of like verbalisms—often improperly referred to as legal "fictions" although they are employed without complete awareness of their artificiality—many legal critics have denounced all legal fictions as unmitigatedly evil. Bentham thought a legal fiction "the most pernicious and basest sort of lying":

"It affords," he wrote, "presumptive and conclusive evidence of moral turpitude in those by whom it was invented and first employed. . . . Not a fiction but is capable of being translated, and occasionally is translated into the language of truth. Burn the original . . . and employ the translation in its stead.

[3] There can be no objection, in the interest of saving time, to the temporary verbal omission of the "as if" when using a fiction, provided the "as if" is not ignored. But such shorthand expressions are dangerous to clear thinking unless the fact that they are abbreviations is kept clearly in mind. See Part One, Chapter XV and especially Appendix VII, "Notes on Fictions."

Fiction is no more necessary to justice, than is poison to sustenance. . . . Fictions are falsehoods, and the judge who invents a fiction ought to be sent to jail. . . . 'Swearing,' says one of the characters in a French drama, 'constitutes the ground-work of English conversation.' Lying, he might have said, without any such hyperbole—lying and nonsense compose the ground-work of English Judicature. . . . In English law, fiction is a syphilis which runs in every vein, and carries into every part of the system the principle of rottenness."

And more recently, Professor Jeremiah Smith has joined in this condemnation:

"The use of fiction," he asserts, "tends not only to impair, in a general way, reverence for truth; but also to diminish the respect which would otherwise be felt for the courts and for the law itself. These objections, in substance, have been urged, not by mere theorists, but by experienced lawyers and judges. We believe that, at the present day, the use of fiction in law should be entirely abandoned. . . . If a fiction does not, in any degree or to any extent, represent a legal truth, then its continued use can result only in evil. If, on the other hand, it represents—in part at least—some clumsily concealed legal truth, then it is capable of being translated into the language of truth, and we should adopt Mr. Bentham's remedy—'Burn the original, and employ the translation in its stead.' In short, we would entirely discard the use of fiction phrases and fiction reasons."

These are strong words. They are too sweeping. Neither in law nor elsewhere could we afford to do away with fictional contrivances. One might almost say that the capacity for sustained valid "as if" thinking is the mark of the civilized man.[14] "Juridical theory," says Tourtoulon pithily, "is all the more objective when it presents itself as fictitious, and all the more delusive when it claims to do without fictions." To the extent that fictions are recognized as such, that their "as if" or "let's pretend" element is kept clear, that the omission of qualifications from such abbreviated or metaphorical statements is not taken to mean the permanent irrelevance of such qualifications—just to that extent fictional representations should be encouraged as invaluable thought-tools. Objection properly arises only when the partial, metaphorical, artificial character of the fiction is overlooked—when, that is, the fiction becomes a myth or semi-myth.[4]

Such misuse of the legal fiction has produced that fiction-phobia among lawyers manifested in the condemnatory expressions of Bentham and Smith. Justified in their assaults on bastard fictions, they have, unfortunately, gone too far and have assailed valid fictions as well.[15]

Valid fictions are defensible—more, they are indispensable. But what is significant for our purposes is the defense of the bastard fictions, the semi-myths. To Blackstone, they were among the cherished beauties of the law. To Mitchell,[16] it seems that the common law is largely indebted to these verbal mechanisms for its rapid development and its ability to follow closely social needs. Why this praise? Because, says Mitchell, these devices make "less noticeable, both to the world and to the judges themselves (and therefore more easy) the legislation that is being accomplished by the judges."[17] Such judicial legislation he considers essential to the life of the law. But no less essential, he contends, is the necessity of concealing what is going on. Wherefore to him these misleading, inaccurate and trouble-making phrases are well worth the price of "the discredit which their apparent falsity brings upon the law."

Stated thus baldly, how childish is such a defense: Judges must continue to create law, but they and the public must be kept unaware of their accomplishment. Untruths must continue to be told to the laity about the essential function of law, and law must continue to be made by men befuddled by myths and only partially aware of what they are doing. And why? Because, apparently, many full-grown men, whether they be laymen or lawyers, cannot

[4] Unfortunately many writers (some of them quoted in this book) use the word "fiction" in the sense of "myth" or "semi-myth."

bear to learn the truth, and must be kept in a world of make-believe where they can continue to cherish the illusion that the law of an adult civilization is, in spirit, of a kind with the authoritative rules laid down for children by their father.[5]

The genealogy of legal myth-making may be traced as follows: Childish dread of uncertainty and unwillingness to face legal realities produce a basic legal myth that law is completely settled and defined. Thence springs the subsidiary myth that judges never make law. That myth, in turn, is the progenitor of a large brood of troublesome semi-myths. One is reminded of Morley's comments with respect to a like development in Church history:

"Subordinate error was made necessary and invented, by reason of some pre-existent main stock of error, and to save the practice of the Church. Thus we are often referred to the consolation which this or that doctrine has brought to the human spirit. But what if the same system had produced the terror which made absence of consolation intolerable? How much of the necessity for expressing the enlarged humanity of the Church, in the doctrine of Purgatory, arose from the experience of the older, unsoftened doctrine of eternal hell?"

[5] This is a *"partial* explanation"; see Part One, Chapter II, note 8 and Appendix X, Section 1. As to the validity of psychological fictions, see Appendix X, Section 2.

CHAPTER V

LEGAL REALISM

We have talked much of the law. But what is "the law"? A complete definition would be impossible and even a working definition would exhaust the patience of the reader. But it may not be amiss to inquire what, in a rough sense, the law means to the average man of our times when he consults his lawyer.

The Jones family owned the Blue & Gray Taxi Company, a corporation incorporated in Kentucky. That company made a contract with the A. & B. Railroad Company, also a Kentucky corporation, by which it was agreed that the Blue & Gray Taxi Company was to have the exclusive privilege of soliciting taxi-cab business on and adjacent to the railroad company's depot.

A rival taxi-cab company, owned by the Williams family, the Purple Taxi Company, began to ignore this contract; it solicited business and parked its taxi-cabs in places assigned by the railroad company to the Blue & Gray Company and sought in other ways to deprive the Blue & Gray Company of the benefits conferred on it by the agreement with the railroad.

The Jones family were angered; their profits derived from the Blue & Gray stock, which they owned, were threatened. They consulted their lawyer, a Louisville practitioner, and this, we may conjecture, is about what he told them: "I'm afraid your contract is not legally valid. I've examined several decisions of the highest court of Kentucky and they pretty clearly indicate that you can't get away with that kind of an agreement in this state. The Kentucky court holds such a contract to be bad as creating an unlawful monopoly. But I'll think the matter over. You come back tomorrow and I'll try meanwhile to find some way out."

So, next day, the Joneses returned. And this time their lawyer said he thought he had discovered how to get the contract sustained: "You see, it's this way. In most courts, except those of Kentucky and of a few other states, an agreement like this is perfectly good. But, unfortunately, as things now stand, you'll have to go into the Kentucky courts.

"If we can manage to get our case tried in the Federal court, there's a fair chance that we'll get a different result, because I think the Federal court will follow the majority rule and not the Kentucky rule. I'm not sure of that, but it's worth trying.

"So this is what we'll do. We'll form a new Blue & Gray Company in Tennessee. And your Kentucky Blue & Gray Company will transfer all its assets to the new Tennessee Blue & Gray Company. Then we'll have the railroad company execute a new contract with the new Tennessee Blue & Gray Company, and at the same time cancel the old contract and, soon after, dissolve the old Kentucky Blue & Gray Company."

"But," interrupted one of the Joneses, "what good will all that monkey-business do?"

The lawyer smiled broadly. "Just this," he replied with pride in his cleverness. "The A. & B. Railroad Company is organized in Kentucky. So is the Purple Taxi which we want to get at. The Federal court will treat these companies as if they were citizens of Kentucky. Now a corporation which is a citizen of Kentucky can't bring this kind of suit in the Federal court against other corporations which are also citizens of Kentucky. But if your company becomes a Tennessee corporation, it will be considered as if it were a citizen of Tennessee. Then your new Tennessee company can sue the other two in the Federal court, because the suit will be held to be one between citizens of different states. And that kind of suit, based on what we lawyers call 'diversity of citizenship,' can be brought in the Federal court by a corporation which organized in Tennessee against corporations which are citizens of another State, Kentucky. And the Federal court, as I said, ought to sustain your contract."

"That sounds pretty slick," said one of the Joneses admiringly. "Are you sure it will work?"

"No," answered the lawyer. "You can't ever be absolutely sure about such a plan. I can't find any case completely holding our way on all these facts. But I'm satisfied that's the law and that that's the way the Federal court ought to decide. I won't guarantee success. But I recommend trying out my suggestion."

His advice was followed. Shortly after the new Tennessee Blue & Gray Company was organized and had entered into the new contract, suit was brought by the Joneses' new Blue & Gray Corporation of Tennessee in the Federal District Court against the competing Purple Company and the railroad company. In this suit, the Blue & Gray Taxi Company of Tennessee asked the court to prevent interference with the carrying out of its railroad contract.

As the Joneses' lawyer had hoped, the Federal court held, against the protest of the Purple Company's lawyer, first that such a suit could be brought in the Federal court and, second, that the contract was valid. Accordingly the court enjoined the Purple Company from interfering with the depot business of the Joneses' Blue & Gray Company. The Joneses were elated, for now their profits seemed once more assured.

But not for long. The other side appealed the case to the Federal Circuit Court of Appeals. And the Joneses' lawyer was somewhat worried that that court might reverse the lower Federal court. But it didn't and the Joneses again were happy.[1]

Still the Purple Company persisted. It took the case to the Supreme Court of the United States. That Court consists of nine judges. And the Joneses' lawyer couldn't be certain just how those judges would line up on all the questions involved. "Some new men on the bench, and you never can tell about Holmes and Brandeis. They're very erratic," was his comment.

When the United States Supreme Court gave its decision, it was found that six of the nine judges agreed with counsel for the Joneses. Three justices (Holmes, Brandeis and Stone) were of the contrary opinion. But the majority governs in the United States Supreme Court, and the Joneses' prosperity was at last firmly established.

Now what was "the law" for the Joneses, who owned the Blue & Gray Company, and the Williamses, who owned the Purple Company? The answer will depend on the date of the question. If asked before the new Tennessee company acquired the contract, it might have been said that it was almost surely "the law" that the Joneses would lose; for any suit involving the validity of that contract could then have been brought only in the Kentucky state court and the prior decisions of that court seemed adverse to such an agreement.

After the suggestion of the Joneses' lawyer was carried out and the new Tennessee corporation owned the contract, "the law" was more doubtful. Many lawyers would have agreed with the Joneses' lawyer that there was a good chance that the Jones family would be victorious if suit were brought in the Federal courts. But probably an equal number would have disagreed: they would have said that the formation of the new Tennessee company was a trick used to get out of the Kentucky courts and into the Federal court, a trick of which the Federal court would not approve. Or that, regardless of that question, the Federal court would follow the well-settled Kentucky rule as to the invalidity of such contracts as creating unlawful monopolies (especially because the use of Kentucky real estate was involved) and that therefore the Federal court would decide against the Joneses.[2] "The law," at any time before the decision of the United States Supreme Court, was in-

deed unsettled.[1] No one could know what the court would
decide. Would it follow the Kentucky cases? If so, the law
was that no "rights" were conferred by the contract. Would
it refuse to follow the Kentucky cases? If so, rights were
conferred by the contract. To speak of settled law governing that controversy, or of the fixed legal rights of those
parties, as antedating the decision of the Supreme Court,
is mere verbiage. If two more judges on that bench had
agreed with Justices Holmes, Brandeis and Stone, the law
and the rights of the parties would have been of a directly
opposite kind.

After the decision, "the law" was fixed. There were no
other courts to which an appeal could be directed. The
judgment of the United States Supreme Court could not
be disturbed and the legal "rights" of the Joneses and the
Williamses were everlastingly established.

We may now venture a rough definition of law from
the point of view of the average man: For any particular
lay person, the law, with respect to any particular set of
facts, is a decision of a court with respect to those facts
so far as that decision affects that particular person. Until
a court has passed on those facts no law on that subject
is yet in existence. Prior to such a decision, the only law
available is the opinion of lawyers as to the law relating
to that person and to those facts. Such opinion is not
actually law but only a guess as to what a court will decide.[2]

Law, then, as to any given situation is either (a) actual
law, i.e., a specific past decision, as to that situation,[3] or

[1] That is, it was unsettled whether the Williamses had the energy, patience and money to push an appeal. If not, then the decision of the lower Federal court was the actual settled law for the
Jones and Williams families.

[2] The United States Supreme Court has wittily been called the
"court of ultimate conjecture."

[3] That is, a past decision in a case which has arisen between the
specific persons in question as to the specific facts in question. Even
a past decision fixes the rights of the parties to the suit only to a
limited extent. In other words, what a court has actually decided

(b) probable law, *i.e.*, a guess as to a specific future decision.

Usually when a client consults his lawyer about "the law," his purpose is to ascertain not what courts have actually decided in the past but what the courts will probably decide in the future. He asks, "Have I a right, as a stockholder of the American Taffy Company of Indiana, to look at the corporate books?" Or, "Do I have to pay an inheritance tax to the State of New York on bonds left me by my deceased wife, if our residence was in Ohio, but the bonds, at the time of her death, were in a safety deposit box in New York?" Or, "Is there a right of 'peaceful' picketing in a strike in the State of California?" Or, "If Jones sells me his Chicago shoe business and agrees not to compete for ten years, will the agreement be binding?" The answers (although they may run "There is such a right," "The law is that the property is not taxable," "Such picketing is unlawful," "The agreement is not legally binding") are in fact prophecies or predictions of judicial action.[4] It is from this point of view that the practice of law has been aptly termed an art of prediction.[3]

Actual specific past *decisions,* and guesses as to actual specific future *decisions.* Is that how lawyers customarily define the law? Not at all.

---

as between the parties may in part still be open to question by other courts and therefore may continue to be the subject of guesses.

[4] The emphasis in this book on the conduct of judges is admittedly artificial. Lawyers and their clients are vitally concerned with the ways of all governmental officials and with the reactions of non-official persons to the ways of judges and other officials. There is a crying need in the training of lawyers for clear and unashamed recognition and study of all these phenomena as part of the legitimate business of lawyers.

But one job at a time. Inasmuch as the major portion of a lawyer's time is today devoted to predicting or bringing about decisions of judges, the law considered in this book is "court law." "Actual law" and "probable law" here discussed mean "actual or probable court law." This limitation, while artificial, is perhaps the more excusable because it roughly corresponds to the notion of the contemporary layman when consulting his lawyer.

Of course, anyone can define "law" as he pleases. The word

"law" is ambiguous and it might be well if we could abolish it. But until a substitute is invented, it seems not improper to apply it to that which is central in the work of the practising lawyer. *This book is primarily concerned with "law" as it affects the work of the practising lawyer and the needs of the clients who retain him.*

From that point of view, court law may roughly be defined as *specific past or future judicial decisions which are enforced or complied with.*

CHAPTER VI

BEALE, AND LEGAL FUNDAMENTALISM

"The decision and judgment of a court, determining a particular controversy . . . can in no sense be regarded as in itself law, whether it be the doom of an ancient monarch, the decision of a popular court, or the judgment of a modern tribunal."[1]

Thus Professor Beale, one of America's most influential legal writers from whom, at Harvard Law School, many of the leading lawyers of this country have received valued instruction. Beale's opinion, which is representative of the conventional doctrine, commands attention.

Beale, you see, repudiates the notion that law consists of past decisions and predictions as to future decisions. Why? Why does he assert that all the particular judgments, rendered or ever hereafter to be rendered by the courts, are not law? Because, he answers, such judgments or decisions fail to correspond to the correct definition of law. Whatever the practical effect on the person or property of the litigants—although it may mean hanging for the defendant in a criminal action or the loss of all his worldly goods to the defendant in a civil suit—Beale seems to consider that the judgment of any court is too finite, too lowly, of too little real import, to be worthy the name Law. Law, by definition, must apparently have a noble aspect, a breath-taking sweep. Law must be, Beale asserts, UNIFORM, GENERAL, CONTINUOUS, EQUAL, CERTAIN, PURE.

[1] Most of the quotations in this chapter are from Beale's "Treatise on the Conflict of Laws." One of the leaders of the bar has said of this work, "It gives the strongest promise of being the best legal work done in this generation."

Take, for instance, a condition that once prevailed in Michigan. The Supreme Court of that state at one time held that it would allow so-called "exemplary" or "punitive" damages (*i.e.* it held that, if a person were injured under certain circumstances, he could collect from the wrongdoer a sum of money which would not only adequately compensate for the injury, but which would also punish the wrongdoer). In subsequent cases the Michigan Court held that it would not assess such exemplary damages. Later, the decisions again swung the other way and exemplary damages were held proper.

Now, argues Beale, each of these decisions could not have been law, for, "if we assume that each decision made the law, we would have the singular result that the law was changed in Michigan backwards and forwards a dozen times within a few years." Beale, of course, could not deny that for the respective persons who sued or were sued in these several cases, each decision was final and unchanged, and that what was decided one way or the other on the question of allowing damages in each of these cases made a real difference to the parties to each particular case. But, despite this practical difference resulting from these changes, these decisions could not be law. Why? Because, says Beale, by definition, the Law cannot change backwards and forwards a dozen times within a few years. The law must remain unchanged, whatever the mere mundane happenings. Its purity is unsullied by mere decisions, whatever the practical consequence of the decisions.

Or again: Congress in 1870 enacted a statute providing, in effect, that paper notes issued by the government must be accepted by all creditors at their face value in payment of debts, although these notes were worth considerably less than their face. In a case which came before the United States Supreme Court, by a five-to-three decision, this statute was held unconstitutional. Soon after this decision, one of the five majority judges resigned and (pursuant to a statute enlarging the number of Supreme Court judges from eight to nine) two new judges were appointed. Within a year another case, identical in facts with the first, came before the Supreme Court. The Court overruled the earlier decision by a five-to-four decision (the two new judges having united with the former minority of three).

The first and second decisions were in flat contradiction. What then was the law on this subject? Apparently the statute was invalid after the first decision and became valid after the second decision. But Beale would say "the Law" had always been the same and that the Court, in one decision or the other, had made a mistake.

In 1917, the question of the validity of minimum-wage legislation came before the United States Supreme Court. One of the nine judges, Brandeis, did not take part in the decision. The remaining eight judges were evenly divided, so that a tie vote resulted and the question was left open so far as the United States Supreme Court was concerned. In 1923, the question again came before that Court. Meanwhile the personnel of the Court had changed several times, with the consequence that by a five-to-three vote (Brandeis again not voting) minimum wage legislation was now held invalid. The changes in personnel were such that had the question been passed upon between November 1921 and June 1922, the decision would almost surely have been the other way.[2] What at any particular moment was the law on that subject? Would the answer not vary with the date when the question was asked? And prior to the year 1923, would the answer not have varied with the accuracy of the guesses as to the Court's personnel? Not so, Beale presumably would say; the law never was in doubt, only the decision was in doubt; as Beale sees it,

[2] See the brilliant article of Professor Powell in 37 Harvard Law Review, 545. He points out that between 1917 (the date of the first decision) and 1923, such legislation had been held valid by several state courts. In all (including the judges who participated in both U. S. Supreme Court decisions) thirty-two judges were of the opinion that minimum wage laws were valid and nine judges were of the contrary opinion.

the decision and the law are not the same, by any manner of means.

Consider the Blue and Gray taxi-cab litigation. According to Beale (and his views are precisely those of the majority of the United States Supreme Court as expressed in the opinion in the taxi-cab suit) the Federal Supreme Court was merely declaring the law of Kentucky. Now it is true that if the suit had been brought in the Kentucky State Court, that court would have declared the law of Kentucky to be the exact opposite. The two courts had different views of the law of Kentucky. But, says Beale of such a situation, "this cannot mean that there are two laws, but merely that one court or both is (*sic*) mistaken in its statement of the law." To be sure the mistake cannot be rectified. The decision of the Kentucky Supreme Court would be final, if the suit were brought in the state court; and the decision of the Federal Supreme Court would be equally final if the suit were brought in the Federal court. Whichever court gives the decision, that decision is all the law there is, in any practical sense, for the parties to the suit. But one or the other (or neither) is *the* Law of Kentucky, according to Beale. Why? Because, "every political society . . . must have only one law. If two laws prevail at the same time, they might be mutually destructive. It is impossible that a single event should be followed by two contradictory consequences."

Of course, Beale does not mean that such a result is impossible in the world of actual happenings. There are at least several dozen instances where the Federal court has attached legal consequences to events in flat contradiction to the views of the courts of the state in which the events occurred. *Beale means that what actually and irremediably happens in existing concrete cases is impossible in the world of law-by-definition. What actually happens doesn't matter in that latter world.*

What is the Law as Beale defines it? It consists of three parts: (1) Statutes, (2) rules and (3) "the general body of principles accepted as the fundamental principles of jurisprudence." This third element is "the one most important feature of law: that is . . . a body of scientific principle. . . . Law, therefore, is made in part by the legislature; in part it rests upon precedent; and in great part it consists in a homogeneous, scientific, and all-embracing body of principle. . . ." This all-embracing body of homogeneous scientific principle constitutes a "philosophical system." Such systems are "truly law" even "though no court has lent its sanction to many of their principles." Of course, he adds, "the application of its principles is the work of a tribunal, which being human, may err, and the common law, being mistakenly applied, the positive law of the State becomes different from the basic system. . . . But it must be obvious that neither by legislative nor by judicial legislation can the basic system of law be changed." Even the "positive law of the state" is not changeable by the courts. For "another characteristic of law is its continuity. . . . The law of today must remain the law of tomorrow, except for such changes as may be made in the law by legislative action before tomorrow."[1]

With law so defined, it is plain why Beale and those who agree with him cannot consider for an instant that the decisions and judgments of courts can be law: An "*essential characteristic* of law is its *generality;* since justice requires equality of treatment for all persons, and this means generality." "Another *necessary characteristic* of law is *continuity* . . . because society needs to know the law in advance of judicial action upon it. . . . *It must be possible* for every person, of his own knowledge or by the help of others' knowledge, to discover the application of the law to any contemplated act. . . . If there were discontinuity in the law—if, for instance, a judicial tribunal had the power to change the law as it liked, or the discretion as to the application of law to the facts—the client would seek advice in vain, for counsel however learned could only vaguely guess what the law would be at the time of possible future litigation. *Predictability of judicial decision is necessary* if the law is to serve its true social purpose; and this predictability is possible only if the law is continuous."

See now. Law *must* be predictable and continuous. It is *essential* that law be general, for without generality there could not be equality, and justice *requires* equality, and that means generality. It is *impossible* that a single event should be followed by two contradictory legal consequences, for any political society *must* have only one law; if it had two, what price predictability? ("If two laws were present at the same time and in the same place upon the same subject we should have a condition of anarchy.") Judges cannot make law, for, if they did, the law might change rapidly and it *must not* change rapidly.

These things cannot be, must not be, according to Beale. But they are—if you look at the actual decisions. Particular judgments of particular controversies are only vaguely predictable. Counsel, however learned, can only guess how the courts will "apply the law" to acts. Decisions in the courts of any given state do vary. The Federal courts and state courts attach different consequences to identical facts occurring in the same place. If there must be certainty, continuity, generality and the like, and if you cannot have them in respect of the decisions of the courts, then how obtain them? By insisting that "the Law" consist not of decisions but of general principles and rules. For these rules and principles can be made stable, continuous and predictable. Lawyers can then advise clients with reasonable accuracy what "Law" is applicable to any set of facts. That is, they can advise what this body of principles would lead to, if the courts didn't make "mistakes." "Purity of doctrine may be lost through wrong decisions of courts, thus warping legal principle by bad precedent," concedes Beale. These "wrong decisions" may bring about "peculiar local law . . . as distinguished from the general doctrine of the prevailing legal system." The "application of its principles is the work of a tribunal which, being human, may err." The law may be "mistakenly applied." Therefore learned lawyer A may often erroneously predict to client B what the decision of the court in State C will be with reference to facts X, Y and Z. But lawyer A can, with little likelihood of mistake, determine "the Law"; that is, he can determine the correct *principles* which constitute what is "truly law." Where that law prevails, in the domain of abstract rules and principles, there exist those characteristics of law which "must be," and there one avoids all those unpleasant and anarchic occurrences which are "impossible"—except in the world where mere human beings dwell.

If you must have law with the characteristics which Beale demands, then inevitably you will refuse to recognize judicial actualities as Law. If the facts about what happens in the courts disagree with your requirements, you will refuse to acknowledge those facts as constituting valid Law and will frame a definition of Law which will meet your requirements.

And this Bealish Law can approximate perfection. It can have, to use Beale's phrase, "purity of doctrine," free from "warping by bad precedent." It can be rid of disturbing novelties and aberrations. It can be a harmonious closed system of principles, not marred by discontinuities, a system from which correct rules can be infallibly and unhesitatingly worked out. In this realm of pure Law, the answer to a particular problem can always be correct. In the sub-lunar world in which the courts dwell, mistakes will happen. But such mistaken decisions are not Law. For such apparent law is not real. Mistaken law is not "truly law," even if the courts stubbornly act as if it were.

In short, real Law, for Beale, is superhuman. This Beale acknowledges when he states that the *"application of principles is the work of a tribunal which, being human, may err."* So Blackstone taught when he portrayed positive law as a copy of natural law: "The law of nature . . . is binding all over the globe in all countries, and at all times; *no human laws are of any validity if contrary to this;* and such of them as are valid derive all their authority, mediately or immediately, from this original."[2] And so the bulk of our bar believes to this day: "The American lawyer, as a rule," says Pound, "still believes that the principles of law are absolute, eternal and of universal validity." Recently (in utter sobriety and with no satirical intention) the conventional view was stated thus: "Every jurist whether he has been some leader of savages at the time of the dawn of civilization, or a modern judge sitting in a court of last resort, has sought for the principles which should determine his judgment in something apart from and above the experience of the race."[3]

"The Law," then, is extra-experiential. It is "the breath of God, the harmony of the world," as Hooker put it; it is "invested with a halo,"[4] a "brooding omnipresence in the sky," to use Holmes' derisive phrase. Such, in effect, are the views expressed by Beale. We may, for convenience, refer to this attitude as legal Absolutism or "Bealism."[3]

From the point of view of the ordinary human being that kind of Absolutist law is meaningless. For the ordinary human being is interested, legitimately, in what happens in court. The decisions of the courts directly affect his life and property. The law in the sky, above human experience, is valueless to the wayfaring man. Principles, rules, conceptions, standards, and the like, may be law for lawyers, regardless of whether such law ever comes into contact with the affairs of life. But not for the rest of humanity. To mere humans, law means what the courts have decided and will decide, and not vague, "pure" generalizations.

But lawyers are intensely practical men and their concern is with the lives and property of their clients. Why, then, is the language of abstract Bealism so dear to the profession? Why are fixed principles and rules elevated to the highest place in the so-called science of law, while the vital realities, the acts of the judges which directly

[3] Beale, it is fair to say, is not a consistent Bealist. But in his more didactic and philosophic writings he expresses so pronounced an absolutist point of view that the term Bealism is justifiable as a label.

touch the lives and property of human beings, are relegated to a subordinate position—as mere "illustrations" or "particular outward manifestations" of "the invisible law whence they proceeded," as "data from which we may obtain by induction the jural rule which they prove to exist"? Why is *generality* so highly prized by lawyers at the expense of *particularity?* How explain the fact that Beale, who believes that "society needs to know the law in advance of judicial action upon it," that "it must be possible for every person, of his own knowledge or by the help of others' knowledge, to discover the application of the law to any contemplated act" and that "for this purpose it must be possible for one learned in the law to speak with authority on the application of law to proposed acts and to predict with a reasonable degree of certainty the decision of courts in case the legality of the acts should be called in question"—why is it that a person thus apparently interested in predicting future judicial decisions can yet stoutly maintain that such decisions are relatively unimportant and that the rules or principles from which they are said to derive are the real jural realities? What explains the hold of Bealism or Absolutism on a large majority of the legal profession?[4]

[4] The writer has perhaps expressed himself somewhat intemperately on the subject of Beale's views. Any psychologist would suspect that the writer's lack of calm indicated a mental conflict on this subject, and, doubtless the suspicion would be justified. The slightly excessive language is to be explained, perhaps, by the writer's effort to rid himself of Bealistic tendencies to which he, like most lawyers, is subject.

Of course, there is no intention to deny Beale's exceptional acuteness of intellect. The criticism is directed against the emotional attitude exemplified in his writings. Compare what is said of Plato, below, Chapter IX. Beale might be called the lawyers' Plato.

It should be added that no competent lawyer is ever completely Bealistic. He could not possibly serve his clients or, as the case may be, perform his function as a judge, unless his Bealism were tempered by a large measure of shrewd common sense. But the *avowed* philosophy of the average lawyer is precisely Bealism, and his common sense is so frequently distorted by that philosophy that the latter deserves serious attention.

CHAPTER VII

VERBALISM AND SCHOLASTICISM

"We do not often," writes Ingraham,[1] "have occasion to speak, as of an indivisible whole, of the group of phenomena involved or connected in the transit of a negro over a rail fence with a melon under his arm while the moon is just passing behind a cloud. But if this collocation of phenomena were of frequent occurrence, and if we did have occasion to speak of it often, and if its happening were likely to affect the money market, we should have some name as 'Wousin' to denote it by. People would in time be disputing whether the existence of a Wousin involved necessarily a rail fence, and whether the term could be applied when a white man was similarly related to a stone wall."

Does this not resemble the Absolutism we have been describing? What are vague, abstract, sky-dwelling, super-experiential principles and rules of law but so many legal analogues of "Wousins"? Shall we say that in the bad habit of Wousining we have found the explanation of the prevalence of Absolutism or Fundamentalism in legal thinking?

That has been said, in effect, by several critics. The possibility of developing a true science of law, according to Dean Leon Green, has been retarded because lawyers have not risen above the word level.[2] Word ritual has been one of the primary methods of law administration. We lawyers are still held in the bonds of "holy words" in the form of rules, principles, formulas and standards, reduced to well-polished phrases. The first requisite of intellectual freedom in law is, according to Green, a wholesome fear of words. Judges seem to solve legal problems by realignments of word patterns, but those problems are not to be solved by formulas, rules, principles, phrases, definitions, or other like devices. Nothing will so promote a legal science as the recognition of the limitations of language as a control of judgment. If we are to make progress in the law, we must no longer canonize words such as "rights" and "duties"; words, says Green, must surrender their sanctity. "There is no other science which has quite the same degree of difficulty in immunizing its language."[3]

Legal Absolutism, then, is word-worship? A suggestive hypothesis. Particularly so when we compare the legal Absolutists with another group of persons to whom the abstract term is well-nigh divine—the metaphysical reasoners of whom Plato is the archetype. Plato saw that beautiful things become corrupted or die, that men who seem to be noble in character do evil deeds. The evanescence of values was painful to him. How make them permanent? Plato found an ingenious answer: The "Beautiful" endures even when beautiful roses wither or beautiful youths become old and ugly. The "Good" remains good when good men grow wicked. Such terms are the names of imperishable entities. Absolute Beauty, for instance, is described by him as "everlasting, not growing and decaying, or waxing and waning; . . . not fair in one point of view and foul in another, or at one time or in one relation or at one place fair, at another time or in another relation or at another place foul, as if fair to some and foul to others, or in likeness of a face or hands or another part of the bodily frame, or in any form of speech or knowledge, or existing in any other being, as for example, in an animal, or in heaven, or on earth, or in any other place; but beauty absolute, separate, simple, and everlasting." And this Absolute Beauty, "without diminution and without increase, or any change is imparted . . . to the perishing beauties of all other things." Beauty *makes* beautiful things beautiful, as Greatness makes great things great, and as Duality produces the things that are two in number.[4]

These immortal entities or Ideas or Universals are "the absolute essence of all things." They alone are possessed of reality.

The notion of the "Real" as impermanent is unendurable. These universals are stable; they are therefore the Real. Thus Plato found relief from unbearable chance and change in the stable meaning of words; thus, by fooling himself with words, he reached "the region of purity, eternity, immortality and unchangeableness" at which he aimed, finding it in what was most abstract. "Abstraction was the Jacob's ladder by which the philosopher ascended to certainty. The further he was from the facts, the nearer he thought himself to the truth."[5]

In variant forms metaphysicians, before and since Plato, have verbalized ugliness and evil out of existence. They experience an irresistible need to conceive the world, not as it is, but as they wish it to be. They assert that life, properly envisaged, has certain attributes and they "prove" their assertions by denying validity to whatever aspects of experience are in conflict with these attributes. They explain away, instead of trying to do away with, whatever they find distressing.

Such "wishful" metaphysicians turn the world upside down. Observation discloses that the environment is unfriendly to their desire for peace and quiet, that evil and dangers are at large, that wars and pestilence and strikes and stock-market panics exist, that often nature is not as human nature would have it. Experience frustrates human hopes, which turn out to be illusory. But the metaphysician says, No. Those shortcomings of experience are the illusions; our hopes are the Real. Life is congenial to the human spirit and only error makes it appear otherwise. Things as you observe them are a mirage. The True Reality is in accord with our values. It is stable, restful, complete, unchanging, devoid of complexities and sudden disruptions. Those evils are the unreal, the imaginary. They are mere "appearance." They contain no hurts for the man with proper insight; he can behold the invisible world which is One, Eternal, Unchanging.[6]

And, to repeat, the key to such legerdemain is the Word. It is with language that the philosopher can seem to convert values into reality and bruising events into mere appearances; with language that he makes his dreams come true and suppresses the unpleasant; with language that he turns compensatory fables into the actual. Ugliness, pain, distressing mutability are destroyed with speech. Evil and all obstructions to happiness are obliterated, danger and chaos are negated, nature is made congenial to human nature,—all by Word-Magic.

"You know," wrote William James, "how men have always hankered after magic and you know what a great part in magic words have always played. If you have his name or the formula or incantation that binds him, you can control the spirit, genie, afrite, or whatever the power may be. . . . So the universe has always appeared to the natural mind as a kind of enigma of which the key must be sought in the shape of some eliminating or power-bringing word or name. That word means the universe's principle, and to possess it is after a fashion to possess the universe itself. 'God,' 'Matter,' 'Reason,' 'Absolute,' 'Energy,' are so many solving names. You can rest when you have them. You are at the end of your metaphysical quest."

So Wousining, Word-Magic, the use of solving names, are at the heart of compensatory metaphysics. For virtually empty concepts seem to give to the metaphysician the stable world he requires. The attributes which the metaphysician cherishes can procure the appearance of permanence and actuality by being described in terms sufficiently meaningless and elastic so that the contradiction of these attributes by reality can be satisfactorily concealed. The more "dematerialized" such terms are, the less friction there will be developed when they collide with facts. They are the indispensable element of such "wishful" philosophy. "Does not the word," asked Plato, "express more than the fact, and must not the actual, whatever a man may think, always, in the nature of things, fall short of the truth?" Where would your philosophic Absolutist be if he were unable to describe the Absolute as One and Only, Metaphysically Simple, Immutable, Eternal, Omnipotent, Omniscient, Omnipresent, Infinitely Perfect, Absolutely Unlimited?

"As the old carapace," writes Rignano,[1] "abandoned by the crustacean after shedding, retains the appearance of the animal which moulded it and which now inhabits it no longer, so the word which continues to represent a quite dematerialized metaphysical concept, is no more than a verbal carapace now completely abandoned by the intellectual content for whose symbolization it had been originally created. Without this verbal carapace, the disappearance of all intellectual content would involve the disappearance of all traces of the past existence of such content. But the carapace preserves something which, just because it proves the past existence of a concept, which formerly had a real life, may quite well be taken for one still existing. So that this something, although devoid of all intellectual content, always constitutes a valuable point of attachment and support for the corresponding emotion, which is so intense that it does not perceive that the cherished resemblances no longer clothe the beloved object."

In this way, many abstract terms, which once had content, but now have little of substance, acquire an intense "emotive value"; they stimulate not intellection but strong feelings. They acquire an "affective resonance" and represent "emotional abstractions."

It is clear by now, surely, that legal Absolutism is akin to the metaphysics we have been describing. For the Bealist, as we have seen, refuses to admit that law is not in accord with his desires. Law as he and his fellow men encounter it in practical effect—in the decisions of the

[1] See "The Psychology of Reasoning"; the description of wishful metaphysical thinking in the text is largely indebted to Rignano's treatise.

courts—conflicts with what he desires law to be. Wherefore he strives by the use of empty but mouth-filling words so to represent law to himself that it will be unburdened by what he considers the crude courtroom actualities that thwart his desires. The method of the wishful metaphysician, who so describes the universe by discreet omissions as to satisfy his personal longings, is of a piece with that of Beale & Co. in defining the law. Both are perfectionists who "achieve the illusion of avoiding the arbitrary character inherent in their assertions" by asserting the truth of what they desire "not in all its nudity and crudeness, but in another form of a more general order so that the desired fact may appear as a consequence of this more general assertion, which just because of its greater generality and greater indetermination can appear less arbitrary."

Language, then, in its emotive aspect, makes legal Absolutism possible. It furnishes a "profound" terminology which seems to yield what the Absolutist demands, while it conceals the difficulties to the realization of his demands. With this terminology he dematerializes the facts he purports to describe; the vagueness of his vocabulary aids him to avoid recognizing contradictions and absurdities which his assertions involve. Contentless words supply "a stable verbal support for inexact, nebulous and fluctuating conceptions." Such dematerialized but sonorous terms as Uniformity, Continuity, Universality, when applied to law by the legal Absolutist, have the same capacity for emotional satisfaction that terms like Oneness, Eternity, or The True, have when applied by the metaphysician to the Absolute. Although the Bealist's arguments may be full of contradictions—as when he affirms that the purpose of legal reasoning is to enable the lawyer to predict decisions, and yet holds that actual decisions are not really law—they acquire, by means of the emotive value of his words, a compensatory significance. Because he wants law to be other than it is, he purports to go behind the actual legal decisions to what he deems the underlying "essential nature" of law. He thus seems to rescue law from what he considers the maltreatment which it receives at the hands of the judges. This he does by the use of satisfying words: with their aid, and not otherwise, he can give himself the illusion of possessing the kind of law which he desires to have. He "perceives with a dictionary instead of with his retina."

His "solving words" create a hallucinatory satisfaction. They become substitutes for action. Eager to possess the Law, which is superior "to law as it is," the Bealist uses compensatory verbiage. This verbiage he tends to rely on, in place of trying to ascertain how far, by direct attention to legal realities, he can bring the actual law with which he is dissatisfied somewhat in line with his aspirations.

In short he is a "wishful" thinker and, in his wishful thinking, Wousining, or Word-Magic, plays an indispensable part.

We can see now why there is so much talk about the certainty of law. That talk is not descriptive of facts; it is made up of magical phrases. Law being so largely lacking in the certainty which is desired, resort is had to those twangings of the vocal chords which will yield compensatory satisfaction.

The emotive and non-descriptive treatment of law has its dangers for the young lawyer; it tends to breed nihilistic skepticism. To those like the writer, who, in their student days, were taught, by means of legal verbalisms, to believe in a perfectionist kind of law, subsequent acquaintance with law as it confronts the practising lawyer brings a shock of disillusionment which for a time provokes a depressing disbelief in the possibility of any kind of continuity, certainty, or uniformity in law. Bealism, which is the verbal expression of excessive optimism, is sure to breed excessive cynicism. To many a young Bealish-trained lawyer the judges seem to be traitors to the true law; when the promised juristic paradise turns out to be a fairy story, the whole juristic world seems drab and dull;

or worse—intellectually or perhaps even morally dishonest.

But why are lawyers peculiarly infected with what has been called "verbomania"? Is there some historical explanation of the fact that our profession is especially subject to this malady?

There is another charge directed against the Bar which seems to furnish such an historical basis: Legal thinking, it is said, is affected by a "belated scholasticism," by "a blighting medieval prepossession. . . . In no other field of human thought is that prepossession to be found in a more exaggerated and persistent form."[7] Lawyers have inherited the attitude of the Middle Ages which consider concepts, abstractions, "general names" as more real than concrete occurrences and things. Legal technique, it is argued, needs liberation from the mental outlook of the Dark Ages; only thus will lawyers learn to stop using abstractions as substitutes for specific events; only then will they cease trying to do justice in particular cases by the sole method of reasoning deductively from such abstractions.

There is a measure of some truth in such strictures. The explicit thought-ways of lawyers, when they take the form of Bealism do resemble the thought-ways of Scholasticism. And Scholasticism did, indeed, worship the Word, borrowing and exaggerating the most unsound tendencies of Plato and his pupil Aristotle. Plato's trick of converting general terms, which describe common attributes of particular things, into immutable Ideas, "real entities eternally fixed in the order of nature," and of treating individual "things" as impermanent and therefore mere unworthy and imperfect copies of these eternal universals—a trick resulting from "a confusion of the subjective and objective in the conception of things and from a belief in the inherent agreement between names and things"—was carried on, with modifications, by Aristotle. Although there was far more of the practical in Aristotle than in Plato, he, too, lent himself, more or less, to the same snobbishness towards concrete, individual, sensible things, so that, at times, he pictured the "hatchetness" of hatchets as more real than any real hatchet. For him, scientific knowledge was based, in theory, not upon a knowledge of individual things but upon man's intuitive knowledge of the several fixed kinds of things and this knowledge was embedded in and to be extracted from language, so that science could "start from the name of such a kind, technically called a Species, and interrogate language about it."[8]

And, via a distortion of Aristotle, this proclivity to infer existence from a name and to exalt universals at the expense of particulars became the foundation of Scholasticism.[9] Under its influence men could seriously accept the thesis that the "Nothing" out of which God created the world is an existing thing (because "Nothing" has a name and every name must refer to some corresponding thing), or could reason that the absence of a thing and the thing itself are of like kind.

Thus arose that scholastic faith in the superiority of abstract terms, that tendency to establish "a hierarchy of ideas in which what is most void in content is placed highest," which we lawyers, it is said, have inherited. A thesis plausible enough if one contemplates the popularity of Bealism among lawyers.

Especially plausible, if, too, one considers the slavish adherence of lawyers to that instrument of reasoning which was worshipped by all men of the Middle Ages[10]—formal logic.[11] How that logic "has kept students of the law going about in circles" is neatly set forth in a recent writing of Professors Oliphant and Hewitt, partly summarized in the following paragraphs:

The school board of Seattle is reported to have insisted that all teachers, as a condition of procuring employment in the Seattle schools, should sign a contract by which they would agree not to join a teachers' union. Suppose that a suit were brought to compel the school board to hire teachers without imposing this condition. If a court were to decide such a suit in favor of the school board, an analysis of its opinion would show that its reasoning was apparently based upon a "fundamental principle." The court would argue that one who is under no duty to enter into a contract with another may stipulate any condition he pleases as a condition to entering into a contract. This principle the court would take as its major premise. It would then state, as a minor premise, that the school board is under no duty to enter into a contract with any particular teachers. The court would then reason syllogistically—that is, it would apply its major premise to its minor premise—and thus reach the conclusion that the school board has a right, as a condition to entering into contracts with teachers, to impose any terms which it pleases, including the stipulation that teachers are not to become members of the teachers' union.

The court would find its major premise in one of two ways. It might state that this liberty of contract was an "abiding and eternal principle of justice,"—a method of finding major premises which many courts employ. Or the court might refer to prior decisions not involving teachers or contracts with governmental officials, and purport to derive this principle "indirectly" from such decisions.

But however the principle is derived, this method of syllogistic reasoning, which is that of formal logic, is the method used by the courts today. Because of its use, the courts' conclusions appear inescapable and inevitable. This seeming machine-like certainty, however, is artificial and conceals a fatal weakness. For a decision against the school board might have been rendered and, if so, could have been justified, with reasoning which would have seemed similarly inevitable. The court could have argued thus: Officials administering the trust of public office may not unreasonably discriminate between applicants for employment. That is an eternal principle of justice or a principle to be found in numerous earlier cases. (There is your major premise.) To deny employment to a teacher because he refuses to agree not to join an organization of teachers is an unreasonable discrimination. (And there is your minor premise.) The ineluctable conclusion is that the school board cannot rightfully refuse to hire a teacher because of his refusal to sign a contract by which he agrees not to become a member of the teachers' union.

The weakness of the use of formal logic is now exposed. The court can decide one way or the other and in either case can make its reasoning appear equally flawless. Formal logic is what its name indicates; it deals with form and not with substance. The syllogism will not supply either the major premise or the minor premise. The "joker" is to be found in the selection of these premises. In the great run of cases which come before the courts, the selection of principles, and the determination of whether the facts are to be stated in terms of one or another minor premise, are the chief tasks to be performed. These are difficult tasks, full of hazards and uncertainties, but the hazards and uncertainties are ordinarily concealed by the glib use of formal logic.[12]

This practice of concealing the real job to be performed in thinking—concealing it not only from others but from the thinker himself—was, it is said, the curse of scholasticism. Wherefore among those, such as Oliphant and Hewitt, who are dissatisfied with current modes of legal thought it is becoming almost a convention to ascribe this dissatisfaction to the persistence of scholasticism in the law.

It is quite easy to make this diagnosis even more credible. F. C. S. Schiller has written a book in which he makes a devastating catalogue of the vices of formal logic. And a deadly parallel can be drawn between the *bad* traits of that logic (as portrayed in the following amusing phrases of Schiller) and those of legal thinking:

(1) The ideal of perfection for formal logic, says Schiller, is fixity. To the scholastic-minded, who worship this logic, the attainment of "perfect truth" is the *summum bonum*. Since there can be no change in the perfect truth, any change in a system of beliefs is symptomatic of its

falsity. Therefore the less we change our beliefs the better. It follows that the ideal of proof is that it should proceed from, and arrive at, certainty. "If certainty is not obtainable in life, then so much the worse for life. Let the Logical Ideal break off all relations with it."

(2) Bound up with these beliefs is the belief that the absolute system of immutable truth is one. For Formal Logic not more than one view can be true. To the formal logician you either have the truth or you have it not. Moreover, since truth is absolute, it is true without regard to circumstances. Experience reveals the fact that concrete situations are always individual, so that Truth, with respect to them, is always relative. Confronted with such relativity and being told that it is impossible to preserve the integrity of absolute truth while continuing to apply it, the formal logician replies simply—"Let us cease to apply it." And if some unpleasant person then argues that a truth which is not applied becomes unmeaning, the answer is that we must abstract from meaning also. For the ideal of our formal thinker is to be independent. Truth is not designed to be relative to man and human uses: Truth is necessary and eternal. The absence in such truth of human meaning and its lack of application to human uses are not therefore important, for Truth would not be absolute if man were allowed any part in its making.

(3) Formal logic is inveterately verbalistic. At its base is a belief in the superior reality of the so-called Universals, a belief that they are real entities which are more real than the objects of perception, entities whose virtue is "that they are free from the vicissitudes of events and the risks of misapplication." With the aid of verbalisms, formal logic maintains its faith in the absoluteness of a limited number of authoritative rules without regard to concrete cases, and satisfies its craving for uniformity and its aversion to novelty. With the aid of absolute words it makes the new seem old and builds up "a superhuman coherent system of eternal truths which are rigid and immutable"

while particular cases appear to exist merely in order to exemplify these eternal truths.[2]

There does indeed seem to be a parallel between the *vices* of formal logic (commonly associated with scholasticism) and the *vices* of legal logic. In that sense scholasticism and Bealism are seemingly related.

But before we accept as sufficient the diagnosis that the major obstacle to clear legal thinking is belated scholasticism or excessive verbalizing, let us ask *why "scholasticism" and verbalizing have survived in lawyerdom when they have become obsolescent (if not obsolete) in the natural sciences.* Are lawyers more stupid than the scientists? Do they have lower I. Q.s? Are they, in their daily activities, characterized by unusual dullness, lack of shrewdness, blindness to the minutiae of everyday affairs? Surely not. No sensible person would assert that the weaker intellects in the community gravitate to the bench and bar. Is it perhaps true, however, that lawyers in dealing with the law are more——?

But let us postpone the completion of that sentence until we have first reviewed rapidly some current descriptions of the thought processes of another very numerous group of human beings.

[2] Of course neither Schiller nor any other intelligent critic of formal logic denies the value of syllogistic reasoning, provided it is not abused by employing it to conceal the fact that the choice of premises is the most important task of the thinker.

The references to scholasticism are to scholasticism at its worst and ignore the more scientific nominalists of the Middle Ages. See Appendix VII, note 5.

CHAPTER VIII

CHILDISH THOUGHT-WAYS[1]

Let us consider childish thinking more in detail.

The young child's thinking is predominantly "wishful" thinking: the wish is, for him, the father to the thought. The new-born infant knows little thwarting of his desires. His adult environment usually sees to it that fulfillment follows quickly upon his wishes. Wishes indeed seem to fulfill themselves.

As the child develops, this expectation that his desires will receive immediate and unlimited satisfaction, abates, as experience gradually teaches him that such an expectation is often disappointed. But, although it gradually gives way to recognition of the relative indifference of the outside world, wishful thinking permeates childhood. The young child tends to regard his desires as realized immediately they are conceived. He puts his thoughts at the

---

[1] The description of childish thought-ways in this and the succeeding chapter is based almost entirely on Piaget's brilliant studies of child psychology, "The Language and Thought of the Child," "Judgment and Reasoning in the Child" and "The Child's Conception of the World." This description is, indeed, to some extent a composite made by the writer, from Piaget's works, consisting in part of excerpts from those works. Because the excerpts are taken from three separate books, juxtaposed to suit the writer's own purposes and mingled with his interpretations, quotation marks have usually been omitted.

Piaget is not responsible for the emphasis given by the writer to certain aspects of childish thought-processes nor for the summary of such ways given at the end of this chapter. He is especially to be absolved from responsibility for the inferences drawn from his material and for the application of those inferences to adult thinking in general and to legal thinking in particular.

service of the instant realization of these desires. He is slow to learn that the actualization of his wishes is frequently impossible or possible only at the cost of effort directed towards making changes in the external world. He blinds himself to the hindrances interposed by reality; he deforms reality in thought in such a way that these hindrances seem to disappear. He is the slave of his wishes, a day-dreamer, a builder of castles in the air.

The drive of his wishes is so strong that he is often unable to distinguish between phantasy and truth. He does not, indeed, often try to prove whether his ideas correspond to fact. "When that question is put to him, he evades it. It does not interest him, and it is even alien to his whole mental attitude."

The young child's world is essentially a world of play as distinguished from a world based on observation. Of course, as he develops, he becomes more and more aware of the latter world. But he does not frequently distinguish between these two worlds. They merge. The mature adult has his play-world, but he knows that it is unreal; for him it is a realm of "voluntary illusion." Not so for the child. For the child play is a reality, whereas objective reality, adult reality, is often a game which he plays with grown-ups. "True" reality is far less true for the child than for adults. The child's universe "is made up almost in its entirety by the mind and by the decisions of belief." The reality to which he clings is the outcome of his own mental construction.

If a young child is asked to draw a picture of a table, he does not copy the table but what he already knows about the table; he copies an "inner model." And so with childish observation generally. The young child usually sees only what he already knows. He is largely impervious to experience. He schematizes things in accordance with his own beliefs. His vision is distorted by his ideas. If he believes that rivers flow backwards, then all the rivers he actually sees seem to him to run upward toward their sources. "In short, he sees objects . . . as he would have imagined them, if, before seeing them, he had *per impossible* described them to himself." His curiosity is affective. He makes the world over to his heart's desire. "I wish it so" becomes "It must be so," and in turn, "It is so."

This kind of thinking has been variously labelled. It has been called "autistic," or "de-reistic," or wishful, or phantasy, or undirected, or unadapted, thinking. All these adjectives indicate that such thinking is subjective, unadapted to or turned away from reality, uncontrolled or undirected by experience.

To comprehend childish thought-ways, it is useful to employ the concept of two levels of thinking. The first or "lower" level is that just described. The other or "upper" level is that "directed" or "adapted" or "realistic" thinking which does not turn away from but deliberately seeks reality to which it tries to adapt itself and which it strives, too, to subjugate and control.

To break up thinking into these two levels is, of course, artificial. These classifications are merely convenient ways of describing tendencies. No one, not perhaps even the new-born, is completely a de-reistic or autistic or wishful thinker. And no one ever comes to a time when all his thinking is on the level of realistic or adapted thinking; all persons think on both levels, now more on one and now more on the other.

But these two categories may be used as indicia of development. The infant, we may say, is primarily a wishful thinker. As he develops, larger and larger areas of his thought become adapted and objective. Maturity means that a proportionately larger part of thought is done on the upper level. Immaturity, childishness, is indicated by the fact that a larger proportion of one's thinking is wishful.

Now closely related to the wishful nature of the child's thinking is another characteristic, already noted: the notion of chance is alien to the child. He believes that life is a harmoniously regulated whole in which chance has no place. There are no "gaps" in the course of events. There is a "reason" for everything. "The world is conceived as an assemblage of willed and regulated actions and intentions, which leave no room for fortuitous and, as such, inexplicable events." Everything can be justified, must be justified, at any price.

Everything, too, is connected with everything else. There is, for the child, no feeling of discontinuity, chaos or disharmony. There is a powerful feeling of unity; all sorts of subjective and inexpressible patterns ("feelings of relation") bind things together. Childish ideas arise through comprehensive subjective schemas, i.e. schemas that do not correspond to analogies or causal relations that can be verified by others. Things are connected by means of a great wealth of incommunicable allusions and implications.

And, in a certain sense, the child knows not novelty. He is constantly assimilating new experiences to his former subjective schemas. New phenomena are forced into earlier habit patterns; new-found objects are "deformed"—crudely assimilated to and identified with what the child already knows. His attitude towards new and unexpected objects is that these new elements in his experience can be made to fit into old frameworks; he often asserts that there are pre-existing "rules" which explain the new as being just like the old. These assertions are accompanied by a feeling that "it must be so" even though he is unable to find any precise justification for the resemblance.

The child, that is, has a greater consciousness of resemblance than of difference. He adopts an identical attitude to all objects that lend themselves to assimilation. He is slow in formulating exceptions to his unconscious groupings of things. He applies as often as he can, through sheer economy of thought, an explanation which he has found adequate in some previous case. He condenses various images, fusing together heterogeneous elements, and without any feeling of the necessity of verification has "an unquestioning belief in the inter-implications of elements condensed in this way."

There is for him no "why" that does not have an answer. He has astonishing capacity for answering any question, satisfying his mind by means of arbitrary justifications of events. He can always find a "reason," whatever is in question. "I know" is his ever-ready response. He disposes of difficult problems with unexpected solutions. He is amazingly fertile in framing explanations, writes Piaget, in a way "that recalls the intellectual vagaries of 'interpreters' rather than the imaginative constructions of normal adults."

An interesting experiment illustrates this proclivity. The child is given a list of simple proverbs together with a list of sentences; each sentence corresponds to and explains one of the proverbs, but all are jumbled together. The child is asked to select the sentence which corresponds to a given proverb. The experiment shows that accident or purely superficial analogy determines the selection. But more important is the child's justification of his choice. Thus a child of nine assimilates the proverb, "White dust ne'er came out of a sack of coal" to the sentence, "People who waste their time neglect their business." According to him, these two propositions mean the same because "coal is black and can't be cleaned," while people who waste their time neglect their children who then become black and can no longer be cleaned. "We have here," writes Piaget, "a syncretistic capacity which at first seems to be due to pure invention; but analysis shows that it comes from the child's inability to disassociate comprehensive perceptions or to restrain the tendency that wants to simplify and condense everything." In short, he conceives the world as more explicable, more "logical" than it is.

Thus the child, without reference to external reality, is able to make for himself the kind of world he wishes, a world which satisfies his desire for stability, continuity and uniformity.

Integrally bound up with these tendencies is another: the child is a confirmed verbalist. He is guilty of a persistent confusion between names and things. Every object seems to him to possess a necessary and absolute name, one which is a part of the object's very nature. The name of an object is regarded as a property inherent in its essence, as real a part of it as its visual characteristics. For the child, to think is to speak, and speaking consists of acting on things by means of words, the words showing the nature of the things named as well as the voice producing them. In learning the name of a thing, the child believes he is reaching to the essence of the thing and discovering its real explanation; as soon as he knows the name, the problem of what the thing is no longer exists. Names belong to things and emanate from them. "Was the sun there before it had its name?"—"No."—"Why not?" —"Because they didn't know what name to give it."— "There must really be God, because he has a name." A country is "a piece of land that has a name."

The name is in the object, not as a label attached to it, but as an invisible quality of the object. The thing includes its name in its intrinsic character although it is invisible. To touch the name of the sun would be to touch the sun itself. Names come from the things themselves. They were discovered by looking at things.

Later, when the child advances beyond such primitive notions and begins to believe that names are "in the air," he still ignores completely the fact that their origin lies within ourselves. The name, he now believes, comes from the object and "appears in the voice": it is then "driven forth again by the voice" but in no case does it spring directly from an internal "thought."

And even when the child becomes aware of the human origin of name-making, he still believes that names have an intrinsic logical value. Could names be changed? "Could the moon have been called 'sun' and the sun 'moon'?"—"No."—"Why not?"—"Because the sun makes it warm and the moon gives light." Even later when the child learns that names are not tied up to the things they represent, he still believes there is a necessary harmony between the name and the thing: the name "fits," "goes well," etc. The sun is so called because "it behaves as if it were the sun," the stars "because they are that shape," a table "because it is used for writing," clouds "because they are all grey," a stick "because it is thick."[1]

Word-magic is a natural consequence of these beliefs of the young child as to the nature of words. Failing to recognize words as symbols, the child's conception of words as adhering to things leads to the further belief that names are the causes of things and can be used directly to influence them. This is natural enough as long as the sign and the thing signified are not distinguished. So the child has a conviction that reality can be modified by names and that, through words, thought can insert itself into the real world and thus directly control events.

In sum, the child[2] is (1) a *wishful* thinker who, (2) in the interest of his desires for *harmony, chancelessness, security and certainty,* builds for himself an over-simplified, over-unified, novelty-less world to conform to his desires, heedless of the lack of correspondence of this construction with the world of actual experience, and (3) who is aided in contriving this world by his implicit *belief in the magic efficacy of words.*

If, now, you were to put in parallel columns the distinctive *vices* of scholasticism and the distinctive traits of childish thinking, the resemblances would be striking. Misuse in modern times of scholastic logic, despite its harmful social consequences[2] is apparently not due, as Schiller would have it, to the fact that "nothing has a greater hold on the human mind than nonsense fortified by technicality, because the more nonsensical it is the more impervious it becomes to rational objection, the more impossible it is to amend it, and so the better it lasts."

---

[2] The word "child" is here, for convenience, used as if it were a constant. Of course, as Piaget and others point out elaborately in their studies, there are developmental periods in the growth of any child. The characteristics of any one period may, however, be partially carried over into later periods.

"Scholasticism," it would seem, is with us today not because it is "consecrated by a tradition of 2000 years," but because all men now alive were once children and many of them continue to remain emotionally childish even in advanced years. "Scholasticism" and platonism— using those terms in a derogatory sense—alike appear to be cleverly elaborated formulations of the emotional attitude of childhood, ingenious rationalizations of the world outlook of the child.[3] To say of a man's thinking that it is scholastic or platonistic, is to say that it is tinged with childish emotions.[3]

[3] The reader will remember that we are using a "partial explanation." See Appendix X.

CHAPTER IX

GENETICS

Can we now complete the sentence left unfinished several pages back? Shall we say that, if we lawyers are preponderantly absolutistic, then we are scholastic or platonistic—and therefore childish?

Scarcely. To say that lawyers are childish in their thinking would be to utter an absurdity. Lawyers are not, as a class, simpletons. Our profession can boast many of the world's keenest minds, many of its most brilliant intellects. There is unquestionably a resemblance of some sort between legal Absolutism and childish thinking. But the resemblance is in illusory aims, in unconscious outlook, not in intellectual processes.

Plato was not childish in terms of intellectual power; he was an intellectual genius. But his thinking had this in common with that of the child: His intellect served his desires in creating a dream-world[1] which satisfied longings strikingly like those of the child. It is with respect to its emotional attitudes that Platonism can be said to resemble childish thinking.

It is in this same sense, and only in this sense, that it can be said that if and to the extent that we lawyers are Bealists (*i.e.* platonists with regard to law), then our thinking resembles childish thinking, not because our intellection is defective, but because our intellects are at times controlled in part by an emotional attitude and guided by an aim more appropriate to childhood than to adult years.

But, even if that be true, it leaves unanswered this question: Why are lawyers in their thinking about law more frequently guided by childish (*i.e.* platonistic) aims than biologists, for instance, in their thinking about biology?

To answer that question adequately, we shall need to inquire more closely into the genetics of childish thought-ways:

First of all, we must observe a central feature of the child's mode of thinking. It is "egocentric." This description is justifiable because the child assumes that everything centers in himself. "His reality is impregnated with self." The desires and commands of the self, the thoughts and point of view of the self, are absolute for the child. He believes that all the world thinks like himself and that all his own explanations are shared by others, since his are the only possible explanations. In every conceivable way the child confuses the self with the universe, assimilates the world to the self, and the self to the world.

Not that the child differentiates between himself and the world and deliberately prefers the former. The exact opposite is the case: the child is not dualistic but adualistic. His confusion of self with the universe arises out of his *unconsciousness of self*. And the curious characteristics of childish thinking stem off this unawareness. It is this ignoring of his self that leads to the countless unobserved intrusions of his self into his thinking and thence to his numerous illusions and errors. "So long as thought has not become conscious of self, it is a prey to perpetual confusions between objective and subjective, between the real and the ostensible; it values the entire content of consciousness on a single plane in which ostensible realities and the unconscious interventions of self are inextricably mixed."

It is the child's naïve egocentricity, his unconsciousness of self, which leads him to regard his own perspective as immediately objective and absolute; to assimilate external processes to schemas arising from his own internal experiences, attributing to the outer world characteristics which properly belong to his mind; to deal with the instruments of his thought as if they were a part of things or situated in things or as a genus of things situated both in the body and in the surrounding air; and, generally speaking, to fail to differentiate between internal and external, psychical and physical, mind and body, subjective and objective.

It is this unconsciousness of self which makes the child a wishful thinker, a verbalist, a fatuous believer in an impossibly chanceless world, devoid of novelty, and gratifyingly secure and harmonious.

And as these childish modes of thought are due to the child's unconsciousness of self, it is precisely the progressive awareness of his self and of his own thought that frees him from them. Wishful thinking; personalization of reality; absoluteness of point of view; imperviousness to experience; belief in word-magic; confusion of self and the world, of inner and outer, thought and things—all these adualisms, illusions and errors diminish proportionately to the growth of the child's awareness of his self, to his breaking away from his egocentricity. To the extent that he becomes self-conscious and thereby learns the internal nature of thought and the motives which guide thinking, just to that extent he comes to desubjectify reality, to think about thinking, to conceive of words not as parts of things but as instruments of thought, to accept chance and change as often unavoidable, to differentiate between his wishes and the actualities of experience.

But what wakes the child to consciousness of self? To answer that question properly we must first observe how the unawareness of self is caused and how it is fostered:

The baby can barely distinguish his own movements from movements outside itself. He and the outer world seem to him to be at one. "When the infant sees his limbs move at his own will, he must feel that he is commanding the world. Thus on seeing a baby joyfully watching the movements of his feet, one has the impression of the joy felt by a god directing from a distance the movement of the stars. Inversely, when the baby takes delight in movements in the outside world, such as the movement of the ribbons of its cradle, he must feel an immediate bond

between these movements and his delight in them. . . .
There is thus in the beginning neither self nor external
world but a *continuum*." And the parents foster the baby's
sense of direct participation in the environment, for their
reactions to the baby make their acts seem a direct continuity of the infant's acts. They respond to almost every
cry of the infant and anticipate many of the desires which
he cannot communicate. The young child, naturally
enough, assumes that the thoughts and actions of others
are directed to his well-being; that his every desire is
shared by the world, his slightest wish understood, the
least of his thoughts common to all.

Thus the parentally created atmosphere keeps alive the
infant's feeling of a *continuum*, the feeling of communion,
which colors all his vision of the world, and so prolongs
the absence of differentiation between the world and the
self.

This sense of *immediacy* of his participation with, and
control of, the outside world is, of course, reduced, as the
child grows up, by repeated experiences of his lack of
direct power over things. It is through the parents, the
child begins to realize, that he maintains his power. His
participation, as we have said, is mediate, indirect, vicari-
ous. The parents seem to be able to do all things, to know
all things; the whole of nature seems to be obedient to
them. The child sees himself, also, as dependent on them.
But they use their magical power for his welfare, in the
interest of his needs. "The most natural idea for him, the
idea he cannot escape from without doing violence to his
habits, is that all nature centers around him and has been
organized by his parents. . . ."

Now, as we noted once before, the father, inevitably,
comes to be accepted as the fundamental repository of
the magnificent parental power. It is primarily the father
who is thought to be omniscient and omnipotent; it is he
who has created all and knows all. He is conceived as possessing sanctity, supreme power, omniscience, eternity and
ubiquity. So that the child's egocentricity is now derivative.

It is as son of his father that the child now maintains his belief that he is the center of the world. Egocentricity is now dependent on father-centricity. The naïve sense of communion with the world, the feeling of a continuum, is a function of the child's belief in the "godhood" of his father. And since the child's unawareness of his self, of his own subjectivity, of the differentiation between psychical and physical and between names and things—his whole emotional attitude—are functions of this sense of continuum, of participation, it follows that his whole artificial scheme of things is related to the continuance of his belief in this godhood of his father.

And so it is that the discovery of the humanity, the fallibility, of his father is the beginning of wisdom for the child. With that staggering discovery comes the child's awareness of his self. "So long as he believes in his father's omniscience, his own self is non-existent." The moment he realizes that his father is imperfect, he discovers the existence of his subjective self. "If Papa does not know everything how can I?" cries the child.

We have quoted before Edmund Gosse's account of his shock when, as a child, he detected his father in an untruth. This was soon followed by another similar incident. Gosse describes the consequences:

"In the first place, the theory that my Father was omniscient or infallible was now dead and buried. He probably knew very little; in this case he had not known a fact of such importance that if you did not know that, it could hardly matter what you knew. My Father, as a deity, as a natural force of immense prestige, fell in my eyes to a human level. In future, his statements about things in general need not be accepted implicitly. But of all the thoughts which rushed upon my savage and undeveloped little brain at this crisis, the most curious was that I had found a companion and a confidant in myself. There was a secret in this world and it belonged to me and to a somebody who lived in the same body with me. There were two of us, and we could talk with one another. It is difficult to define impressions so rudimentary, but it is certain that it was in this dual form that *the sense of my individuality now suddenly descended upon me."*

Such is the typical crisis in the life of the child. *This diminution of respect for and veneration of father dates the liberation of the child from his own naïveté.* The world now is alien, different from himself. There is an I and a not-I. The ostensible and the real, inner and outer, thoughts and things, begin to separate. Dualisms arise, objectivity commences. The inescapability of change and chance, of disharmony and discontinuity, forces itself on him. The subjectivity of thought dawns upon the youngster. The whole world outlook of the child begins to be transformed.

But the disillusionment is by no means at once complete. Skepticism has set in, but it does not follow through. For, although he has deposed his own father, the child has not relinquished fatherliness. Substitutes for the father, substitutes which shall not be fallible and weak, are still sought after. To the extent that they are found, the individual's sense of communion, the delicious ease of selflessness, are maintained. And, too, to that extent, he can still conceive of the world as a harmoniously organized whole where chance is excluded and everything is justified, and where he can preserve his adualisms, his egocentricity, his verbalism, his wishful thinking.

The emotional attitudes of any person are spotty. Just as in the developing child the degree of objectivity varies, so in the grown-up there may be inconsistent emotional attitudes, varying with the subject-matter he is confronting. In relation to those subjects where father-substitutes have been obliterated, adult objectivity will make these thought-processes objective, while in relation to other subjects, where father-substitutes have not been dissipated, the unconscious childish aims will survive and, to a disproportionately large extent, thought mechanisms of a childish character will continue; and thinking to that extent will be done on the "lower" level, rather than the "upper" level.

Since, then, the Law is easily personified as a father-substitute[1] and it is only with difficulty that the father image is dislodged from that stronghold, it is not difficult to understand the relative lack of objectivity in thinking with regard to law as compared with thinking with regard to physics.[2]

Here apparently is the reason why legal thinking is, in part, scholastic, why legal thinkers are still much given to Platonizing: Children are incipient, unsophisticated Platonists. Not only lawyers, but all men in their approach to the law are still somewhat childish emotionally and therefore are prone to Platonizing—not, of course, in the crude manner of children, but in a polished and sophisticated fashion. Verbalism and word-magic; fatuous insistence on illusory certainty, continuity and uniformity; wishful intellection which ignores, or tries to obliterate from cognizance, unpleasant circumstances—these are the marks of childish thought and often affect legal thinking.

We can now more adequately complete our uncompleted sentence: "Scholasticism" has survived in lawyerdom while it is on the wane among natural scientists because the *emotional* attitudes of childhood have a more tenacious hold on men when their thinking is directed towards the law than when they are thinking about the natural sciences, and not because lawyers have intellects inferior to the scientists. If and to the extent that you are controlled by a childish emotional need for strict authority, to that extent your thought-processes will be restricted and will retain something of the childish pattern. The natural sciences, as we shall see, are not so easily as law converted into a father-substitute. Hence in the natural sciences, authoritarianism is less potent and the aims of the child have been more rapidly abandoned. The complete liberation of lawyers from the so-called tradition of scholasticism can come only through their liberation, with respect to law—like that of scientists with respect to science

[1] See Part One, Chapter II.

—from the emotional attitudes of the child. Hallucinatory satisfactions will cease being sought in law when men learn to cease regarding law as the embodiment of fatherly authority.

It is worth while, perhaps, to rephrase this conclusion:

Most of us learn how to conceal, verbally, our "egocentricity" both from ourselves and from others. That it is concealed does not mean that it has ceased to exist. In so far as there are still areas of our thinking primarily on the lower or wishful level, we may be said to be emotionally childish.

Now there are certain aspects of experience where we react more egocentrically, more wishfully, than in others. It is to be suspected that those aspects of experience for some reason evoke childish attitudes. In this sense it seems proper to say that with respect to law there is more of the kind of thinking charged with childish emotional attitudes than with respect to natural sciences. In the natural sciences, directed or objective thinking is patently more active than in law. Here, it would seem, is the explanation of the charge that legal thinking is eminently "scholastic." It is not a "blighting medieval prepossession" that "has kept students of the law going about in circles." It is rather that the subject of law evokes youthful illusory aims,[2] aims which are at cross-purposes with the important practical function of law, aims that are hidden away and therefore bafflingly interfere, at times, with the operations of the often gifted and singularly brilliant minds of lawyers.

[2] Evokes such illusory aims, it is important to remember, *less in the mind of the lawyer than in that of the layman* who tries to think about the nature and function of law. A pre-eminent physicist, Frederick Soddy, writes that lawyers are "charlatans" who "mystify the public" when they could quite easily, if they would, make law simple, predictable and intelligible to all men.

The reader will recall that we are using a partial explanation. See Part One, Chapter II, note 8 and Appendix X.

As to the use of the blanket word "child," see note on page 81.

CHAPTER X

WORD-CONSCIOUSNESS

But what of the possible argument that it is not the prolongation of childish emotional attitudes which is responsible for the survival in adult years of the certainty illusion and other related mental traits, but that, on the contrary, it is verbalism that is accountable for the persistence of what seem to be childish attitudes and that, therefore, release from a state of retarded thinking must be sought in a direct attack on verbalism?

While writers on law, such as Green, have made some such suggestion, yet for development of that idea we shall need to turn to the writings of C. K. Ogden and his associates,[11] since they are the principal exponents of the notion that the original sin in all inadequate thinking is to be found in the misuse of words. They portray as a "disease of language" the difficulty the human mind experiences in dealing with abstractions. Words, they say, become our masters because the very nature of language fosters a belief in the independent reality of what are merely verbal contrivances. In order to save time, we contract and condense language. We therefore make up words like Virtue, Liberty, Democracy, Freedom, and then forget that they are merely handy abbreviations. So we come to treat them as if they were independent entities, more real than the aspects of the circumstances they were used to describe or classify. But if we view them as mere symbols or labels we shall be rid of all the troubles such bogus entities have cost mankind. We shall then see that these entities are "phantoms due to the refractive power of the linguistic medium; they must not be treated as part of the furniture of the universe, but are useful as symbolic accessories enabling us to economize our speech material." If once we are thus oriented, we shall no longer "regard ourselves as related to a variety of entities, properties, propositions, numbers, functions, universals and so forth—by the unique relation of knowledge. Recognized for what they are, i.e., symbolic devices, these entities may be of great use."

The hindrance to the detection of the merely verbal character of those abstractions is, we are told, due to a belief in word-magic, a conviction that words have power over things, a theory of an inherent connection between symbols and the things to which the symbols refer, a "common, inherited scheme of conception" traceable to the attitude of savages. Primitive man has a deeply rooted belief that "a word has some power over a thing, that it is akin or even identical in its contained 'meaning' with the thing or its prototype. . . . The word acts on the thing and the thing releases the word in the human mind. . . . A word is used by the savages when it can produce an action and not to describe one, still less to translate thoughts. The word therefore has a power of its own, it is a means of bringing things about, it is a handle to acts and objects and not a definition of them."[2] Unfortunately this belief is imported into the thinking of today by language itself.[3] "The various structural peculiarities of a modern, civilized language carry an enormous deadweight of archaic use, of magical superstition and of mystical vagueness." Through language, it is said, we inherit "the pragmatic Weltanschauung of primitive man"; through language "the barbarous primitive categories have deeply influenced the later philosophies of mankind." Thus our present behavior is molded by the unseen hand of the past and our thought is encompassed by "ineluctable verbal coils." Primitive man's outlook persists in the work of the profoundest thinkers because this outlook is inherent in language: "Through language all of our intellectual, and much of our social, heritage comes to us." "The primitive, magical attitude towards words is responsible for a good deal in the general use and abuse of language."

Accordingly the release from the dominance of the primitive, the elimination of the sway of word-magic, the destruction of wousining, the cure for the diseases of language, are to be sought in "word-consciousness," in a perception of the true use of words,[4] and in a study of the genesis of current language habits. Why, ask our word-doctors, do primitive language practices dominate our current speech? Because "the extreme vitality of the magic attitude to words is explained . . . not only by a reference to the primitive usages of language by savages and, no doubt, by prehistoric man, but also by perpetual confirmation in infantile uses of language. . . . The pragmatic (primitive) function of language is carried on into its highest stages, especially through infantile use and through backsliding of adults into unsophisticated modes of thinking and speaking."

There is much optimism latent in such a theory of language. If it be true that (a) "so far from grammar being of the structure of the world, any supposed structure of the world is more probably a reflection of the grammar used"; and (b) if "we can say that the fundamental categories, universal to all human languages, can be understood only with reference to the pragmatic Weltanschauung of primitive man, and that, through the use of language, the barbarous primitive categories must have deeply influenced the later philosophies of mankind"; and (c) if this influence is due to the fact that when we learn words as children we are subjected to the primitive attitudes encysted in language and therefore often succumb to these attitudes in later life—! Then there is vast hope for progress away from illusion and towards realism. For, thus considered, what appears to be the childish insistence upon possessing a world seemingly without chance or change, a tight universe into which no novelties can leak, is due to the primitiveness of the language we learned in childhood; a language expressive of the savage's dreams, a language therefore little adapted to any awareness of a chancy, changing world; a language committed to predilections for the inert, the static, the certain. This language, this barbarous certainty-loving language, is the language we employ as adults. Of course we have difficulty in thinking, against the grain of primitive man's language, of a modern civilized man's world. Hopeful indeed, this vista. For the static tendency of our intellection, if it be not inherent in our mental structure but merely in our inherited speech forms, may be largely modifiable. We may be able to revise our language, to devise a vocabulary replete with dynamic words and phrases, and thereby enhance our powers of thinking dynamically.[5] We may then discover that Bergson's antithesis of static "intellect" and fluid "intuition" is false. Our intellect may become intuitive, closer to the "nature of things." Our mental sifting-machine[6] may become surprisingly adjustable. Word-consciousness may deliver us from primitivity in thinking by enabling us to look beyond our speech forms to the things we are talking about.[7]

Let us now return to Dean Green's contention that backwardness in legal thinking is ascribable to the misuse of words. We might adapt and support his argument thus: The cause of certainty-illusion and other obstructions to realistic thinking about law is the crystallization of primitive attitudes in the language which children learn and grown men employ. Certainty-hunger and other superstitious notions thereby affect grown man's approach to everything—including law. Accordingly the way to get rid of the blight on legal thinking is through that science of symbolism which will exorcise the age-old superstitions from our use of words.

Now it must be plain that such an argument would prove too much. If it were correct, then such manifestations as the certainty-illusion would be no more pronounced or injurious in law than in other fields. But this, as we have seen, is not the case.[8] Although primitiveness does, indeed, lurk in our language, yet in some fields men have moderately well succeeded in combating archaic thought-ways, in spite of the hindrance of a language still infected with the world-outlook of savages. Granting that misuse of language retards progress towards a mature view of experience generally, we still have to answer why the rate of that progress is slower in respect to law; why (to rephrase the statement of the problem) the desire is relatively weak and impotent, in thinking about law, to overcome the handicaps imposed by a language suffused with paleolithic notions.

The answer must begin with a revised statement of the genetic theory of language: [9] The error which lies behind and explains the child's addiction to word-magic is not acquired by the child from language but is a native attribute of the child's thought-ways. The child's confusion of thought and things antedates his learning of language; the language which he learns from adults fosters and gives definite form to this confusion, but is not its cause. The indications are that, even if language were purged of all the magical superstition and mystical vagueness which it contains because of its anthropological origins, children would none the less create for themselves word-magic as they create non-verbal magic and animism.

The child, says Piaget, does not merely imitate adult language. He does not swallow grown-up speech raw, but digests it according to mental digestive processes of his own. His imitation is selective and recreative.

So that, while there is what may be called a primitive outlook in the language which the child learns, this outlook is not created in the child by language but corresponds to the child's natural trends. "It is not the child that is molded by language; it is the language which is already childish."

If we employ the metaphor of disease, we may say that the difficulties which words seem to engender do not constitute a disease of childhood, but rather that these difficulties result from a disease of childhood of which the misuse of language is a symptom. Or again we may say that, if language is diseased, then each generation of children reinfects it.

Indeed it is a question whether, so far as the child is concerned, we should refer to word-magic as a disease. It is normal to the child and "abnormal" only in the adult.[10] The real disease is emotional infantilism unduly prolonged. Of that disease, verbomania is merely one symptom. Our word-doctors have confused the symptom with the disease.

See, for instance, the child's relation to the "emotive" use of words as reported by Piaget. Language is not for the young child primarily a means of communicating thought. The child's first words are bound up with his acts. As they are originally a part of his acts, so, even after they become a means of communicating thoughts (become, that is, "symbols of reference"), they continue to contain definite emotional charges associated with certain acts. It is in this way that many words retain for a child not only an affective, but also a sort of magical significance. For this reason, too, words frequently become, for the child, a substitute for action. He obtains from them a hallucinatory satisfaction: When he cannot get what he wants by acting, he often turns to words as a method for obtaining what he desires. With words he creates his own reality which is frequently for him as good as, or better than, objective reality.

Now this use by the child of words as a means of hallucinatory satisfaction is not due to any aboriginal Weltanschauung buried in the words themselves. The child, quite on his own, is a wishful thinker and, without any suggestion from external sources, finds that words are an invaluable aid for creating a desired picture of events in place of unpleasant reality.[11] No one needs to teach him that word-magic, the wizardry and spells of speech, the employment of talismanic phrases, are excellent modes of escape from the harsh ways of actual events. He is a natively wishful thinker and his wishful thinking is aided, but is not created, by his misuse of words.[12]

If word-magic is not the cause of childish emotional attitudes, it seems unlikely that a mere development of word-consciousness will dissipate those attitudes.

Francis Bacon's case is useful material. He was explicitly word-conscious. One of the chief indictments he brought against the schoolmen was their preoccupation with words as against observation of things. This preoccupation, he wrote, was one of three "distempers of learning." He railed against what he described as "delicate learning" where words usurp the place of substance and polished phrases are accepted for real weight of meaning: "Of this vanity, Pygmalion's frenzy is a good emblem; for words are but the images of matter, and except they have life of reason and invention, to fall in love with them is all one as to fall in love with a picture." "Men believe that their reason governs words, but it is also true that words, like arrows from a Tartar bow, are shot back and react upon the mind."

But this word-consciousness did not help Bacon to escape from the most hampering characteristics of scholasticism: At the basis of his "scientific" method was the assumption that "certainty at all costs and by the shortest route is the sole aim of inquiry."[13] He formulated principles of science but was contemptuous of the true scientific work of his contemporaries, Harvey, Gilbert and Galileo. Despite Bacon's insight into the dangers of canonizing words, he did not develop a scientific, that is an adventurous, a risk-taking type of mind. Word-consciousness was not, in itself, sufficient to release him from the dominance of so-called primitive thought-ways.

The real "cure" probably must be sought in whatever causes an undue prolongation of a childish emotional outlook. It seems likely that instead of such an outlook succumbing to an attack on verbalism, verbalism will give way completely only when the childish emotional point of view is outgrown. In the "pre-symbolistic" thinking of the child do we not see the origins of the failure "to deal with anything more than words, and to substitute classification of verbal distinctions for the study of actual thinking" which, according to Schiller, is the curse of formal (*i.e.* scholastic) logic? That assumption of an imaginary identity of name and thing, that proclivity to explain the inexplicable by means of phantom words, "to infer the existence immediately from the name," which Lange describes as the fundamental errors of Platonism—are they not unmistakably akin to the natural errors of childhood?

Such a conclusion does not, however, preclude enthusiasm about the crusade of Ogden *et al.* They would surely be justified in urging that, if man becomes word-conscious, if he stops confusing words with "things," if he frees himself from bondage to Word-Magic, he will be far better able to throw off the attitudes of the child whenever and wherever he develops the will so to do. If a war on words, or word-revolution, will not destroy childish illusions, such a war or revolution may well be a necessary step in accomplishing the ultimate destruction of such illusions. The work that Ogden and his associates have begun, even though it may not be striking at the roots of the evil which they hope to eliminate, is of great importance.[14]

And such a war on words is to be welcomed in the province of law. It will assist in demolishing many a legal myth. But there, too, it will, unaided, probably prove to be insufficient. For the subject-matter of law excites a hunger for certainty even in men generally wary of the snares of language. A great physicist, like Soddy, loses his scientific caution when he confronts the law and talks like any naïve absolutist metaphysician. If adults of keen mind become "scholastic" and verbalistic in dealing with the law, we would seem to be justified in surmising that the subject-matter of the law is one which evokes, almost irresistibly, regressive emotions. It is not, then, the clouding of the critical faculties through the power of words that betrays us lawyers; it is rather that, confronted by the law, men tend to be baffled by feelings stimulated by the father-substitute which law represents, and therefore use narcotizing and paralyzing words to pursue what are relatively childish aims.[15]

The trouble with legal thinking is not the mental inadequacies of the lawyers. It is the very nature of law, its rôle as a father-substitute, that stirs up unconscious attitudes, concealed desires, illusory ideals, which gets in the way of realistic observation of the workings and significance of law. For law appears to arouse these emotional deterrents to clear thinking in almost all men whenever they direct their attention to legal problems. The lawyers, on the whole, are better able to fight off these deterrents than the laymen. For, notwithstanding the obstructing illusions, the lawyers must daily perform that practical task of adjusting conflicting interests which is the function of the legal profession; the performance of that task compels them to win ponderable victories over those illusions by which the layman is more likely to be victimized. But if the lawyers are less deluded than the laymen about the character of law, their realism is not as vigorous as it might be, else Bealism would be as outmoded among lawyers as Platonism is among the first-rate scientists.

CHAPTER XI

SCIENTIFIC TRAINING

It would be natural enough to find that one of the ablest critics of legal Platonism, Professor Walter Wheeler Cook, a man singularly free of the vicious tendencies of that tradition, is convinced that the way out of the legal Dark Ages is through acquainting law students with the logic of the natural sciences. Then, Cook believes, we shall have lawyers with a scientific habit of thought, then the artificialities of judicial thinking will gradually disappear. Cook's activities in legal pedagogy are constructively revolutionary and the advancement of learning in the law already owes a vast deal to his efforts. But whether his program for an attack on Platonism will accomplish all that he anticipates may be doubted.

Consider, for instance, the case of Plato himself. Before his time Greek science had made rapid strides. Relativism and healthy skepticism were developing, men were being freed from bondage to authority in thinking about nature and were pushing on to that fearless observation of experience and that analysis of natural processes which centuries later—the delay being in part due to Plato—was to produce what we call modern science. Plato, in his youth, was taught and was greatly impressed by the views of the earlier scientific-minded Greek thinkers. From their teachings he became acquainted with doctrines which would now sound modern, for the atomic theory, relativity and pragmatism then had their beginnings.

But Plato did not help to foster those beginnings. On

the contrary he was the great leader of the reaction.[1]
While Protagoras stressed the particular and the individual
and maintained that, as Lange puts it, "the expression
that something is, always needs a further determination in
relation to what it is or is becoming," while Heraclitus
taught of the all-pervasiveness of change, Plato fled to
an opposite position. From his more scientific-minded
predecessors he had learned that sensible things are ever-
changing, ever in flux, that there are no absolutes, and
that all standards are relative. Very well then, he concluded, the sensible world is not real; such reality as it has
is secondary and subordinate to the Universals (like absolute greatness or absolute health or absolute beauty or
absolute goodness) which are Eternal, True and Real.[1]

Thus "Platonizing" was born.[2] Plato's acquaintance
with incipient relativistic and nominalistic thinking did not
rescue him from mystical absolutism, but only enabled
him the more subtly and seductively to expound in articulate form that exalted verbalism, that expression of the
confusion between subjective and objective, which, at its
worst, became Scholasticism. Plato's course demonstrates
that the yearning for authority[2] is insidious. It will find
satisfaction at all costs, twist any material to its ends. It
can rationalize into supports to its aims the very concepts
that seemingly are the aids to its antithesis, the adventurous progress of science.

This is peculiarly true in relation to law. Let us see what

[1] Plato did foster mathematics for its religious and ethical value.
Some think that the Golden Age of Greek mathematics was due
to the emancipation of the mathematicians from Platonic influences.

[2] Plato, of course, was not 100 per cent Platonist. He was a
genius, therefore a complicated man. (For an excellent but perhaps
over-enthusiastic statement of his many-sidedness, see A. E. Tay-
lor's "Plato.") But he gave the world a beautifully worded statement of "Platonism" and this statement, as in part revised by
Aristotle but interpreted by less scientifically educated minds, became the heritage of the Middle Ages, taking on forms which Plato
would, doubtless, have repudiated.

certainty-hunger in law has done in distorting some of the philosophies which it has encountered.

The eighteenth century was surely friendly to science. However inadequate its formulations may seem as a final program for scientific thought, the Age of Reason which produced such men as Lavoisier was one which in its science challenged authority and gave free play to the impulse to question all theretofore accepted axioms with regard to the processes of nature. Whatever of concealed authoritarianism the postulations of eighteenth-century science contained, that authoritarianism was sufficiently weak, so far as scientific inquiry was concerned, to be negligible.

Now see in what manner the lawyers adopted this eighteenth-century scientific world-outlook. In physics, astronomy and chemistry, men were making significant use of mathematics. It became the mode that law should be made scientific. Very well then, mathematical reason would be employed in the law, and law would become as scientific as physics and astronomy. But the resemblance was only on the surface. In the sciences, mathematical reasoning was being used as an aid to bold conjectures, as a method of checking up on impudent guesses about nature. Mathematics did not hamper, it aided creative work in physics and chemistry. It did not impede inquiry into the happenings of actual, concrete events. The purpose of eighteenth-century science was to observe and understand and control the actual. It was progressive, reconstructive, restless, manipulative. It was adventurous, incessantly curious. And mathematical reasoning was not used by the eighteenth-century scientists to stifle but to foster skepticism of authoritative pronouncements.

Not so with the lawyers of that period. The "mathematical reason" they enshrined was that which Plato had worshipped.[3] Their purpose was to find a few self-evident,

[3] Plato believed that mathematics had "an elevating effect, compelling the soul to reason about abstract number and rebelling against the introduction of visible or tangible objects into the ar-

never-changing principles. From these unalterable axioms of "legal science," the mathematical reason, they assumed, could work out flawless solutions of every problem arising from the multitude of factual occurrences. The emphasis in legal science was the exact reverse of that in natural science: it was not on observation of the particular but on the attainment of universals which were above and independent of experience. Not novelty, but fixity, was the goal. Certainty, stability, rigidity were to be procured by reason. And this was to be accomplished through the overlordship of arid abstractions. With the lawyers, the reign of Reason became a new Absolutism.

And the nineteenth century. For all that twentieth-century scientists may question the sufficiency of nineteenth-century notions of the nature of things, for all that they may smile at the complacency of the scientific views of Spencer and Mill, no one can deny that those views were, in effect, the work-songs of an era which, whatever it said in church, went blithely ahead in the laboratory heedless of the fact that its inventions and "discoveries" were in flat contradiction of time-honored truths. But what did the lawyers do with the postulates which were helping the nineteenth-century scientists? Did acquaintance with the ways of contemporary science make the law equally pliant and bold? Did juristic philosophy become infected with the iconoclasm of the scientists? Let us see.

Again the lawyers took over some of the jargon of the science of the day. Law was to be "inductive":

"The common law," wrote Hammond in 1880, "must be learned, like the laws of the world, inductively. The decided cases of the past are so many observations upon the practical workings of these laws, from which the true theory is to be inferred,—precisely as the astronomer infers the planet's orbit from his observation of its position at many different times. The observed facts are authoritative: our inferences from

gument" and "that the knowledge at which geometry aims is knowledge of the eternal, and not of aught perishing and transient." See Appendix III.

them are theory; but it is the formation of that theory which enables us to carry our observations farther and more intelligently, and thus to arrive gradually at *the true understanding of the laws that govern the moral as well as those that govern the material universe.*

. . . The belief in *a common law of which all precedents and decided cases are merely the evidence and exposition,* cannot be a delusion or a fiction, so long maintained. . . . The old doctrine rested on the assumption that there were fixed principles of jural as well as moral right, which every man was bound to obey, and which every magistrate was bound to recognize and enforce to the best of his knowledge and ability. . . . We can improve upon the fathers of the common law, not by rejecting their belief in the existence of such a law, but by recognizing the fact that it must be learned, like the laws of the physical world, inductively.

. . . The explanation of the true office of precedents, as data from which we may obtain by induction the jural rule which they prove to exist, is not only the most reasonable in itself, but has been recognized by high judicial authority."[3]

And Bishop, in 1889, gave the following classic exposition of law as an inductive science:

"The investigator into our jurisprudence, precisely like the student of physical matter and forces, seeks to find the laws however invisible to outward sight, which in real fact govern the movements, the things, the instances, the cases, or however otherwise the idea is expressed, under his inquiry. *The combined decisions and statutes are often, for convenience, and without practical misleading, spoken of as the law. Yet, in truth, beyond them may be, invisible to the illumined understanding, what in more accurate language is termed the law, whereof they are but particular manifestations. . . . So the law of the motions of the physical heavens is invisible to the unillumined sight;* but, since it has become a part of human knowledge, it is contemplated as quite separable from the motions themselves. . . . Legal investigation, therefore, . . . consists of looking into the outward manifestations—that is into the statutes, and more particularly into the decisions—and formulating to the mind *the invisible law* whence they proceed."[3]

So the jargon of the nineteenth-century philosophy of science was taken over by the lawyers, not in the interest of aiding an open-minded observation of what law is, but to support once again the worship of an "invisible law" consisting of vague jural rules which are vastly superior to specific decisions, such decisions being governed by, or mere evidence of, those ultimate legal truths which constitute the real and true law. The purpose of the "inductive science of law" was to climb, by the same Jacob's ladder as Plato had used, to certainty. Like Plato, the further the legal philosopher of the nineteenth century was from facts, the nearer he thought himself to truth.

The fact is that the practice of the sciences has usually been in advance of the contemporary philosophy of science. The scientific philosophies gradually work around to formulations, based on scientific practices, which formulations make increasing concessions to the dwindling of authoritarianism expressed in the exploits of the scientists. But whatever of authoritarianism remains in the language of scientific philosophy, the philosophy of law will make the most of it.[4]

While lawyers would do well, to be sure, to learn scientific logic from the expositors of scientific method, it is far more important that they catch *the spirit of the creative scientist,* which yearns not for safety but risk, not for certainty but adventure, which thrives on experimentation, invention and novelty and not on nostalgia for the absolute, which devotes itself to new ways of manipulating protean particulars and not to the quest of undeviating universals.

The experimental approach would be peculiarly serviceable in law. For the practice of law is a series of experiments, of adventures in the adjusting of human relations and the compromising of human conflicts. The paradox is that where this approach is most needed it is all too frequently repudiated. In one sense it is constantly in use, for the daily job of the lawyers would fail without it. But while we lawyers use it, we discount it. We do our job with an unfortunate unconsciousness of the nature of that job or of the technique we employ. For the practical work in which we are engaged is at variance with the illusory ideals we strive, at the same time, fruitlessly to serve.

Can the scientific *spirit* be inculcated by instruction in the ways of the scientists?[4] It would seem not. That spirit is adult. It involves an abandonment of the spirit of the child which demands a guaranteed, certainty-insured world.

Is it formal education that in the development of the child himself breaks down his egocentricity, his wishful thinking, his devotion to verbal magic, his confusion of thought and things? No, nor observation of phenomena nor knowledge gained from experience. None of these, neither adult teaching nor "the direct pressure of reality" causes the child to give up these distinctive modes of dealing with his problems. It is, writes Piaget, "a change in the general trend of his mind" that explains the relatively diminished use of these childish habits of thinking. And what causes that change in the general trend of his mind? That, we have seen, is due to the growth of consciousness of self which depends in turn largely on the liberation from the bonds that tie him to his father.

If any subject-matter, such as law, still possesses marked power to excite a spirit of devotion to fatherly authority, that subject-matter will be one where the spirit of the child is difficult to eradicate and the spirit which characterizes the scientist difficult to instill.

What blocks a clearer understanding by lawyers of what they are about is not dull-mindedness. Nor is it, for the most part, inadequacy of educational training. It is, it seems, an *emotional blocking* due to the very character of law, to the facility with which the law is converted into a substitute for fatherly authority.[5] If any lawyer can meas-

[4] This is Cook's belief.

[5] The reader will again recall that this is a partial explanation. The same "emotional blocking" has often affected the thinking of natural scientists; see Appendix III on the unscientific conception of science. But the "emotional blocking" is less potent today

urably prevent himself from making that substitution, his thinking about law will become realistic, experimental —adult.[6]

---

in scientific than in law thinking; see pages 262–264, Part Three, Chapter I.

[6] See Part Three, Chapter II, on Mr. Justice Holmes.

CHAPTER XII

THE JUDGING PROCESS AND THE JUDGE'S PERSONALITY

We have considered decisions from the point of view of the lawyer and his client. We can now add to our realistic comprehension of the character of law by looking at decisions from the point of view of the judges who render them. As the word indicates, the judge in reaching a decision is making a judgment. And if we would understand what goes into the creating of that judgment, we must observe how ordinary men dealing with ordinary affairs arrive at their judgments.

The process of judging, so the psychologists tell us, seldom begins with a premise from which a conclusion is subsequently worked out. Judging begins rather the other way around—with a conclusion more or less vaguely formed; a man ordinarily starts with such a conclusion and afterwards tries to find premises which will substantiate it.[1] If he cannot, to his satisfaction, find proper arguments to link up his conclusion with premises which he finds acceptable, he will, unless he is arbitrary or mad, reject the conclusion and seek another.

In the case of the lawyer who is to present a case to a court, the dominance in his thinking of the conclusion over the premises is moderately obvious. He is a partisan working on behalf of his client. The conclusion is, therefore, not a matter of choice except within narrow limits. He must, that is if he is to be successful, begin with a conclu-

[1] A convenient analogy is the technique of the author of a detective story.

sion which will insure his client's winning the lawsuit. He then assembles the facts in such a fashion that he can work back from this result he desires to some major premise which he thinks the court will be willing to accept. The precedents, rules, principles and standards to which he will call the court's attention constitute this premise.

While "the dominance of the conclusion" in the case of the lawyer is clear, it is less so in the case of the judge. For the respectable and traditional descriptions of the judicial judging process admit no such backward-working explanation. In theory, the judge begins with some rule or principle of law as his premise, applies this premise to the facts, and thus arrives at his decision.

Now, since the judge is a human being and since no human being in his normal thinking processes arrives at decisions (except in dealing with a limited number of simple situations) by the route of any such syllogistic reasoning, it is fair to assume that the judge, merely by putting on the judicial ermine, will not acquire so artificial a method of reasoning. Judicial judgments, like other judgments, doubtless, in most cases, are worked out backward from conclusions tentatively formulated.[1]

As Jastrow says, "In spite of the fact that the answer in the book happens to be wrong, a considerable portion of the class succeeds in reaching it. . . . The young mathematician will manage to obtain the answer which the book requires, even at the cost of a resort to very unmathematical processes." Courts, in their reasoning, are often singularly like Jastrow's young mathematician.[2] Professor Tulin has made a study which prettily illustrates that fact.[3] While driving at a reckless rate of speed, a man runs over another, causing severe injuries. The driver of the car is drunk at the time. He is indicted for the statutory crime of "assault with intent to kill." The question arises whether his act constitutes that crime or merely the lesser statutory crime of "reckless driving." The courts of several states have held one way, and the courts of several other states have held the other.

The first group maintain that a conviction for assault with intent to kill cannot be sustained in the absence of proof of an actual purpose to inflict death. In the second group of states the courts have said that it was sufficient to constitute such a crime if there was a reckless disregard of the lives of others, such recklessness being said to be the equivalent of actual intent.

With what, then, appears to be the same facts before them, these two groups of courts seem to have sharply divided in their reasoning and in the conclusions at which they have arrived. But upon closer examination it has been revealed by Tulin that, in actual effect, the results arrived at in all these states have been more or less the same. In Georgia, which may be taken as representative of the second group of states, the penalty provided by the statute for reckless driving is far less than that provided, for instance, in Iowa, which is in the first group of states. If, then, a man is indicted in Georgia for reckless driving while drunk, the courts can impose on him only a mild penalty; whereas in Iowa the judge, under an identically worded indictment, can give a stiff sentence. In order to make it possible for the Georgia courts to give a reckless driver virtually the same punishment for the same offense as can be given by an Iowa judge, it is necessary in Georgia to construe the statutory crime of assault with intent to kill so that it will include reckless driving while drunk; if, and only if, the Georgia court so construes the statute, can it impose the same penalty under the same facts as could the Iowa courts under the reckless driving statute. On the other hand, if the Iowa court were to construe the Iowa statute as the Georgia court construes the Georgia statute, the punishment of the reckless driver in Iowa would be too severe.

In other words, the courts in these cases began with the results they desired to accomplish: they wanted to give what they considered to be adequate punishment to drunken drivers: their conclusions determined their reasoning.

But the conception that judges work back from conclusions to principles is so heretical that it seldom finds expression.[2] Daily, judges, in connection with their decisions, deliver so-called opinions in which they purport to set forth the bases of their conclusions. Yet you will study these opinions in vain to discover anything remotely resembling a statement of the actual judging process. They are written in conformity with the time-honored theory. They picture the judge applying rules and principles to the facts, that is, taking some rule or principle (usually derived from opinions in earlier cases) as his major premise, employing the facts of the case as the minor premise, and then coming to his judgment by processes of pure reasoning.

Now and again some judge, more clear-witted and outspoken than his fellows, describes (when off the bench) his methods in more homely terms. Recently Judge Hutcheson essayed such an honest report of the judicial process. He tells us that after canvassing all the available material at his command and duly cogitating on it, he gives his imagination play,

"and brooding over the cause, waits for the feeling, the hunch —that intuitive flash of understanding that makes the jump-spark connection between question and decision and at the point where the path is darkest for the judicial feet, sets its light along the way. . . . In feeling or 'hunching' out his decisions, the judge acts not differently from but precisely as the lawyers do in working on their cases, with only this exception, that the lawyer, in having a predetermined destination in view,—to win the law-suit for his client—looks for and regards

[2] Years ago the writer, just after being admitted to the bar, was shocked when advised by S. S. Gregory, an ex-president of the American Bar Association—a man more than ordinarily aware of legal realities—that "the way to win a case is to make the judge want to decide in your favor and then, and then only, to cite precedents which will justify such a determination. You will almost always find plenty of cases to cite in your favor." All successful lawyers are more or less consciously aware of this technique. But they seldom avow it—even to themselves.

only those hunches which keep him in the path that he has chosen, while the judge, being merely on his way with a roving commission to find the just solution, will follow his hunch wherever it leads him. . . ."

And Judge Hutcheson adds:

"I must premise that I speak now of the judgment or decision, the solution itself, as opposed to the apologia for that decision; the decree, as opposed to the logomachy, the effusion of the judge by which that decree is explained or excused. . . . The judge really decides by feeling and not by judgment, by hunching and not by ratiocination, such ratiocination appearing only in the opinion. The vital motivating impulse for the decision is an intuitive sense of what is right or wrong in the particular case; and the astute judge, having so decided, enlists his every faculty and belabors his laggard mind, not only to justify that intuition to himself, but to make it pass muster with his critics." Accordingly, he passes in review all of the rules, principles, legal categories, and concepts "which he may find useful, directly or by an analogy, so as to select from them those which in his opinion will justify his desired result."

We may accept this as an approximately correct description[3] of how all judges do their thinking. But see the consequences. If the law consists of the decisions of the judges and if those decisions are based on the judge's hunches, then the way in which the judge gets his hunches is the key to the judicial process. Whatever produces the judge's hunches makes the law.

[3] Which confirms what was said above, Chapter III, about judicial "rationalizations." See Hutcheson, "The Judgment Intuitive: The Function of the 'Hunch' in Judicial Decisions," 14 Cornell Law Quarterly, 274.

A century ago a great American judge, Chancellor Kent, in a personal letter explained his method of arriving at a decision. He first made himself "master of the facts." Then (he wrote) "I saw where justice lay, and the moral sense decided the court half the time; I then sat down to search the authorities. . . . I might once in a while be embarrassed by a technical rule, but *I almost always found principles suited to my view of the case. . . .*" Cf. p. 302.

What, then, are the hunch-producers? What are the stimuli which make a judge feel that he should try to justify one conclusion rather than another?

The rules and principles of law are one class of such stimuli.[4] But there are many others, concealed or unrevealed, not frequently considered in discussions of the character or nature of law. To the infrequent extent that these other stimuli have been considered at all, they have been usually referred to as "the political, economic and moral prejudices" of the judge.[5] A moment's reflection

[4] If Hutcheson were to be taken with complete literalness, it would seem that such legal rules, principles and the like are merely for show, materials for window dressing, implements to aid in rationalization. They are that indeed. But although impatience with the orthodox excessive emphasis on the importance of such devices might incline one at times to deny such formulations any real value, it is necessary—and this even Hutcheson would surely admit—to concede them more importance. In part, they help the judge to check up on the propriety of the hunches. They also suggest hunches. See Chapter XIII for a further discussion of this matter.

[5] Most of the suggestions that law is a function of the undisclosed attitudes of judges stress the judges' "education," "race," "class," "economic, political and social influences" which "make up a complex environment" of which the judges are not wholly aware but which affect their decisions by influencing their views of "public policy," or "social advantage" or their "economic and social philosophies" or "their notions of fair play or what is right and just."

It is to the economic determinists and to the members of the school of "sociological jurisprudence" that we owe much of the recognition of the influence of the economic and political background of judges upon decisions. For this much thanks. But their work has perhaps been done too well. Interested as were these writers in problems of labor law and "public policy" questions, they over-stressed a few of the multitude of unconscious factors and over-simplified the problem.

Much the same is to be said of the views of the "historical school" with respect to the effect of custom on judicial decisions. "Whether a custom will or will not be ratified by the courts depends after all on the courts themselves," says Dickinson, "The Law Behind Law," 29 Columbia Law Review, 113, 285. "Whatever forces can be said to influence the growth of the law, they

would, indeed, induce any open-minded person to admit that factors of such character must be operating in the mind of the judge.

But are not those categories—political, economic and moral biases—too gross, too crude, too wide? Since judges are not a distinct race and since their judging processes must be substantially of like kind with those of other men, an analysis of the way in which judges reach their conclusions will be aided by answering the question, What are the hidden factors in the inferences and opinions of ordinary men? The answer surely is that those factors are multitudinous and complicated, depending often on peculiarly individual traits of the persons whose inferences and opinions are to be explained. These uniquely individual factors often are more important causes of judgments than anything which could be described as political, economic, or moral biases.[4]

In the first place, all other biases express themselves in connection with, and as modified by, these idiosyncratic biases. A man's political or economic prejudices are frequently cut across by his affection for or animosity to some particular individual or group, due to some unique experience he has had; or a racial antagonism which he entertains may be deflected in a particular case by a desire to be admired by some one who is devoid of such antagonism.

Second (and in the case of the judge more important), is the consideration that in learning the facts with reference to which one forms an opinion, and often long before the time when a hunch arises with reference to the situation as a whole, these more minute and distinctly personal biases

---

exert that influence only by influencing the judges. . . . Current *mores* . . . are things about which there is room for considerable difference of opinion and . . . when it is a question of their writing themselves into law, the opinion which prevails is the judges' opinion." See Cardozo, "The Nature of the Judicial Process," 174: "In every court there are likely to be as many estimates of the 'Zeitgeist' as there are judges on its bench." See also Gray, "The Nature and Sources of Law," Chapter XII.

are operating constantly. So the judge's sympathies and antipathies are likely to be active with respect to the persons of the witness, the attorneys and the parties to the suit. His own past may have created plus or minus reactions to women, or blonde women, or men with beards, or Southerners, or Italians, or Englishmen, or plumbers, or ministers, or college graduates, or Democrats. A certain twang or cough or gesture may start up memories painful or pleasant in the main. Those memories of the judge, while he is listening to a witness with such a twang or cough or gesture, may affect the judge's initial hearing of, or subsequent recollection of, what the witness said, or the weight or credibility which the judge will attach to the witness's testimony.[6]

That the testimony of witnesses is affected by their experiences and temperaments has been often observed. While as yet the courts have not availed themselves of the mechanisms of the laboratory, such as have been suggested by Münsterberg and others, for the detection of the willful or unconscious errors of witnesses, yet the legal textbooks and judicial opinions are full of shrewd observations about the fallibility of human testimony:

"Men are prone to see what they want to see."

"It must be admitted that at the present day the testimony of even a truthful witness is much over-rated."

[6] Judges, we are advised, are far more likely to differ among themselves on "questions of fact" than on "questions of law":

"In my experience in the conference room of the Supreme Court of the United States, which consists of nine judges, I have been surprised to find how readily those judges come to an agreement upon questions of law, and how often they disagree in regard to questions of fact. . . ." said Mr. Justice Miller.

"We have before us several cases where our decisions turn entirely upon the evidence and I am aware how much more likely judges are to hold different opinions in such cases than where legal questions are at issue," said another judge.

"The same evidence which to one may be convincing, to another may seem absurd," said Judge Pitney. Many judges have declared that sharply contested questions of fact are usually more difficult to solve than so-called questions of law.

"No doubt the eyes of some witnesses are livelier than those of others and the sense of sight may be quickened or diminished by the interest or bias of him who possesses it."

"Even where witnesses are upright or honest, their belief is apt to be more or less warped by their partiality or prejudice for or against the parties. It is easy to reason ourselves into a belief in the existence of that which we desire to be true, whereas the facts testified to, and from which the witness deduces his conclusions, might produce a very different impression on the minds of others."

"It frequently happens that a person, by long dwelling on a subject, thinks that a thing may have happened, and he at last comes to believe that it actually did occur."

And the courts have noticed that—

". . . a witness may have a strong bias from what he conceives to be the justice of the case, so that with entire innocence he may recall things which have never occurred, or forget important instances which have occurred, through the operation of sympathy for a good man threatened with a loss."

The courts, too, have observed that testimony is not a mere mechanical repetition or transcription of past events and that testimony often involves fallible inferences; in other words, a witness in testifying to things seen or heard or felt is inevitably making judgments on or inferences from what he has seen, heard or felt. And numerous experiments, made out of court, go to strengthen the conviction that, without any improper motives, witnesses, in forming such inferences, may badly misrepresent the objective facts. The reader perhaps recalls the instances reported by Münsterberg:[5]

"A few years ago a painful scene occurred in Berlin, in the University Seminary of Professor von Liszt, the famous criminologist. The Professor had spoken about a book. One of the older students suddenly shouts, 'I wanted to throw light on the matter from the standpoint of Christian morality!' Another student throws in, 'I cannot stand that!' The first starts up, exclaiming, 'You have insulted me!' The second clenches his fist and cries, 'If you say another word——' The first draws a revolver. The second rushes madly upon him. The Professor steps between them and, as he grasps the man's arm, the revolver goes off. General uproar. In that moment Professor Liszt secures order and asks a part of the students to write an exact account of all that has happened. The whole had been a comedy, carefully planned and rehearsed by the three actors for the purpose of studying the exactitude of observation and recollection. Those who did not write the report at once were, part of them, asked to write it the next day or a week later; and others had to depose their observations under cross-examination. The whole objective performance was cut up into fourteen little parts which referred partly to actions, partly to words. As mistakes there were counted the omissions, the wrong additions and the alterations. The smallest number of mistakes gave twenty-six per cent. of erroneous statements; the largest was eighty per cent. The reports with reference to the second half of the performance, which was more strongly emotional, gave an average of fifteen per cent. more mistakes than those of the first half. Words were put into the mouths of men who had been silent spectators during the whole short episode; actions were attributed to the chief participants of which not the slightest trace existed; and essential parts of the tragi-comedy were completely eliminated from the memory of a number of witnesses."[6]

The courts have been alive to these grave possibilities of error and have therefore repeatedly declared that it is one of the most important functions of the trial judge, in determining the value and weight of the evidence, to consider the demeanor of the witness.[7]

They have called attention, as of the gravest importance, to such facts as the tone of voice in which a witness's statement is made, the hesitation or readiness with which his answers are given, the look of the witness, his carriage, his evidences of surprise, his gestures, his zeal, his bearing, his expression, his yawns, the use of his eyes, his furtive or meaning glances, or his shrugs, the pitch of his voice,

[7] At this moment we are describing only trials by a judge without a jury; see below, Part One, Chapter XVI, for a discussion of the jury process.

his self-possession or embarrassment, his air of candor or of seeming levity. It is because these circumstances can be manifest only to one who actually hears and sees the witnesses that upper courts have frequently stated that they are hesitant to overturn the decision of the trial judge in a case where the evidence has been based upon oral testimony; for the upper courts have recognized that they have before them only a stenographic or printed report of the testimony, and that such a black and white report cannot reproduce anything but the cold words of the witness. "The tongue of the witness," it has been said, "is not the only organ for conveying testimony." Yet it is only the words that can be transmitted to the reviewing court, while the story that is told by the manner, by the tone, by the eyes, must be lost to all but him who observes the witness on the stand.

It is, then, a legal commonplace that a witness cannot mechanically reproduce the facts, but is reporting his judgment of the facts and may err in the making of this judgment.

Strangely enough, it has been little observed that, while the witness is in this sense a judge, *the judge, in a like sense, is a witness.* He is a witness of what is occurring in his courtroom. He must determine what are the facts of the case from what he sees and hears; that is, from the words and gestures and other conduct of the witnesses. And like those who are testifying before him, the judge's determination of the facts is no mechanical act.[8] If the witnesses are subject to lapses of memory or imaginative reconstruction of events, in the same manner the judge is subject to defects in his apprehension of the testimony;[9]

[8] In a case in Indiana a new trial was granted upon proof that the eyesight of one of the jurors was so defective that he was unable to distinguish the faces of the witnesses. We may expect that some day the courts will likewise hold that a judge, hearing a case without a jury, cannot give a fair trial if he is so near-sighted that he is unable to observe the expression, deportment and demeanor of the witnesses.

[9] It is no easy task for the judge to bring together in his mind,

so that long before he has come to the point in the case where he must decide what is right or wrong, just or unjust, with reference to the facts of the case as a whole, the trial judge has been engaged in making numerous judgments or inferences as the testimony dribbles in.[7] His beliefs as to what was said by the witnesses and with what truthfulness the witnesses said it, will determine what he believes to be the "facts of the case." If his final decision is based upon a hunch and that hunch is a function of the "facts," then of course what, as a fallible witness of what went on in his courtroom, he believes to be the "facts," will often be of controlling importance. So that the judge's innumerable unique traits, dispositions and habits often get in their work in shaping his decisions not only in his determination of what he thinks fair or just with reference to a given set of facts, but in the very processes by which he becomes convinced what those facts are.

The peculiar traits, disposition, biases and habits of the particular judge will, then, often determine what he decides to be the law. In this respect judges do not differ from other mortals: "In every case of actual thinking," says F. C. S. Schiller, "the whole of a man's personality enters into and colors it in every part." To know the judge's hunch-producers which make the law we must

---

for the purpose of finally reaching his conclusions as to the facts, what is frequently a voluminous body of testimony. For many years the judge has been able to avail himself of the devices of stenography and typewriting so that, after the close of the case, he can, after a fashion, rehearse what has occurred, through reading at his leisure the typewritten statement. This statement, however, omits those important facts such as the demeanor of the witness and the like, to which we referred above. And if the judge was inattentive during the giving of any of the testimony, the mere words on paper will not adequately make up for his inattention. It may well be that the courts will some day adopt a recent mechanical innovation and that we shall have *"talking movies"* of trials which will make possible an almost complete reproduction of the trial so that the judge can consider it at his leisure.

know thoroughly that complicated congeries we loosely call the judge's personality.[8]

If the personality of the judge is the pivotal factor in law administration, then law may vary with the personality of the judge who happens to pass upon any given case. How much variation there is, as we pass from judge to judge, is not, as matters now stand, discoverable, because of the method of reporting cases and the verbal contrivances used by the judges which conceal judicial disharmony. We have little statistical material in this field. For the most part, we must fall back on the impressions of lawyers, impressions of the kind which do not often find their way into print. Occasionally, however, they are made public. The following is from the reminiscences of a man who has served both as prosecuting attorney and as judge:

"The jockeying for a judge is sometimes almost humorous. Lawyers recognize the peculiarities, previous opinions, leanings, strength and weakness, and likes or dislikes of a particular judge in a particular case. Some years ago one of the bright lawyers of Chicago conferred with me as an assistant state's attorney, to agree on a judge for the trial of a series of cases. We proceeded to go over the list. For the state's attorney, I objected to but one judge of all the twenty-eight Cook County judges, and as I went through the list I would ask him about one or another, 'How about this one?' As to the first one I named he said, 'No, he decided a case a couple of weeks ago in a way that I didn't like, and I don't want him to use my client as a means to get back to a state of virtue.' As to another, he said, 'No, he is not very clear-headed; he is likely to read an editorial by the man who put him on the ticket, and get confused on the law.' Of another he said, 'No, he might sneer at my witnesses, and I can't get the sneer in the record.' To another he objected that 'If my clients were found guilty this judge would give them the limit.' To still another he said, 'No, you can't get him to make a ruling in a case without creating a disturbance in the court room, he is so careful of the Supreme Court.' Again he replied to one, 'No, if the state's attorney should happen to sit in the court room I won't get a favorable ruling in the entire case.' And so we went along."[9]

One bit of statistical evidence as to the differences between judges is available: A survey was made of the disposition of thousands of minor criminal cases by the several judges of the City Magistrate's Court in New York City during the years 1914 to 1916 with the express purpose of finding to what extent the "personal equation" entered into the administration of justice. It was disclosed that "the magistrates did differ to an amazing degree in their treatment of similar classes of cases."[10] Thus of 546 persons charged with intoxication brought before one judge, he discharged only one and found the others (about 97%) guilty, whereas of the 673 arraigned before another judge, he found 531 (or 79%) not guilty. In disorderly conduct cases, one judge discharged only 18% and another discharged 54%. "In other words, one coming before Magistrate Simons had only 2 chances in 10 of getting off. If he had come before Judge Walsh he would have had more than 5 chances in 10 of getting off." In vagrancy cases, the percentage of discharges varied from 4.5% to 79%. When it came to sentences, the same variations existed. One judge imposed fines on 84% of the persons he found guilty and gave suspended sentences to 7%, while one of his fellows fined 34% and gave suspended sentences to 59%. Everson concludes that these figures show to what a remarkable degree the individuality of the magistrates is mirrored in their disposition of cases. "Justice," he says, "is a very personal thing, reflecting the temperament, the personality, the education, environment and personal traits of the magistrate."

But if we determine that the personality of the judge has much to do with law-making, have we done enough? Can we rest content with this mere recognition? Can we stop with the blanket statement that our judicial process at its best will be based upon "the trained intuition of the judges," on the hunches of experienced men? Perhaps it will be found that we must stop there, but who can tell? When only a small fraction of the bench and bar as yet admit, and then timidly, that concrete human beings and not abstract rules make the law, it is too early to decide that a new technique of wise and discriminating judging cannot be developed. That those jungles of the mind which we are just beginning to discover will soon be reduced to a high state of civilized order is not likely, but that they must ever remain in their present chaotic state is equally far from certain.

Just what form a new technique of judging will take, it is too soon to guess. And the same may be said of conjectures as to how long it will be before such a technique can become effective. It would not be wise to be over-optimistic. Schroeder, one of the few lawyers who has thought deeply and courageously about this problem, has fallen into the error of assuming that a blending of law and psychology will promptly produce remarkable results.[111] He anticipates that, with the insight that modern psychology affords, we shall quickly be able to ascertain, from the language employed by a judge in his opinions, the hidden predispositions and impulses which brought about his decision. He believes that "every choice of conclusion, argument, precedent, phrase or word," in a judge's opinion, "is expressive of an unconscious, a dominant personal motive in the judge. Every such choice is a fragment of autobiography because it reveals not only the present conscious motive, but also the still potent, past and immature experimental causes, which determined the unconscious impulses submerged in, but controlling the avowed motive. . . . So we may read the life of the judge backwards. Every opinion thus amounts to a confession."[10]

---

[10] The particular case which Schroeder chose as an illustrative instance was loaded with an unusual amount of evidence of the peculiar character of the particular judge who decided it. Moreover, in analyzing that judge's opinion, Schroeder was forced to fall back on sources of information about the judge's personal life which

If Schroeder were right, the discovery of the hidden causes of decisions would be fairly simple. But the job is not so easy. The directing impulses of judges will not so readily appear from analyses of their rationalizing words. We shall not learn how judges think until the judges are able and ready to engage in ventures of self-discovery.

Which is not to say that, as a preliminary, it will not be valuable to make studies, from the outside, of the motives and biases of judges—studies based on their biographies and on shrewd surmises as to the buried meanings obliquely expressed in their language. Haines[12] has outlined a plan for such a study of the several judges of the United States Supreme Court. He enumerates the following factors as likely to influence judicial decisions: The judges' education, general and legal; their family and personal associations, wealth and social position; their legal and political experience; their political affiliations and opinions, their intellectual and temperamental traits.[11]

Now, such investigations might prove of immense value if they would stimulate judges to engage in searching self-analysis. For the ultimately important influences in the decisions of any judge are the most obscure, and are the least easily discoverable—by anyone but the judge himself. They are tied up with intimate experiences which no biographer, however sedulous, is likely to ferret out, and the emotional significance of which no one but the judge, or a psychologist in the closest contact with him, could comprehend. What we may hope some day to get from our judges are detailed autobiographies containing the sort of material that is recounted in the autobiographical novel;

---

would ordinarily be inaccessible. Nevertheless, and despite its over-sanguine outlook, Schroeder's article deserves warm commendation as a pioneering effort.

[11] Even to recognize that the judges' "temperamental traits" are operative is not enough. What we need to see is that there are at work innumerous "subjective" factors of which the phrase "temperamental traits" is only a very rough description. Schroeder has gone furthest in referring to them but is over-hopeful in his belief that they can be easily brought to light.

or opinions annotated, by the judge who writes them, with elaborate explorations of the background factors in his personal experience which swayed him in reaching his conclusions. For in the last push, a judge's decisions are the outcome of his entire life-history. Judges can take to heart the counsel Anatole France gave to the judges of literature:

"All those who deceive themselves into the belief that they put anything but their own personalities into their work are dupes of the most fallacious of illusions. The truth is that we can never get outside ourselves. . . . We are shut up in our own personality as if in a perpetual prison. The best thing for us, it seems to me, is to admit this frightful condition with a good grace, and to confess that we speak of ourselves every time we have not strength enough to remain silent. To be quite frank, the critic ought to say: Gentlemen, I am going to speak of myself apropos of Shakespeare, apropos of Racine, of Pascal, or of Goethe."

Everson, in his report on the statistics of the decisions by the judges of the City Magistrate's Court, expressed the belief that the publication of these records would cause a better understanding by the judges of their own work and lead them to

"a viewpoint somewhat tempered by the knowledge of what the other judges are doing and with a broader viewpoint of the problems before them. Each magistrate will come to recognize his own personal peculiarities and seek to correct any that cannot be justified in the light of the records of his associates."

But a different result ensued. The disclosures "were so startling and so disconcerting that it seemed advisable to discontinue the comparative tables of the records of the justices."[12] The bench and bar did not want to have called to their attention the extent to which judging is affected by the temperament, training, biases and predilections of the respective judges.

[12] Haines, loc. cit. Disconcerting indeed, for see how such a revelation disposes of predictable law. The lawyers' guesses bear little resemblance to controlled experiments.

No one can know in advance what a judge will believe to be the "facts" of a case. It follows that a lawyer's opinion as to the law relating to a given set of facts is a guess as to (1) what a judge thereafter will guess were the facts and (2) what that judge will consider to be the proper decision on the basis of that judge's guess as to the facts. Even that is too artificial a statement. The judge, in arriving at his hunch, does not nicely separate his belief as to the "facts" from his conclusion as to the "law"; his general hunch is more integral and composite, and affects his report—both to himself and to the public—concerning the facts. Only a superficial thinker will assume that the facts as they occurred and as they later appear to the judge (and as he reports them) will invariably—or indeed often—correspond. The judge's decision is determined by a hunch arrived at long after the event on the basis of his reaction to fallible testimony. It is, in every sense of the word, *ex post facto*. It is fantastic, then, to say that usually men can warrantably act in reliance upon "established law." Their inability to do so may be deplorable. But mature persons must face the truth, however unpleasant.

Why such resistance to the truth? Why has there been little investigation of the actualities of the judging process? If we are right in assuming that the very subject-matter of the law activates childish emotional attitudes, we can perhaps find an answer to these questions.

It is a marked characteristic of the young child, writes Piaget, that he does very little thinking about his thinking. He encounters extreme difficulty if asked to give an account of the "how" of his mental processes. He cannot reflect on his own reasoning. If you ask him to state how he reached a conclusion, he is unable to recover his own reasoning processes, but instead invents an artificial account which will somehow seem to lead to the result. He cannot correctly explain what he did to find this result. "Instead of giving a retrospect he starts from the result he has obtained as though he had known it in advance and then gives a more or less elaborate method for finding it again. . . . He starts from his conclusion and argues towards the premises as though he had known from the first whither those premises would lead him."

Once more these difficulties find their explanation in the child's relative unawareness of his self, of his incapacity for dealing with his own thoughts as subjective. For this obtuseness produces in the child an overconfidence in his own ideas, a lack of skepticism as to the subjectivity of his own beliefs. As a consequence, the child is singularly non-introspective. He has, according to Piaget, no curiosity about the motives that guide his thinking. His whole attitude towards his own thinking is the antithesis of any introspective habit of watching himself think, of alertness in detecting the motives which push him in the direction of any given conclusion. The child, that is, does not take his own motives into account. They are ignored and never considered as a constituent of thinking.

It would not be surprising, then, to find that, in dealing with a subject-matter which stimulates childish emotional attitudes, the inclination towards a critical analysis of the motives which lie behind thinking is not very vigorous. If we view the law as such a subject-matter, we have a key to our puzzle. Lawyers are constantly looking into the motives and biases of clients and witnesses, but are peculiarly reluctant to look into the motives and biases of judges. Yet such inquisitiveness, deliberately cultivated, is at the very core of intelligent dealing with the law. That it is virtually non-existent is perhaps due to the survival of childish resistance to introspection with reference to thinking about law. The suggestion that judicial thinking can be motivated thinking is usually met with derision or amusement, as if the notion that judges had hidden motives were absurd.[13] One recalls a dictum of Piaget in talking of the child:

"The less a mind is given to introspection the more it is the victim of the illusion that it knows itself thoroughly."

[13] It should be obvious from the above that *we do not think psychological studies are likely to make decisions markedly more predictable.* See Addenda to Second Printing, number 3.

CHAPTER XIII

MECHANISTIC LAW; RULES;
DISCRETION; THE IDEAL JUDGE

We have been inquiring into the reason for the persistence of the basic illusion. It might be asked whether our question is worth answering. If an illusion helps men live, if by acting on an erroneous dogma, men arrive at valuable results, for the most part unmixed with evil, then to insist upon exposing the falsity of the illusion or dogma is at best pedantry or bad manners and at worst malicious mischief or sadistic morbidity. If then the illusion or dogma of legal certainty were essentially useful, to attack it would be inexcusable, regardless of its patent deviation from reality.

But its harmful consequences are not few. We have observed how it breeds disrespect of law, how it leads to the wasteful technique of circumlocution, turning lawyers into a profession of rationalizers who appear to laymen like a guild of professional hypocrites.

Many more are the unfortunate sequels or corollaries of the fundamental error. Notably, there is the insistent effort to achieve predictability by the attempt to mechanize law, to reduce it to formulas in which human beings are treated like identical mathematical entities. Under such influences, there is proclaimed the ideal of "a government of laws and not of men." The law is dealt with as if it were settled once and for all; its rules are supposed to operate impartially, inflexibly: justice must be uniform and unswerving. In other words, the stress is on generalizations, not on concrete happenings; on averages, not on details. Little allowance can be made for justice in the particular case: thus the law is written and thus it must be applied. Novelty and creativeness must not be permitted. Adaptation of the rules to peculiar individual circumstances is frowned upon. Discretion in the judge must be avoided for fear that it would lead to dangerous arbitrariness. Individualization of controversies, response to the unique human facts of the particular case, would make the law uncertain, unpredictable.

Let us observe the consequences of such an attitude, taking as typical the following comments of even so enlightened a thinker as Salmond:

"The law presents itself primarily and essentially as a system of rigid rules. . . ." This "has brought grave evils in its train. It is the source of the technicality and formalism, the complexity and esoteric mystery, which have at all times been made a ground of reproach against judicial administration. Nevertheless, the good sense of all communities has at all times recognized that in spite of these grave evils the balance of advantage lies beyond question on the side of administering justice in obedience to a rigid and elaborate system of binding legal rules. . . . The evils which accompany and elaborate any technical legal system are many and obvious but they are the necessary price which a community pays for the release from greater evils. It is true that the administration of justice according to law is notoriously uncertain. Yet the extensive substitution of unrestricted judicial discretion for preëstablished rules of law would add to this uncertainty rather than diminish it. . . . It is true that the law necessarily lays down general rules which cannot take due account of the special circumstances of the individual case, whereas a court which is permitted to do justice at its good pleasure can take all those circumstances into consideration and act accordingly, observing that equity which, according to the old definition, mitigates the rigor of the law. Yet it is certain that this advantage is bought at too great a price. *The same principle which allows a judge to take account of the individual merits of the particular case exposes him at the same time to all the perverting impulses of his emotional nature, to all his prejudices, and to the unconscious bias of his mental constitution.* For one case in which, in any reasonable system of law, a court was constrained to do injustice because of necessary conformity to preëstablished rules, there would be many in which, un-guided by such rules, he would be led astray by the tempta-tions which beset the "arbitrium judicis." . . .

"The law is impartial. It has no respect of persons. Just or unjust, wise or foolish, it is the same for all, and for this reason men readily submit to its arbitrament. Though the rule of law may work injustice to the individual case, it is neverthe-less recognized that it was not made for the individual case and that it is alike for all. 'Durum sed ita scriptum est' is allowed as a sufficient justification for its imperfect operation in the individual instance. The law-abiding spirit so created in a community is a public advantage that far outweighs the benefits which may accrue in particular cases by allowing to courts the opportunity of substituting what they conceive to be natural justice in lieu of justice according to law. An elaborate and technical system of law is doubtless in many respects an evil but it is the only road to freedom from greater evils. *We are in bondage to the law,*' said Cicero, '*in order that we may be free.*' '*Legibus servimus ut liberi esse possimus.*' "[1]

This is very pretty, but is it not mostly rhetoric? The law is not a machine and the judges not machine-tenders. There never was and there never will be a body of fixed and predetermined rules alike for all. The acts of human beings are not identical mathematical entities; the in-dividual cannot be eliminated as, in algebraic equations, equal quantities on the two sides can be cancelled.[2] Life rebels against all efforts at legal over-simplification. New cases ever continue to present novel aspects. To do justice, to make any legal system acceptable to society, the ab-stract preëstablished rules have to be adapted and ad-justed, the static formulas made alive. It is impossible to do as Salmond would have judges do, that is, eliminate "the influence of illegitimate considerations applicable to the particular instance."

Note that Salmond significantly calls these considera-tions "illegitimate." There we touch the nerve of the vice in the conventional attitude expressed by him. For these considerations "applicable to the particular instance" must and do make themselves felt. And, because they are considered "illegitimate," these influences are buried and concealed.

The judges, that is, are asked to perform in the dark what is the very essence of the judicial function. The task of the judge, if well done, is no simple one. He must balance conflicting human interests and determine which of several opposing individual claims the law should favor in order to promote social well-being. As each case comes before him, he must weigh the claim of the parties. He must determine whether to fit a particular case into the terms of some old rules (either because they are working well, or because men have acted in reliance upon them and he considers the protection of such reliance socially valuable) or to "legislate" by revising and adjusting the preëxisting rules to the circumstances of the instant controversy. If these powers of the judiciary are unwisely exercised, the community will suffer.

Now, the task of judging calls for a clear head. But our judges, so far as they heed the basic myth, can exercise their power with only a muzzy comprehension of what they are doing. When they make "new rules," they often sneak them into the *corpus juris;* when they individualize their treatment of a controversy, they must act as if engaged in something disreputable and of which they themselves cannot afford to be aware. But the power to individualize and to legislate judicially is of the very essence of their function. To treat judicial free adaptation and law-making as if they were bootlegging operations, renders the product unnecessarily impure and harmful.

To do their intricate job well our judges need all the clear consciousness of their purpose which they can summon to their aid. And the pretense, the self-delusion, that when they are creating they are borrowing, when they are making something new they are merely applying the commands given them by some existing external authority, cannot but diminish their efficiency. They must rid themselves of this reliance on a non-existent guide, they must learn the virtue, the power and the practical worth of self-authority.[3]

While the majority of lawyers deny that judges make law, a vigorous minority assert, realistically, that they do.[1] But when does a judge make law? The minority here splits into two groups.

John Chipman Gray is typical of the first group. His contribution to hard-headed thinking about law was invaluable. He compelled his readers to differentiate between *law* and the *sources* of law.[2] "The Law of the State," he wrote, "is composed of the rules which the courts, that is the judicial organs of that body, lay down for the determination of legal rights and duties." He felt it absurd to affirm the existence of law which the courts do not follow: "The Law of a State . . . is not an ideal, but something which actually exists." His thesis was that "the Law is made up of the rules for decision which the courts lay down; that all such rules are Law; that *rules for conduct which the courts do not apply are not Law;[3] that the fact that courts apply rules is what makes them Law; that there is no mysterious entity 'The Law' apart from these rules; and that the judges are rather the creators than the discoverers of the Law.*"

According to Gray, the "law of a great nation" means "the opinions of a half-a-dozen old gentlemen, . . ." For, "if those half-a-dozen old gentlemen form the highest tribunal of a country, then no rule or principle which they refuse to follow is Law in that country." Of course, he added, "those six men seek the rules which they follow not in their own whims, but they derive them from *sources* . . . to which they are directed, by the organized body

---

[1] See Part One, Chapter IV.

[2] The title of his great work on that subject is "The Nature and Sources of Law."

[3] "If the judges . . . come to a wrong result, and give forth a rule which is discordant with the eternal verities, it is none the less Law."

(the State) to which they belong, to apply themselves."

And those sources of law—*i.e.,* sources of "the rules for decision which the courts lay down"—are statutes, judicial precedents, opinions of experts, customs and principles of morality (using the term morality to include "public policy"). That none of these factors is, in and of itself, Law is best exemplified by a consideration of a most important source—statutes. For, says Gray, after all it is only words that the legislature utters when it enacts a statute. And these words can get into action only through the rules laid down by the courts: it is for the courts to say what those words mean. There are limits to the courts' power of interpretation, but those limits are vague and undefined. And that is why statutes are not part of the Law itself, but only a source of law: "It has sometimes been said that the Law is composed of two parts—legislative law and judge-made law, but in truth all the Law is judge-made law. The shape in which a statute is imposed on the community as a guide for conduct is that statute as interpreted by the courts. The courts put life into the dead words of the statute. To quote . . . from Bishop Hoadly: 'Nay, whoever hath an *absolute authority* to *interpret* any written or spoken laws, it is *He* who is truly the Law Giver to all intents and purposes, and not the Person who first wrote and spoke them.' "[4]

Gray was indeed a hardy foe of the Bealist fundamentalists. Judges, he saw, make the law and, until they make it, there isn't any law, but only ingredients for making law. When a handful of old gentlemen who compose the highest court announce the law, that is the Law, until they change it, whether anyone else, however wise, thinks it good or bad, right or wrong. *But,* for all his terse directness, you will detect more than a trace of the old philosophy in Gray's views. You will note his constant reiteration of the words "rules" and "principles." Gray defines law not as what courts decide but as the *"rules* which the courts lay down for the determination of legal rights and duties" or "the *rules of decision* which the courts lay down." If a court in deciding a particular case fails to apply the "rule generally followed," that decision is not law. The rule for decisions usually laid down by the courts in Massachusetts is that a payment made on Sunday discharges a debt. "A judge in Massachusetts once decided that payment on Sunday was no discharge of a debt, but that has never been the Law of Massachusetts," said Gray. Judges make law, according to Gray, when they make or change the rules; law-making is legal rule-making, the promulgation by a judge of a new rule for decision.

Now this stress on generality as the essence of law is a remnant of the old myth. And a vigorous remnant. It is found in the thinking of perhaps ninety percent of even those who, like Gray, scoff at the idea that law-making occurs anywhere except in the courtroom. Unless, they say, a court announces a new rule—announces it expressly or impliedly—it is not making law. Law equals legal rules —rules which the courts use, not anyone else's rules, but rules nevertheless; such judge-made rules constitute the law.[5]

But in 1897 a new attitude[6] was expressed when Holmes wrote, "A legal duty so called is nothing but a prediction that if a man does or omits certain things he will be made to suffer in this or that way by a judgment of the court; and so of a legal right. . . . *If you want to know the law and nothing else, you must look at it as a bad man, who cares only for the material consequences which such knowledge enables him to predict.* . . . What constitutes the law? You will find some text writers telling you that it is something different from what is decided by the courts of Massachusetts or England, that it is a system of reason, that it is a deduction from principles of ethics or admitted axioms or what not. But if we take the view of our friend the bad man we shall find that he does not care two straws for the axioms or deductions, but that he does want to know what the Massachusetts or English courts are likely to do in fact. I am much of his mind.

The prophecies of what the courts will do in fact, and nothing more pretentious, are what I mean by law."

That was in 1897. In 1899 Holmes said, "We must think things not words, or at least we must constantly translate our words into the facts for which they stand if we are to keep to the real and the true. I sometimes tell law students that the law schools pursue an inspirational method combined with a logical method, that is, the postulates are taken for granted upon authority without inquiry into their worth, and then logic is used as the only tool to develop the results. It is a necessary method for the purpose of teaching dogma. But inasmuch as the real justification of a rule of law, if there be one, is that it helps to bring about a social end which we desire, it is no less necessary that those who make and develop the law should have those ends articulately in their mind. . . . *A generalization is empty so far as it is general. Its value depends on the number of particulars which it calls up to the speaker and the hearer."*[4]

Holmes's description of law can be stated as a revision of Gray's definition, thus: Law is made up not of rules for decision laid down by the courts but of the decisions themselves. All such decisions are law. The fact that courts render these decisions makes them law. There is no mysterious entity apart from these decisions. If the judges in any case come to a "wrong" result and give forth a decision which is discordant with their own or anyone else's rules, their decision is none the less law. The "law of a great nation" means the decisions of a handful of old gentlemen, and whatever they refuse to decide is not law. Of course those old gentlemen in deciding cases do not

---

[4] In 1917, Holmes said from the bench of the United States Supreme Court, that "general propositions do not decide concrete cases."

In 1918, he said, "But for legal purposes a right is only the hypostasis of a prophecy."

For a further discussion of Holmes' attitude, see Part Three, Chapter II.

follow their own whims, but derive their views from many sources. And among those sources are not only statutes, precedents, customs and the like, but the rules which other courts have announced when deciding cases. Those rules are no more law than statutes are law. For, after all, rules are merely words and those words can get into action only through decisions; it is for the courts in deciding any case to say what the rules mean, whether those rules are embodied in a statute or in the opinion of some other court. The shape in which rules are imposed on the community is those rules as translated into concrete decisions. Your bad man doesn't care what the rules may be if the decisions are in his favor. He is not concerned with any mysterious entity such as the Law of Massachusetts which consists of the rules usually applied by the courts; he regards only what a very definite court decides in the very definite case in which he is involved; what is the "usual rule" is a matter of indifference to him. To paraphrase Bishop Hoadly, whoever has an absolute authority to translate rules into specific judgments, it is he who is truly the law-giver to all intents and purposes, and not the persons—be they legislators or other judges—who first wrote or spoke the rules.[5] What lawyers are engaged in is predicting or procuring determinations of concrete problems. Clients want those concrete determinations rather than generalizations. Judges are called on not to make rules, but to decide which side

[5] "I think that lawyers and judges too often fail to recognize that *the decision consists in what is done, not what is said by the court in doing it,*" said Judge Cuthbert W. Pound recently. "Every opinion is to be read with regard to the facts in the case and the question actually decided. This is common learning, yet the fondness of the bar for formulas which are substitutes for thought leads its members at times to complain that precedents have been disregarded when in fact no authoritative decision has been ignored." He goes on to say that precedents are to be construed *"as meaning what they ought to mean, rather than what the judge who writes the opinion says about their meaning. . . .* General principles are few; particular cases are many. . . . A bad reason may be given for a good decision." New York Bar Association Bulletin, September 1929, p. 279, 282–3.

of some immediate controversy is to win. The rules are incidental, the decisions are the thing.

Whenever a judge decides a case he is making law: the law of that case, not the law of future cases not yet before him. What the judge does and what he says may somewhat influence what other judges will do or say in other cases. But what the other judges decide in those other cases, as a result of whatever influences, will be the law in those other cases. The law of any case is what the judge decides.

Often when a judge decides a case he simultaneously publishes an essay, called an opinion, explaining that he used an old rule or invented a new rule to justify his judgment. But no matter what he says, it is his decision which fixes the legal positions of the litigants. If Judge Brilliant decides that Mr. Evasion must pay the federal government $50,000 for back taxes or that Mrs. Goneril is entitled to nothing under the will of her father, Mr. Lear, the contents of the judge's literary effusion makes not one iota of practical difference to Mr. Evasion or Mrs. Goneril. Opinion or no opinion, opinion-with-a-new-rule-announced or opinion-with-old-rules-proclaimed—it is all one to the parties whose contentions he adjudicated.

To be sure, this opinion may affect Judge Conformity who is later called on to decide the case of Rex vs. Humpty Dumpty. If Judge Brilliant in Mr. Evasion's case describes a new legal doctrine, his innovation may be *one* of the factors which actuates Judge Conformity to decide for Humpty Dumpty, if Judge Conformity thinks the facts in Humpty Dumpty's case are like those in Mr. Evasion's case. But—need it be reiterated?—the new doctrine will be but one of the factors actuating Judge Conformity.[7]

The business of the judges is to decide particular cases. They, or some third person viewing their handiwork, may choose to generalize from these decisions, may claim to find common elements in the decisions in the cases of Fox vs. Grapes and Hee vs. Haw and describe the common elements as "rules." But those descriptions of alleged common elements are, at best, some aid to lawyers in guessing or bringing about future judicial conduct or some help to judges in settling other disputes. The rules will not directly decide any other cases in any given way, nor authoritatively compel the judges to decide those other cases in any given way; nor make it possible for lawyers to bring it about that the judges will decide any other cases in any given way, nor infallibly to predict how the judges will decide any other cases. Rules, whether stated by judges or others, whether in statutes, opinions or text-books by learned authors, are not the Law, but are only some among many of the sources to which judges go in making the law of the cases tried before them. Because Gray was still obsessed by the belief that the essence of law is generality, he refused to see that rules formulated by judges are, like statutes, only one of the sources of law. As Edmund Burke put it: "No rational man ever did govern himself by abstractions and universals. The major (premise) makes a pompous figure in the battle, but victory depends upon the little minor of circumstances."[6]

[6] Suppose Judge Mild hears the case of Jack vs. Jill and gives judgment for Jack. When so doing he states that he is applying what often theretofore has been announced by judges whenever the facts of a case are A, B and C. Judge Mild states the facts of the suit of Jack vs. Jill so that they appear to be A, B and C. Gray would say Judge Mild had made no law.

Now, suppose that instead of being heard by Judge Mild the case is heard by Judge Bold. He likewise decides in favor of Jack; but Judge Bold so states the facts that they appear to be D, E and F. Judge Bold announces that in earlier cases where similar facts have been found, courts have adopted a rule unfavorable to Jack; but Judge Bold has decided that the old rule is unjust, or unwise, or based on outmoded considerations, and therefore he announces a new rule. Gray would say Judge Bold had made law. The results for Jack and Jill are the same whether the decision is rendered by Judge Mild or Judge Bold. The judge made the law for them whether he purported to fit the facts into an old rule or to make a new rule to fit the facts.

Gray is not primarily interested in what happens to Jack and Jill but in rules of decision which will aid Judge Meek in deciding a later dispute between Tit and Tat; and when Judge Meek decides

There is no rule by which you can force a judge to fol-low an old rule or by which you can predict when he will verbalize his conclusion in the form of a new rule, or by which he can determine when to consider a case as an ex-ception to an old rule, or by which he can make up his mind whether to select one or another old rule to explain or guide his judgment.[7] His decision is primary, the rules he may happen to refer to are incidental.

The law, therefore, consists of *decisions*,[8] not of rules. If so, then *whenever a judge decides a case he is making law*. The most conservative or timid judge, deny it though he may, is constantly engaged in law-making; if he were to see himself objectively he would doubtless feel like Molière's M. Jourdain who was astonished to learn that all his life he had been talking prose.

Many a case is decided without the writing of an opin-ion. The trial judge usually does not bother to tell why he thinks John Doe should lose to Richard Roe. But does he any the less make the law of the case because he has not tried to tell the story of his reactions to the evidence in the shape of legal formulas?[9] Surely law does not come into

that case, Gray would not consider that any law has been made unless it involved the application of a new rule of decision.

For a further discussion of this matter, see Appendix II.

[7] Dewey, in speaking of everyday thinking, says, "The individ-ual's good judgment is the guide. There is no label on any given idea or principle which says automatically, 'Use me in this situa-tion'—as the magic cakes of Alice in Wonderland were inscribed 'Eat me.' "—See "How We Think."

[8] And predictions as to future decisions. See Part One, Chapter V. As there noted, the discussion in this book is largely confined to court law.

[9] "The trial judge is the most important officer of government. . . . The trial court is absorbed in law administration at first hand. The appellate court is so far removed from the real controversy that it more and more becomes concerned primarily with fashion-ing harmonious rules and doctrines for use by trial courts." Dean Green, 28 Columbia Law Review, 1014, 1037.

being only in those cases that are appealed to an upper court which will write an opinion reciting some rules.

Holmes has convinced but a small part of the bar, for his statement of the nature of law is a frontal attack on the basic legal myth and all the sub-myths. But he has some brilliant disciples. Perhaps the hardest-hitting is Professor Walter Wheeler Cook. He expresses the realistic view of law thus:

"We as lawyers," writes Cook, "like the physical scientists, are engaged in the study of objective physical phenomena. Instead of the behavior of electrons, atoms or planets, however, we are dealing with the behavior of human beings. As lawyers we are interested in knowing how certain officials of society—judges, legislators, and others—have behaved in the past, in order that we may make a prediction of their probable behavior in the future. Our statements of the 'law' of a given country are therefore 'true' if they accurately and as simply as possible describe the past behavior and predict the future behavior of these societal agents. . . . 'Right,' 'duty,' and other names for legal relations are therefore not names of objects or entities which have an existence apart from the behavior of the officials in question, but merely terms by means of which we describe to each other what prophecies we make as to the probable occurrence of a certain sequence of events—the behavior of the officials."[8] "The practicing lawyer . . . is engaged in trying to forecast future events. What he wishes to know is . . . what a number of more or less elderly men who compose some court of last resort will do when confronted with the facts of his client's case. He knows how they or their predecessors have acted in the past in more or less similar situations. He knows that if without reflection the given situation appears to them as not differing substantially from those previously dealt with, they will, as lawyers say, follow precedent. This past behavior of the judges can be described in terms of certain generalizations we call rules and principles of law. If now the given situation appears to the court as new, i.e., as one which calls for reflective thinking, the lawyer ought to know, but usually does not, because of his unscientific training,[9] that his case is 'new' because these rules and principles of law do not as yet cover the situation. . . . As it is the lawyer finds competing analogies or principles which are possibly applicable. A familiarity with modern studies of human thinking would reveal to him that his job is not to find the preëxisting meaning of the terms in the rules and principles which he wishes the court to apply, but rather to induce the court to give those terms for the first time a meaning which will reach the desired result. If we shift our point of view from that of the practicing lawyer to that of the judge who has to decide a new case, the same type of logical problem presents itself. The case is by hypothesis new. This means there is no compelling reason of pure logic which forces the judge to apply any one of the competing rules urged on him by opposing counsel. His task is not to find the preëxisting but previously hidden meaning in these rules; it is to give them a meaning. . . . The logical situation confronting the judge in a new case being what it is, it is obvious that he must legislate, whether he will or no.[10], 10

What then is the part played by legal rules and principles? We have seen that one of their chief uses is to enable the judges to give formal justifications—rationalizations—of the conclusions at which they otherwise arrive.[11] From that point of view these formulas are devices for concealing rather than disclosing what the law is. At their worst they hamper the clear thinking of the judges, compelling them to shove their thoughts into traditional forms, thus impeding spontaneity and the quick running of ideas; they often tempt the lazy judge away from the proper task of creative thinking to the easier work of finding platitudes that will serve in the place of robust cerebration.

At their best, when properly employed, they have undeniable value. The conscientious judge, having tentatively arrived at a conclusion, can check up to see whether such a conclusion, without unfair distortion of the facts, can be linked with the generalized points of view theretofore acceptable. If none such are discoverable, he is forced to

10 For a further discussion of legal realism, see Appendix II.
11 Cf. Cardozo, "The Nature of the Judicial Process," 167–176.

consider more acutely whether his tentative conclusion is wise, both with respect to the case before him and with respect to possible implications for future cases.[12]

But it is surely mistaken to deem law merely the equivalent of rules and principles. The lawyer who is not moderately alive to the fact of the limited part that rules play is of little service to his clients. The judge who does not learn how to manipulate these abstractions will become like that physician, described by Mill, "who preferred that patients should die by rule rather than live contrary to it." The number of cases which should be disposed of by routine application of rules is limited. To apply rules mechanically usually signifies laziness, or callousness to the peculiar factors presented by the controversy.

Viewed from any angle, the rules and principles do not constitute law. They may be aids to the judge in tentatively testing or formulating conclusions; they may be positive factors in bending his mind towards wise or unwise solutions of the problem before him. They may be the formal clothes in which he dresses up his thoughts. But they do not and cannot completely control his mental operations and it is therefore unfortunate that either he or the lawyers interested in his decision should accept them as the full equivalent of that decision. If the judge so believes, his thinking will be the less effective. If the lawyers so believe, their opinions on questions of law (their guesses as to future decisions) will be unnecessarily inaccurate.

It is sometimes asserted that to deny that law consists of rules is to deny the existence of legal rules. That is specious reasoning. To deny that a cow consists of grass is not to deny the reality of grass or that the cow eats it. So while

[12] Here, in fact, is where formal logic performs its proper task. As Balfour says, "It never aids the work of thought, it only acts as its auditor and accountant-general." Schiller states that "to put an argument in syllogistic form is to strip it bare for logical inspection. We can then see where its weak points must lie if it has any, and consider whether there is reason to believe that it is actually (*i.e.* materially) weak at these points. We thereby learn where and for what the argument should be tested further."

rules are not the only factor in the making of law, *i.e.* decisions, that is not to say there are no rules. Water is not hydrogen; an ear of corn is not a plow; a song recital does not consist of vocal cords; a journey is not a railroad train. Yet hydrogen is an ingredient of water, a plow aids in the development of corn, vocal cords are necessary to a song recital, a railroad train may be a means of taking a journey, and hydrogen, plows, vocal cords and railroad trains are real. No less are legal rules.[13]

If we are to learn the law by observing the conduct of judges, then we shall want to take legal principles into account, for they are among the causative factors affecting such conduct. But if we are not to be befogged by words we will not assume that the "principles of law" are similar to the "principles of biology." The principles of biology are based directly on the biologist's description of the conduct of animal organisms; the principles of law are often only remotely related to judicial conduct. Accurately to describe that conduct requires close watching of many other factors.

What lies back of the prevalent obsessive interest in legal rules we have already seen; it is naïvely expressed in the utterance of a well-known law teacher: "The law is a normative science and the investigator of this science has more interest in perfecting his generalization as a part of a unified and coherent whole than in observing the application and misapplication of a legal technique," a statement which is reminiscent of the spectator of Racine's comedy who wished to laugh according to the rules. By narrowing the observed data of the so-called science of law, certainty and predictability can seemingly be guaranteed, whereas such a guaranty is impossible if one is required to observe the "application and misapplication of a

[13] See Appendix II for a fuller discussion. On the use of rules as quasi-fictions, see below, Part One, Chapter XV.

legal technique."[14] But, alas, this latter is precisely the task of the lawyer.

The unwisdom of confining attention to rules and principles can perhaps be made more clear by such questions as these:[11] Will these rules and principles suffice as the sole or chief bases of predicting future decisions? Are they the only mode of describing all future probabilities for the purpose of predicting future decisions? Do they, in other words, constitute sufficient explanations of past decisions or causes or indications of the course of future decisions? Are they adequate as records of what has heretofore happened in the courts and of what will happen? To what extent are they helpful as histories of past law or as guides to the law that is to come?

An answer to these questions must lead to a vision of law as something more than rules and principles, must lead us again to the opinion that the personality of the judge is the pivotal factor. Where, then, is the hope for complete uniformity, certainty, continuity in law? It is gone except to the extent that the personalities of all judges will be substantially alike, to the extent that the judges will all have substantially identical mental and emotional habits.

And here we come to a curious conclusion: it is perhaps just possible that we could get stereotyped results from our judges by picking stereotyped men for the judicial office. If we were to elect or appoint to the bench the most narrow-minded and bigoted members of the community, selected for their adherence to certain relatively fixed and simple prejudices, willing to be and remain ignorant of those niceties of difference between individuals the appre-

---

[14] This is what Salmond and others really mean when they state that the great value of following principles and rules in law is that thereby we diminish the effect of the personal biases and prejudices of the judges. What is nearer the truth is that by habituating the judges to the practices of expressing themselves as if the primary emphasis in their thinking were on rules and principles, we make it appear, contrary to the truth, that the individual attitudes and predilections of the judge are inoperative. See Addenda to Second Printing, number 3.

hension of which makes for justice, and insensitive to the rate of social change—we then might have stability in law. There is little hope of such stability, however, if our judges are the more enlightened, sensitive, intelligent members of the community, for then there will be small likelihood that all judges will react identically to a given set of circumstances or will be obtuse to the recognition of unique facts in particular legal controversies. In a deeper sense, however, uniformity of point of view among judges is likely to increase to the extent that judges are the more enlightened, the more quick to detect and hold in check their own prejudices, the more alive to the fact that rules and precedents are not their masters but merely agencies to be utilized in the interest of doing justice. The outward semblance of certainty may diminish but the conviction that justice will be done will be more certain when decisions are rendered by such judges as Holmes, Cardozo, Hutcheson, Lehman and Cuthbert Pound.[15]

"No rational man," to quote Edmund Burke again, "ever did govern himself by abstractions and universals. The major (premise) makes a pompous figure in the battle, but the victory depends upon the little minor of circumstances." Even that wise statement is perhaps oversimplified, for it implies that, although decisions are governed rather by one's beliefs about the facts than by abstract rules, yet the act of deciding can be divided into two parts, the determination of the facts and the determination of what rules are to be applied to those facts. *But these two parts of judging are usually not separated, but intertwined.* Generally, it is only after a man makes up his mind, that he attempts, and then artificially, to separate these two operations.

This must be true of the judge as of other men. It is sometimes said that part of the judge's function is to pick

[15] That awareness by judges of the law's inherent uncertainty and the conscious use of discretion in individualizing controversies will, curiously enough, augment legal certainty, so far as possible, see Appendix II and below, at the end of Part One, Chapter XIV.

out the relevant facts. Not infrequently this means that in writing his opinion he stresses (to himself as well as to those who will read the opinion) those facts which are relevant to his conclusion—in other words, he unconsciously selects those facts which, in combination with the rules of law which he considers to be pertinent, will make "logical" his decision.[16] A judge, eager to give a decision which will square with his sense of what is fair, but unwilling to break with the traditional rules, will often view the evidence in such a way that the "facts" reported by him, combined with those traditional rules, will justify the result which he announces.

If this were done deliberately, one might call it dishonest, but should remember that with judges this process is usually unconscious and that, however unwise it may be, upright men in other fields employ it, and sometimes knowingly. William James relates that, when a young man, he was assisting a professor who was giving a popular lecture on the physiology of the heart for which purpose he was employing a turtle's heart supporting an index-straw which threw a moving shadow, greatly enlarged, upon the screen, while the heart pulsated. The lecturer said that,

[16] What F. C. S. Schiller says of ordinary reasoning may be measurably true of the reasoning of the judiciary: "What does in fact generate and hold good in actual inference is the personality of the man who draws it in a particular context, and the nature of his intelligence, interest, purposes, and ends; its value is determined partly by its relevance to this, partly by the impression it makes on others whose thinking is similarly personal. . . . The only way of really explaining the course of thought is to go to its antecedents, *i.e.,* the motives, character, circumstances of the thinker. . . . *The relevant . . . is what is selected by a knower as 'helpful' for his purpose."*

What are the "relevant facts" in any case? One judge may say they are facts a, b and c. It may well be that most other judges would agree that there could be but one proper decision *if* they agreed that a, b and c were the relevant facts. But suppose another judge holds that the evidence also discloses fact d and that fact d is "relevant." On that basis he may reach a different decision, which most other judges would concede to be correct *if* they agreed that a, b, c and d were the relevant facts.

when certain nerves were stimulated, they would act in certain ways which he described. To James's horror the turtle's heart refused to function as the lecturer had predicted. "There was no time for deliberation," says James, "so, with my forefinger under a part of the straw that cast no shadow, I found myself impulsively and automatically imitating the rhythmical movements which my colleague had prophesied the heart would undergo. I kept the experiment from failing; and . . . established in the audience the true view of the subject. . . . The heart's failure would have been misunderstood by the audience and given the lie to the lecturer."[17]

To many persons, like Salmond, it is unthinkable that not the rules but the personalities of the judges are of transcendent importance in the working of the judicial process. They suggest that the judge's peculiar biases must and can be obliterated by having the judge "follow the law" or consider himself "bound by the law."[18] Often such writers ascribe the intrusion of the judge's personality to what is called an unwarrantable exercise of "discretion." If, they argue, the bench is deprived of the power to ex-

[17] James gives another instance of how scientific men will cheat at public lectures rather than let an experiment fail: "I have heard of a lecturer on physics who had taken over the apparatus of the previous incumbent consulting him about a certain machine intended to show that, however the peripheral parts of it might be agitated, its center of gravity remained immovable. 'It *will* wobble,' he complained. 'Well,' said the predecessor apologetically, 'to tell the truth, whenever *I* used that machine, I found it advisable to *drive a nail* through the center of gravity.' "

These references to James are not to be taken as an approval of the policy of fooling the laity; see Part Two, Chapter V.

[18] Even one of the most unillusioned commentators is found remarking that "to be ruled by a judge is, to the extent that he is not bound by law, tyranny or despotism. It may be intelligent or benevolent, but it is tyranny just the same." A conscientious judge is, of course, "bound by law" in the sense that he does not act capriciously, but since, in the last analysis, his decision is his decision, we must face the fact that we are ruled by judges, not by abstract law. If that be tyranny or despotism, make the most of it.

ercise discretion, then the personal equation can be eliminated and the law will be uniform, definite and certain. "The discretion of a judge," said Lord Camden, "is the law of tyrants; it is always unknown; it is different in different men; it is casual, and depends on constitution, temper and passion. At best it is often caprice. In the worst it is every vice, folly, and passion to which human nature can be liable."

In an amusing opinion[12] Judge Peters of Alabama quotes Lord Camden's language with approval:

"It may be extreme," he says, "but every practitioner of experience knows that it is not without much truth. The writer of this opinion has known a popular judicial officer grow quite angry with a suitor in his court, and threaten him with imprisonment, for no sensible reason save the fact that he wore an overcoat made of wolf skins. Moreover, *it cannot safely be denied that mere judicial discretion is sometimes very much interfered with by prejudice, which may be swayed and controlled by the merest trifles such as the toothache, the rheumatism, the gout, or a fit of indigestion, or even through the very means by which indigestion is frequently sought to be avoided.*" And the opinion then goes on to decry "the uncertain security of a power so uncontrollable and liable to error as mere judicial discretion—a power that may possibly be misdirected by a fit of temporary sickness, a mint julep, or the smell or look of a peculiar overcoat, or things more trivial than those."

Now, Judge Peters was close to the truth. He set forth, with what many lawyers would think unbecoming candor, some of the unnamed and often undiscerned springs of judicial conduct. But, although he was unconventional in his manner of describing them, he represented the typical point of view in assuming that they were to be done away with by destroying discretionary judicial powers and requiring the judges to apply undeviating rules. He is at one with Salmond, who, we have seen, is apprehensive that, if a judge were allowed to take account of the merits of a particular case, he would be exposed "to all the perverting impulses of his emotional nature, to all his prejudices, and to the unconscious bias of his mental constitution and . . . would be led astray by the temptation which beset the 'arbitrium judicis.'"

Surely here again we are confronting mythical thinking. All judges exercise discretion, individualize abstract rules, make law. Shall the process be concealed or disclosed? The fact is, and every lawyer knows it, that *those judges who are most lawless, or most swayed by the "perverting influences of their emotional natures," or most dishonest, are often the very judges who use most meticulously the language of compelling mechanical logic, who elaborately wrap about themselves the pretense of merely discovering and carrying out existing rules, who sedulously avoid any indications that they individualize cases.* If every judicial opinion contained a clear exposition of all the actual grounds of the decision, the tyrants, the bigots and the dishonest men on the bench would lose their disguises and become known for what they are.

It is time that we gave up the notion that indirection and evasion are necessary to legal technique and that in law we shall better achieve our ends if lawyers and judges remain half-ignorant, not only of these ends, but of the means of achieving them.

No, the pretense that judges are without the power to exercise an immense amount of discretion and to individualize controversies, does not relieve us of those evils which result from the abuse of that judicial power. On the contrary, it increases the evils. The honest, well-trained judge with the completest possible knowledge of the character of his powers and of his own prejudices and weaknesses is the best guaranty of justice. Efforts to eliminate the personality of the judge are doomed to failure. The correct course is to recognize the necessary existence of this personal element and to act accordingly.

Indeed, as Ehrlich puts it, this personal element "should not be tolerated as something unavoidable but should be gladly welcomed. For the one important desideratum is that his (the judge's) personality must be great enough to be properly intrusted with such functions." The central problem of adequate administration of justice is "how to organize the judiciary so as to give plenty of scope to strong personalities."[13]

The attempt to cut down the discretion of the judge, if it were successful, would remove the very creativeness which is the life of the law.[14] For try as men will to avoid it, judging involves discretion and individualization. The judge, in determining what is the law of the case, must choose and select, and it is virtually impossible to delimit the range of his choice and selection. But many have feared that discretionary element in justice, and even when they come to see that it is unavoidable, treat it as something to be deplored and not altogether *comme il faut*.

This attitude was nicely disclosed in the writings of Aristotle. His description of judicial discretion, which he called "equity," is classical, and through the ages men, liberally disposed towards such discretions, have recurred to that description. Legal rules, he pointed out, are necessarily general, designed to meet the average situation, but the circumstances of most actual cases are particular. Human rule-makers cannot lay down in advance rules which will fit all particular cases thereafter arising. Wherefore the rules of law must often be modified in their application. Where the provisions of the law would result in injustice, owing to the special circumstances of a particular case, the law must be supplemented and adjusted by equity:

"The reason is that all law is couched in general terms," he wrote, "but there are some cases upon which it is impossible to pronounce correctly in general terms. Accordingly, where a general statement is necessary, but such a statement cannot be correct, the law embraces the majority of cases, although it does not ignore the element of error. Nor is it the less correct on this account; for the error lies not in the law, nor in the legislature, but in the nature of the case. For it is plainly impossible to pronounce with complete accuracy upon such a subject-matter as human action.

"Whenever then the terms of the law are general, but the particular case is an exception to the general rule, it is right, where the legislator's rule is inadequate or erroneous in virtue of its generality, to rectify the defect which the legislator himself, if he were present, would admit, and had he known it, would have rectified in legislating.

"That which is equitable then is just, and better than one kind of justice, not indeed better than absolute justice, but better than the error of justice which arises from legal generality. This is in fact the nature of the equitable; it is a rectification of law where it fails through generality. For the reason why things are not all determined by law is that there are some things about which it is impossible to lay down a law and for which a special decree is therefore necessary. For where the thing to be measured is indefinite the rule must be indefinite, like the leaden rule that is used in Lesbian Architecture; for as the rule is not rigid but adapts itself to the shape of the stone, so does the decree too to the circumstances of the case."[19]

For all that, Aristotle feared that equity which his description had ennobled. It was something extraneous, a necessary evil, a concession, so he says in effect, to the inevitable untidiness of mortal affairs:

"There may indeed be cases which the law seems unable to determine, but in such case can a man? . . . He who bids the law rule, may be deemed to bid God and Reason rule, but he who bids man rule adds an element of the beast; for desire is a wild beast, and passion perverts the minds of rulers, even when they are the best of men. The law is reason unaffected by desire."[20]

[19] Ethics, V., xiv. In the Politics, II, he wrote, "As in other sciences, so in politics, it is impossible that all things should be set down precisely; for enactments must be universal, but actions are concerned with particulars."

[20] "Politics," III, xvi; he also wrote, "Whereas the law is passionless, passion must ever sway the heart of man." "Magistrates do many things from spite and partiality."

In our day, Roscoe Pound has done much to call attention to the beneficence of discretion and the evils that flow from the attempts to deny or suppress it. And yet Pound, like Aristotle—but more subtly—has done much by his phraseology to perpetuate the feeling that there is something in equity and discretion which is out of line with the course which law should take. In the very article in which he deplores the "decadence of equity," he describes equity or discretion sometimes as the "anti-legal" and sometimes as the "non-legal" element in the administration of justice.[21]

Pound, that is, for all his sound wisdom as to the great worth of the use by judges of equity and discretion, holds to the old tradition in so labelling discretion that it appears as something foreign to law, thus confirming the conventional impression that discretion is alien to and opposed to law.[15], [22]

Now it may be desirable for some purposes and at some times to use terminology which will make it appear that there is a sharp cleavage between something which we call law and something which we call discretion; to appear to break up what goes on in the courts into two separate elements. But words have an emotive value and to say that a part of what a judge does is not law or "non-legal" or "anti-legal" is to create the impression that that part of the judge's conduct is tinged with impropriety.

The truth is, of course, that what Pound calls law and what he calls non-legal cannot be separated. They are so thoroughly intermingled that it is impossible to divide

[21] See below, Part Two, Chapter I, and Appendix II, for a further discussion of Pound's views on this subject. There was more excuse for Aristotle in setting off "law" against "discretion" for "law" to Aristotle meant statutory legislation which is inherently general.

[22] He repeatedly opposes "justice according to law" and "justice without law." The conflict between these two ideas "will not down," he writes. "Justice may be administered according to the discretion of the person who administers it for the time being, or according to law." "Law means uniformity of judicial action—generality, equality, and certainty in the administration of justice."

them; nothing but false attitudes can be engendered by labelling either of these components as if it were not a necessary, ever-acting, and therefore desirable part of the processes of law. It is as if one were to treat thirst or hunger, or sexual desire, as not proper. Such treatment of human appetites has a long history—a history which should serve as a warning to those who continue to deal in like spirit with legal processes.

Moreover, when, more or less detachedly, one observes what goes on in court one is led rather to say that, if there must be a better or a worse, a more or less important aspect of legal processes, then what Pound calls the non-legal is the dominant, the more important, the more truly legal, for it is found at the very core of the whole business; as against Aristotle and Pound it would be wiser to go to the other extreme and to say that the law is at its best when the judges are wisely and consciously exercising their discretion, their power to individualize cases.[23]

Let us take stock at this point. The childish desire to rediscover an all-knowing, strict father-judge in the law leads to a demand for impossible legal inflexibility and infallibility. Thence follow assiduous efforts to make law static and therefore to reduce the power of the judge, to deny to him creativeness. These efforts are unavailing—fortunately so, since justice depends on a creative judiciary. But the compulsion to make the appearances deny the fact of judicial innovation and individualization means that the most important task of the judge must be done in a sneaking, hole-in-corner manner. The judicial genius must do his work on the sly: a Mansfield modernizes and vastly improves English commercial law, but, while doing so, feels obliged to reiterate that the certainty of the law is of much more importance than its reasonableness.

The methods of the lawyers depart markedly in this respect from those of the natural scientists. Among scientists there is a determination to eliminate the personal equation

23 See further on this matter, Appendix II.

not by concealing it but, on the contrary, by the most persistent efforts to drag it into the light, carefully note its effects and thereby to reduce its consequences. If this is the practice in astronomy where the personal equation is relatively slight, does it not seem clear that it should be the method in the law, where the personal equation inevitably looms large? The unavoidable intrusion of the judge's personality has its evil aspects. But the evils are not to be abated by the method of covering up the fact of this intrusion but by going in precisely the opposite direction—by bringing into the sunlight of free and unembarrassed discussion the truth that the obscure personal traits of our judges are of vast significance in shaping our law.

Not, of course, that it will ever be possible for judges to become completely emotionless. The nature of the subject-matter with which the judge deals makes the elimination of the personal equation peculiarly difficult. There are few tangled emotions involved in determining the parallax of a distant star. Passion and prejudice may play some part in deciding whether one will adhere to or break away from a particular theory about electrons or light waves, but the emotions involved are less numerous and far more simple than those of the judge deciding a complicated dispute about the conduct of the officers of a corporation, the rate of fare to be charged by a street-railway company, the constitutionality of a statute affecting labor, the meaning of a tax law. The judge is trying to decide what is just; his judgment is a "value judgment" and most value judgments rest upon obscure antecedents. We cannot, if we would, get rid of emotions in the field of justice. The best we can hope for is that the emotions of the judge will become more sensitive, more nicely balanced, more subject to his own scrutiny, more capable of detailed articulation.

As we have seen, judges and lawyers are astute enough in their observation of the effect of non-rational factors in the thought-processes of *witnesses,* while as to the effect of these factors on the thought-processes of *judges,* they are singularly blind. Such consciousness as exists of these components of the judicial process is usually vague and only partly articulate; such few references as are made to them are made surreptitiously or by way of gossip. For the most part, awareness of these factors seldom rises above the level of unavowed knowledge.

They are scarcely mentioned in the law schools. "The art of manipulating judges properly," it has been said, "is important, and yet does not, and rightly should not, receive the attentions of the law schools. . . . The primary object of the university as a public institution can only be the advancement of our legal institutions through the development of a liberal understanding or science of the law." It is fair to ask how there can be any such understanding, liberal or otherwise, which omits consideration of any part of the process by which judges arrive at their decisions.

Unfortunately, our thinking about law is ruled by just such sentiments as are expressed in the above quotation. The random references which are made to the actualities we have just been considering are made shamefacedly. With few exceptions, our discussions of law posit an "ideal," super-human, passionless, judge. In an occasional aside we admit that a judge may be affected by "weakness" when he allows his feelings to enter into his reasoning. But the manner of referring to these "weaknesses" indicates a belief that they are exceptional and pathological. Now even if the humanness of judges were pathological, it would deserve explicit attention as part of "a liberal understanding or science of the law." But calm observation discloses that such "frailties" are normal, not diseased; recurrent, not exceptional. And a study of law which shoves the consideration of the normal and usual into a footnote and labels it "unusual and morbid" cannot lead to anything like an adequate understanding of the subject.

Ideals and counsels of perfection which are not remotely realizable lead to vicious betrayals of those who come under their influence. If law students are taught law in terms of the conduct of ideal or non-existent judges, then when later those students become practitioners or judges, they are unlikely to be at their best in coping with the ways of the actual judging process.

What the attitude of the average lawyer is when he first confronts the real nature of law has been well described by Judge Lehman:

"When I first became a student in the Law School, many years ago, I thought that the Law, developed through the centuries by judges and lawmakers, to meet the changing conditions and problems of life, was founded on principles that must be immutable because they must be right. I held to the idea that the judge did not create or change, but merely applied, rules which any right-thinking man could have evolved for himself; and that a lawyer who gave advice which proved wrong, or took the part of an unsuccessful litigant, must either be ignorant of established precedent and statutory enactment, or else he had failed to reason correctly; for surely each decision must be securely founded on statute or precedent. The rule of law was there and constituted the major premise of a syllogism, the facts of the case the minor premise, and the conclusion could be drawn by correct reasoning. I pictured the judge, selected because of his wisdom and high character, sitting in the court room or in his study and applying to any given case the true rule of the law. If error occasionally crept in, I thought that this must be due to human frailty and such error would unfailingly be corrected by an appellate court. . . . My dismay, when, as a law student, I first realized that Law was not an exact science founded on immutable principles, but that the decisions of judges even though at times wrong must necessarily, to a great extent, constitute premises from which other deductions must be drawn, was as nothing to the dismay I felt as a judge when I first realized that in many cases there were no premises from which any deductions could be drawn with logical certainty."[16], 24

24 See a similar statement by Judge Cardozo, referred to in Part Two, Chapter VI.

And Judge Hutcheson was long in learning the function of the "hunch" in judicial decisions. He describes an early experience:

"Many years ago, at the conclusion of a particularly difficult case both in point of law and of fact, tried to a court without a jury, the judge, a man of great learning and ability, announced from the Bench that since the narrow and prejudiced modern view of the obligations of a judge in the decision of cases prevented his resort to the judgment aleatory by the use of his 'little, small dice' he would take the case under advisement, and, brooding over it, wait for his hunch.

"To me, a young, indeed a very young lawyer, picked, while yet the dew was on me and I had just begun to sprout, from the classic gardens of a University, where I had been trained to regard the law as a system of rules and precedents, of categories and concepts, and the judge had been spoken of as an administrator, austere, remote, 'his intellect a cold logic engine,' who, in that rarified atmosphere in which he lived coldly and logically determined the relation of the facts of a particular case to some of these established precedents, it appeared that the judge was making a jest, and a very poor one, at that."[17]

Is it not absurd to keep alive the artificial, orthodox tradition of the "ideal judge?" The rational alternative is to recognize that judges are fallible human beings. We need to see that biases and prejudices and conditions of attention affect the judge's reasoning as they do the reasoning of ordinary men. Our law schools must become, in part, schools of psychology applied to law in all its phases.[18] In law schools, in law offices and law courts there must be explicit recognition of the meaning of the phrase "human nature in law."[25] The study of human nature in law (to paraphrase Graham Wallas, who has done

---

[25] *Indeed the dishonesty of judges and other governmental officials is a proper subject-matter for study by lawyers.* That a certain judge is corrupt is highly important to the honest lawyer and his client. It may be imperative to avoid trying a case before a judge suspected of being dominated by a political boss interested in the case.

so much to emphasize the evil of divorcing the study of human nature from the study of politics) may not only deepen our knowledge of legal institutions but open an unworked mine of judicial wisdom.[19]

It has been argued that judges will go far towards abandoning "medievalism" when they begin to procure, and to rely on, carefully prepared factual data as to the social setting of the cases which come before them for decision. Something of the sort has occasionally been done, as for instance in cases dealing with statutes regulating the hours of labor for women or with the inapplicability to wage contracts of the rules growing out of mercantile contracts. This technique has, indeed, wide possibilities. Our judges can well afford to get expert advice as to the customs and usages (and the consequences of such customs and usages) of business men in dealing with commercial paper, banking credit, reorganizations of financially embarrassed corporations and other like and unlike situations. More than that, there deserves to be studied the possible employment, throughout the field of law, of that method of patient investigation, by disinterested experts, of the facts and background of individual cases now used by our more enlightened juvenile courts and courts of domestic relations. Today the judge's knowledge of the individual aspects of cases comes to him off the record, sometimes improperly, sometimes accidentally, sometimes through his reading between the lines of the evidence formally presented. We need to develop a more explicit technique for individualizing cases.[26]

[26] The dishonest judge learns much that does not appear in the record. The honest judge, in certain kinds of cases, permits himself the privilege of procuring backdoor information, as, for instance, in receivership cases, where the receiver consults with the judge in chambers, often in the absence of the parties to the proceedings. Also, judges fitfully and sporadically avail themselves of the doctrine of judicial notice to obtain knowledge privately from experts whose names and opinions are usually not revealed to the litigants.

Why cannot all cases be given the same careful study (openly

But the systematic, deliberate and openly disclosed use of the unique facts of a case will not be of much service until the judges develop the notion of law as a portion of the science of human nature. And that development cannot come to fruition until the judges come to grips with the human nature operative in themselves.[27]

disclosed), *with respect to the facts, which is given to cases, say, of juvenile delinquents in our best juvenile courts?* Lawyers need to learn more of the ideals of Hippocratic medicine in which the cure of the patient is considered of more importance than the ("æsthetically" satisfying) cataloguing of diseases.

[27] What this implies is that the judge should be not a mere thinking-machine but well trained, not only in rules of law, but also in the best available methods of psychology. And among the most important objects which would be subject to his scrutiny as a psychologist would be his own personality so that he might become keenly aware of his own prejudices, biases, antipathies, and the like, not only in connection with attitudes political, economic and moral but with respect to more minute and less easily discoverable preferences and disinclinations.

CHAPTER XIV

ILLUSORY PRECEDENTS: THE FUTURE: JUDICIAL SOMNAMBULISM

Lawyers and judges purport to make large use of precedents; that is, they purport to rely on the conduct of judges in past cases as a means of procuring analogies for action in new cases. But since what was actually decided in the earlier cases is seldom revealed, it is impossible, in a real sense, to rely on these precedents. What the courts in fact do is to manipulate the language of former decisions.[1]

[1] There are the two following effective methods employed by the courts for "distinguishing" (*i.e.* evading or sterilizing) a rule laid down in an earlier case:

(1) The rule is limited to the "precise question" involved in the earlier case. *"Minute differences in the circumstances of two cases,"* said a well-known English judge, *"will prevent any argument being deduced from one to the other."* The "decision consists in what is done, not in what is said by the court in doing it," writes Judge Cuthbert Pound. The United States Supreme Court has stated that every "opinion must be read as a whole in view of the facts on which it was based. The facts are the foundation of the entire structure, which cannot safely be used without reference to the facts." The generality of expressions used by a court must, according to Lord Halsbury, "be governed and qualified by the particular facts of the case in which such expressions are found. . . . I entirely deny that [a case] can be quoted for a proposition that may seem to follow logically from it."

(2) It is often asserted that the "authoritative" part of a decision is not what was decided or the rule on which the court based its decision but something (lying back of the decision and the rule) called the "ratio decidendi"—the "right principle upon which the case was decided." In determining whether an earlier decision is a precedent to be followed, a judge need pay scant heed to what the court in the earlier case decided, nor even to what that court

They could approximate a system of real precedents only if the judges, in rendering those former decisions, had reported with fidelity the precise steps by which they arrived at their decisions. The paradox of the situation is that, granting there is value in a system of precedents, our present use of illusory precedents makes the employment of real precedents impossible.

The decision of a judge after trying a case is the product of a unique experience. "Of the many things which have been said of the mystery of the judicial process," writes Yntema,[1] "the most salient is that *decision is reached after an emotive experience in which principles and logic play a secondary part.* The function of juristic logic and the principles which it employs seem to be like that of language, to describe the event which has already transpired. These considerations must reveal to us the im-

---

stated or believed to be the "ratio decidendi" for its judgment. "It is," says Allen, a defender of the doctrine of "stare decisis" (*i.e.* standing by the precedents), "it is for the court, of whatever degree, which is called upon to consider the precedent, to determine what the *true* ratio decidendi was." The "authoritative" part of a former decision, on this theory, is not the rule announced by the judge in the former case, nor what that judge thought was the principle back of the rule he was applying. What "binds" the judge in any later case is what that judge determines was the "true" principle or "juridical motive" involved in the prior decision. *The earlier case means only what the judge in the later case says it means.* Any case is an "authoritative" precedent only for a judge who, as a result of his own reflection, decides that it is authoritative.

See Allen, "Law in the Making," for a discussion of these two more or less inconsistent theories of the use of precedents. Allen is as unaware of this inconsistency as of the casuistry involved in the process of "distinguishing" cases. He points out that in arriving at the true principles behind the precedents, the judge may and often does employ not only his own reasoning powers but the views of text-writers and scholars. This leads to the result (which Allen fails to perceive) that *anyone can make a legal rule or principle.* When a case comes before a judge, your rule or mine may be more acceptable to him than any theretofore announced from any bench. The authoritative (*i.e.* compulsory or dictatorial) character of legal rules, principles, precepts or other legal generalities, is therefore non-existent. See further, Appendix II.

potence of general principles to control decision. Vague because of their generality, they mean nothing save what they suggest in the organized experience of one who thinks them, and, because of their vagueness, they only remotely compel the organization of that experience. The important problem . . . is not the formulation of the rule but the ascertainment of the cases to which, and the extent to which, it applies. And this, even if we are seeking uniformity in the administration of justice, will lead us again to the circumstances of the concrete case. . . . The reason why the general principle cannot control is because it does not inform. . . . It should be obvious that when we have observed a recurrent phenomenon in the decisions of the courts, we may appropriately express the classification in a rule. But the rule will be only a mnemonic device, a useful but hollow diagram of what has been. It will be intelligible only if we *relive again the experience of the classifier.*"

The rules a judge announces when publishing his decision are, therefore, intelligible only if one can relive the judge's unique experience while he was trying the case—which, of course, cannot be done. One cannot even approximate that experience as long as opinions take the form of abstract rules applied to facts formally described. Even if it were desirable that, despite its uniqueness, the judge's decision should be followed, as an analogy, by other judges while trying other cases, this is impossible when the manner in which the judge reached his judgment in the earlier case is most inaccurately reported, as it now is. You are not really applying his decision as a precedent in another case unless you can say, in effect, that, having relived his experience in the earlier case, you believe that he would have thought his decision applicable to the facts of the latter case.[2] And as opinions are now written, it is

---

[2] "The plea that by admitting a principle in one case," says F. C. S. Schiller, "we have admitted it in all, is an attempt to cheat us out of a recognition that circumstances alter cases and that cases must be considered on their merits."

"All of us," warned Anatole France, "judge everything by our

impossible to guess what the judge did experience in trying a case. The facts of all but the simplest controversies are complicated and unlike those of any other controversy; in the absence of a highly detailed account by the judge of how he reacted to the evidence, no other person is capable of reproducing his actual reactions. The rules announced in his opinions are therefore often insufficient to tell the reader why the judge reached his decision.

Dickinson admits that the "personal bent of the judge" to some extent affects his decisions. But this "personal bent," he insists, is a factor only in the selection of new rules for unprovided cases. However, *in a profound sense the unique circumstances of almost any case make it an "unprovided case" where no well-established rule "authoritatively" compels a given result.* The uniqueness of the facts and of the judge's reaction thereto is often concealed because the judge so states the facts that they appear to call for the application of a settled rule. But that concealment does not mean that the judge's personal bent has been inoperative or that his emotive experience is simple and reproducible.[3]

Oliphant has argued that the courts have been paying too much attention to the language of prior cases and that the proper use of the doctrine of following the precedents should lead the courts to pay more attention to what judges in earlier cases have *decided* as against what they

---

own measure. How could we do otherwise, since to judge is to compare, and we have only one measure, which is ourselves; and this measure is constantly changing."

[3] See further, Appendix II. Of course there are cases where the facts are so simple and undisputed and stereotyped that the judge must either apply a settled rule or frankly over-rule the precedents. The indications are that there are fewer such cases than most persons assume. *When the judges develop their processes so as more adequately to individualize all cases to the extent they do now in many "socialized" courts, such type cases will become markedly fewer. Today the judicial conventions artificially simplify many cases, so that they appear to come within settled rules, with resulting injustice to one or the other of the parties.*

have *said* in their opinions.[2] It may be true that in a limited number of simple cases we can guess what the judge believed to be the facts, and therefore can guess what facts, in any real sense, he was passing on. But usually there are so many and such diverse factors in the evidence which combine in impelling the judge's mind to a decision, that what he decided is unknown—except in the sense that he gave judgment for A, or sent B to prison for ten years, or enjoined C from interfering with D.

At any rate, that will be true while the present method of reporting and deciding cases is adhered to. If and when we have judges trained to observe their own mental processes and such judges with great particularity set forth in their opinions all the factors which they believe led to their conclusions, a judge in passing on a case may perhaps find it possible, to some considerable extent, intelligently to use as a control or guide, the opinion of another judge announced while passing on another case. But as matters stand, reliance on precedents is illusory because judges can seldom tell precisely what has been theretofore decided.

Every lawyer of experience comes to know (more or less unconsciously) that in the great majority of cases, the precedents are none too good as bases of prediction. Somehow or other, there are plenty of precedents to go around. A recent writer, a believer in the use of precedents, has said proudly that "it is very seldom indeed that a judge cannot find guidance of some kind, direct or indirect, in the mass of our reported decisions—by this time a huge accumulation of facts as well as rules." In plain English, as S. S. Gregory or Judge Hutcheson would have put it, a court can usually find earlier decisions which can be made to appear to justify almost any conclusion.[4]

[4] Judge Cuthbert Pound quotes the doctrine that "when a court has once laid down a principle of law as applicable to a certain state of facts, it will adhere to that principle and apply it to all future cases where the facts are substantially the same, and this does for the stability and certainty of the law." Judge Pound adds, "The courts and judges state this doctrine of stability with repetitious and tedious emphasis. Yet it is not infrequently reasoned

What has just been said is not intended to mean that most courts arrive at their conclusions arbitrarily or apply a process of casuistical deception in writing their opinions. The process we have been describing involves no insincerity or duplicity. The average judge sincerely believes that he is using his intellect as "a cold logic engine" in applying rules and principles derived from the earlier cases to the objective facts of the case before him.

A satirist might indeed suggest that it is regrettable that the practice of precedent-mongering does not involve *conscious* deception, for it would be comparatively easy for judges entirely aware of what they were doing, to abandon such conscious deception and to report accurately how they arrived at their decisions. Unfortunately, most judges have no such awareness. Worse than that, they are not even aware that they are not aware. Judges Holmes, Cardozo, Hand, Hutcheson, Lehman and a few others have attained the enlightened state of awareness of their unawareness. A handful of legal thinkers off the bench have likewise come to the point of noting the ignorance of all of us as to just how decisions, judicial or otherwise, are reached. Until many more lawyers and judges become willing to admit that ignorance which is the beginning of wisdom and from that beginning work forward painstakingly and consciously, we shall get little real enlightenment on that subject.[5]

---

away to the vanishing point. One may wade through a morass of decisions only to sink into a quicksand of uncertainty. The decisions . . . are mere illustrations of the common law as applied to particular cases and unless the precedent cited is 'on all fours' with the case at bar the principle relied on does not necessarily apply, if some other principle is found to be more applicable. . . . The courts state general principles but the force of their observations lies in the application of them and this application cannot be predicted with accuracy."

[5] One wishes, for instance, that Judge Hutcheson would not stop with the mere statement that his decisions are the result of inspirational hunches, but would some day give a detailed statement of his reactions throughout the course of a trial and during the time when he was hunching and gathering together the materials for

Perhaps one of the worst aspects of rule-fetichism and veneration for what judges have done in the past is that the judges, in writing their opinions, are constrained to think of themselves altogether too much as if they were addressing posterity. Swayed by the belief that their opinions will serve as precedents and will therefore bind the thought processes of judges in cases which may thereafter arise, they feel obliged to consider excessively not only what has previously been said by other judges but also the future effect of those generalizations which they themselves set forth as explanations of their own decisions.[3] When publishing the rules which are supposed to be the core of their decisions, they thus feel obligated to look too far both backwards and forwards. Many a judge, when unable to find old word-patterns which will fit his conclusions, is overcautious about announcing a so-called new rule for fear that, although the new rule may lead to a just conclusion in the case before him, it may lead to undesirable results in the future—that is, in cases not then before the court.[6] Once trapped by the belief that the announced rules are the paramount thing in the law, and that uniformity and certainty are of major importance and are to be procured by uniformity and certainty in the phrasing of rules, a judge is likely to be affected, in determining what is fair to the parties in the unique situation before him, by consideration of the possible, yet scarcely imaginable, bad effect of a just opinion in the instant case on possible unlike cases which may later be brought into court. He then refuses to do justice in the case on trial because he fears that "hard cases make bad laws." And thus arises what may aptly be called "injustice according to law."

---

his "opinion," or as he has happily called it, the "apologia" for his decision.

[6] See Appendix II as to Bingham's notion that the effort to lay down rules for future cases is inconsistent with the avowed refusal of the courts to decide "moot" cases, *i.e.*, cases in which there is no real present controversy before the court.

Such injustice is particularly tragic because it is based on a hope doomed to futility, a hope of controlling the future. Of course, present problems will be clarified by reference to future ends; but ends, although they have a future bearing, must obtain their significance in present consequences, otherwise those ends lose their significance. For it is the nature of the future that it never arrives. If all decisions are to be determined with reference to a time to come, then the law is indeed chasing a will-o'-the-wisp. "Yesterday today was tomorrow." To give too much attention to the future is to ignore the problem which is demanding solution today. Any future, when it becomes the present, is sure to bring new complicating and individualized problems. "Future problems" can never be solved. There is much wisdom in Valéry's reference to the "anachronism of the future."

Indeed, alleged interest in the future may be a disguise for too much devotion to the past, and a means of avoiding the necessity for facing unpleasant risks in the present. If the decision of a particular case takes the form of the enunciation of a rule with emphasis on its future incidence, the tendency will be to connect the past by smooth continuities with the future, and the consequence will be an overlooking of the distinctive novelties of the present. There will be undue stress on past, habitual ways of doing things.

What is more significant is that this regard for the future serves also to conceal that factor in judging which is most disturbing to the rule-minded—the personality of the judge. Thus in a recent book[4] the author finds an advantage in the technique of abstract logic which judges purport to employ in that it requires the judges to

"raise their minds above the facts of the immediate case before them and subordinate their feelings and impressions to a process of intricate abstract reasoning. *One danger in the administration of justice is that the necessities of the future and the interest of parties not before the court may be sacrificed in favor of present litigants.* . . . Nothing is so effective to prevent this outcome as that judges should approach the decision of a controversy with minds directed to considerations having no connection with the immediate situation or interest in the parties. Judges are human instruments, with prejudices, passions, and weaknesses. As it is, they often decide a new point or a doubtful point, ignore a principle, narrow a rule, or explain a concept under the influence of these human limitations. But this influence is enormously diminished by the necessity of centering their attention on a mass of considerations which lie outside the color of the case at bar; and by the habit of coming at every question from the angle of a dry and abstract logic."

It might be more accurately said that the influence of this point of view promotes judicial self-delusion and produces that ineffectual suppression of the judge's personality which leads to the indirect, unobserved and harmful effects of his personality on judicial decisions.

Present problems should be worked out with reference to present events. We cannot rule the future. We can only imagine it in terms of the present. And the only way to do that is as thoroughly as possible to know the present.[7]

We come to this: The desire to regulate the future is in part a desire for impossible uniformity, security and certainty, for over-simplification, for a world regulated and controlled as a child would have it regulated and controlled.

In the interest of preserving the appearance of such a world, much effort is devoted to "keeping the record straight"; that is, to making it appear that decisions and opinions have more of the logical and less of the psychological than is possible. This desire manifests itself in many curious comments and suggestions.

[7] Many of our judges have become golfers; they would do well to take over into the law something of the golfing technique of keeping the eye on the ball. The golfer wants to know where the ball is to go; but to play well he must concentrate to a large extent on the ball itself. So the judge with regard to present facts and future consequences.

Thus a writer, not long since, suggested that there was growing an unfortunate tendency of courts to decide cases on their merits, that this was making the law chaotic, but that a return to certainty and predictability could be procured, in spite of this tendency, if the courts would cease writing opinions. The suggestion was made naïvely and without cognizance of the fact that it meant merely that the failure of the courts to adhere to mechanical applications of rules would be less obvious, if the courts merely recorded their judgments without opinions and thus made it more difficult to scrutinize the means by which they arrived at their judgments.

And, again, it has been urged that, in the interest of maintaining respect for the courts, dissenting opinions should never be rendered, the intent being that thereby the public will not be made aware that able judges, sitting side by side and passing on the same set of facts, can disagree about the law.

The point of all such proposals is that they tacitly concede the impossibility of obtaining legal conformity, but seek to cover up the more obvious manifestations of this lack. The healthier method would be not only to recognize the gross evidences of uncertainty but to make evident the actual but now concealed circumstances which make certainty an impossibility, to the end that by describing accurately the real nature of the judicial process we may learn to better it.

The judge, at his best, is an arbitrator, a "sound man" who strives to do justice to the parties by exercising a wise discretion with reference to the peculiar circumstances of the case. He does not merely "find" or invent some generalized rule which he "applies" to the facts presented to him. He does "equity" in the sense in which Aristotle— when thinking most clearly—described it. "It is equity," he wrote in his Rhetoric, "to pardon human failings, and to look to the law giver and not to the law; . . . to prefer arbitration to judgment, for the arbitrator sees what is equitable, but the judge only the law, and for this an arbitrator was first appointed, in order that equity might flourish."[8] The bench and bar usually try to conceal the arbitral function of the judge. (Dicey represents the typical view. A judge, he says, "when deciding any case must act, *not as an arbitrator, but strictly as a judge; . . . it is a judge's business to determine not what may be fair as between A and X in a given case,* but what according to some principle of law, are the respective rights of A and X.") But although fear of legal uncertainty leads to this concealment, the arbitral function is the central fact in the administration of justice. The concealment has merely made the labor of the judges less effective.[9]

We must stop playing ostrich, one is tempted to say. And then one remembers the amusing remarks of Stefansson on that cliché and its cognates: There is, he says, an African ostrich, a zoölogical bird. There is also the ostrich

[8] The reader will recall the discussion of Aristotle's unfortunate separation of "law" and "equity."

Is not the present-day growth of non-judicial arbitration largely due to an attempt to have that equity flourish which the courts have seemed to deny?

Interestingly enough, the tendency is to set up non-governmental arbitration tribunals which are required to follow their own precedents. The judges (who are really trained arbitrators) are to be superseded by seeming arbitrators who are instructed to act as judges (*i.e.,* as judges seem to act). Unfortunately, as the system develops, the precedents are sure to accumulate and the untrained arbitrators will be baffled by a lack of an effective technique for skilfully evading their own former decisions. *We shall, in effect, be exchanging moderately expert arbitrators for quite inefficient judges.*

[9] Among the numerous resulting harms is the fact that the judges must think one way and talk another. This would be bad enough if they did so consciously and hypocritically. But it is far worse because they are unaware or only half aware of the difficulty.

On the continent there is a movement in favor of "free legal decision" which emphasizes the "subjective sense of justice inherent in the judge." (See page 301 ff.) The question is not whether we shall adopt "free legal decision" but whether we shall admit that we already have it. See Addenda to Second Printing, number 3.

of literature, philosophy and morals. The latter buries his
head when frightened. The former does not. The literary
ostrich, however, has for two thousand years survived all
attacks from careful first-hand observation of the zoölogical bird. He has survived because, like the literary wolf or
the literary Eskimo, he is a part of "knowledge-by-definition" which is more stable than constantly changing em-
pirical knowledge. The average human has a passion for
order and symmetry[10] in the universe, a craving for absolute knowledge, an abhorrence of chaos. Let us, then,
suggests Stefansson with nice sarcasm, find a new basis for
all knowledge. Let us in all fields have knowledge that is
incapable of being contradicted. Knowledge-by-definition
(defined facts; truths that are standardized errors, but are
not allowed to be contradicted) will eliminate the embarrassment of adaptation to the discovery of newly observed
facts.

The plan of standardizing error, which Stefansson ridicules, has a purpose: the complete exclusion from attention of all facts which annoyingly interfere with our
theories does create the appearance of a thoroughly controlled and ordered universe.[11] But the belief in such a
disciplined universe is consistently acted upon only by
primitive men, children and the insane.[5] To the extent
that anyone relies on such a belief he becomes the victim
of the very uncertainties which he ignores and which he
therefore fails to allow for.

To be sure, whoever rejects the childish habit of standardizing error attains increasing knowledge of the ways

[10] Several writers note, as the explanation of the excessive desire
for a legal certainty, the "aesthetic impulse" or "the sense of symmetry." But is not an excessive demand for symmetry perhaps the
result of an undue prolongation of emotional infancy? The aesthetic impulse, when it takes that form, should be more accurately
called "the anaesthetic impulse." It is related to that undue desire
for rest which is regressive; see below Chapter XV.

[11] Cf. Zane's statement that "the machinery of justice must provide some method of *decently veiling violations of the general rule
in particular cases.*"

of the objective world, and makes his world picture ever more complex. Life will then disclose itself to him as far more precarious and difficult to conciliate than it appeared to primitive man or than it appears to the idiot or to the child. But just in proportion as he learns more about what was previously unknown, he reduces his chances of being crushed by unobserved dangers. That is the paradox of wisdom: In so far as we become mindful that life is more dangerous than we had naïvely supposed in childhood, we help ourselves to approach nearer to actual security.[6] We should never have had steam-engines if men had been content with dream-engines. Airplanes were not invented by believers in wishing rugs.[12]

And so in respect to the law: If we relinquish the assumption that law can be made mathematically certain, if we honestly recognize the judicial process as involving unceasing adjustment and individualization, we may be able to reduce the uncertainty which characterizes much of our present judicial output to the extent that such uncertainty is undesirable. By abandoning an infantile hope of absolute legal certainty we may augment markedly the amount of actual legal certainty.[13]

To the somnambulist, sleep-walking may seem more pleasant and less hazardous than wakeful walking, but the latter is the wiser mode of locomotion in the congested traffic of a modern community. It is about time to abandon judicial somnambulism.[14]

[12] That, within limits, dreaming has value, see page 181.
[13] The reader will recall that this is a *"partial* explanation."
[14] "In some cases," says Bentham, "jurisprudence may be defined the art of being methodically ignorant of what everybody knows."

CHAPTER XV

PAINFUL SUSPENSION

As everyone knows, it is indispensable to adequate thinking that the thinker should be able to keep his mind in suspense. Reflective thinking necessitates inquiry into the rightness of established habits, interruption of routine, selection of alternatives, detection of ambiguities, choice of roads at the crossways.[1]

Now reflective thinking is what we want of our judges. If the judging process is to be well conducted, then our judges should know what are the obstacles to reflective thinking and the causes of these obstacles.

The psychologists usually report that the suspense required to arrive, by reflection, at adequate judgments is painful. So that the judge whose judgments are routine, is, in this sense, avoiding the pain of suspended judgment. Since routineer judges are undesirable, it is worth while to inquire into the nature of the unpleasantness which the more desirable judges, the reflective judges, must apparently encounter.

If to withhold judgment is disturbing, to rush to a conclusion seems to bring peace. Yet there is one group of human beings, the scientists, who apparently seek to avoid that peace. They go out in search of disturbing problems. They provoke for themselves situations which compel them to anguish themselves recurrently with suspended choices, with the retention of an open mind, with refusals to accept the first suggestions, refusals to rush to customary conclusions. The scientists are professional doubters, men devoted to breaking up tradition. They seem deliberately to be courting the kind of pain said to be involved in reflective thinking.

If the quest of the new has been the concern of science, as much cannot be said of the law. For there, precedent is honored. The advocate and the judge rely on "authorities"; the juristic vocabulary is not rich with words that suggest experimentation. And yet, as we have said, law must be far more tentative and adaptive than chemistry. Cook and his group are surely right in saying that lawyers must learn to look upon their work as a vast series of experiments. We will want to know, then, why the scientist has learned to welcome all that makes for the suspended judgment necessarily involved in conducting experiments, how he has come to enjoy what the psychologists tell us is painful. Let us look at some of the suggested explanations.

Vaihinger[2] detects three stages in human development.[1] First, there is the stage of dogmatism. This is proper, he says, to primitive man. Dogmatism is a form of logical optimism which trustfully assumes that whatever occurs in thought therefore exists, that thought is infallible.[2]

This is followed by negative skepticism which is pessimistic and insists on the hopeless subjectivity of thought, its uncertainty, invalidity and unreality. At this stage, thought is regarded as an extremely defective instrument which falsifies reality and leads us astray.

Such logical pessimism is barren, but it has its value, for it destroys naïve dogmatism and leads to a third stage of "true criticism" in which it is recognized that although thought may not be in complete correspondence with factual reality, it may lead to ultimate practical coincidence with the facts of existence.

This critical attitude, says Vaihinger, can appear only

[1] He is here following Kant.
[2] It was perhaps the naïve dogmatist of whom Vaihinger was thinking when, in his youth, he described man as a "species of ape afflicted by megalomania."

at a high stage of intellectual development. It involves the ability to think in a contingent manner, to accept thoughts, ideas, concepts, rules, principles, as provisional, tentative, relative, elliptical.

Vaihinger asks what retards growth in the direction of "true criticism." He apparently finds the answer in what he calls the "equilibratory tendency of the psyche which is impatient to rid itself of the uncomfortable condition of tension" produced by the existence of an idea which is only provisionally accepted. If an idea is accepted as objective, it has a stable equilibrium, whereas an hypothesis has an unstable one. The mind tends to make stable every psychical content and to extend this stability, because the condition of unstable mental equilibrium is uncomfortable. This tendency towards the stabilization of ideas is quite "natural," says Vaihinger.

The origin of this "natural" tendency of the psyche[3] Vaihinger does not explain. But his use of the word "natural" connotes something enduring and ineradicable in human thought-processes. Barry in his excellent discussion of the difficulties of scientific thinking,[4] has more recently advanced a similar thesis:

"Our desire for an immediate solution of ultimate problems is not a childish weakness," he writes, "but an inescapable predisposition. The psychologist[3] now realizes that one of the two or three primary human instincts—those which appear to involve no process of inference—is the fear occasioned by loss of bodily support. The same fear operates intellectually.[5] We demand first of all security in our convictions; after that, if we are courageous, we venture to criticize them. It is easy to see that all the prejudices which operate to retard the progress of free inquiry, whether it be religious, moral, economic, political, or purely intellectual, may be largely thus accounted for; and it is likewise evident that among all these prejudices there is none more powerful than that of intellectual conviction."[6]

[3] He apparently means Watson. This theory may therefore be labelled the Barry-Watson theory.

For Vaihinger the desire to express truths dogmatically is "natural." For Barry this desire is an "inescapable predisposition" having its roots in an "instinct" which is present at birth—a fear of loss of bodily support. "It is not childish," says Barry, thus implying that it is an organic tendency (the analogue of physical inertia, he suggests) which is inescapable and incessant throughout the life of any human. Even granting that it "involves no process of inference" and appears at birth, does it follow that this desire is not childish, i.e. appropriate to childhood, but not to maturity? Are all the tendencies of the infant, because they appear without effort on its part, to be taken as "not childish" and therefore destined to last throughout adult life? May there not be responses appropriate to childhood and inappropriate to mature years? What of the glands that cease functioning in early years? What of the milk-teeth which we outgrow as we develop? Surely to say that a child is born with a desire for physical (and therefore mental) support does not justify the further statement that such a desire "is not childish"[7]—i.e. that it is a desire which cannot be modified or sloughed off in adult life.

Barry, however, gives his thesis a scientific cast by basing it on what, he says, "the psychologist now recognizes" as "one of the two or three primary human instincts." To what authoritative psychologist is he referring?

"It appears," writes Grace Addams, "turning from one authority to another, that there are no human instincts, that there are two fundamental instincts, that there are eight principal instincts, and many minor ones, that there are sixteen (unclassified), that there are forty-two . . . or more than can be counted. According to which authority is accepted, these instincts are: common to all men or never duplicated; transitory or permanent; indistinguishable from simple reflexes or complex mental processes; aimless or consciously purposeful."

And Miss Addams quotes Dunlap:

"Practically, we use the term instinctive reaction to designate any reaction whose antecedents we do not care, at the time, to inquire into; by acquired reaction, on the other hand, we mean those reactions of whose antecedents we intend to give some account. But let us beware of founding a psychology, social, general, or individual, on such a definition."

We need not, then, be too much impressed by Barry's reference to the instinctual basis of the "equilibratory tendency." Moreover, although Vaihinger calls this tendency "natural" and Barry thinks it "not childish" but derived directly from "instinct," both apparently believe that it can be vastly reduced in intensity.[8] How? By advanced intellectual development, says Vaihinger, by a high degree of mental training;[9] by the production of a highly developed logical mind that does not surrender to the "equilibratory impulse," that does not care to purchase relief from mental discomfort by "mental slumber."[10]

Let us see whether the views of Vaihinger and Barry cannot be made more acceptable by reinterpretation. The child, says Piaget, has great difficulty in dealing with any hypothesis which is not adapted to his personal conception of reality. You ask him, "Assume a dog has six heads, how many heads will fifteen dogs have?" He refuses to answer, because "he knows a dog does not have six heads." You ask him, "If you could touch the sun, would you feel it?" His answer is, "You can't touch him."

The child, that is, up to a certain age, will not assume a hypothesis unless you can force him to believe it. He will not reason from an assumption unless he can turn it into an affirmation. He will not posit a statement without believing it, merely for the sake of seeing where it will lead.

Now why is the child incapable of reasoning from premises which he does not thoroughly believe? In answering this question Piaget links it up with a related question: Why does the child experience difficulties in dealing with questions of relation? Why does he think of north or south, or right or left, or up or down, as absolute? Why is it hard for him to see that a brother must necessarily be a brother of someone, or that to some people the child himself is a foreigner? For the child, north is north, up is up, a brother is a brother, a foreigner is a foreigner. The relative significance of these terms he cannot comprehend.

This is due, says Piaget, to the child's illusion of point of view. The child is in a state of "egocentric immediacy." His own point of view is absolute, and he therefore has the greatest difficulty in grasping someone else's belief or assuming imagined ideas which are not a part of his own established reality. This, in turn, is due to the fact that he has not yet desubjectified thought, that he has not yet become so aware of himself as to distinguish between the self and the not-self. When that consciousness of self—the source of which we have already referred to—develops, he is then able, to a far greater extent than theretofore, to modify the absoluteness of his own, and to approach a completely relational, point of view.

The development of resistance to what Vaihinger calls the equilibratory tendency of the mind, the resistance to that tendency which impels the thinker to rush to conclusions, may therefore properly be considered as a product not of high *intellectual* progress but rather as a product of *emotional* maturity. The unwillingness to accept all concepts as relative and subject to qualifications is not due to intellectual retardation but to emotional backwardness. The desire for intellectual support is appropriate to an early period of emotional development; it is a desire which in childhood it would be undesirable too vigorously to modify. It is satisfied in large measure during childhood by dependence on the parents and, it would seem, particularly by dependence on the father; it can be reduced in intensity as the child grows older to the extent that he is gradually weaned from reliance on fatherly authority—to the extent, that is, that the individual arrives at emotional and not merely intellectual maturity.

As we have noted, there is a powerful nostalgia in the infant for the relatively undisturbed state of security which it enjoyed prior to birth. The environment, after birth, forces the infant away more and more from a condition patterned after this early serenity. The development of the child may be viewed as a struggle between a powerful tendency to return to a pre-birth tranquillity and a tendency, of a dynamic character, away from such a state of rest.[4] Neither of these opposing tendencies wins a complete victory until death, but an approach to maturity would seem to involve increased yieldings of the regressive tendency (toward rest), and more frequent victories of the opposed dynamic tendency.

Now the equilibratory tendency, the desire for intellectual support, may be considered as part of the regressive tendency to return to the early undisturbed security. It is, in that sense, normal to infancy in which the opposed dynamic factor is proportionately weaker.

In these terms, then, the pain involved in suspended judgment is a product of the regressive and more infantile tendencies. Development should mean a diminution of such pain, should mean that the dynamic tendency becomes a larger component. In other words, with maturity doubt and inquiry should no longer be unpleasant, but should rather become a source of interest and satisfaction. Maturity is wakeful and vital. The constant effort to achieve a stable equilibrium, resembling sleep, is regressive, infantile, and immature. The acceptance of everything as transitory, the welcome of new doubts, the keen interest in probing into the usual, the zest of adventure in investigating the conventional—these are life-cherishing attitudes. They are the attitudes of the so-called scientific mind—which we may now translate as the emotionally adult or mature mind.

For the emotionally mature mind, then, the suspense of judgment involved in critical thinking is a source of pleasure, not of pain. It is related by Graham Wallas that, in a debate with Bernard Shaw, a critic remarked, "Mr. Shaw, you seem to talk like two people," to which Shaw

4 See Appendix VIII. Cf. Bernfeld, "The Psychology of the Infant."

replied, "Why only two?" Shaw, a man possessed of remarkable emotional maturity, positively enjoys a state of mind in which he is not at rest, in which there is a struggle of many persons within him, and in which he arrives at judgments as the result of prolonged and wakeful combat between opposing possibilities.

We need judges possessed of this Shavian spirit who will enjoy thinking as experimentation, to whom a wakeful attitude of intelligent doubt will be a source of pleasure. Such men will not talk of "rules" and "principles" as finalities while unconsciously using them as soporifics to allay the pains of uncertainty. They will treat rules and principles as shorthand expressions, ingenious abbreviations, metaphors, short-cuts, figures of thought, intellectual scaffoldings, and the like; they will find positive satisfaction in hypothetical, relative, fictional and provisional thinking.

Where the courts are aware that they are using a fiction, they admirably define its limited purpose. A fiction, they have said, is "an assumption that a thing is true which is not true, or which is probably false as true; the rule being that the court will not endure that a fiction, intended for the sake of justice should work 'contrary to real truth or substance of the theory.'" "Fictions of law," they have said, "shall not be permitted to work any wrong."

But what, with unfortunately few exceptions, judges have failed to see is that, *in a sense, all legal rules, principles, precepts, concepts, standards—all generalized statements of law—are fictions.* In their application to any precise state of facts they must be taken with a lively sense of their unexpressed qualifications, of their purely "operational" character. Used without awareness of their artificial character they become harmful dogmas. They can be immensely useful and entirely harmless if used with complete recognition that they are but psychological pulleys, psychical levers, mental bridges or ladders, means of orientation, modes of reflection, "As-Ifs," convenient hypostatisations, provisional formulations, sign-posts, guides.[5] We want judges who, thus viewing and *employing all rules as fictions,* will appreciate that, as rules are fictions "intended for the sake of justice," it is not to be endured that they shall work injustice in any particular case, and must be moulded in furtherance of those equitable objects to promote which they were designed.

All of which means that, if justice is to be capably administered, judges must be so trained that they will put a premium on their dynamic tendencies and struggle against the drag of childish nostalgia for the oversecure and the impossibly serene—for a father-governed world.

It might seem that thinking supported by the dynamic tendency is related to directed, realistic thinking, while thinking characterized by the opposing tendency is related to "autistic," de-reistic, wishful or phantasy thinking. Although there are doubtless such inter-connections, it would be a grave error to conclude that all phantasying is relatively immature or fruitless with respect to realistic thinking.[6] Poincaré has told us something of how the mind of a great mathematician operates, of "the inspirations which are the fruits of unconscious work" done by "the subliminal ego" with "an absence of discipline" and a "disorder born of chance." "This very disorder," he advises, "permits of unexpected couplings."

No, we cannot dispense with imagination, flashes of insight—phantasy, if you will. But there are different kinds of phantasy. There is the day-dream that denies, and seeks escape from, reality: the compensatory, castle-in-the-air kind of imagining, perhaps proper to a certain youthful period and always to be allowed to grown-ups in a holiday spirit. And then there is the creative, inventive phantasy, projecting in imagination possibly useful rearrangements of experience.

This is a crude statement of the difference between what is valuable and what is harmful in adult day-dreams but it

[5] For further discussion of this point of view, see Appendix VII.
[6] Of course phantasy has an important place in poetry. See Richard's "Science and Poetry."

will serve to indicate that to deplore the persistence of infantile longings does not mean the advocacy of a "hard-boiled" matter-of-factness. On the contrary, there is ground for the belief that phantasying of the childish order is backward-looking and that, just to the extent that such childish phantasying is diminished, will inventive, forward-looking phantasying become effective.[11] It is the more constructive type of speculating which needs to be cultivated among legal thinkers.

To decry, as we have done, the quest in law of the demonstrably unattainable does not mean that we advocate giving up "ideals" in law. What the law ought to be constitutes, rightfully, no small part of the thinking of lawyers and judges. Such thinking should not be diminished, but augmented. For the most part it has been unconscious; it should, as Holmes has said, be made more largely conscious. There can be, as Morris Cohen has aptly put it, a "scientific character to questions as to what the law ought to be."

But there is a nice difference between ideals (or "oughts") and illusions. The approximately possible differs from vain hopes founded on unprofitable day-dreaming. Such day-dreaming often, indeed, prevents the pursuit of the possible.

We may well want judges "with a touch in them of the qualities which make poets,"[12] who will administer justice as an art and feel that the judicial process involves creative skill. This means that we want to encourage, not to discountenance, imagination, intuition, insight. But it does not mean that we should not frown upon pure phantasy thinking. "This unconscious work," says Poincaré, "is not possible or in any case not fruitful, unless it is first preceded and then followed by a period of conscious work. . . . All that we can hope from these inspirations which are the fruits of unconscious work,[7] is to obtain points

[7] The reader who is emotively disturbed by the use of such phrases as "unconscious work" is referred to Hart, "Psychopathology"; see also Appendixes VIII and X.

of departure for (our) calculations. As for the calculations themselves, they must be made in the second period of conscious work which follows the inspiration. They demand discipline, attention, will, and consequently, consciousness." Demand, that is, an abundance of free energy, not absorbed by wasteful infantile musings on how to reach a never-never land, but capable of being devoted primarily to soluble adult problems.[8]

[8] G. N. Lewis notes that much of the knowledge of the organic chemist "does not fully emerge into his scientific consciousness, and has been called the chemical instinct." Cf. the remarks of the great chemist Kekule, who, in reporting two important discoveries made by him "inspirationally," said, *"Let us learn to dream, gentlemen. Then, perhaps, we shall find the truth . . . but let us beware publishing our dreams before they have been put to the proof by the waking understanding."* (Quoted by Leuba, "The Psychology of Religious Mysticism," 242.)

Leuba, discussing such scientific "inspirations," points out that "they take place only after a period of conscious work and that they complete or continue something already begun. When the solution is complex, it does not come to mind with all the details worked out. The key is at hand, but it still has to be used." Poetical inspiration, he adds, follows the same law. Compare W. I. Thomas's contribution in "The Unconscious, a Symposium"; Graham Wallas, "The Art of Thought"; Valéry, "Variety," 60.

CHAPTER XVI

THE BASIC MYTH AND THE JURY

The demand for excessive legal certainty produces, it has been seen, a violent prejudice against a recognition of the practical need for flexible adaption and individualization of law based upon the unique facts of particular cases. Yet the life and growth of society make imperative such flexible individualization of the rules. Not allowed to operate in the open, such individualization has been worked out by surreptitious methods. Notable among such surreptitious methods is our amazing use of the jury.

The function of the jury is supposed to be fact-finding. According to the official or naïve theory, when a case is tried before a judge and jury, there is a nicely divided tribunal: to the judge is left the determination of the rules of law; to the jury is left solely the ascertaining of facts. The jury, so the story goes, must in no manner encroach upon the powers of the judge. It must not concern itself in any manner with the authority or wisdom of the law. What the judge announces as law must be taken by the jury as completely authoritative.[1]

If practice followed theory, the judge would ask the jury to determine, from the evidence, specific facts. "Do you believe from the evidence that Jones fell through the elevator shaft and broke his leg?" "Do you believe from the evidence that Smith represented to McCarthy that there was an oil well on the premises?" "Do you believe from the evidence that Robinson agreed to marry Miss Brown?"

[1] See Appendix V for a discussion of the "naïve," the "sophisticated" and the "realistic" views of the function of the jury.

After the jury had reported its specific "findings," the judge would then decide, in the light of these findings, the respective legal rights and liabilities of the parties.

But seldom is anything approximating such a plan followed. In the great run of cases the "general verdict" is used. Briefly described, the usual process is this: After the evidence has been heard, the judge gives the jury what are known as "instructions on the law" which in effect tell the jury that, if they believe from the evidence that facts A and B exist, then the law requires them to bring in a verdict for the plaintiff, but if they believe facts C and D exist, then the rules of law are thus and so, and require them to find for the defendant. Thus they are told that, if they believe that Smith did not represent to McCarthy that there was an oil well on the premises, they must, as a matter of law, bring in a verdict for Smith and against McCarthy.[2]

The jury then retire and later report back to the judge —what? That they believe from the evidence that Smith did represent there was an oil well and that, therefore, they have found for McCarthy? Not at all. They bring in a "general" verdict; they report simply that their verdict is for McCarthy. No details are given. No one knows and no one is permitted to ask the jury how they arrived at this verdict. It may be, indeed, that their verdict would have been against McCarthy and for Smith, had they applied the legal rules, contained in the judge's instructions, to what they honestly believed to be the facts. But their beliefs on the question of fact are not disclosed. Whether they applied or disregarded the rules of law cannot be ascertained.[3]

[2] Of course, the instructions are often more intricate and state rules largely unintelligible to the jury.

[3] "In a vast majority of cases, the verdict is a complete mystery, throwing a mantle of impenetrable darkness over the operations of the jury. Whether the jurors deliberately and openly threw the law into the discard, and rendered a verdict out of their own heads, or whether they tried to apply it properly but failed for lack of understanding—these are questions respecting which the verdict

The truth is (as anyone can discover by questioning the average man who has served as a juror) that usually the jury are neither able to, nor do they attempt to, apply the instructions of the court. The jury are more brutally direct. They determine that they want Jones to collect $5000 from the railroad company or that they don't want pretty Nellie Brown to go to jail for killing her husband, and they bring in their general verdict accordingly. Ordinarily, to all practical intents and purposes, the judge's views of the law might never have been expressed.

In most jury cases, then, the jury determine not the "facts" but the legal rights and obligations of the parties to the suit. For the judgment of the court follows the general verdict of the jury, so that the verdict, since it produces a judgment which determined the respective rights and obligations, decides the law of the particular case.[4] But this decision is made by persons with little understanding of the pre-existing "rules of law" and scant will

---

discloses nothing. . . . No one but the jurors can tell what was put into it and the jurors will not be heard to say. The general verdict is as inscrutable and essentially mysterious as the judgment which issued from the ancient oracle of Delphi. Both stand on the same foundation—a presumption of wisdom. The court protects the jury from all investigation and inquiry as fully as the temple authorities protected the priestess who spoke to the suppliant votary at the shrine." Sunderland, "Verdicts, General and Special," 29 Yale Law Journal, 253, 258.

The courts usually hold that no evidence can be introduced to show that the jury misunderstood the judge's instructions; or that they so understood the facts that, in the light of the judge's instructions, they should have brought in a different verdict; or that they reached their verdict without deliberation, or by lot or some other gaming device.

[4] In criminal cases the verdict, if for the accused, is conclusive and, therefore, there should be little doubt that the jury, in such cases, decides the law. See Appendix V, "Notes on the Jury."

In civil jury cases, the judge has a limited power to set aside the verdict. This is at best, however, a negative power—a power to veto but not to decide. It is a veto based upon a guess. Even this limited power can be exhausted. See Appendix V.

to adhere to or employ these rules even so far as they are comprehended.

The general-verdict jury trial, in practice, negates that which the dogma of precise legal predictability maintains to be the nature of law. A better instrument could scarcely be imagined for achieving uncertainty, capriciousness, lack of uniformity, disregard of former decisions—utter unpredictability. A wise lawyer will hesitate to guarantee, although he may venture to surmise, what decision will be rendered in a case heard and decided by a judge alone. Only a very foolish lawyer will dare guess the outcome of a jury trial.[5]

Why, then, has the general-verdict jury system developed? In large part, it would seem, because it serves two purposes: It preserves the basic legal dogma in appearance and at the same time (albeit crudely and bunglingly) circumvents it in fact, to the end of permitting that pliancy and elasticity which is impossible according to the dogma, but which life demands.[6]

An English judge, Mr. Justice Chalmers, not at all satirically, but with delightful simplicity and naïveté, has lauded the jury system because it leads to just such results:

[5] See where the jury leaves the "art of prediction." The lawyer must guess, at a minimum, what the judge will say to the jury; what heed the jury will pay to what the judge says; what elements in the evidence the jury will consider; what factors not in the record (their feelings about the judge, the lawyers, the clients, the witnesses) the jury will consider; what the attitude of the jurors may be to one another. . . .

Surely, if any law is retroactive—unknowable at the time of action—it is jury law. As long as the jury system flourishes it will be peculiarly absurd to say that any man warrantably acted with reference to a known state of law.

[6] Probably because this use of the jury seems to square the legal circle, it has been said that "the whole machinery of the state, all the apparatus of the system and its varied workings, end in simply bringing twelve good men into a box."

"Again," he writes, "there is an old saying that hard cases make bad law. So they do when there is no jury. The Judge is anxious to do justice to the particular parties before him. To meet a particular hard case he is tempted to qualify or engraft an exception upon a sound general principle. When a judge once leaves the straight and narrow path of law, and wanders into the wide fields of substantial justice, he is soon irretrievably lost. . . . *But hard cases tried with a jury do not make bad law, for they make no law at all, as far as the findings of the jury are concerned. The principle is kept intact while the jury do justice in the particular case by not applying it.*"[7]

By such use of the jury, you can eat your cake and have it too. You can preserve your rules and principles unswerving and unyielding—in the form of the judge's instructions—and you can have a jury's decision (which determines the rights of the parties to the case) that is based upon scant respect for those abstractions as against emotional appeals. The rules and principles remain pure and unsullied—because, while clearly enunciated, they are not applied.

This attitude is expressed in varying fashions. "The jury

---

[7] That juries decide the law is a statement which does not satisfy the Bealist. For he thinks of the law as expressed in rules, generalizations, principles. But the law of a particular case issues in a decision as between the contestants. To them the law of their case has its value and significance solely in the determination of their respective rights and liabilities. If Jones, as a result of a jury verdict, at the end of a lawsuit collects $5,000 from Smith, he cares little about the general legal principles which may have been involved.

Jury-made law, as compared with judge-made law, is peculiar in form. It does not issue general pronouncements. You will not find it set forth in the law reports or in text-books. It does not become embodied in a series of precedents. It is nowhere codified. For each jury makes its own law in each case with little or no knowledge of or reference to what has been done before or regard to what will be done thereafter in similar cases. Yet jury law, although not referred to as law, is real law none the less. If all cases were general-verdict jury cases and if judges never directed a verdict, the law of all decided cases would be jury law.

system," said a well-known judge, "is generally regarded as deriving one of its chief advantages from having the law applied by persons having no permanent offices as magistrates and who are not likely to get into the habit of forcing cases into rigid forms and arbitrary classes." And another judge speaks in favor of the jury as against the judge because "it is a matter of common observation that judges and lawyers, even the most upright, able and learned, are sometimes too much influenced by technical rules."

More bluntly, it has been said that the public wants its conduct to be judged by laymen, by the man in the street. "It cannot be doubted," says Chamberlayne, "that a principal claim of the jury to popular favor is its traditional ability to defy, in a general verdict, the law of the land as announced by the judge." And you will find many persons defending the jury with that argument. Such a defense has at least the virtue of candor. But if it be sound, what a mockery it makes of our judicial system! Jurors, it says in effect, are better able to dispense justice than those who have been ostensibly selected for that purpose. You see, of course, on what that view is founded: the judges have too successfully created the belief that they are sincerely dominated by the basic dogma of legal inflexibility, that they will not individualize cases, that they will give decisions according to rigid rules. This belief both satisfies and alarms.

For while men want the law to be father-like, aloof, stern, coldly impartial, they also want it to be flexible, understanding, humanized. The judges too emphatically announce that they are serving the first of these wants. The public takes the judges seriously, assumes that the judges will apply hard-and-fast law to human facts, and turns to the jury for relief from such dehumanized justice.

The conventional image of the law is, of course, a mask, a false-face, made to suit unconscious childish desires. But that false-face terrifies even the persons who have made it. The law, as they picture it, will not allow the

judges to indulge their feelings, their sympathies, for the
persons appearing as suitors in the courtroom; the law,
they believe, when properly administered, creates impersonal and artificial rules, which command respect because
they guard against any human "weakness" in the judge
by requiring him to come at every question from the angle
of dry and abstract logic; this abstractness may produce
hardship by requiring the omission of seemingly pertinent
considerations, it may be artificial, inadequate and harsh,
but it safeguards the law from deflection from its all-important generality.[1] Flesh and blood cannot stand that
kind of law. Judges, so conceived, are too terrifying. We
dare not, says the public, let them act thus in our affairs.
The public turns, therefore, to a humanizing agency—the
jury. Then they can have it both ways. The judge, wearing
a false-face, which makes him seem like the child's stern
father, gravely recites the impersonal and artificial rules
which command respect; but the juries decide the actual
legal controversies.

Now there are thousands of cases decided every year by
judges in juryless courts.[2] Flexibility and individualization are not wanting in the decisions rendered by judges
in cases tried without the intervention of the jury. But the
judges do not usually admit—even to themselves—the wide
margin of discretion they employ in arriving at those decisions. They purport to be governed largely by rules and
principles, standards and such,[8] and thus perpetuate the
public apprehension of the cold formalism of their decisions.[9] As long as the judiciary goes on thus verbally com-

[8] The judges when sitting in equity (without a jury) admit that
they exercise discretion, but purport to be governed by "principles"
—which, however, are, in most instances, fortunately vague.

[9] The jury are sometimes credited with liberalizing strict law
because they ignore instructions. An often-cited illustration is the
refusal of the juries to apply the harsh fellow-servant rule which
the courts evolved. But is it not possible that the courts failed to
abolish the fellow-servant rule by "judicial legislation" just because
the juries made that abolition unnecessary? In other words, the
courts could maintain their attitude of strictness and "pass the

plying with the demand for illusory legal certainty, formulating the law of the land with an appearance of excessive rigidity, just so long will palliating methods, such as the general-verdict-jury-system, be used. The original sin is to be found in the perpetuation of the basic dogma. Until we are rid of that sin, we are not likely to do away with the secondary evils that flow from it.

Especially in criminal law is the jury highly regarded as a means of necessary humane individualization. Not easily would our people relinquish to the judges the power to pass on the guilt or innocence of one accused of crime. The jury is assumed to be more merciful to the alleged criminal, more responsive to unique extenuating circumstances. Yet it may be doubted whether the popular estimate of the benevolent character of jury law in criminal cases is altogether correct. "Parties charged with crime," it has been wisely said, "need the protection of the law against unjust convictions quite as often as the public needs it against groundless acquittals."[10]

---

buck" to the jury. The jury is an unnecessarily cumbersome agency for the process of nullifying undesirable rules. The courts are adept enough in that process when they can't "pass the buck."

[10] "A judge who has long sat at *nisi prius* ought gradually to acquire a fund of experience which enables him to represent the common sense of the community far better than an average jury," said Mr. Justice Holmes.

The subject of the value of the jury in criminal law is bound up with the entire problem of penology and criminology. And some people question whether most judges, as now educated, can expertly cope with these problems.

The way out in Criminal Law may be to train our judges in criminology, giving them wide discretion to individualize punishment, and then, if we are to retain the jury, leaving to the jury merely the power of finding the facts through answers to interrogatories or through the special verdict. Pending that development, it would be well to consider carefully the suggestion (made by Prof. Glueck and advocated by former Governor Alfred E. Smith) that judge and jury in criminal cases, as now, determine the guilt or innocence of the accused, leaving to expert criminologists the determination of the treatment of those found guilty. See Sheldon Glueck, "Principles of a Rational Penal Code," 41 Harvard Law Review, 453, 476.

But the childish belief in the inflexibility of legal rules and the related belief that the judges represent the spirit of unswerving law, make most men fear any proposal to leave the last word to the bench where life or liberty is at stake.[3]

We have thus arrived at an almost unbelievable result. The dogma of precise legal predictability requires the denial of any large measure of discretion in the judge adequately to vary and adjust the abstract legal formulations to meet the unique and novel aspects of particular cases. This dogmatic denial of novelty and creativeness in the making and adjustment of law in turn traces back, as we have seen, to an unsatisfiable childish longing for certainty, finality and predictability. In jury trials this longing is largely satisfied—in appearance—and hopelessly thwarted in practice.[4] The result is that, to preserve the self-delusion of legal fixity, certainty and impartiality, in many cases we hand over the determination of legal rights and liabilities to the whims of twelve men casually gathered together. Seeking to escape judge-made law, we have evolved jury-made law.

The jury, and not the judge, determine the rights of the respective parties and the jury's determination of these rights is guided by no real regard for "rules," abstract or otherwise. The decisions of many cases are products of irresponsible jury caprice and prejudice. That the defendant is a wealthy corporation and the plaintiff is a poor boy; that the principal witness for one of the parties is a Mason or a Catholic; that the attorney for the accused is a brilliant orator—such facts often determine who will win or lose.

The jury system means that the illusion of the existence of an inflexible body of rules ostensibly has been maintained, whereas, in fact, uniformity and inflexibility are negated. Proclaiming that we have a government of laws, we have, in jury cases, created a government of often ignorant and prejudiced men. To satisfy cravings for unrealizable certainty, a technique has been devised which, when employed, makes impossible such moderate legal certainty as is reasonable, desirable and practically obtainable. To keep alive a pretense of the rigidity of the law, the work of dispensing justice is often left to the altogether too flexible moods of twelve untrained men. This is individualization and adaptation of legal rules to particular cases at their worst, producing the very arbitrariness which the dogma of legal certainty aims to avoid.

The demand for an impossible legal stability, resulting from an infantile longing to find a father-substitute in the law, thus actually leads, in the use of the jury, to a capriciousness that is unnecessary and socially harmful.

It has been urged by some lawyers that the worst evils of the jury system can be avoided by abolishing general verdicts and restricting verdicts to fact-finding verdicts, in which the jury merely finds the constitutive "facts," leaving it to the judge thereafter to apply the law to the facts thus found.[5] And there can be little doubt that there would be less uncertainty resulting from jury trials if fact verdicts in some form were always employed and the general verdict abolished, for the judge thereby would more nearly become the sole arbiter of the law.

But are jurors good fact-finders? What adequate fact-finding involves we have already observed.[6] It requires devoted attention, skill in analysis, and, above all, high powers of resistance to a multitude of personal biases. But these qualities are obviously not possessed by juries. They are notoriously gullible and impressionable.[7]

"Jurors called upon to sit as judges come into the jury box unused to the surroundings, and naturally have a feeling of strangeness and general timidity," says Judge McEwen. "They distrust themselves and distrust their ability to judge as to the truth. A perfectly competent business man or mechanic, were the same question presented to him in his business or occupation, would have no doubt or misgiving as to a decision, but place the same man with the same question in a court room, and he becomes a timid, questioning, indecisive creature."[8]

Is it likely that twelve men, summoned from all sorts of occupations, unaccustomed to the machinery of the law, unacquainted with their own mental workings and not known to one another, can, in the scant time allowed them for deliberation, do as good a job in weighing conflicting testimony as an experienced judge? Can they as well see through the story of the glib liar,[11] or of the unconsciously biased but conscientious witness, or as ably allow for the stage fright which often makes the honest but cautious man speak falteringly on the witness stand?[9] It is hard to conceive that any astute person can take seriously the stereotyped praise of the jury, uttered daily by sophisticated lawyers, of which the following classic, by Judge Cooley of Michigan, is typical:

"The jurors, and they alone, are to judge of the facts and weigh the evidence. The law has established this tribunal because it is believed that, from its numbers, the mode of their selection and the fact that the jurors come from all classes of society, they are better calculated to judge the motives, weigh possibilities, and take what may be called a common-sense view of a set of circumstances involving both act and intent, than any single man, however pure, wise and eminent he may be."

The truth is that the very judges who seem to estimate the jury as superior triers of the facts pragmatically reveal little sincerity in their jury worship:

[11] "A judge who has sat for ten or fifteen years on the criminal bench is usually keener to detect a liar or see through a 'faked' defense than any twelve men drawn indiscriminately from different walks of business activity," writes Arthur Train.
"Some of the opinions of Sir William Scott and of Sir John Nicoll reveal marvelous sagacity and skill in co-ordinating little circumstances, separately innocent to the untrained mind, so as to produce a powerful special impeachment of a witness." Moore, "On Facts," 10.

"It is well known," observes Moore,[12] "that on appeals in chancery cases . . . the admission of illegal evidence by the chancellor does not cause a reversal of his decree upon the facts, if there remains in the record sufficient legal evidence, in the judgment of the appellate court, to sustain the findings of fact. The judges of the appellate court, after reading and digesting the illegal evidence, deem themselves capable of weighing the legal evidence without partiality of prepossession; while in common-law cases tried by a jury, the same judges frequently declare a mistrial, grant new trials, or reverse on appellate review, upon the ground that illegal evidence was heard by the jury and gained such lodgement in their minds that no instruction by the trial judge to disregard it could possibly be faithfully executed by conscientious jurymen. The same judges who profess to regard jurors as pre-eminently qualified to decide questions of fact, write opinions in appellate courts in law cases pointing out in stirring language the prejudicial evidence which they believe must have fatally infected the judgments of jurors, but never suggest recusing themselves after pondering any kind or quantity of illegal evidence in chancery appeals."

The judicial jury-worshipers are not hypocritical; their eulogies are reflections of semi-myths growing out of the self-delusion involved in the central legal myth, and are not to be considered as in any manner fair appraisals of the jury.

The jury, then, are hopelessly incompetent as fact-finders. It is possible, by training, to improve the ability of our judges to pass upon facts more objectively. But no one can be fatuous enough to believe that the entire community can be so educated that a crowd[13] of twelve men chosen at random can do, even moderately well, what painstaking judges now find it difficult to do. It follows that the use of fact-verdicts, while it may slightly reduce the evils of the jury system, cannot eliminate them.[14] The

[12] "On Facts," 36.

[13] The jury as a "crowd" and therefore subject to "crowd impulses," would repay study by psychologists.

[14] Sunderland, who urges the use of fact verdicts, admits that they would merely palliate the fundamental difficulty.

jury makes the orderly administration of justice virtually impossible.[15]

What a crop of subsidiary semi-myths and mythical practices the jury system yields![16] Time and money and lives are consumed in debating the precise words which the judge may address to the jury, although everyone who stops to see and think knows that these words might as well be spoken in a foreign language—that, indeed, for all the jury's understanding of them, they are spoken in a foreign language. Yet, every day, cases which have taken weeks to try are reversed by upper courts because a phrase or a sentence, meaningless to the jury, has been included in or omitted from the judge's charge.

Do not those unintelligible words[10] uttered by the judge in the presence of the jury resemble the talismanic words of Word-Magic? Since the twelve men in the box do not comprehend what the man on the bench is telling them to do, what he is telling them must be assumed to be self-efficacious, capable of working automatically by "transforming the suggested idea into accomplished fact by means of the suggestion itself." Such an assumption smacks of child-magic, which hopefully employs formulas and key-words to conquer the environment without substantial effort.[11]

Of course, the belief in the magic efficacy of the judge's words is at most only half-hearted. What has happened is that the judge's instructions have become part of an elaborate ceremonial routine.[12] Once, in simpler times, there was perhaps a thorough belief that what the judge said about the law had marked effect on the jury. But today, although that belief has atrophied, the elaborate ceremony continues, just as, we hear, religious or magical rites,

[15] The absurdity of the jury system doubtless has played a large part in the movement for arbitration. Unfortunately precedent-worship has injected itself into that movement and is likely to destroy whatever of value there is in the experiment.

[16] Some of these semi-myths are discussed in Appendix V.

once performed with entire conviction as to their power, often degenerate into formalism until "right" or "wrong" come to mean merely the exact execution or neglect of all the details of a prescribed ritual. So the judicially intoned formulas are now like debased or devitalized magic incantations, which "depend for their efficacy on being uttered rather than on being heard."[13]

The so-called "cautionary instructions" to the jury—are they not, too, like debased magic spells or cabalistic formulas? Here are some gems from the court-room liturgy:

"You sit here as judges of the facts, and as judges of the facts you must not put yourself in the place of either the plaintiff or the defendant, because, if you do, you bring into play a kind of sympathy either for the plaintiff or the defendant. You are to sit here in the solemn capacity of judges, absolutely free from any bias or prejudice or sympathy or any like human emotion, sit here calmly and judicially and determine first what the facts are and then determine from those facts the things I have instructed you you must determine, what things can properly and reasonably be inferred from the facts that have been adduced here from the witness stand."

"I may add that it is usual and appropriate for questions of law to be argued to the court and for the jury to take the law from the court. I am sure I need not reiterate or elaborate to you a proposition which every one must understand. You will only do your duty to the public, and as well to the accused, in this case, by excluding from your minds promptly, manfully, and sternly all impressions which may have been placed there, or which may have unconsciously found their way there, which are not made by the evidence or the law. The certainty, the regularity, and inexorable firmness and justice of the action of courts and juries are the absolute and indispensable requisites to the preservation of our civilization. The certainty ceases to exist when the juries are to be moved by appeals to the tender emotions of human nature, to the distress of the unfortunate, to sympathy for the helpless, to the sorrows of the prisoner's family. The regularity of jury trials vanish when juries can be misled into antagonism to constituted authorities, upon feigned issues when no sort of antagonism should exist, and when all are animated simply by an anxious desire to

ascertain the truth, and to give due weight and importance
to evidence. The firmness and justice of juries are as intangible
and uncertain as the viewless winds when they will consider
as a guide anything save the law, commanding that which is
right, and prohibiting that which is wrong."

"I take it that it is unnecessary to say to an intelligent jury
that we are not here in the administration of public justice to
be actuated by the feelings of sentiment; that may do very
well outside of this courthouse, but we are here to see that
the law, which is laid down as a rule of conduct for all citizens,
is enforced. Whenever a party is charged with violation of
law, it is my duty to give you the law; it is your duty to apply
the facts to the law, and if the state has established the guilt
of the party accused beyond a reasonable doubt, you should
find a verdict of guilty; and you cannot allow your judgments,
according to your oaths, to be influenced by sentiment or anything of that kind."

Now, no one believes that these admonitions work. If
they do, why does the jury lawyer in his address to the
jury not confine himself to clear and concise logical arguments based on a passionless summary of the evidence?
He does the reverse; he uses every trick of oratory and
acting to appeal to the crudest emotions of the twelve good
men and true. He knows only too well that they will not
nicely weigh the testimony nor discriminatingly consider
what the judge has told them of the law. The jury lawyer
is a realist, seeking a result, and he plays upon every
weakness of the dozen men who will decide the fate of his
client.

Yet judges will solemnly instruct a jury that "No juror
should permit the admiration, the ill feeling or prejudice
he may entertain for any counsel connected with the case,
to influence him." Do the judges honestly believe that
those words will take effect? Hear what an experienced
judge, when off the bench, has to say on that question:

"A book could be written on the subject of the influence of
the personality of the lawyer in the court room," says Judge
McEwen. "Each workman must use his own tools, and so the
lawyer must fight with his natural weapon. We have winners

in all fights. There are men who walk into the court rooms with so much dignity and weight, who speak with such gravity and solemnity that they create for themselves a funereal atmosphere that over-shadows everything. They carry an impression of such deep learning that the words they speak seem to have tenfold weight, and if there were a crime in the law for obtaining a verdict by false pretenses, this type would many times be subject to prosecution; such as a pious lawyer, or the pious acting lawyer, who selects a jury that does not attend the ball games on Sunday, and gets the whole case into such a solemn atmosphere that a jury cannot help but return a verdict of guilty for the reason that the defendant ought to be punished for his sins if not for the crime mentioned in the indictment. Then we have the lawyer who plays the farmer, deliberately slaughters the King's English, chews tobacco prodigiously, offers his plug to the jurors and gets their sympathy and good will by appearing to be one of them, and by making it seem that their interests are common against the oppressor on the other side of the table."

What, then, one may ask, is the function of these apparently functionless "cautionary instructions"? They are not sincerely supposed to control the jury. They are part of a rite, and it has been said of rites: "The particular meanings of a complicated piece of ritual tend to lose themselves in a general sense of the efficacy of the rite as a whole to bring blessing and avert evil. Nay, unintelligibility is so far from invalidating a sacred practice that it positively supports it by deepening the characteristic atmosphere of mystery. Even the higher religions show a lingering predilection for cabalistic formulas."

These instructions are like exorcising phrases intended to drive out evil spirits; phrases once earnestly thought to be efficacious, now no longer believed in, yet an inextricable part of a conventionalized system of observances. Perhaps, too, the more unintelligible and technical instructions on the law may be considered as part of this mechanism of exorcism, resembling the "tremendous words" from Hebrew and Greek, such as Schemhamphora or Tetragrammaton, which the medieval exorcists employed to scare away the minions of Satan.

Thus the basic legal myth produces an intricate, technical ritual, practically useless, but the subject of endless and wasteful disputation.[17]

[17] "In Australia councils of the older men are held day by day during the performance of their ceremonies, at which traditions are repeated and procedure determined, the effect being mainly to perserve custom, but undoubtedly in part also to alter it. . . . A man of a more original turn of mind will claim to have a new ceremony imparted to him in a vision, and such a ceremony will even be adopted by another tribe which has no notion of its meaning. Meanwhile, since little is dropped while so much is being added, the result is an endless complication and elaboration of ritual. Side by side with elaboration goes systematization, more especially when local cults come to be merged in a wider unity. . . . At these higher stages there is more need than ever for the expert in the shape of the priest, in whose hands ritual procedure becomes more and more of a studied discipline, the naive popular elements being steadily eliminated, or rather transformed." See article on "Ritual," Encyclopedia Britannica (11th Ed.), Vol. 22, p. 372.

Our complicated and cumbersome rules of evidence could be simplified immeasurably if we did away with the jury. The hearsay rule, for instance, is largely due to the mistrust of the jury's competence to weigh evidence.

CHAPTER XVII

CODIFICATION AND THE COMMAND THEORY OF LAW

"Let us end all this confusion by adopting a code. Let us once and for all by statute enact a carefully prepared body of rules sufficiently complete to settle all future controversies." That is the remedy for legal uncertainty recurrently proposed by men of strong common sense.

Frederick the Great tried it. He intended that in the code prepared under his directions "all contingencies should be provided for with such careful minuteness that no possible doubt could arise at any future time. The judges were not to have any discretion as regards interpretation, but were to consult a royal commission as to any doubtful points, and to be absolutely bound by their answer."[1] And the decisions of the courts in applying the code were to have no weight whatsoever as precedents. The plan failed. The code did not automatically solve all legal problems. The royal commission was obliged to issue many volumes of supplementary rules, and the courts were unable to obey the injunction that in deciding cases they should not be influenced by the decisions of their predecessors. Finally, it was formally recognized that the code could not successfully stereotype the law so as to make it, at one stroke, available for all possible combinations of circumstances; the royal commission was dissolved, and the judges were explicitly given the right to "interpret" the law "so as to give effect to changes in the general condition of things."

[1] Schuster, "The German Civil Code," 12 Law Quarterly Review, 17, 22.

Napoleon likewise endeavored to have enacted a code which would end what he considered lawyers' quibbling. He believed that the Code Napoleon anticipated all possible future cases. Elaborate interpretation of the code, he thought, would be chicanery; "good sense and willingness to respect the law could and should serve every purpose."[2] The circumstances under which that code was drafted made his expectations unusually plausible. The political and social situation was singularly stable. The industrial revolution had not yet begun. "At that time the legislator did not need to concern himself how, in the future, law was to be made to accord with social requirements."[1]

And the French lawyers and judges, on the whole, strove conscientiously to apply the code, in the spirit in which Napoleon had conceived it, as a complete formulation of rules adequate to solve all legal problems. "No sooner had the Civil Code been promulgated, than observation of the incessant action of periodical evolution was laid aside for the easier study of legislative tests," says Lambert.

"Scientific study gave way to mere commentary. Interpretation was deluded into the belief that the Civil Code and the few laws which had completed it and modified it, would serve indefinitely to answer all the juridical problems which the practice of affairs gives rise to each day. Expounders of the statutes believed that from their provisions, exclusively, by processes of analogy and by induction and deduction, they must control the development in detail, even of principles whose advent the legislator could not have foreseen. They were not concerned whether such control was equitable and adequate to the purposes of the principle, or such, indeed, as

[2] Charmont, "La Renaissance du Droit Naturel," in "Modern French Legal Philosophy," 113. Not that Napoleon was naïve in his views. "Upon one occasion he acknowledged: 'I first thought it would be possible to reduce laws to simple geometrical demonstrations, so that whoever could read and tie two ideas together would be capable of pronouncing on them; but I almost immediately convinced myself that this was an absurd idea'"—Lobingier, "Napoleon and his Code," 32 Harvard Law Review, 114, 120.

would assure its proper operation. Despite the clear and repeated lessons of history, they would not admit the inability
of the legislator to render the law stationary; they denied that
codification could at best modify the conditions of future
juridical evolution, and that it cannot halt or suspend its
course. They raised to the level of a dogma the concept of
the rigidity and immobility of the law and of its capacity to
anticipate and control everything. They considered all other
sources of law as dead, and, in spite of the daily contradictions
of experience, proclaimed that henceforward the adjustment
of the existing system of law to the transformations in social
and economic environment could be realized only when and
as the legislator decreed. Powerless to prevent the inevitable,
spontaneous and extra-legislative production of law, they yet
bound themselves to ignore it. They adopted as the fundamental basis of their method a premise which is the very
negation of one of the most universal laws of social evolution,
the perpetual mobility of law. . . . The principal consequence
of the method which took root in France immediately after
codification, has been to *screen more and more from public
observation the true operation of existing, living institutions,
by concealing them behind the masks of dead institutions of
the past.*"[2]

More recently Germany adopted a "modernized" code.
It is generally conceded that any hopes entertained that
it would banish legal contingency and ensure certitude
have been sharply disappointed:

"When on January 1, 1900," wrote Justice Gmelin,[3]
"throughout those parts of Germany where the Roman civil
law had prevailed, the Roman law ceased to be in force, and
the controversies raging around it disappeared together with
the local statutes supplementing it, which frequently were just
as hard to interpret, a good many people may have imagined
that a new epoch had begun, an epoch in which a code, easy
to use, would facilitate the decision of law cases which
practical life produces in ever novel forms, by means of a
few easily framed pronouncements intelligible to everybody.
That hope has not been fulfilled. The number of controversies
is legion. The necessary tools of the practitioner include thick

commentaries and a flood of published decisions by the highest courts that is rising in an actually menacing manner."

Again the hope of attaining a large measure of legal certainty by codification proved vain. It produced not certainty, but sterile logic-chopping.

Where code-worship has prevailed in code-governed countries, the real judicial process of adaptation has been concealed under the guise of formal exactness, the principal effect of which has been, writes Lambert, to create a chasm,

"that widens each day, between the theory of text-writers and the rules created by judicial decisions. Theory was bound to feel the effect of its own policy of obstructing the natural path of the law, and of refusing to allow its principles and reasoning to be made elastic, or its classification of juridical elements to grow and multiply, as the increasing complexity of social and economic relationships required. By declaring the law to be stationary, theory condemned it to part company gradually with reality. Its place had to be taken little by little in practice by a new system of law formed slowly through the repetition of judicial precedent, and adjusted to the actual needs of society: the body of judicial decisions.

"Meanwhile the gap between theory and practice is now rapidly widening. The law expounded in classroom and textbook differs more and more from that applied in the courts."[4]

Codification, whatever its real worth, cannot create a body of rules which will exclude judicial innovation and thereby guarantee complete predictability. In attempts to achieve a perfect code covering all imaginable cases, we encounter again the old dream of legal finality and exactitude. Once this dream took the form of a belief in a list of rules directly God-derived.[5] Belief in a man-made code, which shall be exhaustive and final, is essentially the same dream in another form, but a form which hides from superficial study the nature of the dream. But a dream it is, nevertheless. For only a dream-code can anticipate all possible legal disputes and regulate them in advance.

As the history of Continental law has disclosed, a code cannot be stable, it must be adaptive. Even in a relatively static society, no one can foresee all future combinations of events. The "specific facts in individual cases produce 'gaps' in every legislative provision."[6] Situations are bound to occur which the legislature never contemplated when enacting the statutes. Then the incompleteness of the code calls for judicial law-making. Such law-making is customarily designated judicial "interpretation," but that is a false label, for it indicates that the process is merely one of ascertaining the meaning and intention of the maker of the statute. As Gray[7] put it,

"A fundamental misconception prevails and pervades all the books as to the dealing of the courts with statutes. Interpretation is generally spoken of as if its function was to discover what the meaning of the legislature really was. But when the legislature has had a real intention, one way or another on a point, it is not once in a hundred times that any doubt arises as to what its intention was. If that were all that the judge had to do with the statute, interpretation of the statutes, instead of being one of the most difficult of a judge's duties, would be extremely easy. The fact is that the difficulties of so-called interpretation arise when the legislature has had no meaning at all; when the question which is raised on the statute never occurred to it; when what the judges have to do is, not to determine what the legislature did mean on a point which was present to its mind, but to guess what it would have intended on a point not present to its mind had the point been present."

Even if, conceivably, in a society which was stable, a definitive code could be drafted which would so settle the law that the code would forever after solve all legal problems, "yet where, as in our time, customs are constantly changing under the pressure of a lively industrialism and commercialism, no code, however adequate for today, could possibly be sufficient for the problems of tomorrow or the day after tomorrow." "Nothing changes more easily than statutes intended by their own expressions to be eternal, for nothing runs greater risk of becoming out of date, of accommodating itself badly to new circumstances," says Demogue.[8]

Unvarying application of the text of codes is impossible; the attempt to apply such a principle of "interpretation" is delusional and produces the very opposite of the result aimed at by the rigid codifier. For it is notorious that the attempt to have the courts apply statutes as if indeed they were all-sufficient, as if all cases not explicitly provided for could be worked out by logical deduction from the express terms of the code, leads to no small measure of uncertainty. The "technicalism" which has usually been engendered by code-making creates the false theory that all cases must find their solution in the literal language of the statutes and rules worked out by analogy therewith. According to this theory, "the legislator is to be credited with having foreseen and settled all things; if the text does not contain a specific solution for every difficulty which may present itself, it at least embodies a principle, by the aid of which all difficulties may be solved. An interpreter needs only to discover this principle, and from it to deduce its consequences—consequences which are derived logically from the law itself."[9]

This theory is but another instance of legal myth-making. Except in those cases which happen to be explicitly covered by the code, the judicial interpreter takes out of the code provisions exactly what he puts in. In spite of, or, perhaps more accurately, because of, this false appearance of purely logical interpretation, the decisions become unpredictable. For where the code is silent, the conventional theory of so-called "interpretation" requires the judge to decide cases by analogy to some code rule, and the selection of the rule thus to be applied by analogy involves, of course, the exercise of a flexible discretion to a far larger extent than is acknowledged by the exponents of the theory or by the judges who believe that they are adhering to the theory.

"The interpreter's respect for texts is only a vain appearance, for he himself actually creates the principles which, in order to gain for them a semblance of authority, he ascribes to the legislators."[10] These "principles" are no less subjective because the judiciary insists on pretending, even to itself, that they are objective. Such self-delusion merely means that the factors of most importance in judicial thinking are employed furtively and clandestinely; it creates the outward semblance of certainty but (so say competent observers of the workings of the codes) increases legal contingency and doubt. "It is possible to 'deduce' all sorts of legal results, which may be wholly inconsistent with each other, out of the same state of facts, because the selection of a starting point for the process of deduction is not hindered by any regard for realities." The result of the concept of a written law to cover all cases is a process of logomachy plus a concealing of the real bases of decisions, with the result "that a law suit is purely a lottery."[11]

The more astute among contemporary commentators on the Continental code systems agree that in the framing of future codes the orthodox principles of codification should be frankly abandoned. The recent Swiss Civil Code is constructed on new lines: it seeks simplicity and flexibility, not detailed, complete regulation. It is "more like an outline of legal principles than a body of provisions purporting to regulate all legal relations."[12] Acute critics of the German and French codes now accept approximately the following attitudes: A code should respond to the multiplicity, complexity and elasticity of present-day legal relationships; the idea of regulating, by anticipation, all possible legal relationships is to be abandoned; the provisions of a code "should be conceived in *very general terms,* flexible enough to be constantly adapted by the courts to the circumstances which they face"; in meeting "new problems, the interpretation must not seek, as formerly, to determine the intention of the legislator, irrespective of the nature of the problem, but to keep adjusting the law to new judicial relationships, so that it conforms to the nature which social changes impart to them."

In other words, judicial law-making is being accepted by the more alert Continental lawyers not only as an unavoidable, but as a desirable and most important element of any code system. If any there be, in this country, who assume that by codification we could rid ourselves of legal indefiniteness and uncertainty, their hopes in this respect should be corrected by the experience of Continental Europe.[3]

The childish belief in legal finality is not to be realized by codification. It is and will ever be based upon illusion.

It is a significant fact that many of the persons who fatuously believe in an all-sufficient code also espouse the "command theory" of law.

John Austin is typical. He was one of the principal English advocates of the adoption of "a code, or systematic and complete body of statute law, intended to supersede all other law whatever."[13] He did not go so far as the codifying committee of the French National Convention of 1796 who "aimed . . . . to realize the dream of philosophers—to make the laws simple, democratic, and accessible to every citizen."[14] But he did think that law "could be so condensed and simplified that *lawyers* may know it: And that, at a moderate expense, the rest of the community may learn from lawyers beforehand the legal

[3] This conclusion is not to be taken as indicating a general hostility to legislation nor as a blanket indictment of wise codification which aims at simplicity and flexibility rather than completeness and finality. See Appendix VI, "Notes on Codification."

It may well be that codification produces greater rather than less flexibility. See Goodhart, "Case Law in England and America," 15 Cornell Law Quarterly, 173, 191 for a suggestion that the adoption of the "restatements of the law" now being formulated by the American Law Institute may lead to increasing disregard for precedents.

effect of transactions in which they are about to engage."[15]

At the same time Austin is known as the principal exponent of the notion that "every law is a command—the command of a monarch or sovereign to persons in a state of subjection to its authority. Law," he wrote, "proceeds from superiors and binds inferiors. . . . The term command is the key to the science of jurisprudence."

Now if the belief in an all-sufficient code is a child's dream, the notion of law as a list of commands is no less a child's notion, a hopelessly over-simplified analysis of the nature of law.[16] Austin's definition of the "command" which, he contends, is of the essence of all laws, displays a striking likeness to the child's conception of the admonitions of the father: "If you express or intimate a wish that I shall do or forebear from some act, and if you will visit me with evil in case I comply not with your wishes, the expression or intimation of your wish is a command," said Austin. "If you are able and willing to harm me in case I comply not with your wishes, the expression of your wish amounts to a command."[4]

There appears to be more than chance in this combination of the advocacy of an exhaustive code and the espousal of the command theory of law. That every law is a command becomes a more plausible assumption when law takes on the form of a seemingly complete body of enacted statutes; judicially created law does not in form lend itself so easily to that assumption.

That the demand for legal certainty and the command theory are naturally concomitant is sensed by Wurzel. In answer to the question why the legal-certainty illusion persists, he replies, as we have seen, that there exists, in the psychology of the occidental administration of justice, a

---

[4] Austin, as noted above, states that "Law proceeds from superiors and binds inferiors" and defines "superiority," as used in this context, as follows: "Superiority signifies might: The power of affecting others with evil or pain, to fashion their conduct to one's wishes."

"social want" that the law should appear to be "a complete body of commands sufficient, by the use of formal logic, to settle all controversies." The consequence of such a conception of law, he keenly observes, is that to most laymen and lawyers jurisprudence is improperly considered to be "a science of obedience, of submission to commands."

Wurzel proceeded no further with this analysis. But we may. The "social want" to which he refers—which manifests itself in a conception of laws as commands to be obeyed and in a desire for a complete body of such commands—is almost a replica of the child's want that his father shall be an omniscient, omnipotent law-maker and giver of commands.

Austin's description, given above, of the command which inheres in all laws, puts in striking phrases the social want to which Wurzel refers. Accepting this description as a moderately accurate portrayal of the public's attitude towards law, it goes to show that the public is still dominated by a childish myth. Although there are gaps in the law, although the law is never complete and always provisional, although it is plain to the eye of any realistic observer that it is being made and remade constantly by the courts, the social want demands that every artifice be used to conceal the existence of gaps in the law, its essential tentativeness. Law must at all costs preserve the appearance of a complete body of commands handed down by a sovereign who possesses superior might and has the power of affecting inferiors with evil or pain, to fashion their conduct according to his desires.

If such wishful thinking is the pivotal fact in the occidental psychology of judicial administration, it is more than accidental that similar wishful thinking is the pivotal fact in the psychology of the child. A childish phantasy is one important element of the juridical attitude of grown men.

CHAPTER XVIII

THE RELIGIOUS EXPLANATION

"Come to security. Come to security. God is great. God is great. There is no god but God." Thus the muezzin, calling the faithful to prayer. "Take me out of the anarchy in which my soul lies," prayed Newman. And Pusey: "Lift up my soul above the weary round of harassing thoughts to thy Eternal presence . . . that there I may breathe freely, there be at rest from myself and from all things that weary me and thence return arrayed with Thy peace. . . ."

The spirit of these supplications suggests another possible answer to our question as to why men seek complete legal certainty: perhaps this search is but one aspect of the religious impulse. For observe the nature of that impulse. "The gods," writes a wise student of religion, "the gods pass across the stage of history in forms innumerable: one note of pathos dominates the drama, man's longing for support, security, companionship and help from the environing universe."[1] Men, whatever their activities, recurrently ask to be safe, to be sure, to be free of undue strain. In all departments of life, not in law only, they want peace, comfort, protection from the dangers of the unknown; they long to have the universe friendly, controllable, definite and knowable. And the conviction that it is possible to attain such security and certainty is of the essence of religion.

Thus viewing our problem, it could be said that when we speak of the longing for illusory certainty in law, we are unwarrantably narrowing a more generic truth. Man, we might conceivably say, driven by fear of the vague-nesses, the chanciness of life, has need of rest. Finding life distracting, unsettling, fatiguing, he tries to run away from unknown hazards. He strives to rise above the struggle for existence, to be rid of all upsetting shifts and changes and novelties. Whether that serenity is practically attainable or not, he demands it. That, we might say, is his religion: *i.e.,* the belief in a universal steadfastness, in an uninterrupted connection between apparently disjunctive events, in cosmic certainty. On this basis it is arguable that in law, as everywhere else, this religious impulse is operative; it drives men to postulate a legal system touched with the divine spirit and therefore free of the indefinite, the arbitrary and the capricious.

The history of law can be made to lend plausibility to such a conjecture. It can be urged that in primitive and ancient times law and religion were virtually one; that, to the early Greeks, for instance, "law was nothing more than one phase of religion";[2] that, in terms of its social origins, law is a gift of the gods.

Notably, too, it was just when law was most closely identified with religion and most dominated by the belief in its divine origin that men apparently made the greatest effort to procure the most detailed and exhaustive laws. Among the primitive Germans, the period when law seemed merely a constituent part of religion was, too, the period of strict formalism in law, dominated by an almost fanatical effort to procure the maximum of nice legal exactness. "Our forefathers," writes Heusler,[3] "desired to be able, themselves, to measure accurately their expectations before going into court; they desired to know all factors out of which judicial discretion was to be constructed, in order that a trial might not be, as today, a lottery where one has an equal chance to win or lose." Folk-law, when law and religion were identical, contained an "extraordinary minuteness and detail of crimes and their amercements; . . . the primitive German who had a splinter of bone knocked out of his cranium wanted to know the result before he went into a lawsuit, and the folk-law told him exactly what he would get if the splinter made a sound thrown against a shield at a distance of twelve feet. There was no room for judicial abberation or discretion."[1]

Shall we conclude, then, that the relation between religion and the demand for excessive legal exactness is clearly established? Is the explanation of the legal-certainty illusion to be found in the religious origins of law? Shall we decide that the contemporary desire for too much definiteness and predictability in law is a "survival" of the earlier identification of law and religion?

If we were prepared to adopt such a thesis we would stress the fact that man once "believed that the question of right and wrong was unconditionally solved with absolute certainty by divine interpretation, so that all doubt disappeared and man bowed to the infallible decision";[4] and we would contend that, as man once thus consciously believed that the gods made him the gift of a divinely certain system of law, so man unconsciously craves that legal system today. And we would go on to argue that this continued unconscious mingling of religion and law is the source of current difficulties with the problem of legal cer-

[1] This characteristic of early Germanic law is neatly illustrated in the following extracts from the Lex Salica (circa 400 A.D.):

"If three men carry off a freeborn girl, they shall be compelled to pay 30 shillings.

"If there are more than three, each one shall pay 5 shillings.

"Those who have been present with boats shall be sentenced to 3 shillings.

"If any person strike another on the head so that the brain appears, and the three bones which lie above the brain shall project, he shall be sentenced to 1200 denars, which makes 30 shillings.

"But if it shall have been between the ribs or in the stomach so that the wound appears and reaches to the entrails, he shall be sentenced to 1200 denars which makes 30 shillings—besides 5 shillings for the physicians' pay.

"If any one steal a suckling pig and it be proved against him, he shall be sentenced to 120 denars which makes 3 shillings.

"If any one steal a pig that can live with its mother, and it be proved on him, he shall be sentenced to 40 denars—that is one shilling. . . ."

tainty. Man, we would say, must no longer search for God in law, for law is not the place to seek religious satisfaction. We would disagree with Heusler, who thinks that some belief in the divine origin of law is essential to its continued existence. We would urge that as men have learned to separate religion and science, leaving the latter to its own devices, so they must learn not to let religion interfere with law; that so far as the administration of justice is concerned, there must be a twilight of the gods; that law cannot function at its best if it must still also in some degree do the work of religion; that we must master the wisdom of refusing to render unto God the things that are Caesar's.

But, without denying all value to such a solution of our problem, we can at once observe its insufficiency. The close and avowed relation of law to religion is a matter of the distant past. The legal profession has long since been split off from the priesthood. To speak of the longing for unattainable legal exactness as due to a "survival" of the bygone domination of law by religion is to be betrayed by word-magic. The word "survival" implies that ancient and obsolete group attitudes, although without present meaning, continue inertly to express themselves. The term "survival," after all, is a metaphor which has acquired false worth from the physiological analogy of vestigial organs—and we must beware of employing such physiological analogies too rigorously in so complex a field as law. When one is seeking an explanation of contemporary social attitudes, a so-called "survival" may be suspected to indicate the existence of some undiscovered or unconscious present meaning, of some concealed contemporary needs or aims, be they conscious or unconscious.[5]

In the preceding chapters we have suggested that one cause of the longing for excessive legal certainty in modern times is the operation of a "force" which acted powerfully in the past and acts powerfully now. It would go to confirm the validity of our thesis if the "force" we have selected for emphasis could be shown to be related to the so-called religious impulse.

We recall again that it could be said as truthfully at any time in the past as it can be said today: society is made up of persons who now are or recently have been children. We recall, too, that, while the persistence of the childish desire to recapture or recreate a father-controlled world has been little observed in its effect on law, the effect of this desire on religion is almost a platitude.

"There exists," writes Flügel, in his study of the family, "a close and obvious correspondence between the attitude of the young child towards his parents and that of man towards the superhuman powers which he personifies as God, the Divine Father." Pertinent here is Schleiermacher's famous definition of religion as a sense of infinite dependence upon God. This definition has been enlarged on by later critics. "It is," writes Menzies,[6]

"his inability to help himself or to supply his own needs that send the worshipper to his god, who has a power he himself has not. . . . Where the sense of need has sent a human being to hold intercourse with a higher power, there . . . religion is making its appearance. . . . At all states of his existence, the world of which man is aware outside him, and the world of feelings and desires within him are in conflict. But the conviction lives within him that in some way they can be brought into harmony, and that a power exists which rules in both these discordant realms and in which, if he can identify himself with it, he will also escape from their discord." The discrepancy between what primitive man "wanted and what the world would give him, between the inner man, so full of desires and plans, and that outward nature which denied him his desires, thwarted his plans and before which he felt so feeble and insecure"—this discrepancy drove him, "if this life was to go on at all on any tolerable basis, to believe in something that had to do with the world outside him and with the world of his heart, in a being which both had sympathy with his desires and power to give effect to them outwardly."

Perhaps this is not an accurate description of the way all primitive men reacted. But it is an adequate picture of a phenomenon daily observable in civilized communities. It is the child, without doubt, who finds that the outside world and the world of feelings and desires within him are often in conflict, who has a conviction that in some way they can be brought into harmony through the aid of someone more powerful than himself. When the child is thwarted in his plans, when he feels himself feeble and insecure, does he not turn to his parents who sympathize with his desires, and, so the young child believes, have power to give effect to them outwardly?

Menzies, indeed, describing the relation of the worshiper to the higher power (whom he "worships from a sense of need" and "whom he conceives, no doubt, after his own likeness, but nevertheless as greater than he is") compares this relation to that "between a parent and a child." And G. B. Foster, speaking of the "old and original . . . gods that fear created," characterizes primitive man, in the words of Tennyson, as an "infant crying in the night, an infant crying for the light and with no language but a cry."

"The essence of the religious emotion is a mingling *sui generis* of love and of fear which one can call respect," says Piaget. "Now this respect is not to be explained except by the relations of the child with its parents. It is the filial sentiment itself. . . . The child in extreme youth is driven to endow its parents with all those attributes which theological doctrines assign to their divinities—sanctity, supreme power, omniscience, eternity, and even ubiquity. . . . It is a common observation that babies attribute to their parents complete virtue. . . . Such then seems to be the starting-point of the filial emotion—that parents are gods. M. Bovet has very justly remarked in this connection how the notion of God, when imposed in the early stages of education, is useless and embarrassing. Insistence on divine perfection means setting up in God a rival to the parents, and M. Bovet has quoted some very curious facts to illustrate this point. If, on the other hand, such insistence is not made and the child is left to his spontaneous conceptions he finds nothing very sacred about God. He is just a man like anyone else, who lives in the clouds or in the sky, but who, with this exception, is no different from the rest. . . . Then comes the crisis. There is necessarily a limit to this deification of the parents. M. Bovet says: For a long while the existence of this rationalistic and philosophical period round about the sixth year has been affirmed; it is generally put forward as an *awakening* of intellectual curiosity; we believe it should be regarded rather as a *crisis*, intellectual and moral at the same time, similar in many ways to that of adolescence. The consequences of such a phenomenon are evident. The feelings experienced by the child up till now towards his parents must be directed elsewhere, and it is at this period that they are transferred to the God with which his education has provided him. *It has been said that the child 'divinifies' his parents. M. Bovet retorts with reason that it can better be said that he 'paternalizes' God at the moment when he ceases to regard his parents as perfect."*

Many other writers have called attention to the significance of the paternal attributes of God who is hailed as "Our Father Who Art in Heaven." E. H. Martin is typical:

"When the growing youth about the time of adolescence finds himself a new being, face to face with a new and wider environment, with new tasks and duties and dangers to face, it is natural that he should strive so far as possible to meet the new situation in habitual ways. The youth needs security. He wishes to feel at home in the new situations into which he has suddenly grown. He, therefore, strives to conceive of the world as an *imaginary family affair*, and regains the feeling of security by constructing an *imaginary father* who will be to this larger family what the actual father was in the circle of his childhood experiences."[2]

[2] Leuba quotes a mystic who reported the following as the essence of the mystic trance: *"The world suddenly seemed like one big family, taking away somewhat one's loneliness."* Cf. Edwyn Bevan's suggestion that men are seeking a psychic kinship with a "Friend behind phenomena": see Otto, loc. cit., 285–297. See Freud, "The Future of an Illusion."

Even the relatively sophisticated current reinterpretations of religion so "view the vast cosmic process of which man is so tiny a segment, as to engender some degree of *at homeness* . . ." says

Of course the child's social environment will affect the form which these childish notions will take. So it follows that, to the extent that theology remains crudely anthropomorphic, the Father in Heaven is likely to absorb a large measure of the attributes originally ascribed by the child to his earthly father. In the anthropomorphic period of social development, law-giving, law-making, the punishing of misdeeds, which the child first conceived as parts of the father's function, become parts of God's function, and law then derives its authority from the father-God.

But when society relinquishes the cruder forms of the anthropomorphic God-concept (due to increased critical knowledge of the character of the universe) not only do the father-substitutes become less obvious and more disguised and abstract in form,[7] but the unconscious yearning for the father seems to seek more directly other channels than religion. Then the carry-over to the law of the "legal" characteristics of the childish father-image becomes less and less roundabout. Finally, as in our times, the longing for a father-who-lays-down-the-law (for the Father-as-Judge) can "short-circuit" the Heavenly Father. No longer, mediately as a derivative of religion, but now immediately, the Law is looked to as a substitute for the infallible Father-Judge of childhood.[8] The law is "paternalized," not "divinified."

We would seem more or less justified, then, in asserting that, not to the survival of a period when law was dominated by a belief in its religious or divine origin, but to a more powerful and still operative influence, underlying both law and religion, is to be ascribed the continued craving for excessive legal stability. Not in religion as

Witcraft, "A Critical Analysis of the Theory That Theism is Essential to Moral Motivation." C. A. Beckwith, in a recent book on "The Idea of God," puts it this way: "We need to know that at the heart of things is a steadfast, righteous, almighty *Will* which tolerates no deviation from its rigid way, but sometimes violently arrests the transgressor and tenderly draws him back into the paths of peace."

such, but in undisposed of childish longings for a father-substitute, longings which play their part in religion as in law,[9] we must seek one of the important causes of the basic legal illusion.[10]

Part Two

THE BASIC MYTH, AND CERTAIN
BRILLIANT LEGAL THINKERS

CHAPTER I

DEAN ROSCOE POUND AND THE SEARCH FOR LEGAL CERTAINTY

American jurisprudence will ever be indebted to Roscoe Pound. In the service of quickening our legal institutions and making the law effective for the task of wise "social engineering," he has combined profound insight, vast legal erudition, thorough acquaintance with the work of early and contemporary legal philosophers in England and the Continent, and a wide knowledge of the social sciences. And, in particular, any student interested in the problem to which this essay has been devoted, must be thankful to Pound for the light he has thrown on various phases of the strange quest of legal certainty.[1]

Not the least of his accomplishments has been the exposure of the evil consequences of the theory of mechanical jurisprudence. Seemingly, he is unalterably opposed to regarding the judges' function as nothing more than that of applying "to an ascertained set of facts a rigidly defined legal formula definitely prescribed as such or exactly deduced from authoritatively prescribed premises."[1]

And yet anything more than a casual reading of Pound discloses the fact that he drastically circumscribes his criticism of such a slot-machine theory of judicial administration. He advocates—no one more enthusiastically—that judges should knowingly use wide discretion, should recognize unique circumstances, should employ flexible stand-

[1] See Appendix IV for further discussion of some of Pound's views.

ards as opposed to fixed rules, and should be encouraged to a "free judicial finding of the grounds of decision"; that "certainty attained by mechanical application of fixed rules to human conduct has always been illusory" is his excellent summing up of the futility of the search for juristic certainty and completeness.[1] But flexibility must, one gathers, be confined to limited portions of the law. It is all well enough when questions of "human conduct" are at issue. The situation is different when "property" or "commercial or business transactions and contracts" are under consideration or when the courts are dealing with "commercial law and the creation, incidence and transfer of obligations." Then, Pound seems to say, the judge should employ rules "authoritatively prescribed in advance and mechanically applied." We must thus "insure the certainty required for the economic order." In these portions of the law the general elements (as distinguished from the unique circumstances of the particular case) are decisive. There we can and should cut down the margin of discretion, and apply rules of "general and absolute application." The ideal of stability, rigidity and certainty is apparently "appropriate to property and commercial transactions." Pound's position seems to be that "the social interests in security of acquisitions and security of transactions—the economic side of human activity in civilized society—call for rule or conception authoritatively prescribed in advance and mechanically applied."

So he apparently believes that in what is perhaps the larger portion of "the field of the legal order," there is fully justified, as a good, hard-headed, realistic and realizable demand, the ancient hankering for something definite and absolute. There, seemingly, the "point of view of strict (Germanic) society" with rules "wholly inelastic and inflexible," the Puritan requirement of fixed, unyielding impersonal rule, and the pioneer's "insistence upon the exact working out of" precise formulas can find their undisturbed consummation.[2]

---

[2] See Appendix IV with reference to Pound's analysis of the legal attitudes of the early Germans, the Puritan and the Pioneer.

Pound, that is, would apparently have men "learn to partition the field of the legal order" substantially as follows:

(1) In one partition there should be placed cases relating to "property" and "commercial or business transactions." (In such cases, presumably, the courts should employ judicial slot-machines, the facts being inserted in one end of the machine and the decision, through the use of mechanical logic, coming out at the other end.)

(2) In the other partition we are to place cases raising problems of "human conduct" or involving "the conduct of enterprise" or fraud, good faith, negligence, or fiduciary duties. There thoroughly non-mechanical methods may be utilized by the judges. Thus, for example, "no two cases of negligence have been alike or ever will be." And says Pound in effect, do what you will, courts, in such circumstances, somehow or other pay attention to the uniqueness of the particular case. Regardless of fixed rules, in dealing with "human-conduct" controversies, courts will not and cannot forget that they are administering justice. Absolute certainty, even when desired, has proved impossible when "human conduct" is at issue.

The success of thus dividing the field according to Pound's plan will, then, depend on the possibility of clearly distinguishing between "business transactions" and "human conduct," for apparently it is only where the latter is involved that slot-machine justice should be taboo. To Pound such a division seems easy. Property cases appear to him to be neatly separable from human conduct or good-faith cases.

But are they separable? Is it true, as Pound asserts, that "every fee simple is like every other," that "there is nothing unique in a bill of exchange," while "no two cases of negligence have been or ever will be alike"? Fee simples (interests in real estate) or bills of exchange often come before the courts owned or claimed by men who have been negligent or deceitful. An examination of the facts of a case relating to business transactions often reveals that the case is *sui generis*.

We are, in this theory of Pound's, facing a remnant of the scholastic tendency to treat abstractions as independent entities. The medical profession is certainly learning the dangers of such an approach to patients. Dr. William A. White[2] criticizes the method by which symptoms are classified "under various headings, but almost altogether as separate and distinct affairs out of relation with any particular patient who may have manifested them. It is a method with which we are familiar. The fever curve of typhoid fever is discussed entirely apart from any particular patient, the variations which it may show are recorded and charted as a separate entity." White adds that from now on the development of psychiatry will "have much more to say about the human problem involved in each particular patient and that symptoms" will "be considered . . . in their settings. . . ." And Dr. F. G. Crookshank has exposed the vice of considering diseases as "Platonic realities" or "morbid entities" having an objective existence apart from the persons affected, rather than as convenient groupings of like cases, groupings liable at any moment to supersession or adjustment.[3]

Pound himself has observed the parallel of legal and medical treatment. "It is no more possible to treat negligence in the abstract than rheumatism in the abstract," he says.[3] But while he states that legal abstractions, like medical abstractions, are "vain as anything more than organizings . . . of experience when applied to the indi-

---

[3] "Science and Health," in "Science and Civilization," edited by F. S. Marven. See also Crookshank's appendix on "Language and Medicine," to the "Meaning of Meaning," by Ogden and Richards, 510. Crookshank there writes, "Diagnosis, which, as Mr. Bernard Shaw has somewhere declared, should mean the finding out of all there is wrong with a particular patient and why, has come to mean in practice the formal unctuous pronunciation of a Name that is deemed appropriate and absolves from the necessity of further investigation. And, in the long run, an acute appreciation of a patient's 'present state' is often treated as ignorant because it is incompatible with sincere use of one of the verbal symbols available to us as Proper Names for Special Diseases." Cf. Singer on "Medicine," in "The Legacy of Greece," 201, 213.

vidual human life" and that types of controversy should
not be isolated and standardized "out of their concrete
setting," his position seems to be that suits which involve
"the legal securing of interests of substances, where cases
are alike and the economic order admits of no individualization," are the proper subject of just such standardizing.

But life does not so nicely, as Pound assumes, divide
itself into cases of "individual human lives" and cases of
"interests of substances."[4] "Human conduct" and "the
security of acquisitions" do not come in neat and separate
bundles. The "social interest in the security of transactions" inevitably becomes entangled with "the social interest in the individual claim to free self-assertion." Which
technique is then to govern, that of individualization or
that of authoritative conceptions prescribed in advance
and mechanically applied? Is the judge to look at the legal
patient clinically or to treat as an entity the legal symptoms?

Pound suggests that his apportionment of the field between (rigid) rule and (flexible) discretion "has its basis
in the respective fields of intelligence and intuition" and
applies Bergson's differentiation. Bergson sees intelligence
as more adapted to the inorganic; it deals with "matter"
and treats experience as if it were static; it has the "power
of grasping the general element in a situation and relating it to past situations." Intuition, on the other hand,
deals with life, with the flux aspect of experience; it has
a "perfect mastery of a special situation," stressing its
uniqueness. And so, apparently, we may differentiate between the law in relation to property or commercial transactions and the law in relation to the conduct of human
beings, treating the first with stress on "intelligence"—
which works mechanically and therefore produces ma-
chine-made legal products—and the second with stress on

[4] In espousing this artificial division Pound is doing his best to
make the law, in part, safe for Bealism. Passing strange, for Pound
has done much to call attention to the difference between "law in
books" and "law in action."

"intuition"—which works with specialized skill and therefore produces hand-made legal products.

This comparison is enlightening. It shows Pound viewing property and commercial transactions as if they were divorced from human relations, as if they were inert, lifeless, and to be dealt with just as the static (Bergsonian) intelligence deals with "matter." But surely property and commercial transactions are not lifeless entities which of their own motion come into court. They are brought there by human needs and hopes and fears and desires.[5]

There seems to be in this differentiation what Holmes would call "delusive exactness."[4] Or, to quote him perhaps more appositely, there is here a need "to think things instead of words."[5] Pound gives his case away when he admits that where "human conduct" or "the conduct of enterprises" is involved, we can afford to trust to "the trained intuition and disciplined judgment of the judge" and allow "administrative justice."[6] But all legal con-

---

[5] "Individualization" of controversies, treating them clinically, of course, may introduce annoying doubt and subject the judge to strain in reaching a conclusion. This was the experience of Gilbert's policemen who sang:

> "When a felon's not engaged in his employment,
>   Or maturing his felonious little plans,
> His capacity for innocent enjoyment
>   Is just as great as any honest man's.
> Our feelings we with difficulty smother
>   When constabulary duty's to be done.
> Ah, take one consideration with another,
>   The policeman's lot is not a happy one.
>
> When the enterprising burglar's not a-burgling,
>   When the cut-throat isn't occupied in crime,
> He loves to hear the little brook a-gurgling,
>   And listen to the merry village chime.
> When the coster's finished jumping on his mother,
>   He loves to be a-basking in the sun.
> Ah, take one consideration with another,
>   The policeman's lot is not a happy one."

Compare Dewey, "Human Nature and Conduct," 240–3; Cardozo, "Paradoxes of Legal Science," 79.

troversies, in last analysis, contain some portion of "human conduct." That Pound's division is irrational and difficult to maintain, even verbally, is disclosed in his balancing against "human conduct" what he terms "the economic side of human activity"; that these two phrases are not antithetical but hopelessly overlap becomes obvious, when, in the latter phrase, one notes the words "human activity."[6]

Pound's attempt to narrow the scope of judicial discretion is thus patently based upon an artificial scheme. In all phases of law there are applicable the words which he would apply to only a limited portion: "The trained intuition and disciplined judgment of the judge must be our assurance that causes will be decided on principles of reason and not according to the chance dictates of caprice."[7]

Pound errs, that is, in too sharply differentiating between (a) one department of law which requires the application of abstract rules and (b) another department which calls for the just and painstaking study of the novel facts of the particular case. This as we have seen, is an unreal dichotomy. Every case presents the question of the extent to which the judge should adhere to settled precedents as against flexible modification of the precedents. There must be gradations and degrees of fixity and flexibility.[8]

Where what Pound calls the "economic side of human activity" is the paramount issue in a case, one grants that there may be greater justification for closely adhering to the precedents. Yet even there the judge should not feel obliged to use rigid rules.[7]

[6] Pound thus comes, at times, dangerously close to adopting the old fallacy of treating as real the dichotomy of "rights" into "rights against persons" and "rights in things." Of course all "rights in things" are "rights" with respect to other persons and therefore involve "human activity."

[7] Pound's classification is a sort of elaboration of the traditional division of rules of law into "rules of property" and other rules. Rules of property, the courts are wont to say, are peculiarly sacro-

We may say, then, that the social interest in the security of property will not, to the extent indicated by Pound, save, or justify as an objective, the age-old phantasy of complete legal certainty to be obtained from authoritative rules mechanically applied.[8]

---

sanct; they must be followed, however unjust, because, presumably, men have acted in reliance on them. But, in concrete application, the courts have found it difficult to determine just what rules are rules of property. (The writer expects in the near future to attempt an explanation of this difficulty.)

Also, one rule of property on which Jones presumably has relied collides with another rule of property on which Robinson presumably has relied or still a third on which Smith presumably has relied.

What is more, the "presumed reliance" is often mythical. When a judge desires or feels obliged to apply an unjust but well established rule of property, he "presumes" that it must have been acted upon. He speaks of "the confusion, entanglements and even suffering" which would "presumably" ensue if he over-ruled the earlier decision, of the "property to the amount of millions of dollars which may depend" upon its being re-affirmed. *But in thus "presuming," the judge is not referring to any known facts of actual life. He has no proof of the public reliance by which he justifies his adherence to the earlier unjust ruling. Actual proof of such reliance is dispensed with.* "It is not," says Black, "to be determined by the production of evidence, but by the weighing of presumptions. It is neither necessary nor proper to bring to the attention of the court specific instances" (of reliance on the rules). Now if it be true that the only reason why a judge adheres to what he considers an unjust or mistaken decision is "to avoid the inevitable injury to the rights of innocent persons" who "presumably" have acted upon it, would it not be sensible for the judge to find out, before doing injustice on this basis, whether this presumed reliance is a fact? But this the judges never do.

[8] Pound has never completely freed himself of rule-fetishism. Not only does he try to preserve one portion of the law for mechanical jurisprudence, but he over-emphasizes, now and again, even in the realm of discretion, the importance of the generalized aspect of decisions. Where rules do not work, such things as "standards" are nevertheless in order, he believes. But "standards," as he defines them, are little more than "safety-valve" concepts, so vague as to be meaningless. He calls them "legally defined measures of conduct," giving as examples "due care," "reasonable service," "due process."

Despite their vagueness, such phrases have, for Pound appar-

Pound, who thus decries the slot-machine theory of administering justice and yet tries to justify it in an extensive portion of the law, in the same way deplores the use of the myth of "no judge-made law" and yet defends it. The vice of pretending that judges never create but merely discover preëxisting rules of law is, he writes, that sooner or later men will

"insist upon knowing where the pre-existing rule was to be found before the judges discovered and applied it, in what form it existed and how and whence it derived its form and obtained its authority. And when, as a result of such inquiries, the rule seems to have sprung full-fledged from the judicial head, the assumption that the judicial function is one of interpretation and application only leads to the conclusion that the courts are exercising a usurped authority. The true conclusion is, rather, that our political theory of the nature of the judicial function is unsound. It was never truly the common law theory. In its origin it is a fiction, born in periods of absolute and unchangeable law. . . . Today, when all recognize, nay insist, that legal systems do and must grow, that legal principles are not absolute, but are relative to time and place, and that juridical idealism may go no further than the ideals of an epoch, *the fiction should be discarded.*"[9]

And yet, elsewhere, we find Pound, without recognition of any inconsistency, praising and defending as socially valuable the very "fiction"[10] which, in the above passage, he has severely criticized:

"Thus, the propositions that a judicial decision is only evidence of the law, *the doctrine that judges always find the law and never make it, are not without an important purpose,*" he writes. "They grow out of a sound instinct of judges and lawyers for maintaining a paramount social interest. They serve to safeguard the social interest in the general security by requiring the grounds of judicial decision to be as definite as

---

ently, an emotional value because of their generality. They are, it may fairly be said, "emotional abstractions," contentless categories, dematerialized terms with "affective resonance." As we have seen, the significance of such elastic words is that they are compensatory. See further, the discussion of Dickinson in Appendix II.

is compatible with the attainment of justice in results. They serve to make *judicial action predictable so far as may be*."[9]

And so again we find Pound aware of the judicial realities, yet reluctant to relinquish entirely the age-old legal myths.

What does it mean that a thinker like Pound is unable to make up his mind, seeming to range himself on two opposing sides of these several questions?[11] Why does he denounce the dogma of "no judge-made law" and yet try to preserve it? Why does he expose the folly of mechanical jurisprudence and yet wish to keep in action a considerable measure of it?[10]

[9] "Law and Morals," (2d) 48. This second view is not unlike that expressed by Mitchell, viz: that judicial law-making will be more easily accomplished if made "less noticeable both to the world and to the judges themselves." See above, Part One, Chapter III.

No one knows better than Pound that the refusal to admit the reality of judicial legislation does not improve the process. The "no judge-made law" myth does not "serve to make judicial action predictable so far as may be." It serves only to make it seem more predictable than it can be—and, indeed, less predictable than it could be if it were not conducted in the intellectual semi-darkness created by that very myth.

[10] The criticism above of Dean Pound's partitioning of "the field of the legal order" and the mechanical application of rules in that portion of the field relating to property and commercial law is, of course, based upon the writer's interpretation of Dean Pound's writings. Whether that interpretation is justified, the reader can determine for himself by turning to the following: 36 Harvard Law Review 825, 945, 951, 957; "An Introduction to the Philosophy of Law," 139–143. It will perhaps be sufficient to quote the following from Pound's "Interpretations of Legal History," page 154:

"In matters of property and commercial law, where the economic forms of the social interest in the general security—security of acquisitions and security of transactions—are controlling, *mechanical application of fixed, detailed rules* or of rigid deductions from fixed conceptions is a wise social engineering. Our economically organized society postulates certainty and predictability as to the incidents and consequences of industrial undertakings and commercial transactions extending over long periods. *Individualization of application and standards* that regard the individual circumstances of each case *are out of place here*. In Bergsonian phrase we are here

Before answering these questions it will be well briefly to consider the attitides towards legal certainty of some other penetrating thinkers.

---

in the proper field of intelligence, characterized by its power of 'grasping the general element in a situation and relating it to past situations.' For the general element in its relation to past situations is the significant thing in securing interests of substance, that is, in the law of property and in commercial law. The circumstances of the particular case cannot be suffered to determine the quality of estates in land nor the negotiability of promissory notes. One fee simple is like another. Every promissory note is like every other. *Mechanical application of rules as a mere repetition precludes the tendency to individualization which would threaten the security of acquisitions and the security of transactions.*"

CHAPTER II

JHERING AND THE KINGDOM OF JUSTICE ON EARTH

"Law as Means to an End," the work of the great German jurist, Jhering, is a book that has had a profound influence on important legal thinkers is this country; it is one of the landmarks of nineteenth-century jurisprudence. As the title of this work suggests, Jhering believed that law should be pliant and deliberately purposive, that it should be consciously used as a means to desired social results.

Such a view of the function of law as a developing and adjustable body of doctrine would appear to implicate an entire denial of the possibility of legal exactness. But the reader is puzzled by a confusion in Jhering's thinking on that subject:

(1) On the one hand his notable contribution was his emphasis on the "freedom of adaptability of law to an end"; he ridiculed the absurdity of trying to create "detailed regulations for every case, juristic recipes for the decision of all possible law-suits" and "the impossibility of seeing before-hand the infinite variety and manifold formation of cases" or of making "the application of the law a purely mechanical thing, in which juridical thinking should be made superfluous by the law."

(2) And yet he urged that the judiciary, as distinguished from the legislative and the executive branches of government, be subject to the "idea of constraint." The difference between the executive and the judiciary is that the judge, as distinguished from the executive, is "expected to

be guided *exclusively* by the law, and this requirement makes it necessary that the law should be fixed with the greatest possible completeness and precision." The great value of the segregation of the judiciary as a distinct branch of state activity is, he wrote, that "it means the retirement of the law into itself for the purpose of solving its problems with security and completeness."

So that although Jhering believed that the law should deal realistically with differences between individuals,[1] yet he was at times apparently opposed to the individualization of controversies. Thus he wrote that, to the ideal judge "the parties litigant are not definite individuals" but "abstract persons in the mask of plaintiff and defendant. . . . Abstraction from all concrete accessories; elevations of the concrete case to the height of the abstract situation as decided in the law, treatment of the case in the manner of an example in arithmetic where it is immaterial what is numbered, whether it be ounces or pounds, dollars or cents—is what characterizes the true judge."

And in a striking passage he stated his ideal of the administration of justice:

"If justice could descend from heaven and take a pencil in its hand to write down the law with such definiteness, precision and detail that its application should become a work of mechanical routine, nothing more perfect could be conceived for the administration of justice, and the kingdom of justice would be complete upon earth."

One senses, in reading Jhering, a struggle between two inconsistent attitudes, a conflict between a marked sensitiveness to objective reality and a powerful drive for satisfaction of purely subjective emotional needs. Is it not indeed passing strange that so ardent a champion of the use of law as an adaptable instrument should at times posit

[1] "The law is unjust which imposes the same burdens upon the poor as upon the rich; for it then ignores the difference in the ability to perform. . . . The law is unjust which treats the person of unsound mind like him of sound mind."

as an ideal the maximum of mechanical legal certainty? Even if Jhering were silent as to the basis of his views, one would be tempted to guess that he was only partially cured of his childish longings, that he was sometimes lured on by the hope of rediscovering the father-judge in the law, that his ideal of judicial administration had its genesis in the father-child relation.

But there is no need for conjecture. For in a few words he has stated his own notion of the close connection between familial postures and attitudes towards law:

"The master of the house," he wrote, "who establishes the family must have authority in the house, if it is to remain; and nature herself has indicated this position for him in its essential outlines—in relation to his wife, by the superiority of his physical strength and by the greater amount of work which falls to his share—*in relation to his children by the helplessness and dependence in which they are for years,—the influence of which, even after they are grown up, remains in the same relation in which it was formed during that period.* Thus nature itself has determined that family relation to be one of superiority and subordination; and in making every man without exception pass through the latter relation, has provided that no one shall enter society who has not learned the *lesson of superiority and subordination* upon which the existence of the state depends. *The family is for every man the preparatory school to the state;* for many nations, as is well known, it was even the model of the latter (Patriarchal State)."

This statement, slightly revised, is in form not unlike our thesis: The family is for every man a preparatory school for the law. But Jhering praises where we would deplore. That the influence of the father on the child (with its lesson of subordination based upon the child's helplessness and dependence) actively affects the attitudes of men in later life with respect to law—so far his views and ours concur. But the significant fact is that to Jhering this continued dependence on quasi-father authority is a virtue—a significant fact because it justifies our surmise that Jhering is himself a victim of childlike hankerings for a father-substitute when he pictures as the kingdom of justice on earth a body of law, definite, precise and detailed, which the courts would apply with mechanical routine.

We would be justified in carrying our surmise a bit further: Jhering apparently is seeking, childlike, an unearthly security; wanting inner peace, he postulates as ideal a law that shall be unswerving and altogether certain even though this ideal is at variance with his insistence on the adaptability of law to changing ends. Again our surmise is confirmed by Jhering's own words; in the following self-revelatory passage he gives his analysis of the psychological roots of his desire for legal certainty:

"For the development of character man needs from the beginning the feeling of security; and this man possesses through the law. Man on the law is as firm and unshaken in his confidence in it as the believer in his confidence in God, Or, more precisely, both of them put their trust not merely in something outside of them, but rather they feel God and the law within them as the firm ground of their existence, and as a living part of themselves, which therefore no power on earth can deprive them of but can only destroy in and with them. This is in both of them the source of their power. The anxiety of the ego in the world which is the natural feeling of the animated atom thrown upon itself, is removed with trust in the higher power which supports it. It feels the power within itself and itself in the power. In place of anxiety and fear develops a firm, immovable sense of security. An immovable sense of security: that is, in my opinion, the correct expression for the state of mind which law and religion produce in man when they correspond to the ideas we form of them.[11]

"The security which these two grant is at the same time dependence. There is no contradiction in this, for security is not independence—there is no such for man—but legal dependence. But dependence is the reverse side, security the obverse.

"Therefore I cannot accept the well known definition of Schleiermacher, who defines religion as the feeling of dependence upon God, for it makes the reverse side the face. It may be suitable for that stage in the development of the religious sense which corresponds to the stage of despotism in the history of law—here the feeling of dependence correctly designates the relation but it does not hold for the final conclusion of the development.

"This final conclusion consists, in religion as well as in law, in the fact that the feeling of security overcomes the feeling of dependence. In this sense, therefore, *i.e.*, from the psychological standpoint, law may be defined as the feeling of security in the State; and religion, as the feeling of security in God."

Recall, now, that Jhering considered that the child's helplessness and dependence on the father creates the subordination-superiority attitude of the child-father relation; and that this subordination attitude, surviving childhood, constitutes the pattern for the relation of man to the State. It is, then, not difficult to discern the true character of Jhering's mental processes when, at times, he seeks maximal clarity and certainty in law. It may be described thus:

Father-child means superiority-subordination (because of the child's helplessness and dependence). There results a feeling of dependence which persists in adult years and is relieved by substituting therefor an immovable sense of security, not only in God, but in the law. The consequence, in relation to law, is an ideal of Justice descending from heaven to write down the legal rules with such detailed completeness and absolute finality that their application by the judges becomes a work of mechanical routine.

Undue prolongation of emotional infancy, a childish dependence on a father-substitute—almost confessedly Jhering finds there the reason for his own desire, as a man, for an immovable sense of legal security. And that desire for an immovable sense of security to be attained through the law (although it was totally at odds with his recognition of the necessity for and social value of legal adaptability) led Jhering, now and again, to worship an illusory ideal of absolute legal certainty and finality. Jhering as a man apparently was still not altogether free of the spell of his childhood subordination to father authority. The law served for him, in part, a subjective function: the satisfaction of a lingering eagerness for an omnipotent father-judge.

CHAPTER III

DEMOGUE'S BELIEF IN THE IMPORTANCE OF DELUDING THE PUBLIC

Demogue, a great contemporary French jurist, cuts under the conventional statement of an antithesis between the demand for legal security and the demand for legal change.[1] The conflict, of which Roscoe Pound makes so much, is, according to Demogue, a conflict between demands for two different kinds of security. He discloses the ambiguity of the phrase "legal security."

There is, first, a conception of security which emphasizes the *status quo*. This conception of security favors a lasting situation. It centers about the notion that a person should not be deprived of his existing rights without his consent. It is conservative in a very literal sense. This is *static* security.

But often when we speak of legal security, we are referring to law designed to promote business activity. Typical of this kind of security is the notion that one shall be protected if one deals with a person who has the *appearance* of being the owner of property, provided one has relied in good faith on this appearance. The purpose of such a notion is to make transactions easier. "The security thus assured is a leaven of activity, a bounty given to active individuals." It is, says Demogue, in the spirit of Western European law and Americanism. Because it incites to action, he terms it *dynamic* security.

Static and dynamic security appear to be ever at war. "We see the idea of security turning against itself. Shall we prefer the security of owners of rights or of those who acquire them?"

Suppose that in good faith I buy a negotiable bond payable to bearer from a man who appears to be the owner. Later it turns out that my seller had merely found the bond which "the real owner" had lost. The law protects me and the loser of the bond cannot recover the bond, or its value from me. Dynamic security has triumphed and I am the gainer thereby.

But now that I am the lawful owner of the bond, I want to keep it secure. I give it to my agent for safe-keeping. I want, that is, *static* security. The agent is dishonest and sells the bond to a third person who buys it in good faith believing my agent to be the real owner. I have no redress against the third person. For now his dynamic security has overcome my static security. If the law "favors me when I acquire an instrument to bearer, from one not the owner, it becomes a menace when I confide that instrument to a banker or depositary who may sell it."[1]

The conflict between dynamic and static security to some extent has been mitigated and more can be done in effecting a reconciliation—as for instance by insurance. But Demogue concludes that no complete resolution of this conflict will ever be realized.

The illusory character of Pound's belief that it is an easy task "to insure the certainty required for the economic order" becomes more than ever clear when we are armed with Demogue's analysis. Pound, as we have seen, suggests that we set aside in one separate tract the law dealing with "the security of transactions," "the security of acquisitions," "property," "commercial or business transactions," and the "creation, incidents and transfer of obligations." In this province (where we are dealing with

---

[1] The client who today wants static security, tomorrow wants dynamic security. Putting it differently, the client who today wants an instrument drawn which will inflexibly control the conduct of certain persons, tomorrow wants that instrument interpreted so as to permit of flexible adjustment. But when he comes to formulate, in generalized terms, his views as to what constitutes an ideal system of law, he usually remembers only the first type of want and asks for a static legal world.

what Pound terms the "economic side of human activity in civilized society"), Pound would have the law consider human rights as if they were inert and static and employ rigid rules which are to be mechanically applied. But such simplification becomes mythical and unreal once we see with Demogue that the "economic order" is the battle-ground of dynamic and of static security.

Demogue has some subtle and disturbing thoughts on the subject of retroactive legislation:[2] It is a principle of legislation—in the United States to a large extent em-bodied in our Constitutions—that the legislature shall not enact laws affecting past conduct. Thus statutes, it is be-lieved, should not impair the obligations of contracts al-ready in existence or reduce vested property rights. The theory is that men shall be able to act in reliance upon existing law, knowing that changes thereafter made by legislative bodies will not modify the law upon which they relied. Consequently, as we said above,[3] absolute cer-tainty and predictability are not apparently endangered by new laws made by legislatures—as distinguished from new laws made by judges. New legislative law, it is cus-tomarily remarked, applies only to the future.

But, says Demogue, consider my case if I own land and refuse to buy a house offered to me at a bargain because I intend to build on my own land. Suppose a law is passed by the legislature forbidding the erection, *in the future,* of houses in the district in which my land is situated. I have been seriously injured because I relied on a state of the law as to my *future "rights"* and the law on which I relied has been changed. The conventional reply to my complaint is that the new law does not affect rights but only hopes, that my rights have not been affected; all that has happened is that certain advantages flowing from my rights have been cut off. "As if," remarks Demogue, "a right is not greatly impaired when its contents are taken away."

The point is that the customary prohibition against ret-roactivity is largely directed against impairment of static security. Demogue expresses this customary prohibition thus: "He who by virtue of an old law has acquired a certain situation . . . should keep it, even if a new law forbids such acquisitions." The theory of non-retroactivity in legislation does not usually protect dynamic security: "If I had expected to avail myself of my right to build on my land, to transform a building into a factory, I am at the mercy of a new law regulating construction, the installation of a factory, or obligations towards neighbors. I had counted on doing something under the old law; this I can no longer do, and I shall be more or less in the position of one contracting party who sees the other withdraw his promise." So that even though the statute applies only to the future it does "attack my security, for under the sway of the former law, I already had a kind of mortgage on the future."

Nor is it possible always to distinguish the one type of security from the other, "for the limit between static and dynamic security is not easy to establish. In the complexity of actual life they contain notions which separate or intertwine, according to the particular case in view. . . . The possible statute of tomorrow which may hinder or help our enterprises, while a ground of hope for some, is a direct attack on security either static or dynamic. Is it necessary to do more than state the known fact that the menace of a new tax, the submission of a bill modifying the extent of mining rights, or employers' liability, or imposing measures of preventive hygiene, makes trouble for the persons who have counted on the state of facts arising under former laws and have acted in the expectation of its continuance?"

There seems to be no adequate remedy for such hardships. To do justice in such cases it would be necessary to inquire into subjective intentions. And "such a subjective criterion cannot be applied in practice; it is too vague in extent, too delicate in application. It would also so delay the satisfaction of the need for social arrangement that it would be unfortunate on that account as well."

The notion of security, then, according to Demogue, appears to be something indefinite with only the vaguest outlines, an inadequate guide for arriving at precise legal formulations.

No one with Demogue's clear vision can, of course, have many illusions about the possibility of legal certainty. "Observation of life, essentially changeable as it is," he writes, "makes it evident that an interest so protected by law that its realization is certain is extremely rare, that a right has only more or less probability of practical realization, its force is never absolute but simply relative." The law lies "in the zone of facts arising because there are strong possibilities for them."

Demogue is keenly sensitive to the tendency in all kinds of human thinking to seek over-simplification: "The simplicity which our minds require does not appear to be the law of the exterior world. It is a proceeding for acquiring knowledge, a necessary logical mode of knowledge, a method of teaching, a means of investigation—for hypothesis is the basis of discovery. There is no proof, on the other hand, that it is the law of things. . . . Accordingly, our minds which aspire to precision and the public which demands of science formulae great and small for attainment of exact results, can never be satisfied. Such certainty is impossible."[2]

And more specifically with reference to legal thinking, he writes: "Simplification, through unity of idea and logical deduction, is a mental need which does not completely correspond to reality. . . . Facts are too divergent to be bent to conform to the nature and need of action of our minds."

Speaking of the "rather vague limits" of the law, he says: "Clearness of ideas is more a need of the mind yearning for security than a representation of the complex realities of life." And again: "The expression, 'Law,' for our short-sighted mentality, conjures up the spectre of an

[2] See Appendix III, below.

irresistible power, whose influence is increased by the fact
that we bow before it. The human mind, eager for direction, often for quiet, is easily inclined towards submission;
so the law is no longer in need of exercising force but is
peacefully obeyed, consent succeeding to coercion."

He discusses "the sentiment of false security." This sentiment, he argues, must in a measure be considered good,
for men frequently act, in a manner advantageous both to
themselves and to others, solely because they do not see
the dangers which surround them. "Too acute a perception of redoubtable realities leads to inaction." But his
clear thinking compels him to add that "false security,
however, is often most undesirable and a cause of disas-
ter"; it is "most dangerous to spread a sense of false security by seeming to give rights which are limited by an
undisclosed clause." Moreover, he believes that man has,
as opposed to his desire for security, "a certain taste for
risk. He finds in insecurity a certain joy of strife and tri-
umph. . . . Does not our European law at times lack
something of the philosophy of the 'strenuous life,' a philosophy more virile and less afraid of taking chances?"

Here then is a thinker thoroughly without illusions either as to the attainability or as to the complete desirability of legal security and certainty. He is a thinker who
is not fooling himself.

And yet we find Demogue deliberately counseling
against the disclosure to the layman of the contingent
character of law. He is willing skeptically to analyze the
fundamental legal notions for himself and to report his
analysis to his fellow-augurs. *But his is a benevolently des-
potic skepticism.* In his opinion, it is necessary that the
layman, the business man, be deceived. A false belief in
legal omnipotence has, says Demogue, a socially educat-
ing value. He quotes with approval from Tarde, "The
question is whether a certain amount of untruth and error,
of dupery and sacrifice will not always be needed for the
maintenance of social peace." It is wise to inculcate a false
sentiment of security. "Men frequently decide to act solely

because they do not see the dangers which surround them." To apprise them of the unreality of legal security might, he believes, be disastrous.

Demogue's opinion on the positive social value of legal illusion he has summed up in the following language: "On the whole it is to be desired that this ideal respect for law, although it rests at bottom on a mistake which the shrewd do not make, belief in the omnipotence of law, be developed as far as possible; that it become a sort of religion because of the resulting tranquillity and economy of social forces, for then more profitable and more effective action will be possible in other directions."[3]

[3] Plato believed that in his ideal Republic the "rulers will find considerable doses of falsehood and deceit necessary for the good for their subjects"; they were to be allowed to lie to their own citizens "for the public good."

Compare the following reflections of Pascal who believed it unwise to try to justify law on the basis of reason or justice: "That is why," he wrote, "the wisest of legislators said that it was often necessary to deceive men for their good and another, a good politician said, 'When a man does not understand the truth by which he might be freed, it is expedient that he should be deceived.' . . . *We must make it [the law] regarded as authoritative, eternal, and conceal its origin, if we do not wish that it should soon come to an end.*"

CHAPTER IV

WURZEL AND THE VALUE OF
LAY IGNORANCE

An acquaintance with Wurzel is indispensable to an understanding of the unfortunate consequences of the certainty illusion in law. No other single writer has as carefully observed the relation between the search for a legal Absolute and the peculiarities of juridical thinking. If heretofore we have expressed disagreement with some of his conclusions and dissatisfaction with the superficial character of his fundamental explanation of the perpetual quest of legal certainty, this does not mean any lack of appreciation of the value of his brilliant contribution to the subject of this essay.

Not even Demogue is more skeptical concerning the possibility of arriving at the juridical heaven-on-earth which has for so long teased the minds of men. "One would be inclined to think that the ideal [of certainty] was generated by the very fact that this quality was not found to exist," writes Wurzel. He desires to see lawyers abandon their antiquated assumptions as to the character and function of law, and become conscious of the mental processes which they now employ unconsciously. They should cease to view jurisprudence as "a science of obedience, of submission to commands." With better insight, lawyers will "rise above the state where they are mere adepts in the art of rendering obedience. Instead, they will cease to conceive of the law as mere naked command and learn to comprehend its nature as a social phenomenon. And we have a right to ask that this should be so. A jurist in ancient classical times was expected to know not merely the letter of the statutes but also their meaning and real significance. Of a modern lawyer we should demand even more: knowledge of the soil from which every legal institution must draw its sustenance, and an acquaintance with the social functioning of each institution."

To this end, lawyers should learn to comprehend the economic and political factors which now indirectly and with too little awareness enter into their thinking. They must learn, says Wurzel in effect, that juridical reasoning is inherently inexact, that legal language is replete with self-deception, that in legal logic there must be a large co-efficient of uncertainty.

So much for the lawyers. But with respect to the general public, Wurzel believes, it must be otherwise. The law itself must continue to employ inexact forms of thought, but the public appearance of a static legal universe must be preserved. The laity must not peer behind the scenes. The law "is bound to appear strictly logical in form, even where in the nature of things it cannot really be so." While the profession is to be instructed as to the creative rôle of the judge, the public would be outraged if the truth were made known.

For the laity, law has to come in the guise of a body of previously formulated commands sufficient, by the mere use of formal logic, to settle all controversies:

"When an injured party appeals to the court he has in mind, as the reason why it is the duty of the judge to interfere, not his economic advantage, nor the principles of ethics or similar things. Nor does he think of the greater personal sagacity and the greater experience of the judge, by which he may be able to find a way out of a tangle of conflicting wills even where the parties cannot see a solution. A European judge is no Oriental sage who is to point out the right course to the parties by virtue of his own higher wisdom. The only authority on which everybody relies, when they assemble together, the injured party and the wrongdoer, as well as the judge, is exclusively and solely the will of the State, embodied in the laws that have been broken. This being so, the judge would hardly supply the wants of the parties if he allowed any doubt to arise but what these commands of the State are really sufficient to settle every contention. Suppose that a decision were to read something like this: We cannot be quite sure what the legislator had in mind regarding the solution of this particular conflict, or whether he ever imagined that one would arise in this particular form; but making use of the provisions of the law on the one hand, and relying on the other hand upon traditions, economic needs of the community, ethical sentiments, popular customs, and so forth, we hold that the proper way for you to act is so and so. A decision of that sort would not be a legal decision at all. The parties would simply reply, 'That is not what we have asked you to tell us.' "

Some, he adds, will deny that "any clearer conception among the laity regarding the true process of arriving at legal (and for that matter, ethical) judgments, and the influence social forces exercise thereon would destroy the authority of such judgments." But Wurzel is apparently not of that mind. The authority of law must be maintained by keeping the public in the dark as to the actual juridical process.

The lawyers, then, are to become more sophisticated, but the laymen are to remain ignorant and deluded.[1]

[1] Toward the end of Wurzel's searching study, "Methods of Juridical Thinking," there occurs the following strange and significant statement: "There is an erroneous idea, often defended but nevertheless plainly mistaken, according to which legal science is to seek salvation in a more profound and refined knowledge of individual psychology. However, the true reasons for the uncertainty we meet with in the investigation of internal facts is caused by other things than our ignorance of individual psychology."

CHAPTER V

THE MEANING OF COMPROMISE

A half-century ago John Morley[1] considered the case of those who, themselves free of old superstitions, forbear to speak out unfalteringly the truth as they see it. In attempting an explanation of the esoteric attitudes of Wurzel and Demogue, it may be helpful to rehearse Morley's analysis.

Morley had little but scorn for the "slovenly willingness to hold two contradictory opinions at one and the same time," for a shrinking deference to the *status quo*. He detested the "dual doctrine" according to which the more enlightened classes should openly encourage for others opinions which they do not hold themselves, of thinking one thing true and the contrary morally beneficial for the majority. "They do not believe in hell, for instance, but they think hell a useful fiction for the lower classes. . . . In other words, they think error useful, and that it may be the best thing for society that masses of men should cheat themselves in their most fervent aspirations and their deepest assurances." They would "fain divide the community into two great castes; the one thoughtful and instructed and using their minds freely, but guarding their conclusions in strict reserve; the other of the illiterate or unreflecting, who should have certain opinions and practices taught them, not because they are true or really what their votaries are made to believe them to be, but because the intellectual superiors of the community think the in-

[1] "Compromise." Morley was concerned with attitudes towards religion and politics; he did not discuss attitudes towards the law.

culcation of such a belief useful in all cases save their own."

This he called "the reserve of intellectual cowardice . . . dealing hypocritically with narrow minds in the supposed interest of peace and quietness." He refused to concede that "there is no harm in men being mistaken or at least only so little harm as is more than compensated for by the marked tranquillity in which their mistake may wrap them. . . . This is an idea that error somehow in certain stages, where there is enough of it, actually does good, like vaccination. . . . Superstition . . . may accidentally and in some few respects impress good ideas upon persons who are too darkened to accept these ideas on their real merits. But then superstition is the main cause of this very darkness. . . . Superstition does an immense amount of harm by enfeebling rational ways of thinking. . . . An erroneous idea . . . tends at the best to make the surrounding mass of error more inveterate. . . . By leaving the old guide-marks undisturbed, you may give ease to an existing generation, but the present ease is purchased at the cost of future growth."

Morley felt little but contempt for giggling epigrams, elegant Pyrrhonism and light-hearted neutrality about antiquated errors. It is dishonest, he believed, to allow one's fellows to feed on a dream and a delusion.

He conceded that it is wise to be patient about the general *acceptance* of a new idea. "But the time has always come, and the season is never unripe, for the *announcement* of the fruitful idea." If the time has not come for the group to receive it, that is no reason why the possessor of the new truth should conceal it. "No man can ever know whether his neighbors are ready for change or not. He has all the following certainties:—that he himself is ready for the change; that he believes it would be a good and beneficent one; that unless some one begins the work of preparation, assuredly there will be no consummation; and that if he declines to take part in the matter, there can be no reason why every one else should not decline

in like manner, and so the work remain ever unper-
formed."

Finally Morley arrived at the following distinction:
"Compromise," he wrote, "may be of two kinds, and of
these two kinds one is legitimate and the other not. It may
stand for two distinct attitudes of mind, one of them ob-
structive and the other not. It may mean the deliberate
suppression or mutilation of an idea, in order to make it
congruous with the traditional idea or the current prejudice
on the given subject, whatever that may be. Or else it
may mean a rational acquiescence in the fact that the
bulk of your contemporaries are not prepared either to
embrace the new idea, or to change their ways of living
in conformity to it. In the one case, the compromiser rejects the highest truth, or dissembles his own acceptance
of it. In the other, he holds it courageously for his ensign
and device, but neither forces nor expects the whole world
straightway to follow. The first prolongs the duration of
the empire of prejudice, and retards the arrival of improvement. The second does his best to abbreviate the
one, and to hasten and make definite the other, yet he
does not insist on hurrying changes which, to be effective,
would require the active support of numbers of persons
not yet ripe for them. It is legitimate compromise to say:—
'I do not expect you to execute this improvement, or to
surrender that prejudice, in my time. But at any rate it
shall not be my fault if the improvement remains unknown
or rejected. There shall be one man at least who surren-
dered the prejudice, and who does not hide that fact.' It
is illegitimate compromise to say:—'I cannot persuade you
to accept my truth; therefore, I will pretend to accept your
falsehood.'" Illegitimate compromise arises from "unavowed disingenuousness and self-illusion, from voluntary
dissimulation, and from indolence and pusillanimity."

We may entirely agree with Morley in lamenting the
results of what he considered cowardly equivocation. At
the same time we must more cautiously apply his con-

demnatory adjectives. The "hush" policy of such as Demogue and Wurzel has less reprehensible causes than cowardice or hypocrisy or personal expediency. Demogue and Wurzel are not of "those who like to satisfy their intellectual vanity by skepticism and at the same time to make their comfort safe by external conformity." Their attitudes are not to be condemned, but explained, and perhaps in these terms:

Such men, it would seem, fail to speak out unequivocally because they, themselves, are still in some small part enthralled by the myths they have learned to see through. That those myths are shams they well know, but the fascination of the myths still continues and they are therefore not entirely ready to relinquish them. Their own need for authoritarianism is diminished, but, they say, the public cannot stand the full truth. *What such men really mean is that they, themselves, cannot bear to have the shams utterly exposed, the superstitions totally destroyed. They find a lingering comfort in the spectacle of a public still under the spell. Such an attitude is not snobbery or esotericism. It is, perhaps, rather a remnant of childish fears, an attenuated father-worship. For not until a man has himself attained full emotional adulthood can he witness fearlessly the coming-of-age of his children.*[2]

[2] See Part Three, Chapter I for further discussion of this notion. The reader will recall again that this is a *partial* explanation.

CHAPTER VI

THE CANDOR OF CARDOZO

Often we have quoted Cardozo. His words are seldom (if ever) equivocal. He wants to do away with legal mysteries. He would have not lawyers alone, but laymen as well, learn the actualities of the judicial process, its essential humanness. One of the greatest American judges, he is in the forefront of those who realistically face the unavoidable uncertainties in law, the actualities of judicial law-making.

"We tend sometimes," he says, "in determining the growth of a principle or a precedent, to treat it as if it represented the outcome of a quest for certainty. That is to mistake its origin. Only in the rarest instances, if ever, was certainty either possible or expected. The principle or the precedent was the outcome of a quest for probabilities. Principles and precedents, thus generated, carry throughout their lives the birthmarks of their origin. They are in truth provisional hypotheses, born in doubt and travail, expressing the adjustment which commended itself at the moment between competing possibilities."[1] The law "must be satisfied to test the validity of its conclusions by the logic of probabilities rather than the logic of certainty."[2] . . . "Magic words and incantations are as fatal to our science as they are to any other. . . . We seek to find peace of mind in the word, the formula, the ritual. The hope is an illusion. . . . Hardly is the ink dry upon our formula before the call of an unsuspected equity—the urge of a new group of facts, a new combination of events—bid us blur and blot and qualify and even, it may be, erase."[3] "In our worship of certainty we must distinguish between the sound certainty and the sham, between what is gold and what is tinsel; and then, when certainty is attained, we must remember that it is not the only good; that we can buy it at too high a price; that there is danger in perpetual quiescence as well as in perpetual motion; and that a compromise must be found in a principle of growth."[4]

Such was not always his position. "Only late in life," he confesses, did he abandon his "blind faith" that the courts would follow a pertinent authority "inexorably to the limit of its logic. I learned by sad experience that they failed, now and again, to come out where I expected. I thought, however, in my simplicity that they had missed the road or carelessly misread the signposts; the divagations never had the aspect of wilful adventures into the land of the unknown. The problem stood before me in a new light when I had to cope with it as judge. I found that the creative element was greater than I had fancied; the forks in the road more frequent; the signposts less complete."

And what he learned he has made public. He has endeavored to make explicit and intelligible the several methods available to the judge in coping creatively with novel problems.[5] Specifically referring to the need at times of subordinating traditional legal concepts to social experience and justice, he says there is nothing new in this notion, "though as with many an old truth, there is need to re-state it now and again. What is new perhaps is the readiness to avow what has always been practiced, but practiced more or less intermittently, and at times with scant appreciation of the nature of the motive force. Hesitant avowal has begotten conduct that is spasmodic and irregular; there has been a feeling, inarticulate to some extent, that the conduct was something to be deprecated, something calling for excuse."[6]

Cardozo, it would seem, has reached adult emotional stature. Unlike some of the other thinkers we have discussed, he is able to contemplate without fear a public which shall know what he knows. And yet, surprisingly, he is not ready to abandon entirely the ancient dream. Just because he is bravely candid, just because he strives to do away with myth-making, unusual significance is to be attached to his backward glances, his admissions of a reluctance to forego altogether a yearning for an absolute and eternal legal system. He begins his latest book[7] with what he himself calls a "wail," confessing to moments of disquietude when looking upon the work of lawyers and judges: "They do things better with logarithms," he cries, thinking of the more exact products of bridge-builders. The "travail" comes, he tells us, when a rule must be announced for a novel situation "where precedents are lacking with authoritative commands." He knows that the common answer to such "laments" is that the law is not an exact science. "There," he says, "the matter ends if we are willing there to end it." But, for him, the matter does not end there. "One does not appease the rebellion of the intellect by the reaffirmance of the evil against which intellect rebels."

These are significant words. The absence of mathematical legal exactness is what Cardozo laments. He experiences "pangs that convulse," and "travail" when he must announce legal rules for a novel situation, when there are lacking "authoritative commands." He cannot "appease the rebellion of the intellect" and he looks upon this lack of mathematical exactness and authoritative commands as "the evil against which intellect rebels."[1]

He goes on to say that "exactness may be impossible, but this is not enough to cause the mind to acquiesce in a

---

[1] In an earlier work, "The Growth of the Law," he had said, "We need not wonder that there is disappointment, ending in rebellion, when the effort is made to deduce the absolute and eternal from premises which in their origin were relative and transitory." "*The curse of this fluidity,* of an ever shifting approximation, is one that law must bear, or other curses yet more dreadful will be invited in exchange."

predestined incoherence. . . . So I keep reaching out and groping for a pathway to the light. The outlet may not be found. At least there may be glimmerings that will deny themselves to a craven *non possumus*, the sterility of ignoble ease. Somewhere beneath the welter there may be a rationalizing principle revealing system and harmony in what passes for discord and disorder." And then he reveals the true nature of his difficulties in the following statement: "Until deeper insight is imparted to us, we must be content with many a *makeshift compromise*, with many a truth that is approximate and relative, *when we are yearning for the absolute.*"

Here indeed is a seeming legal paradox: No one has expounded more elaborately than Cardozo, for the benefit of the bar and the laity, the fact that law is uncertain and must be uncertain, that overeagerness for legal certainty and denials of legal contingency are harmful. All his writings elaborate this point and urge his readers to its recognition. He is clearer-visioned than Pound. And unlike Demogue and Wurzel, he wants the public to see with him the true nature of the judicial process.[2] But while he admonishes against a belief in the attainability of a perfect and unchanging legal system, he makes it plain that he has learned to accept this belief only with bitterness. And, alas, he implies that, one day, when "a deeper insight is imparted to us," we will need no longer to be content with "makeshift compromise," and truths that are "merely approximate and relative," and can then satisfy our "yearning for the absolute" and be done forever with the curse of "fluidity."

[2] His writings have been of inestimable value in making possible realistic thinking about law. There is perhaps but one judge who is his superior in this respect—Mr. Justice Holmes. See Part Three, Chapter II.

Part Three

CONCLUSION

CHAPTER I

GETTING RID OF THE NEED FOR FATHER-AUTHORITY

No intelligent person can question the wisdom of the revised attitude toward the law which our Pounds, Wurzels, Demogues and Cardozos would have the lawyers and the laity adopt. They want our "courts to perceive what it is they are doing" and thus be "enabled to address themselves consciously to doing it in the best way."[1] They want an effective, intelligent fusion of the two competing tendencies towards stability and change; a working principle of growth; a constant revision of the law's heritage of knowledge and thought; the frequent adaptation of the legal rules so as to relate them to the realities of contemporary social, industrial and political conditions. They desire that traditional premises should be so shaped as to give effect to social interests, with reference not to the abstract claims of abstract individuals, but to the concrete situation; they picture law as continuously more efficacious social engineering, satisfying, through social control, as much as is possible of the whole body of human wants.

They urge that lawyers and judges should deal realistically with their materials and their technique, and that there should be an adult recognition, by the public generally, of the possibilities and limitations of the law with consequent improvement of its legitimate functioning.

All this is no easy task. Men in any of life's relations will never be completely free of delusions.[2] But delusions can be diminished. And those who desire the healthy growth of the law will with courage seek to diminish legal delusions and, to that end, to comprehend the nature and sources of their own weaknesses,[1] and of the powerful yearning in themselves as well as others for unrealities in law.

Just in so far as we ourselves are childish, do we want to keep our children from growing up. So say the modern educators. It is weak, it is unworthy, to over-protect the children. This is the "snare of patronage," the great sin of parenthood: to obstruct the psychological freedom of the child.[3] The prolongation of infancy is essential to the development of the human infant, but to prolong infancy unduly at the expense of the child's development is to violate the eleventh commandment.

A coming-of-age has its perils for the children and its pains for the parents. Yet, if our legal critics are to play the rôle of wise fathers, they must have the courage to let their "children" grow up. Myth-making and fatherly lies must be abandoned—the Santa Claus story of complete legal certainty; the fairy tale of a pot of golden law which is already in existence and which the good lawyer can find, if only he is sufficiently diligent; the phantasy of an aesthetically satisfactory system and harmony, consistent and uniform, which will spring up when we find the magic wand of a rationalizing principle. We must stop telling stork-fibs about how law is born and cease even hinting that perhaps there is still some truth in Peter Pan legends of a juristic happy hunting ground in a land of legal absolutes.

To the extent that lawyers, whether more or less consciously, join the conspiracy of silence about, or denial of, the ineradicable mutability of law, they do an injury to their fellows. For to that extent—and in one of the most important life activities—they are keeping men in subjection to a falsehood and, worse, to the debilitating irresponsibility arising from reliance on supposed safety-conferring external authority. Not only is there involved an injury to

---

[1] One recalls Gilbert's fairies who, chided for falling in love with mortals, exclaimed, "We know it's weakness, but the weakness is so strong."

the maturation of law, but as well to the spirit of men generally. For, if what we have suggested is true, if something of a paralyzing father-worship is one of the hidden causes of men's belief in a body of infallible law, then the perpetuation of that belief means that everywhere the noxious thralldom to mere authority and tradition is strengthened.[2]

Growing up means throwing off dependence upon external authority.[3] It means self-reliance, the acceptance of responsibility. It means questioning—not hastily, angrily, rebelliously, but calmly and dispassionately—our bequests from the past, our social heritage.

A great religious thinker, George Berman Foster, writing of religion, has put the matter in words which, slightly modified, might well be heeded by the leaders of the legal profession:

"The true and wise lover and leader of his brothers will not shield them against doubt, but make them equal to doubt, inspire them with strength to doubt. They will say to their brothers that religious doubt is not a disease of the soul; but is necessary to the health of the soul; that it does not signify decay or degeneration but re-birth—the mounting upward of never-resting, never-rusting life. . . . Whoever fears doubt, fears truth; for it is truth that casts the first shadow of doubt into the human spirit. . . . It is in religious doubt that we begin to acquire the power of a true self-confidence."[4]

Increasing constructive doubt is the sign of advancing civilization. We must put question marks alongside many of our inherited legal dogmas, since they are dangerously out of line with social facts.[5]

Indeed, we may throw some light on our problem by asking what, in general parlance, we mean by a "fact."

[2] See Appendix III as to the effect on Science of the childish desire for cosmic certainty.

[3] It is worth noting once more that prolonged dependence on fatherly authority may exist in adult years even when the childish fears which brought about such dependence are absent. The child-father relation, no longer a necessary means of adaptation, has acquired subjective end value.

Holmes has answered that it is something one can't help believing. "What gives it objectivity is that I find my fellow man to a greater or less extent (never wholly) subject to the same Can't Helps." Barry more recently has defined a fact as a "coercive" or "compulsory" experience "established by common agreement which is indicated by similar behavior with reference to it." And Eddington speaks of it as a "symposium" of presentations to individuals in all sorts of circumstances.

Now these common agreements as to "coercive experiences," these symposia with respect to the nature of Can't Helps, keep changing, even where the subject-matter has reference to what we call the laws of nature.[6] In other words, stubborn facts are, in a sense, not so stubborn as we are wont to suppose. In the natural sciences the rate of change in the accepted symposia is rapid because there the habit of constant questioning, of unremitting doubt, has come to be accepted, at least by the scientists,[7] as a virtue. Even in those sciences, it took thousands of years to justify doubt. And outside of the sciences, most of our facts have remained unchanged for at least several hundred generations. A large part of our accepted or unquestioned "truths" are the "unverified world-pictures of vanished barbaric (prehistoric) peoples." The toughness of these facts is due—to what? To the vast power of the authority behind them. They have become sacred; they are protected from close scrutiny by terrifying taboos.

Primitive man could not endure the terrors that surrounded him. He made masks to conceal the menace they involved, so that now, says Shaw, "every mask requires a hero to tear it off."[4] In each man's infancy, generation after generation, his father has taught him the eternal verity of these masking "truths." Wherefore he is coerced by them and treats them as if they were nature's irreducibles. And if the tendency to tear off the masks, to question

---

[4] "The Quintessence of Ibsenism," 20: "We have plenty of these masks around us still; some of them more fantastic than any of the Sandwich Islanders' masks in the British Museum."

man-made Can't Helps, has progressed far less rapidly in the law than in the natural sciences—if, that is, our "law facts" need to be brought in line with our "science facts"—this is no doubt because in the law father-authority has found a firmer lodgment.

This point is so important that we venture to state it once more in slightly variant terms. As we have often remarked in the foregoing pages, our legal abstractions can only be approximations. They are, by definition, drawn off —abstracted—from the facts. Hence, the results can never be precise, perfect. They must be inexact. If the "environment" were stable, the degree of inexactness could become more negligible and remain relatively fixed.[5] But the economic, political and social problems are ever-shifting. So that, in the very nature of the situation, the approximations must be revised frequently and can never be accepted as final in terms of satisfactory consequences. We must be content with modest probabilities, as Dewey puts it, and not foolishly pretend that our legal abstractions are mathematically accurate, for that pretense obstructs the will to modify and adjust these abstractions in the light of careful observation of their working results.[8]

These abstractions, that is to say, are tools whose whole value is instrumental. They have been contrived to meet particular problems. As new problems arise, the old tools must be adapted to cope with them. But when the old tools have been authoritatively pronounced to be once-and-for-all perfect, when, that is, they have the father-sanction, then to question their everlasting sufficiency is difficult. Then the tools seem not human contrivances but a very part of the nature of things. The questioning, when it begins, has to be oblique, the adaptions surreptitious. Even the questioner, the adapter, must not let himself know that he is daring to depart from the accepted ways. Science made large strides when man began to treat the traditional formulations as no longer completely correct and definite

---

[5] No complete rigidity would be attained, even so, unless and until the personalities of all judges became approximately uniform.

knowledge of objective nature but as hypotheses or fictions;[6] in other words, when men were ready to treat as tentative the guesses about the external world which had been handed down to them. Then only could they fearlessly observe the events, dispassionately consider new guesses about the character of these events.

All the guesses are human and, therefore, subject to question. But the old guesses come to us as the father's truths and are, therefore, sacrosanct. Humanity increases its chances of survival and of progress to the extent that it becomes able to question—neither blindly to accept nor violently to defy—the father's guesses, and to discontinue calling them self-evident truths. In the sciences this attitude has won out. Although the law is a more patently human construction than, say, physics, yet, in the calm reconsideration of the value of inherited truths, law is decades behind physics. Why? Because in law, the father is more deeply entrenched. The law is a near substitute for that father, a belief in whose infallibility is essential to the very life of the child. And in the life of the adult that authority now no longer usefully, but still potently, often holds sway.

The fear of change is an ancient one. We may, with Elsie Clews Parsons, define civilization as man's steps in his escape from that fear. Whitehead puts the same thought somewhat differently: Development in life means wandering. Modern science has imposed on humanity the necessity for increased wandering, for migrations into uncharted seas. The future will disclose dangers. "It is the business of the future to be dangerous; and it is among the merits of science that it equips the future for its duties." We must not confuse civilization and security, for security and stability will, with advancing civilization, grow less. Too much insecurity is perhaps inconsistent with civilization. "But, on the whole, the great ages have been unstable ages."[9]

[6] See Appendix VII.

Whence it follows that, if we are to grow more civilized, we must arrive at a more adult attitude towards chance and change. And here a nice distinction must be made between the adult position with respect to danger and a less developed sentiment which falsely resembles it.

Early in this essay we spoke of the bewilderment of the infant,[7] of his seeking for sureness and security in the confused environment into which he has suddenly been ejected; of his finding, in a reliance upon his idealized father, some measure of relief from his confusion. And we traced the effects of the persistence in adult life of this reliance upon the father. But the child is motivated not only by the desire to escape the terrors of the unknown; he has also within him a store of vital energy, he is a growing dynamic organism. His dynamic capacities constantly assert themselves; the child is never completely a mere creature of parental authority. In a certain sense, danger and risk, as well as safety and security, make their appeal to him. As sometimes he runs away from chance and change, so at other times he seeks them.

Now the curious fact is that such childish courting of danger may be, in part, a product of father-authority. All children have a dual attitude towards the father. The child needs a belief in an all-powerful, all-wise parent. Yet that parent ever and again takes on the aspect of a harsh tyrant who cruelly and unfairly interferes with the child's aims and purposes. Even the most loving and obedient child feels occasional animosity towards the father and, at times, revolts against the father. His conduct, in such circumstances, may be in the direction of healthy growth, but, in so far as it is merely expressive of revolt, it is purely negative in meaning. The child, that is, may not be forging ahead, but only running away from a new terror—the terror of too strict fatherly authority.[8]

[7] See Part One, Chapter II.

[8] M. D. Eder quotes a Japanese proverb which enumerates the four greatest terrors which Japan is called upon to endure: "Earthquakes, thunder, fire and too strict fatherly authority." The Freud-

Recent writings in criminology have a decided bearing here. Many criminals, we learn, are driven to lawlessness by an inner, subconscious revolt against the authority of the father. In opposing the law they are reacting to it as a father-substitute. They, too, so to speak, demand (but "contrary-wise") an authoritarian law in order that they may rebel against it. Fatherly authority in their childhood was too oppressive and as a consequence the anti-authority bias developed as a determining conduct-factor throughout life.[9] The violent rebel against authority is no more "free" than the slave of authority; he is in bondage to a compulsion to revolt; his is a constrained attitude, which Cooley[10] has happily called the "subservience of contradiction."[11]

And so we must distinguish between that growth towards maturity which produces an acceptance of danger and that childish reaction against fatherly authority which takes on the appearance of adult courage. The constrained rebellion against paternalism is not a symptom of development but of prolonged infantilism. It is another form of slavish obedience. The person engaged in such rebellion is not free of paternal authority, but is still subjectively dependent upon it.[12]

---

ians, in explaining the "ambivalent" attitude towards the father, properly consider other important factors which are not given attention here.

[9] One is reminded of those wretches in the Divine Comedy who "all the while felt themselves drawn onwards by a *fear which became a desire* towards the cruel riverside which awaits everyone destitute of the fear of God."

[10] "Life and the Student," 124.

[11] Compare Gilbert's observation:

> "I often think it's comical
> How nature always does contrive
> That every boy and every gal
> That's born into the world alive
> Is either a little Liberal
> Or else a little Conservative."

[12] There is a measure of deep insight in the facetious remarks of Mr. Justice Darling: "I cannot avoid noticing an error into which they fall who complain of the uncertainty of law as though

True growth involves healthy encouragement of the inherent spontaneity of the child, an encouragement of wakeful vitality and the discouragement of half-blind adherence to, or half-blind breaking away from, the traditional.

And so in law. If the search for the father-judge is ended,[13] if the authority-ridden mode of regarding law is eliminated, if men see law as a human adjustment and not as a gift or mandate from some external source, no violent transformation need or will occur. The relief from fear of chance need not result in the adoption of a policy of incessant, hectic change, but should lead to a policy of healthy and vital growth.

Today, excessive regard for certified stability yields to an excessive desire for modification, so that there is a constant unconscious struggle between these two impulses, a struggle unnecessarily violent. There is vacillation in the mind even of the average man between worship and denunciation of legal certainty. The demand for too much change is as little based on practicality as the demand for too much rigidity. Holmes has warned us that continuity with the past is not a duty. It is no less true that there is no obligation to effect discontinuity with the past. A recognition of those two truths, resulting from a thoroughly adult attitude towards fatherly authority, will produce a balanced, not an anarchic, attitude towards law.[14]

---

it were a weakness. Rather should it be considered the chiefest of all sanctions. . . . Many would dare to do wrong, did they know for certain what would follow."

[13] If the child indeed becomes father of the man, *i.e.*, each individual becomes his own father and thus eliminates the need for fatherly authority.

[14] From the genetic point of view, development towards maturity might be roughly schematized as follows:

(1) At first the child's thinking is egocentric, "autistic," unsocialized. He accepts his own thoughts as self-evident; he is totally unaware of any subjectivity in his thinking. (2) Later, doubts arise as to the self-evident character of his own thoughts. Their subjective character becomes somewhat apparent. He now substitutes the father's dogmas for his own. Father's thoughts are objectively real.

When men are free of childish compulsions away from or towards the traditional, it will be possible for them to have an open mind on the question of the advisability of radical alterations of law.

In other words, such a revised attitude will not entail constant inquiry into the sufficiency of all legal formulations. *It is unnecessary and undesirable to attack on all fronts at once.* Certain formulations must have been and will be at any given moment treated as, for the time being, fixed and settled while others are being investigated. But those "rules" that are thus, for the time being, taken for granted, will be only temporarily dealt with as permanent. They will be considered as *temporary absolutes.* Some of them will be accepted because repeated checkings show them still to be working well;[15] others because the attention, at the moment, will be too occupied.[16]

Modern civilization demands a mind free of father-governance. To remain father-governed in adult years is peculiarly *the* modern sin. *The modern mind is a mind free of childish emotional drags, a mature mind.* And law, if it is to meet the needs of modern civilization must adapt itself

---

(3) Still later, other authorities are substituted for the father. But, in this substitutive manner, fatherly authority still continues. Truths which emanate from authority are objectively real. (4) Then all authority may come into question, all human thought being conceived as subjective and therefore invalid and unreal. (5) The stage of complete maturity is reached when the relativity of all truths is accepted but seen to be compatible with the provisional validity and utility of such truths.

Once more, note that we are using a *"partial* explanation."

[15] Compare Dewey, "Human Nature and Conduct," 239.

[16] Whitehead has expressed this idea in generalized terms (loc. cit. 289): "There are two principles inherent in the very nature of things, recurring in some particular embodiments, whatever field we explore—the spirit of change, and the spirit of conservation. There can be nothing real without both. Mere change without conservation is a passage from nothing to nothing. Its final integration yields mere transient nonentity. Mere conservation without change cannot conserve. For after all, there is a flux of circumstance, and the freshness of being evaporates under mere repetition."

to the modern mind. It must cease to embody a philosophy opposed to change. It must become avowedly pragmatic. To this end there must be developed a recognition and elimination of the carry-over of the childish dread of, and respect for, paternal omnipotence; that dread and respect are powerful strongholds of resistance to change. Until we become thoroughly cognizant of, and cease to be controlled by, the image of the father hidden away in the authority of the law, we shall not reach that first step in the civilized administration of justice, the recognition that man is not made for the law, but that the law is made by and for men.

CHAPTER II

MR. JUSTICE OLIVER WENDELL HOLMES, THE COMPLETELY ADULT JURIST

One wise leader pointing the way we have had with us many years. The judicial opinions and other writings of Mr. Justice Holmes—practitioner, teacher, historian, philosopher, judge—are a treasury of adult counsels, of balanced judgments as to the relation of the law to other social relations. There you will find a vast knowledge of legal history divorced from slavish veneration for the past, a keen sensitiveness to the needs of today with no irrational revolt against the conceptions of yesterday, a profound respect for the utility of syllogistic reasoning linked with an insistence upon recurrent revisions of premises based on patient studies of new facts and new desires. He has himself abandoned, once and for all, the phantasy of a perfect, consistent, legal uniformity, and has never tried to perpetuate the pretense that there is or can be one. He has put away childish longings for a father-controlled world and it is for that reason, one suspects, that he has steadfastly urged his fellows to do likewise. As a consequence, whatever clear vision of legal realities we have attained in this country in the past twenty-five years is in large measure due to him. No American thinker working his way forward, against his own and other's prejudices, to sane and honest recognition of how the law works and how its workings can be bettered, but Holmes's adult illusionless surveys are an indispensable aid and an inspiration.[1]

[1] The quotations in this chapter are from Holmes's "The Common Law," his "Collected Legal Papers," and from his legal opin-

Almost fifty years ago Holmes made the famous statement (the implications of which have not yet been thoroughly appreciated) that "The life of the law has not been logic; it has been experience."[1] Intuitions "avowed or unconscious," prejudices, views of public policy, the necessities of the time have had, he wrote, "a good deal more to do than the syllogism in determining the rules by which men should be governed," adding that the law "cannot be dealt with as if it contained only the axioms and corollaries of a book of mathematics."

In many ways he has since developed this attitude. Recently he said, "Certitude is not the test of certainty. We have been cock-sure of many things that were not so." Often he has decried the tendency to deal with law as if it were "a theological working out of dogma." His veneration for the law grows out of its practical achievements: "It has the final title to respect that it exists, that it is not an Hegelian dream, but a part of the lives of men."

As one of our foremost legal historians, he does not underestimate the value of the history of law. "A page of history is worth a volume of logic," he has said, in one of his opinions. Yet he calls attention to history's "almost deceptive charm" and bids us beware of "the pitfall of antiquarianism." His chief interest in the past is for the light it throws upon the present. While learning is a very good thing, he says, it may lead us astray and the law, so far as it depends on learning, "is indeed the government of the living by the dead." To a very considerable extent this is inevitable. "The past gives us our vocabulary and fixes the limit of our imagination . . . but the present has a right to govern itself so far as it can; and it ought always be remembered that historic continuity with the past is not a duty, it is only a necessity." The use of the history of law

ions; the latter, so far as they relate to Constitutional questions, being conveniently collected and brilliantly interpreted in Felix Frankfurter's article, "Mr. Justice Holmes and the Constitution," 41 Harvard Law Review, 121. As to Holmes's realistic view of law and its effects, see above, Part One, Chapter XIV.

for him "is mainly negative and sceptical. . . . Its chief
good is to burst inflated explanations."

He has often weighed and considered the value of rules
of law which are survivals of ancient traditions, when the
ancient meaning has been forgotten. In such cases the
judges strive to give modern reasons for the old rules.
Such reasons, Holmes finds, are, for the most part, artificial
and unsatisfactory. They are "inflated and unreal explanations."

But he concedes that sometimes the old rules have an
actual present use. "If truth were not often suggested by
error, if old implements could not be adjusted to new uses,
human progress would be slow." But it will not do to invent reasons offhand for whatever we find established in
the law. "Scrutiny and revision are justified." History
should not be used to increase our slavishness to the past.
"It is the first step towards an enlightened skepticism, that
is, towards a deliberate consideration of the worth of . . .
rules. . . . It is revolting to have no better reason for a
rule of law than that so it was laid down in the time of
Henry IV. It is still more revolting if the grounds upon
which it was laid down have vanished long since, and the
rule simply persists from blind imitation of the past."

Ever and again he has reverted to his early position that
"in substance the growth of the law is legislative," that
"the secret root from which the law draws all the juices
of life" are considerations of what is expedient for the community concerned, more or less definitely understood views
of public policy. These are considerations "which judges
most rarely mention and always with an apology." They
are "most generally . . . the unconscious result of instinctive preferences and inarticulate syllogisms." The process
of judicial lawmaking "has been largely unconscious." It
is important to insist on a "more conscious recognition of
the legislative function of courts." For the considerations
which are actuating the courts in making law are so important that there is a danger in allowing these considerations to continue "in an inarticulate form as unconscious

prejudice or half-conscious inclination. To measure them justly needs not only the highest powers of the judge and a training which the practice of the law does not insure, but also a freedom from prepossessions very hard to attain. It seems to me desirable that the work should be done with express recognition of its nature. The time has gone by when law is only an unconscious embodiment of the common will. It has become a conscious reaction upon itself of organized society knowingly seeking to determine its destiny."

He has abandoned legal mysticism. "The Common Law is not a brooding omnipresence in the sky. . . ." He believes "in the superiority of the artificial to the natural" and therefore believes that "mankind yet may take its own destiny consciously and intelligently in hand." He looks "forward to a time when the part played by history in the explanation of dogma shall be very small and instead of ingenuous research we shall spend our energy on study of the ends sought to be attained and the reasons for desiring them."

Nor has he been in much doubt as to the source of the general reluctance consciously to recognize the fact of judicial law-making. Many years ago he wrote that perhaps one of the reasons for this reluctance "is that the moment you leave the path of mere logical deduction you lose the illusion of certainty which makes legal reasoning seem like mathematics." And sagely, he added, "But the certainty is only an illusion, nevertheless." For the grounds of decision are taught by experience of life. Lawyers need to use the tool of logic but "there is a fallacy in trusting too much to this tool." He smiles at the remark of a very eminent judge who said that he never let a decision go until he was absolutely sure that it was right. Dissenting opinions, he says amusedly, are often censured as if they "meant simply that one side or the other were not doing their sums right."

What has made lawyers overstress logic he has sensed accurately: "The logical method and form flatter that longing for certainty and for repose which is in every human mind. But certainty generally is illusion, and repose is not the destiny of man." In the following words, he undermines the puerile belief that by compelling judges to render decisions which appear to omit all evidences of judicial legislation you can, in fact, keep them from making new law:

"Behind the logical form lies a judgment as to the relative worth and importance of competing legislative grounds, often an inarticulate and unconscious judgment, it is true, and yet the very root and nerve of the whole proceeding. You can give any conclusion a logical form. You always can imply a condition in a contract. But why do you imply it? It is because of some belief as to the practice of the community or of a class, or because of some opinion as to policy, or, in short, because of some attitude of yours upon a matter not capable of exact quantitative measurement, and therefore not capable of founding exact logical conclusions. Such matters really are battle-grounds where the means do not exist for determinations that shall be good for all time, and where the decision can do no more than embody the preference of a given body in a given time and place. . . . I cannot but believe that if the training of lawyers led them habitually to consider more definitely and explicitly the social advantage on which the rule they lay down must be justified, they sometimes would hesitate where now they are confident, and see that they were taking sides upon debatable and often burning questions."

He has been sound, too, about the function of doubt: "To have doubted one's own first principles is the mark of a civilized man." Accordingly he can afford to doubt even his own dogmas: "While one's experience thus makes certain preferences dogmatic for one's self, recognition of how they came to be so leaves one able to see that others, poor souls, may be equally dogmatic about something else." And, accordingly, he has developed that remarkable tolerance which is the mark of high maturity. Skeptical about the inevitable validity of existing rules merely because they exist, he is yet no fiery reformer eager to abandon all tradition merely because of its lack of novelty.

His unquenchable zeal for an honest facing of the facts and his uncommon pliancy of mind have led many to think of him as a dangerous radical. Yet thirty years ago he said:

"I do not expect or think it desirable that the judges should undertake to renovate the law. That is not their province. Indeed precisely because I believe that the world would be just as well off if it lived under laws that differed from ours in many ways, and because I believe that the claim of our especial code to respect is simply that it exists, that it is the one to which we have become accustomed, and not that it represents an eternal principle, I am slow to consent to overruling a precedent, and think that our important duty is to see that the judicial duel shall be fought out in the accustomed way. But I think it is most important to remember whenever a doubtful case arises, with certain analogies on one side and other analogies on the other, that what really is before us is a conflict between two social desires, each of which cannot both have their way. The social question is which desire is stronger at the point of conflict. The judicial one may be narrower, because one or the other desire may have been expressed in previous decisions to such an extent that logic requires us to assume it to preponderate in the one before us. But if that be clearly so, the case is not a doubtful one. Where there is doubt the simple tool of logic does not suffice, and even if it is disguised and unconscious, the judges are called on to exercise the sovereign prerogative of choice."

In his constitutional opinions he has been in favor of allowing a wide latitude of freedom in experimentation and has accordingly sustained statutes involving "social experiments" even though, as he has said, they "may seem futile or even noxious to me and those whose judgment I most respect."[2] Now over eighty years of age, just the other day he said from the bench that our Constitution

"is an experiment, as all life is an experiment. Every year, if not every day, we have to wager our salvation upon some prophecy based upon imperfect knowledge.[3] While that experiment is part of our system, I think that we should be eternally vigilant against attempts to check the expressions of opinions that we loathe and believe to be fraught with death unless they so imminently threaten immediate interference with the lawful and pressing purposes of the law that an immediate check is required to save the country."

And most significant for our purposes is his recognition that one's dogmas, the things in which one believes and for which one will fight and die, one's essential attitudes towards the universe, are "determined largely by early associations and temperament, coupled with the desire to have an absolute guide."

The great value of Holmes as a leader is that his leadership implicates no effort to enslave his followers. It would be grossly misusing his example to accept his judicial opinions or views on any question of law as infallible. It may well be assumed that he would be the readiest to urge a critical reconsideration of any doctrines he has announced. He has attained an adult emotional status, a self-reliant, fearless approach to life, and, we repeat, he invites others to do likewise. We might say that, being rid of the need of a strict father, he can afford not to use his authority as if he, himself, were a strict father.

His legal skepticism is clear, sane, vital, progressive—not an easy achievement, as one can see in the examples of Jhering, Pound, Demogue and Wurzel. One is reminded of Vaihinger's comments on the pessimistic character of Greek skepticism: When the Greek skeptics realized the deep chasm between thought and reality, there resulted a marked depression. They despaired of thought. "When the ancient skeptic found thought beginning to pursue its own path and departing from reality, he immediately supposed that he could declare all thinking void, without reflecting that thought yet leads to correct practical results." This was inevitable, says Vaihinger, because "mere subjective thinking" had not "yet achieved these tremendous scientific feats which are distinctive of modern times." Hence, Greek skepticism was negative, paralyzing and led to inaction.

And so in law today, most men still recoil from the admission of the "subjectivity" of law. Many sophisticated lawyers, like Demogue, are skeptics, but, like the Greeks, they fear to accept completely the full meaning of their doubts. Holmes, almost alone[2] among lawyers, adopts that skeptical attitude upon which modern science has builded, that modern skepticism which looks upon thought as instrumental and acknowledges the transient and relative nature of all human thought-contrivances. Holmes has been telling us for fifty years that, in effect, the Golden Rule is that there is no Golden Rule. But the old fascinations lure men away from the essential meaning of his teaching.

For Holmes's thoroughly "scientific" view of law requires courage, more courage than is required in the natural sciences. In those sciences, as Vaihinger points out, skepticism has proved its worth. Not so, as yet, in the law. And it is courageous indeed to face the fact, once and for all, that men have made the law and must take the responsibility for its good or bad workings.

If, like Holmes, we win free of the myth of fixed authoritarian law, having neither to accept law because it comes from an authority resembling the father's, nor to reject it for like reason, we shall, for the first time, begin to face legal problems squarely. Without abating our insistence that the lawyers do the best they can, we can then manfully endure inevitable short-comings, errors and inconsistencies in the administration of justice because we can realize that perfection is not possible. The legal profession will then for the first time be in a position to do its work well.

If that view of the law brings to the lawyer a large sense of the burdens of his responsibility, it may also bring its pleasures—the pleasures of self-confidence, self-authority, of the conscious use of one's abilities in one of the most important areas of human activity.

[2] Except a small group of thinkers (many of them influenced by Holmes) most of whom we have referred to heretofore or in Appendix II.

APPENDIXES

OTHER EXPLANATIONS

Among the many possible additional explanations of the basic legal myth are the following:

1. The religious impulse. This is discussed in Part One, Chapter XVIII.

2. The aesthetic impulse. (Or the sense for symmetry, consistency or logical simplicity.) This explanation deserves a lengthy consideration which would lead to a discussion of the nature of the aesthetic. See Part One, Chapter XIV.

The writer hopes some day to follow up the possibility that a pathologically excessive desire for symmetry in art is not unrelated to the undue prolongation of emotional infancy.

3. Effect of professional habits.

4. The economic interpretation. (Judges belong to the most conservative portion of the community. Protection of vested interests.)

Without here attempting any adequate consideration of this explanation, it may be remarked that the basic legal myth seems to be believed by all sorts and conditions of men, radicals as well as conservatives. Economic factors play a tremendous part in the thinking of all men, lawyers and judges included. But whatever "the state of the industrial arts," in Russia or elsewhere, the legal-certainty illusion will remain an important problem.

5. A human instinct to seek security and certainty (self-preservation). Cf. Part One, Chapter XV.

6. A practical interest in peace and quiet. Cf. Appendix IV.

7. Imitation.

8. Devotion to custom.

9. Inertia.

10. Laziness or physical fatigue.

11. Stupidity. "The essence of stupidity is the demand for final opinions."

12. Mental structure. Cf. Appendix III.

13. Language and word-magic. See Part One, Chapters VII and X.

14. The Barry-Watson theory. See Part One, Chapter XV.

NOTES ON RULE-FETICHISM
AND REALISM

Professor John Dickinson and Dean Leon Green have recently written at some length on the nature of law.[1] They are in interesting contrast. Dickinson represents the older tradition in its most sophisticated and seductive form. Green is one of the most clear-headed yet subtle exponents of the new realistic school.

Dickinson begins with a masterly attack on the various efforts to discover a "law behind law," that is, "to find a mediating principle which will not disturb the conception of law as pre-determined for the judges, while at the same time reconciling this conception with the possibility of change from time to time in any or all of its specific rules"; he examines critically the proposed paths to "a system of independently existing and inherently valid law having its source wholly outside government."[2] He acutely analyzes and exposes the fatal weaknesses of:

1. The 18th Century notion that the mediating principle was to be sought in the "natural reason" or "the reason of the law";

2. The early 19th Century theory that the "law behind

---

[1] Dickinson, "The Law Behind Law," 29 Columbia Law Review, 114, 284; Green, "The Duty Problem in Negligence Cases," 28 Columbia Law Review, 1014; 29 Columbia Law Review, 255. The second half of each of these essays appeared in the March 1929 number of the same magazine.

[2] This essay shows a marked advance in realism over Dickinson's earlier treatise, "Administrative Justice and the Supremacy of Law." See note to Part One, Chapter XIV.

law" was located in popular custom, that social and economic institutions and mores dictate specific legal rules or that the "sense of justice of the people" specifically points to the rule to be applied in any given situation;

3. The later 19th Century theory that law is an inductive science which can discover, in the precedents, authoritative jural principles capable of demonstrating the objective correctness of the rule to be applied to any new situation which may arise;

4. The current conception that there is "a science of human nature and society in such a sense as to dictate in advance with objective precision and authority the specific legal rule . . .";

5. The related idea that the law itself supplies a basic scale of values to serve as a standard for all situations, or that the judgments of policy involved in the work of judges can be "generalized into a coherent system of policy which can be said to underlie the whole law, and dictate all its specific rules," or that there are at any time controlling legal theories which compel specific legal results.

Dickinson's admirable survey leads him—and his open-minded readers—to the conclusion that there is no "higher law" by means of which the law applicable to any particular case can be predicted. He demonstrates the fallacy of confusing (a) some of the considerations which operate on a judge at the moment of making law with (b) the law which is being made by the judge. And he accepts as inescapable the fact that judges make law to meet new situations and that, in doing so, they are guided by their "personality and intellectual equipment," "conditioned by traditional practice, current fashions, and the whole contemporary state of art." "Whatever forces can be said to influence the growth of the law," he writes, "they exert that influence only by influencing the judges," for while judges tend to shape law to their readings of the changing convenience of the society they serve, "such readings are not, and cannot be, absolute, like the readings of a galvanometer." There is, he notes, room for considerable dif-

ference of opinion about the current mores and "when it
is a question of their writing themselves into law, the
opinion which prevails is the judges' opinion." The judges
are not "passive recorders" of social forces. "They do not
create the materials out of which the new rule is built, but
they use them, select, reject, combine, emphasize, in short
give form and life to them, as their personality and intellectual equipment dictate; and if this is not creative activity, no creative activity is performed by human beings."
The "personal bent of the judge is inevitably a strong
factor in the formation of the value-judgments underlying
the selection of new rules for unprovided cases."

With these preliminaries the reader justifiably anticipates a conclusion that law, in last analysis, is what the
judges decide and that, in reaching their decisions, the
judges are not in any wise "authoritatively" controlled.
But such a notion Dickinson repudiates as nihilistic. It
involves, he asserts, an unwarranted confusion of "law"
with "discretion" (or "policy" as he sometimes calls "discretion"). For Dickinson, like Gray,[3] insists that *law consists entirely of rules* which the courts develop. And he
also insists that *these judge-made rules are "authoritative."*
The term law, he says, must not "be so broadened as to
include processes of a necessarily discretionary character;
*a distinction must be maintained between rules and the
discretion which makes and applies rules.* . . ." For the
"basic purpose of law" is "to *control* discretion."[4]

[3] Like many others besides Gray. But the comparison with Gray
is peculiarly interesting because Dickinson ascribes to Gray, of all
men, the notion that "the law by which a case is decided comes
into existence in the act of deciding it." This is no doubt the logical
outcome of Gray's views and especially of his treatment of statutes
as merely a "source of law." But Gray (as pointed out above, Part
One, Chapter XIII) failed to follow his own thesis to its logical
conclusion and, like Dickinson, believed that a court makes new
law only when it evolves a new "rule of decision."

[4] The influence of Roscoe Pound on Dickinson is here manifest.
Pound (see above, Part One, Chapter XIII) sharply differentiates
between "law" and "discretion"; the latter he labels "anti-legal."
Pound has consistently maintained that law is characterized by

Up to the point where he makes this differentiation between "law," (which consists of authoritative rules) and "discretion," Dickinson, in his latest writings, is as clear-visioned as Holmes or any of the realists. But at that point the ancient myth reappears. The very words Dickinson uses remind one of Bealism: A distinction between rules and the discretion which makes rules *"must* be maintained," he insists. Why the "must"? Is there in the nature of the judicial process a precise cleavage between the two? Will the judge do his work more ably, will the lawyer function better if he strives nicely to discriminate between "law" which consists of "rules" and "discretion" which makes rules or applies them? Dickinson scarcely hints at an answer to these questions.[5] His "must" derives apparently from hidden subjective needs, from illusory aims which are attenuated but still active.

Here is an essay devoted to demolishing the belief that there is anything compulsory behind law. And yet in it we find Dickinson quoting with approval a statement that rules are "norms which point *authoritatively* in a particular direction" and asserting that "the courts in extending

---

its generality. In 1919 he stated that law consisted of (1) rules, (2) principles, (3) legal conceptions and (4) standards. In 1923 he said, "there are three elements that make up the whole of what we call law"; *viz.*, (1) Legal precepts [which presumably include (a) rules, (b) principles, (c) legal conceptions and (d) standards], (2) traditional ideas and technique of interpreting, developing and applying legal precepts and (3) philosophical, political and ethical ideas as to the end of law.

Pound has done as much as any Anglo-American jurist to point out the unavoidable and socially desirable rôle of judicial discretion. See especially 20 Green Bag, 401; 5 Columbia Law Review, 20; 13 Columbia Law Review, 696. But Dickinson's harmful distinction between "law" and "discretion" is one of which Pound may fairly be called the chief Anglo-American expositor. *Cf.* Dickinson, "Administrative Justice and the Supremacy of Law," especially p. 128.

[5] Except in so far as (pp. 315–9) he impliedly answers "no" by his exposure of the evil consequences of the traditional hard-shelled Bealist notion that rules are the principal aids in arriving at or predicting legal decisions.

or narrowing a rule by interpretation are not questioning the *authoritative character* of the rule."

What does the word "authoritative" mean? It is defined, usually, as "entitled to acceptance or obedience," "exercising authority," "commanding," "peremptory," "dictatorial." It connotes something "paramount," "supreme," "predominant," "imperious," "imperative," "compulsory," "absolute." In any of those senses are legal rules authoritative? Is that what Dickinson intends? His readers are left in doubt. Dickinson's answer, so far as it can be spelled out of his essay is—yes and no. Rules, he says, are authoritative; yet judges, he admits, can choose—except in the simplest cases—which one of several competing rules is to be applied in any particular case. And Dickinson concedes that, in "applying" a rule, the judges can expand or contract it—can, indeed, change its "meaning." But all such alterations, he submits, "can be said to go only to the application, not to the *authority* of the rule."

The equivocal character of Dickinson's attitude towards rules is disclosed in his treatment of legal "theories" or "doctrines." He smiles at the naïveté of those who assume that any legal theory or doctrine is "law." How can it be law, he argues, since a court may reject it and choose to employ a rival theory—as, for example, when a court refuses to apply the theory that liability should always be predicated upon fault and determines that in some instances social welfare will be better served if, for some acts, men are held absolutely liable regardless of fault, *i.e.,* even when acting with all due care. The courts in making use of one theory rather than another are choosing, says Dickinson, between alternatives. "Their choice is not foreclosed by anything entitled to be called authority." The judges use legal theories and doctrines to explain their conclusions, but such theories "explain a result after it has been reached, but are useless beforehand as a guide for reaching it."

But cannot exactly the same be said of rules? Courts are constantly determining which of several rival rules to apply.[6] Is it any the less true of the choice of rules than of the choice of theories that "the choice is not foreclosed by anything entitled to be called authority"? And do not rules, like legal theories, serve chiefly to "explain a result after it has been reached," and are not rules, like legal theories, usually "useless beforehand as a guide for reaching" the result?[7]

Why then are rules "authoritative" when legal theories

[6] This Dickinson freely admits; indeed his essay contains an admirable discussion of the problem of the judge in selecting from among "competing analogies."

[7] Dickinson in part attempts to anticipate this argument by pointing to the fact that "a vast number of legal rules have beyond dispute settled into at least a temporary fixity although they sprang originally from the creative legislative activity of judges." He refers to such settled rules as "that a contract must rest on consideration, or the rule in Shelley's case." On "the case-to-case application of [such] well-established rules," he asserts, the "personal characteristics of the judges may fairly enough be said to have no appreciable influence. . . . Rules like these possess well understood objective authority in such sense that no competent judge, whatever his temperament or intellectual equipment, feels that he has any choice in giving effect to them." The "personal bent of the judge" is a factor only in "the selection of new rules for unprovided cases."

But cases unequivocally calling for the routine application of such rules seldom come into court. Dickinson has failed to consider the immense importance of the judge's power to find the "facts." He has overlooked that the peculiar circumstances of any particular case cause the judge to favor one conclusion or another, and that the judge then often—more or less consciously—"interprets" those circumstances so that his conclusion can be stated in terms of some well-established rule of law, some rule "beyond dispute settled into at least temporary fixity."

What Dickinson ignores is that in a profound sense *the unique circumstances of almost any case make it an "unprovided case"* where no rule of "well understood objective authority" precludes the exercise of the judge's choice and therefore where no settled rule bars the influence of that "personal bent" of the judge which Dickinson concedes is inevitably a strong factor in the decision of "unprovided cases." *If the judge so states the facts that they appear to call for the application of a "well-established rule" the effect of his "personal bent" is concealed, but that is not to say that it is inoperative.* See above, Part One, Chapters XII, XIII and XIV.

or doctrines are not? Because (the reader is constrained to conclude) Dickinson feels obliged, at all costs, to find something in the administration of justice which is "authoritative," however slightly so. Accordingly he uses all the arts of the keen dialectician to find this compulsory quality in rules. Having by ingenious verbalities convinced himself that rules have some vestigial obedience-compelling character, he then sets the rules apart and appropriates the term "law" exclusively to what appears in the form of rules.[8]

Dickinson attempts to support his position with a sort of *reductio ad absurdum* argument directed against those who stress the ultimate and paramount importance of specific decisions. If, he says in effect, you do not agree that law consists of rules, then you are denying the existence of such rules. And such a denial lands you in juristic nihilism or pyrrhonism. In other words, Dickinson contends that, unless you agree that law is nothing more or less than rules, you must admit "that law in any true sense becomes an impossibility."[9]

[8] With less subtlety but more directness Salmond does the same; see 16 Law Quarterly Review, 376, 386.

[9] See 29 Columbia Law Review, 313: "The result of this" (the realistic) "view is of course to hold that all law must be made in the actual case to which it is applied; and hence that *no rule of law can survive authoritatively from case to case, so that law in any true sense becomes an impossibility.*" See also 29 Columbia Law Review, 116 and note 11; 318-9.

Dickinson cites with approval an article by Corwin (74 University of Pennsylvania Law Review, 638, 656) who criticizes Gray's view that statutes are not part of law but only a source of law because law, so far as affected by statutes, is only what the judges declare the statute means. If that be true, says Corwin, the same must be said of any rule of law announced by a court in a decision, for such a rule, fully as much as any statute, means in later cases only what the courts, in the later cases, say it means. Then, concludes Corwin with what he apparently assumes to be crushing sarcasm, "it is impossible to lay down a decision in unmistakable terms; and so there is no law!" This is precisely correct—if, but only if, law must mean rules set forth in "unmistakable terms" or (to use Dickinson's terminology) set forth "authoritatively."

Even those who believe that "rules are the alphabet of his study

Now there are two fallacies in this argument. As we have said, to deny that law consists of rules is no more to deny that rules exist than to deny that a cow consists of the grass it eats is to deny the reality of grass or the fact that the cow eats it. The basic flaw in this contention—and here we shall borrow from Dickinson's own language—is traceable to an identification of law with but one of the materials which may and often do enter into the making of law, *i.e.,* the making of decisions, which identification seems to be the result of exaggerated legalism which cannot conceive of the ingredients of law as other than law itself, and which thus insists on regarding rules as fully law instead of looking on them as merely one of the phenomena which sometimes powerfully influence the making of law and sometimes aid in predicting what law will be made. In short, what Dickinson claims is that law consists of one of the numerous factors which affect courts when engaged in making law, *i.e.,* in reaching decisions.

As we said (Part One, Chapter XIII), water is not hydrogen; an ear of corn is not a plow; a song recital does not consist of vocal cords; a journey is not a railroad train. Yet hydrogen is an ingredient of water, a plow aids in the

---

to any modern English lawyers" believe also that "Any judgment of any court is authoritative only as to that part of it, called the *ratio decidendi,* which is considered to have been necessary to the decision of the actual case between the litigants. *It is for the court, of whatever degree, which is called upon to consider the precedent to determine what the true* ratio decidendi *was.*" (Allen, "Law in the Making," 148–9.) Not the rule announced by the earlier court but what the later court believes to be the principle back of that rule—there is the authoritative factor, according to the conventional theory.

There is something which approaches willful misunderstanding in Dickinson's discussion of the views of those who deem decisions and not rules to be the central fact in law. See p. 318 and especially p. 116 where he states that the German advocates of "free judicial decision" "deny in substance that there can be general rules, or anything but specific decisions." The injustice of this comment will appear in the discussion of the "free judicial decision" school below in this Appendix.

development of corn, vocal cords are necessary to a song recital, a railroad train may be a means of taking a journey. And hydrogen, plows, vocal cords and railroad trains are real. No less are legal rules.

Dickinson's second fallacy is a belief that you are annihilating law if you refuse to accept the view that law consists of rules. But, as we have seen,[10] Holmes, Cook, Yntema and Green are able to define law without identifying it with rules.

In sum, Dickinson views "law" as but one component of "the administration of justice." The latter is subdivided into (1) "law," (*i.e.* rules), and (2) "policy" or "discretion." The judges exercise discretion or policy in applying law (*i.e.* rules); in determining what law (*i.e.* what rule) is to be applied; in widening or contracting the "meaning" of law (*i.e.* rules); in subsuming the facts of any case under the selected law (*i.e.* rules).

But this power, this discretion, this exercise of policy is not law, says Dickinson—not even when it passes over into law-making, *i.e.*, into the making of new rules.[11] What, then, is it? Dickinson gives us no answer.

Dean Green begins where Dickinson ends. That which to Dickinson is not-law is for Green its essence. Law is precisely "the power of passing judgment through formal political agencies for securing social control," *i.e.*, "control of the conduct of our neighbors and ourselves." This definition he offers as "a starting point from which it is possible to account for the behaviour of judges as a part of a law administration system." Other definitions err, he explains, in confusing this power with the instrumentalities through which the power itself is employed. Thus rules are

[10] Part One, Chapters XIII and XIV.
[11] For Dickinson (pp. 318–9) notes that the discretion involved in making rules is different only in degree and not in kind from the discretion involved in applying rules. But, he argues, the exercise of such discretion is not law; the law consists of the rules which result from the exercise of such discretion.

no more law than a policeman is law. In pointing out this differentiation between law and the machinery through which it operates,[12] he does not intend to minimize the importance of the machinery. "There can be no power without machinery; there can be no law without judges and courts and rules. But machinery without power is impotent. . . . In so far as the sources of law are apparent, they are found in the judgments of the individuals who are entrusted with the power to pass those judgments."

Such a view, of course, makes the judge all-important. "We have looked to the wrong source for dependability. We have sought it through a technic of language instead of a technic of judgment. We rather trust the machinery than its engineers." He maintains that "the judge is the most responsible unit in our social structure—that his judgment is the most vital factor of law administration. . . . About him must be built any program designed to serve a science of law." This means that we must "trust the affairs of men to the fallibility of men's judgments. It has required a long process of painful experimenting to drive home the dreaded fact—if it be even now driven home—that men must rely upon the judgment of men and make the best of it."

"How do judges pass judgment?" It is not possible to answer with any accuracy. Judgment-passing is still a mystery. "The processes of judgment are as obscure as the processes of thought. . . . We play around with our legal technic, make use of robust phrases, as though they disclosed the secret of our judgment. But it is a rare thing that an opinion acknowledges the forces which have impelled the judgment to be pronounced. . . . We are eager to believe that this is a 'government of laws and not of men.' We are pained when we come face to face with the fact that there is nothing more stable in our civilization than the common fund of desires, habits and intelligence

[12] This differentiation, in spirit, resembles Gray's contrast between law and the sources of law. But, of course, Green and Gray are poles apart in their respective attitudes towards rules.

of ourselves and our neighbors. And we refuse to believe that the power of passing society's judgment on the every-day affairs of society can be safely intrusted to the men whom we select as judges."

That the factors which control the judgment of the courts "do not differ in degree from those which control the like power of judgment in other affairs which we nor-mally think of as outside the scope of government is con-stantly becoming clearer. . . . The usages, customs and mores in all realms of society . . . are doubtless con-trolled by the same factors as the judgments we call law judgments. The term law is merely a term which is most generally used to indicate *governmental* control, as op-posed to other sorts of control. But law, as power to sub-ject people to control by passing judgment, is no different in government from what it is in Church, in fashion, in that mass of every-day relations which prevail through human society. . . . My suggestion is that law, wherever found, is in turn controlled by factors common to all sorts of administration, whether of formal government or other forms of group activity."[13]

Where this leaves rules is obvious: "After we have judged, we make use of all sorts of devices to indicate the lines our processes (of judgment) have followed in reach-ing judgment. We employ numberless mediums of expres-sion. It is these that many minds grasp and fondle as though they themselves hid the secret of judging and by some process of devotion could be made to give up their secret. You have observed those who cling to the words of the judge as though they possessed some occult power

[13] Green then discusses as the factors of most significance: (1) The administrative factor [*i.e.* difficulties of administration]; (2) the ethical or moral factor; (3) the economic factor; (4) the pro-phylactic factor; (5) the justice factor.

His views on the effect of word-slavery are discussed heretofore in Part One, Chapters VII and X; his discussion of the jury-ritual is touched upon in the notes to Part One, Chapter XVI; his refer-ence to the importance of the trial judge is quoted in Part One, Chapter XIII.

to determine other judgments. And possibly they do have some such power for the occult judge. There is no gainsaying that the formulas in which judgments have been couched have been highly important factors in men's dealings. Along with other uses they serve as storage cells for a legal science. They range from the tiniest one-cell order to those of the highest multiples. But how are those formulas themselves produced? How are they charged with this power of law? We seldom go behind them; we begin with them. We have our rules, our doctrines, our rights, powers, privileges, immunities, duties, etc., but where did we get them, and why do we use them as we do? When we say in a particular case that a defendant had a right, defendant was under a duty, and the like, this but means that we have already passed judgment. We are merely using these terms to pronounce the judgment passed. The process has been concluded in some unknown way; the result is merely being vocalized."

In another article Green has a trifle more bluntly expressed the same thought: "Sometimes a lawyer scarcely recognizes his case after it has gone through the court of last resort. An opinion may, and frequently does, merely represent an elaboration of the theory which caught the fancy of the judge or court writing the opinion. This fact makes it difficult to look through the well developed essay of the judge and catch even a glimpse of all the competitive theories and data from which the choice of the appellate court was made. Another judge might with equal assurance have reached an entirely different conclusion and thus have written a very different opinion."

Surely this is clearer thinking than Dickinson's. It avoids all the difficulties raised by rule-fetichism. For rule-fetichism leads the brightest and best informed minds, like Dickinson's, to vain attempts to dichotomize the administration of justice into authoritative law and something wayward which is not-law, called discretion or policy. Green sees the whole business as integral. Law is the power to judge, to decide specific controversies. Policy, discretion—these are not something apart from law, but are at the very center of the judicial process. Whoever studies that process unhampered by subjective commitments which deflect accurate observation must note that, while rules enter into the making of law, they are not the whole of it. That process of judging (which is law[14]) is not to be confined within the compass of mere rules. The rules play only a subordinate rôle.

Dickinson unfortunately does not discuss Green—perhaps because their writings in this field were published simultaneously. But it is peculiarly unfortunate[15] that he has paid no heed to the work of Bingham. For Bingham, whose writings antedate Dickinson's, has been at some pains to analyze the erroneous theory that law finds its only authoritative expression in abstract pronouncements in judicial opinions, "that no judgment is of any importance in the field of law unless a rule then or previously formulated by a court . . . is applied by the court as a guide to its decision, and that the importance of a case, therefore, lies not principally in its concrete existence, but in the abstract fact that the rule was then applied and illustrated."[16]

---

[14] From the point of view of the practical work of the lawyer, law may fairly be said to be past decisions (as to past events which have been judged) and predictions as to future decisions. From the point of view of the judge, the law may fairly be said to be the judging process or the power to pass judgment.

[15] Unfortunate, because Dickinson's scholarship and acute observation are leading him more and more in the direction of realism at which he fails to arrive because he is blocked by an obsessive, although diminishing, regard for rules. One ventures to hope that when Dickinson next investigates the nature of law he will overcome those vestigial effects of the basic myth which now mar his valuable work. The elimination from Dickinson's recent articles of perhaps one-fourth of their contents would convert them into a first-rate contribution to legal realism.

[16] Bingham observes that, in its older phase, this theory took the form of a denial that judges ever make law and of an assertion that judges merely discover, announce and apply authoritative rules; in its later phase this theory admits that judges make law but insists upon generality as an essential character of law.

Bingham's thesis may be paraphrased[17] as follows: The lawyer is concerned primarily with determining exactly what will be decided by the courts concerning concrete questions and with ascertaining what sort of facts will induce the judges to make specific decisions. He wants to know "the possibilities of concrete legal effects and their pertinent causes." What courts have done, how they have done it, and why, are important to the lawyer, because such knowledge will enable him more adequately to predict how and what the courts will do in future concrete cases which will come before them, and because it will assist the lawyer in persuading the courts to decide his cases in the manner he desires.

If what courts have done and will do in deciding specific controversies is law, then the knowledge which the lawyer uses to help him in predicting or bringing about decisions is not law, but is knowledge concerning law.[18]

[17] A paraphrase is desirable as Bingham's is a forbidding Austinian style. It is perhaps this style which accounts for the fact that Bingham is little noted by those working in the same field. The writer confesses that he had not heard of Bingham until this book was substantially completed. Bingham's writings on the nature of law appear in 11 Michigan Law Review, 1,109; 9 Illinois Law Review, 97; 25 Green Bag, 162.

[18] "Law at its point of contact with the life of the people consists of the reasoned determinations and the concrete action of men and not of an indefinite, intangible and irresponsible system of rules and principles." Cf. Corbin, 44 Law Quarterly Review, 24, 28-9: "Every jural relation between men can be shown to be a prediction of what, on specified facts, the conduct of organized society, acting by its agents (as it must) will be"; the bases of such predictions are: (1) knowledge of past judicial action and legislation; (2) "the personality and experience of the judges who are to pass judgment on a case"; (3) "a knowledge of the prevailing mores of the time."

Compare also Keyser, "On The Study of Legal Science," 38 Yale Law Journal, 413: "The subject matter of legal science is a certain species of human behavior—I mean the distinctive behavior of those persons whose official role in human society is to answer, for the community they represent, such questions as arise respecting what is just. In a word, the subject matter of legal science is the decisions (the distinctive behavior) of judges. . . . Law (judicial be-

If he or anyone else chooses to compress such knowledge into generalized form, there results a legal rule. But the generalized form does not change the character of this knowledge. A rule tells something about law, but is not law.

For, to repeat, law is what has happened or what will happen in concrete cases. Past decisions are experimental guides to prognostications of future decisions. And legal rules are mental devices for assembling, in convenient form, information about past cases to aid in making such prognostications. Or they may be defined as generalized statements of how courts will decide questions, of the considerations which will weigh with courts in the decision of cases to which the rules are applicable.

Anyone can make a legal rule. That is, anyone can study the precedents and, as a result, can venture predictions of the legal consequences of particular conduct, and can put these predictions into the form of generalizations; anyone can make generalized statements of what (in the light of the past decisions or whatever) the courts should or are likely to do in the future. When we say of any legal rule, "That is the law," we mean that we think it indicates, with a relatively high degree of accuracy, potential concrete decisions. If you or I, or Jack Robinson makes such a rule, it is no better or worse because of its author. Its validity, its utility as a mental tool, depends not on who

---

havior) changes because the stimuli that evoke it and the circumstances that condition it do not remain the same and do not repeat precisely but continually alter under the influence of new things emerging endlessly in the flux of life and the world. . . . Law (judicial behavior) depends upon and varies with a variety of more or less familiar variables." Keyser mentions as among these variables the following: Modes and forms of business; manners, customs, mores; religious opinion and feeling; science and invention; industrial development; political theory; axiology.

Llewellyn's brilliant study, "A Realistic Jurisprudence—The Next Step," 30 Columbia Law Review, 431 (published while this book was at the press) makes no reference to Bingham, who had at several points anticipated Llewellyn, although the latter is most generous to others of his predecessors.

created it, but on the degree of its trustworthiness as a prognostication of future concrete decisions. The more accurate, the more reliable, the forecast contained in it, the more valid the rule.

Judges, obviously, have no monopoly on such rule-making. The fact that a judge, in explaining the grounds for his decision, utters such a generalized prediction, does not vouch for its validity or utility. Wigmore's rules of law with respect to evidence, Gray's with respect to real property, or Mechem's with respect to agency are considered far more reliable than those found in the average judicial opinion. Yet neither Wigmore, Gray nor Mechem was ever on the bench. There is nothing, then, inherently superior about judicially contrived rules of law.

Nor can any rule of law, by whomever made, be "authoritative." For whether a rule be considered as an historical summary—a brief, generalized statement of what courts have done—or as a prediction of what courts will do, it cannot be final, binding, dictatorial. That is, the notion of "authoritativeness" is alien to the character of a rule, looked at either as a bit of historical description or as a bit of prophecy. The announcement of a rule by a court cannot, therefore, confer upon it an authoritative quality.

Even if—by a distortion of the ordinary meaning of words—the word "authoritative," as applied to legal rules, is taken as meaning "accurate," it cannot be said that rules found in judicial opinions are peculiarly authoritative (*i.e.* accurate). Experience shows that judicially uttered rules are often misleading, wholly vague or useless. A judicial opinion may generalize more or less adequately the results of the customary action of the courts but it is usually deficient in explaining the motives for the judge's decisions. "In the first place, the opinion is generally written after the judgment has been determined upon. In the second place, often it is the opinion of only one of the judges of the court. The reasons of the different judges who concur in the decision may vary widely. . . . Thirdly, it is often a difficult task for a man to comprehend clearly and accurately the real motives which have led to his decision. In many cases it requires powers of insight into one's personal mental and psychological machinery, conscious and unconscious, and analytical ability which are possessed by only a small portion of humanity. Fourthly, accurate generalization and expression are difficult tasks in which few are adept, and are not essential to the functions of the judge."

The business of judges is to dispose of litigation, not to formulate rules, that is, not to state accurate generalizations of the result of their decisions or accurate forecasts of future decisions.[19] To generalize accurately the determinations of the courts and the real reasons or motives producing those determinations are tasks for which the judges do not have sufficient time. It can be done better by others.

These are the reasons why "the generalizations of judges so often fail to indicate accurately 'what the law is'—*i.e.*, what would happen or has happened in concrete cases—on all matters covered by the generalization, and why the legal investigator and judges in later cases discard the explanation in a judicial opinion as unsatisfactory, although they agree that the decision itself is sound."

That judicial generalizations have an effect on the thinking of judges, Bingham admits. "I do not deny that statements of judicial generalizations are important facts in the train of legal sequences, which must be carefully studied and interpreted in the course of obtaining a cor-

[19] It is for this reason that Bingham objects to the phrase "judicial legislation" to describe judicial law-making. Legislation sets standards for future cases. The courts do not legislate; they hear, supervise and determine particular concrete controversies.

Bingham points out that the effort of judges, when deciding particular cases, to lay down authoritative rules to govern cases which may arise in the future is inconsistent with the avowed refusal of the courts to decide "moot" cases, *i.e.*, cases in which there is no real controversy presently before the court.

Bingham gives no satisfactory explanation of the desire for "generality" which lies behind the authoritative-rule theory of law.

rect estimate of the indicative value of the decision to which they lead; nor that such statements are potent precedential considerations in the determination of subsequent cases; nor that judges have often decided cases contrary to their judicial inclination because of the existence of such precedents, and have done so sometimes under the influence of an idea that those precedents were authoritative dictates."[20]

But he points out the obvious fact that a belief that a rule is an authoritative dictate does not make the rule authoritative. The belief may and does (often harmfully) influence judicial reasoning. But to admit the potency of the influence of this belief is by no means to say that the belief is not entirely erroneous. Indeed it is this very belief which Bingham attacks because it "clouds the understanding of judges and lawyers, introduces circumlocutions, subtleties, and vagaries into legal reasoning, and encourages in the language of the profession an abundance of misleading, indefinite, and unsound pronouncements."

Bingham is, of course, not unmindful that, as long as judges continue to be dominated by the "authoritative-rule theory" it will be expedient for the lawyer to word his reasoning accordingly: "One who is arguing before a court should so adapt his forms of reasoning and his manner of expression as to convince the judges as thoroughly and easily as possible. Therefore he will find it expedient to employ generalizations and language which are current in the profession and which may be paralleled by quotations from judicial opinions and standard texts. It requires some mental effort to recognize substantially the

[20] As we have observed (Part One, Chapter XIV), the alleged devotion to precedents is illusory. Attempts to explain, in rational and intelligible form, when and how precedents will be followed, inevitably become involved in casuistry and hair-splitting. See for instance, Black on "precedents," or Allen, "Law in the Making," Chapter IV. Compare Bingham's comments (11 Michigan Law Review, 109–13) with Green, 28 Columbia Law Review, 1036–38; Dickinson, 29 Columbia Law Review, 119; Oliphant, 8 American Law School Review, 215.

same consideration in a new garb and to appreciate improvements in arrangements and associations of ideas. One cannot be sure that busy judges will vigorously master such innovations and improvements, and this risk must be carefully weighed before one departs from the beaten paths of legal thought and speech in advocacy, however defective, dark, and inadequate those paths may be."[21]

At the close of the nineteenth century, just about the time when Holmes was first urging Anglo-American lawyers to regard their work realistically, a similar point of view—expressed as the doctrine of "free judicial decision"[22]—began to be advocated, quite independently, on the Continent of Europe and especially in Germany.[23]

The pivotal point of this doctrine is its emphasis on the just solution of the particular case, on right judgments on the merits of a lawsuit as against correct logical deduction from preëstablished rules. It considers equity and discretion the central factors in the work of the judges.

The school which supports this doctrine has its right

[21] Cf. W. Jethro Brown, 29 Yale Law Journal, 399–400: "The really practical lawyer will employ his scientific equipment to aid him in arriving at sound conclusions, but will express these conclusions with due regard to judicial informities! . . . The ancient fiction that judges never added to, but only applied, pre-existing law, has been long since discredited. There are still judges, however, who cherish the fiction that a statutory text or a legal principle or rule may have all the certitude and inelasticity of a mathematical proposition or chemical formula. When a lawyer pleads before such a judge his method of approach will be flank rather than frontal. The tact required of the judge is proverbial. But what of the tact required of the advocate who lives in an age of seemingly rapid transition, and in a world where thought dwelleth not in watertight compartments!"

[22] Also called "free legal decision," "liberty of decision," "free application of law."

[23] Some claim that the founder of this doctrine was Gény, a French jurist, who wrote of it at least as early as 1899; others claim the honor for the German jurist, Ehrlich.

Holmes's work seems to have antedated that of these Continentals.

and left wing and its moderates. The clearest exposition of
its point of view available in English translation is perhaps
a treatise by one of the moderates, Gmelin, Justice of the
Court of Appeals of Stuttgart. He portrays the attitude of
this school as a reaction against scholastic argumentation,
and against deduction of decisions by mere formal logic
from rules embodied in the code. The reaction was due to
the belief that the decisions which resulted from such
scholastic reasoning offended the "sense of justice." And
it is the sense of justice which the new school contends
should in all cases control the judge except in those unusual instances where explicit language in the code compels the judge to reach what he would otherwise consider
an unjust decision. "And would it really be arrogant and
worthy of condemnation," asks Gmelin, "if a . . . judge
should remember his sense of justice and emphasize—even
in express words—what he believes to be just and equitable in the case to be decided, and then proceed to show
that what he thus found to be just is really in harmony
with the established law?"

Gmelin quotes a minister of justice who used to exhort
young judges in this manner: "When a case is to be decided, you had better at first leave your Code alone. After
you have understood the facts thoroughly, consider what
would be right according to your common sense and the
law of nature and equity; then, when you have thoroughly
made up your minds on the case, look at your Code, and
behold! You will find that the statute fits your own conclusion exactly in almost all cases, and that its intention is
nothing but what you intend also." Gmelin adds, "It is
entirely true that by following that method an unbiased
judge will find at first glance what is true and right in
thousands of cases."

The facts of the case are all-important to the free judicial decision proponents.[24] "We need a vivid under-

[24] Other writers of this school refer to "a knowledge of the requirements growing out of the circumstances of the case" or "all
the surrounding circumstances." They see "the rule of law" merely

standing of the facts, a sympathetic treatment of the human destinies that are passing before our eyes. We must strive to penetrate into the needs of the parties who come before the judge as patients come before the physician, so that we may not offer them the stone of bald reasoning but the bread of sympathetic relief." Judges should strive to find "the right judgment on the merits by practical sense and true comprehension of the facts, instead of the correct logical deduction by the help of logical subtleties." Gmelin summarizes the purpose behind this new attitude thus: *"To bring about a just determination by means of the subjective sense of justice inherent in the judge, guided by an effective weighing of the interests of the parties in the light of the opinions prevailing in the community regarding transactions like those in question."*

The will of the judge is to be directed to the just and reasonable results within the limits of the positive rule of law. Such just and reasonable results are to be aimed at consciously. Heretofore they have been sought clandestinely. For the subjective sense of justice has been, in the past, identified with arbitrary discretion. Where decisions have been just, the "true reasons have been relegated to some remote corner in the opinion, so that they appeared like some mere embellishment rather than the basis of the decision which in truth they were." Opinions often "reason backwards," so that there is in them "a sort of hypocrisy, which is frequently enough suspected by the writer of the opinion although he does not realize what the cause of the trouble is." The judge having found the true conclusion, "afterwards fits to it a scholastic chain of merely formal logic as the pretended means of arriving at the result." This semi-hypocritical method should be abandoned in favor of acknowledged "free decision."

---

as "a general guide." "The real duty of the judge is to find the law which dwells in each particular state of facts." They insist on "open *recognition* of the gaps in the law" and examination of "all the surrounding circumstances of the case" in "places of the subterfuge of forced construction of texts."

But "does not the new method imperil most seriously the certainty of the law?" asks Gmelin. "That question I shall answer by the counter-question: Does such certainty exist at present? . . . Any one of us judges who has occasion in some matter to venture a prediction regarding the outcome of a law-suit will, in view of the flood of doubtful points existing today, feel himself overwhelmed by a feeling of uncertainty."

Indeed, the new method is likely to produce more rather than less certainty. "Fruitless wrangling about learned concepts," stubborn pride in the correctness of formal reasoning, lead to needless differences of opinion among judges. "In proportion as a judgment is to be based on legal tact, a sense of morality and the instinct of long experience, each judge will become more tolerant of the differing opinion of his neighbor on the bench." Where considerations of justice are made paramount, the most reasonable and appropriate solution will prevail in most instances, while in scholastic disputation "the most unreasonable and impractical solution has just about an even chance." For by formal logic you "can guarantee the formal correctness of procedure but never the correctness of results." "The idea that decisions based on purely dialectical argumentation have the alleged quality of logical necessity is a figment of the imagination." Decisions which shock the sense of justice "are supported by undoubtedly acute legal arguments that cannot be gainsaid from the standpoint of formal logic." More than that, the unjust judgments are often "supported by greater deductive acumen" than those that do substantial justice. "This fact proves that the prevailing method of finding the decision by logical deduction from the legal rule does not work properly. It seems to be an open secret that in the majority of cases we can support both sides of a contention by deductions and constructions drawn from the rule by faultless logic."

The free judicial decision school has clarified the indispensable factor of the judge's personality in judicial administration. "The central and normal part played by the judge consists in a personal mental activity," writes Gény. "A legal decision is always the result of a number of factors influencing the judge; meaning and text of a rule is one of these factors, but not the only one,"[25] writes Ehrlich. "Each application of a general rule to a particular case is necessarily influenced by the personality of the judge who makes it. . . . The point is that this fact" (the influence of the judge's personality) "should not be tolerated as something unavoidable but should be gladly welcomed."

Free judicial decision will not lead to anarchy in thus acknowledging and welcoming the presence of this personal element.[26] "Free decision," says Ehrlich cogently, "is conservative, as every kind of freedom is; for freedom means responsibility, while restraint shifts responsibility upon other shoulders." And Gmelin notes another important consideration: "In discussing the subjective discretion of the judge we must not forget that his knowledge of the whole body of law and the interdependence of its parts (say *e.g.* with regard to the utility of prescribed formalities and the necessity of enforcing them) will so vitally affect his original sense of justice that a new and particular condition of his mind is the result. Of this condition the judge could not rid himself in any particular case, even if he wished to do so, any more than a medical expert, in testifying, could eliminate his knowledge of medicine."[27]

[25] Here the inaccuracy of Dickinson's comments, referred to above, becomes apparent. The "free law" school does not, as Dickinson states, "deny that there can be general rules, or anything but specific decisions." See the articles by Gény, Ehrlich and Gmelin in "The Science of Legal Method," 4–10, 78, 130, 132. It does deny that these rules can be authoritative, and it deplores the results of the practice of trying to make them appear to be authoritative.

[26] See Part One, Chapter XIII.

[27] Dean Green has more directly answered the argument that liberation from rule-worship will cause anarchy: "The control of judges is not to be found in rules, but in the fact that they are men

The "free-law" doctrine was developed as a response to the problems arising in countries where an effort has been made to codify law. Some of those problems are therefore peculiar to those countries, but the difficulties are essentially similar to those which confront the English or American lawyer. Whether rules are set forth in codes or statutes or decisions, the attempt to make them dogmas is a vain thing. The function of the judge is something more than to know and apply those rules. The task of the lawyer does not end there. The judging of concrete cases —that is "law"; rules, while they enter into that business, are by no means the whole of it or the most important part of it. The notion that rules are authoritative and constitute law hampers the adequate administration of justice. That notion is traceable to the basic legal myth. We shall have better law when, by ridding ourselves of that myth, we come to recognize the relatively subordinate importance of rules.[28]

---

nourished on the same thoughts and other life-giving sources as the rest of us, and are subject to be influenced by the same factors in making their judgments as those which influence their fellows generally. Judges, as other men, are bound by the factors which condition their growth." "There is not much danger of any judge being either likely or able to depart very far from the beaten path, and if so, there is little danger that he can influence others to follow him." 28 Columbia Law Review, 1014, 1020, 1038. Cf. Radin, "Statutory Interpretation," 43 Harvard Law Review, 863.

[28] For other noteworthy attacks on the authoritative character of rules, see Francis in 28 Yale Law Journal, 335; Radin in 11 American Bar Association Journal, 357; Klaus in 28 Columbia Law Review, 312, 441.

SCIENCE AND CERTAINTY: AN UNSCIENTIFIC CONCEPTION OF SCIENCE

Even science is, for many, a new source of illusion, a new escape from change and chance, a new road to the absolute. For, unfortunately, to many persons, science is a charter of certainty, a technique which ere long will give man complete control and sovereignty over nature. Science seems to hold out an expectation that ultimately man will gain total relief from uncertainty and procure elimination of chance.

Of course that is an unscientific conception of science. Science thus falsely conceived becomes, in effect, another father-substitute, a guarantor of that absolute certainty which the child craves and which the fully adult man recognizes as infantile. A scientific conception of science[1] rejects such childishness. For science, rightly employed, requires patient and exact observation of *all* phenomena,

[1] Such a conception involves, first of all, the making of a distinction between (1) scientific results and (2) scientific method and outlook. It is the latter, the scientific habit of thought, to which reference is made when the word "science" is employed in the text above. See an admirable discussion of this distinction by A. E. Heath, "Science and Education" in "Science and Civilization" (edited by F. S. Marvin), 221. Heath there briefly deals with the two chief popular errors concerning scientific method: (a) the belief that the criterion of scientific method is its quantitative character; and (b) the belief that scientific treatment of a field implies that the facts of the field are ultimately reducible to mechanics. See also the works referred to in the notes to Part One, Chapter I, especially Barry, "The Scientific Habit of Thought."

including the human organism itself. And such observation goes to show the inescapable limitations of human observation and of human intellection based upon such observation. We are finite creatures with limited end-organs and therefore with restricted approaches to and apprehension of our environment. Our control of that environment will doubtless grow. But there are facts which must ever be beyond our reach and control.

Karl Pearson[2] (following Kant, but using more modern imagery) has put it thus:

"It is not hard to imagine by extension of existing machinery a great stone-sorting machine of such a character that, when a confused heap of stones was thrown in pell-mell at one end, some sizes would be rejected while the remainder would come out at the other end of the machine sifted and sorted according to their sizes. Thus a person who solely regarded the final results of the machine might consider that only stones of certain sizes had any existence, and that such stones were always arranged according to their sizes. In some such way as this, perhaps, we may look upon that great sorting-machine—the human perceptive faculty. Sensations of all kinds and magnitudes may flow into it, some to be rejected at once, others to be sorted, all orderly, and arranged in place and time. *It may be the perceptive faculty itself, which, without our being directly conscious of it, contributes the ordered sequence in time and space to our sense-impressions. The routine of perception may be due to the recipient, and not characteristic of the material.* If anything like this be the case, then (granted a co-ordination of perceptive and reasoning faculties), it will be less surprising that, when the human mind comes to analyze phenomena in time and space, it should find itself capable of briefly describing the past, and of predicting the future sequences of all manner of sense-impressions. From this standpoint the nomic natural law is an unconscious product of the machinery of the perceptive faculty, while natural law in the scientific sense is the conscious product of the reflective faculty, analyzing the process of perception, the working of the sorting-machine. The whole of ordered nature is thus seen as the product of one mind—

2 "The Grammar of Science" (3rd Edition), 106.

the only mind with which we are acquainted—and the fact that the routine of perceptions can be expressed in brief formulae ceases to be so mysterious as when we postulate a two-fold reason, one type characteristic of 'things-in-themselves,' beyond our sense-impressions, and another type associated with the machinery of nervous organization."

Whether or no Pearson's suggestion, with all its implications, is acceptable *in toto,* it is useful in calling attention to the fact that the limitations of our mental sifting machine exclude the possibility of our coping with all of the environment. Those factors in the environment with which our mental machine cannot deal, which, because of its structure, it is forced to reject and treat as nonexistent, must obviously remain beyond its control. Life then is always to be unavoidably full of uncontrollables, to be chancy, uncertain.

To be sure, the processes of this sifting machine may be less rigid than Pearson apparently believes. All the seeming fixity of our mental apparatus may not be ineradicably determined by our biological heritage but may be, to a very large extent, a product of our social heritage,[3] —traditional stupidities and socially created blindnesses passed on from father to son and likely to be abandoned more and more rapidly as unnecessary father-respect loses its domination over adult thinking. The static aspect of the "intellect," which Bergson sees as its indelible and essential characteristic, may be modifiable in some considerable measure.[4]

But while man's intellection may grow more elastic and "intuitive," closer to the "nature of things," man will never be able to become aware of, let alone control, all the factors in the environment which are affecting him and his fortunes. The belief in ultimate scientific certainty is therefore fatuous. For since there will always be elusive factors, unknowable and unpredictable, the adventitious cannot be removed from human life. The universe will always

[3] In which language plays its part. See Part One, Chapter X.
[4] See Part One, Chapter X.

contain some remnant of what, humanly speaking, is chaos, something which refuses to be reduced to our conception of order, something astray which cannot be formulated in terms of "scientific laws." When all is said and done, this is, for man, a chancy world. Science, wisely considered, is no substitute for the all-wise, all-powerful father. The fact of change and chance must be bravely faced.

As we have said, to face unflinchingly the inevitableness of chance is to be grown up. As childhood recedes, one is forced by events to accept in every-day life the fact that some things are so because they are so. There develops a sort of "adult agonisticism." The "idea of chance," says Piaget, "is derivative: it is a conclusion forced upon us by our powerlessness to explain." But it is a conclusion which the child has not yet learned to adopt. "For lack of a definite idea of chance, he will always look for the why and wherefore of all the fortuitous juxtapositions which he meets with in experience." The idea of the accidental eludes him; it does not exist for him. And, Piaget adds, "a world in which chance does not exist is a far less mechanical and more anthropomorphic world than ours."

The over-simplified world pictured by popular science is therefore a child's world, a dream world in which men seek rest from the contingencies to which they are forced to submit in the stress and strain of daily living.

But the true scientific spirit is not content with such a dream world. It frankly admits the existence of the fortuitous. And, paradoxically, its calm acceptance of the unavoidable imperfection of its technique vastly improves its usefulness. For by this admission it gets rid of an impossible task and can face the environment unburdened by the necessity of stretching its aims beyond their proper scope.

If and whenever a sophisticated scientist postulates a universe completely governed by discoverable unchanging law, he recognizes that such a postulate is a fiction, *i.e.,* a statement of something untrue, made simply to aid in getting work done, made with complete recognition of its unreality.[5]

[5] See the writers on scientific method cited in notes to Part One, Chapter I and in Part Three, Chapter I. Note what Bridgman and Eddington state with reference to the recently formulated "Principle of Uncertainty" or "Principle of Indeterminacy" in physics. Cf. Appendix VII, "Notes on Fictions."

NOTES ON POUND'S VIEWS

1. POUND'S VIEWS ON THE NATURE OF THE DESIRE FOR LEGAL CERTAINTY

To Pound the conflict between the demand for certainty and the demand for change seems to be central in all stages of legal history. To him, "all thinking about law has struggled to reconcile the conflicting demands of the need of stability and the need of change. . . . In one way or another all of the vexed questions of the science of law prove to be phases of the same problem."[1] No one, perhaps, has so industriously portrayed the innumerous aspects of this problem. His interpretation of the nature and causes of the need for legal certainty and stability deserves the most careful study.

Pound views law as a means of securing social interests. In particular, he treats the demand for stability, certainty and uniformity as due basically to the "social interest in the general security," or as he sometimes phrases it, "a paramount social want of general security." He leaves us in no doubt as to the meaning of these phrases, for he

[1] Cf. Sir James Mackintosh: "The science of law is continually struggling to combine inflexible rules with transactions and relations perpetually varying." Coleridge said that "the two antagonist powers or opposite powers of the state, under which all other state interests are comprised, are those of *permanence* and *progression*." Sir Henry Maine wrote that in progressive societies social necessities are always in advance of law so that there is always a gap between the two; he adds, "Law is stable; the societies we are speaking of are progressive. The greater or less happiness of a people depends on the degree of promptitude with which the gulf is closed."

writes, "the paramount social interest in the general security, which as *an interest in peace and order* dictated the very beginnings of law, has led men to seek some fixed basis of a certain ordering of human action which should . . . *assure a firm and stable social order.*"[2]

In other words, he views the stability-uniformity-certainty-security demand as primarily the response to a practical social need for the elimination of war and strife and the procuring of peace and order in the social group. He is saying, in effect, that the law is essentially a parallelogram of two practical forces, the practical need for stability and the practical need for change. That the demand for certainty may become excessive and even self-defeating, he recognizes. But he apparently believes that the vital urge towards juristic absolutism is essentially a justifiable grouping for a firm and stable social order, *a longing having its roots deep in reality.*

Although that appears to be his essential thesis, there is much in his own writing which lends support to an opposite view. Thus he classifies the twelve principal ideas of the nature of law which men have developed:[3]

1. The idea of a divinely ordained rule or set of rules for human action, such as, for instance, the Mosaic law or Hammurabi's code handed him by the Sun-God.

2. An idea of law as a tradition based on the old customs which have proved acceptable to the gods.

3. The recorded wisdom of the wise men of old who had learned the safe course or the divinely approved course for human conduct.

4. A philosophically discovered system of principles which expressed the nature of things and to which man, therefore, ought to conform his conduct.

---

[2] "An Introduction to the Philosophy of Law," 18, 73; "Interpretations of Legal History," 1; cf. "The Spirit of the Common Law," 119; "Juristic Science and the Law," 31 Harvard Law Review, 1047; "Classification of Law," 37 Harvard Law Review, 933.

[3] "An Introduction to the Philosophy of Law," Chapter II.

5. A body of ascertainments and declarations of an eternal and immutable moral code.

6. A body of agreements of men in politically organized society as to their relations with each other. This is a democratic version of the identification of law with the enactments and decrees of the Greek City-State.

7. A reflection of the divine reason governing the universe. (Thomas Aquinas.)

8. A body of commands of the sovereign authority.

9. A system of precepts discovered by human experience whereby the human will may realize the most complete freedom possible, consistent with the like freedom of will of others. This theory assumed that the human experience by which the legal principles were discovered was determined in some inevitable way and was not a matter of conscious human endeavor.

10. A system of principles discovered philosophically whereby the external life of man is measured by reason, or whereby the will of the individual in action is harmonized with those of his fellowmen.

11. A body of rules imposed on man in society by the dominant class for the time being in furtherance, conscious or unconscious, of its interest. (This economic interpretation of law takes legislation as the type of legal precept.)

12. The dictates of economic or social laws with respect to the conduct of man in society, discovered by observation and expressed in precepts developed through human experience of what would work and not work in the administration of justice.

"What common elements," he asks, "may we find in the foregoing twelve pictures of what law is? For one thing, each shows us a picture of *some ultimate basis, beyond reach of the individual human will, that stands fast in the whirl of change of which life is made up.* . . . This fixed and stable starting point is usually the feature upon which the chief emphasis is placed. Next we shall find in all theories of the nature of law a picture of a determinate and mechanically absolute mode of

proceeding from the fixed and absolute starting point. . . .
Third, we shall see in these theories a picture of a system of
ordering human conduct and adjusting human relations *rest-
ing upon the ultimate basis and derived therefrom by the
absolute process.*

"In other words, they all picture, not merely an ordering of
human conduct and adjustment of human relations, which we
have actually given, but something more which we should like
to have, namely, a doing of these things in *a fixed absolutely
predetermined way,* excluding all merely individual feelings or
desires of those by whom the ordering and adjustment are
carried out."

Pound tells us that, as disclosed in these "subconscious
picturings of the end of law," the law seems to have been
conceived "as existing to satisfy a paramount social want
of general security," *i.e.,* to satisfy a practical need for a
stable society. This we may question. Granted that a practical and realistic interest in social order is at work in these
legal cosmogonies, still it is surely true that they also disclose patently an excessive interest in mental peace secured
by a belief in some ultimate authority beyond the reach of
human will—which is not unlike the child's belief in the
character and position of his father.

Again, Pound groups the attempted reconciliations of
stability and change, and notes that they have apparently
employed three main methods—authority, philosophy, history.

(a) The method of authority, he tells us, "puts a single
ultimate unchallengeable author behind the legal order and
as the source of every legal precept whose declared will is
binding as such." This authority may, in some periods of
history, be a God, or the Wise Men, or the State.

Pound would have us believe that when men are thinking thus it is because of their practical interest in a practical security. No doubt practical interest plays a part in
such beliefs. Yet surely "a single . . . unchallengeable authority whose declared will is binding as such" sounds not
unlike a child's notion of his father, and it is surely credible
that such a subconscious infantile notion had something

to do with the conception of legal authority thus aptly described by Pound.

(b) At times, he says, the need of change comes to the fore and then men often use what he terms the method of philosophy—some directing and organizing theory which recognizes change and yet denies its reality. So, the theory of the law of nature and the doctrine of natural rights meet these conditions. The actual changing rules of law get their validity from the ideal, unswerving, natural law which the rules reflect and of which they are more or less perfect copies. Inevitably, such a theory, designed to conceal the reality of change, sooner or later becomes another type of authority. Accordingly, this theory has led to the belief in immutable and eternal legal principles of universal validity which were not merely discoverable, but which, generally speaking, the jurists had discovered.[4]

Again, are we not, in this theory, listening to something like a small boy with a grown-up vocabulary talking of an ideal father?

(c) The method of history, says Pound, was the particular nineteenth-century contribution to the reconciliation of legal stability and change. It rejected the theory that law was deduced from rational principles. It found its principles historically; but, practically, there was slight difference between the result thus reached and that arrived at by the method of natural law. The historical school arrived at "natural law based upon historical premises." It created a new absolutism. It "discovered" the same old fixed, arbitrary, universal, unchangeable standards.

It is clear then, according to Pound's findings, that by whatever route men have traveled, something like external, immutable and absolute authority has turned out to be a

[4] What such a philosophy can produce as its fundamental notion of the nature of law, we may see in Blackstone's Absolutism; for him the law is "a rule: not a transient sudden order from a superior, to or concerning a particular person; but something permanent, uniform and universal." Cf. Pound, "Outlines of Lectures on Jurisprudence," Chapter 3.

large element in the juristic theories at which they have arrived. Ever we encounter this paradox: that even where a new theory or philosophy arises in response to a present need of readjustment (as, for instance, where it is used to overhaul and refit legal precepts in a period of commercial expansion) yet men strive to cover up the transformation, to deny the reality of change, to conceal the truth of adaptation behind a verbal disguise of fixity and universality.

Now Pound sees these facts clearly, but he ascribes the recurring fascination of authoritarianism primarily to a practical social need.[5] If the legal philosophers, even while working out a philosophy that will permit of change and validate it, go on chanting of immutability, the reason is, according to Pound's view, the paramount social interest in the general security. An interest in practical needs fosters the hope of finding "some ultimate unifying idea equal to the task of yielding perfect law which should stand fast forever." Men, he thinks, above all else, need social peace and quietude as the basis of a decent ordering of society. This, he believes, is a wise *practical* requirement; not the sole requirement, and yet the "paramount" requirement, all others being classified by him as "less immediate social interests." Men seek "to make the legal order appear something fixed and settled and beyond question," and have faith in their ability to find an "everlasting, unchangeable legal reality" because such a perfect unchangeable law would be the best safeguard of their paramount practical social interest. But, says Pound in effect, unfortunately life demands changes (*i.e.*, there is "the pressure of *less immediate* social interests"), and the clash of these two types of practical social interest produces the fundamental problems in the philosophy and practice of the law.

[5] Since readjustment, as well as stability, is a practical need, why do the philosophies of law never apotheosize legal change? Is it not because the notion of legal stability has a stronger subjective, non-practical, appeal? Is it "practical" to demand an unrealizable kind of law?

But if the clash had been between two practical interests, each rooted in reality, would not men sooner have recognized the artificial character of the compromises they have contrived? Would each successive theory or philosophy have striven so earnestly to mask the fact of change, paid such excessive tribute to an absolute external authority?

There is clearly something else besides practical needs making itself felt in this clash. Pound himself for a moment approaches such a view. New situations have called continually for modification of legal precepts. "And this," he says, "has led men to seek principles of legal development by which to *escape from authoritative rules which they feared or did not know how to reject,* but could no longer apply to advantage." But Pound does not develop this hint.

Elsewhere in his writings there is another intimation. He is speaking of the various sources of authority to which men have looked for legal finality. He refers to such sources of authority as "juristic gods." One expects, for a moment, that he will here develop the hypothesis (which we suggested and examined above in Part One, Chapter XVIII) of the fatuous search for religious satisfaction in the law. But this lead, too, he fails to follow up.

So that, despite hints to the contrary, one leaves Pound's scholarly dissertations with the feeling that he rests the demand for legal certainty basically on objective practical and not on subjective illusory needs.

2. Pound's Discussion of Some Traditional Elements in American Law

Pound finds that there are three chief traditional elements in American law still operative and tending to promote the demand for rigidity and fixity.[6] Further light may be thrown on our own thesis by a brief survey of these three elements and their inter-relation:

[6] "The Spirit of the Common Law."

(a) There is a *Germanic* element which is "the substratum of our law." This "means that the basis of our American law, the material out of which American judges in the nineteenth century made the law under which we live, represents the state of development which may be called the stage of the strict law." This strict Germanic law has "the point of view of primitive society." Its rules are "wholly inelastic and inflexible."

(b) There is the *Puritan* element,[7] with its insistence on fixed, absolute, unyielding, impersonal rules.

(c) There is the *Pioneer* influence with its policy of governmental action coupled with its requirement of uniformity, equality and certainty leading to an "insistence upon the exact working out of rules and the devotion to that end of the whole machinery of justice."

No one who has read Pound's suggestive work, "The Spirit of the Common Law," can fail to agree that all these factors in our past are still affecting our present legal system. They are "survivals." But why have they survived? Other past influences have little or no present meaning to us. If the attitudes of the primitive Germans, of the Puritans and of the Pioneers were not congenial to our contemporary attitude they would not today be recognized as operative.[8]

In other words, tradition is not self-operative. Its existence as a survival must be related to some present meaning. What is the present meaning? Pound does not ask this question, since he merely describes, but does not seek to explain, the reason for the fact of survival. But of his answer, if this question were put to him, there can be little doubt. There still exists, he would say, "the social interest in the general security," namely, an interest in peace and order, in a firm and stable society. We have a present

[7] Of which further below.

[8] Compare John Dewey in "The Social Sciences and their Interrelations," 24; Professor Morris Cohen, "Law and Scientific Method," 6 American Law School Review, 235; Elsie Clews Parsons, "Fear and Conventionality," XI.

practical need for security, stability and peace. These traditional formulations of the means of satisfying this need are, accordingly, still congenial.

Our answer would be somewhat different. To be sure, "the social interest in the general security" is a value which still maintains. But—no one knows this better than Pound[9] —a false and fatuous conviction that this interest can best be promoted through rigidity and mechanization in the judicial process does not today promote the orderly working of the administration of justice. These traditions, in so far forth, are indeed hostile to social peace and order and stability. For these traditions embody delusional beliefs in the amount of certainty desirable and obtainable. And such beliefs interfere with the competent handling of such questions as the relation of law and morals, the distinction between law and equity, the respective provinces of court and jury, the proper amount of individualization in the treatment of criminals. So that these traditions, for the most part, are opposed to orderly working of the administration of justice.

It seems more likely that there is another explanation of the fact that today we find a place in our legal philosophy for the point of view of primitive society whose rules are

[9] See, for instance, "The Theory of Judicial Decision," 36 Harvard Law Review, 641, 802, 940: The law has been regarded as going back to or derived from something absolute and definite— whether the will of the sovereign, the decrees of God, fundamental metaphysical data or history. This approach to law has led to a conception of the judicial process as one of finding pre-existing grounds of decision, giving them pre-appointed meaning and applying them with logical exactness. This ideal has frequently hindered the effort to arrive at real justice, has induced the courts to be callous to unfortunate results in particular cases, has made unconscious (and therefore often blundering and unwise) the indispensable use of economic and political materials as grounds of decisions, and brought about the use of unfortunate and inadequate devices to permit necessary flexibility and discretion—devices which were often obviously inconsistent with the theory of law-finding which the courts avowed. This inconsistency has produced popular suspicion, criticism and dissatisfaction. See also "An Introduction to the Philosophy of Law," Chapter III.

wholly inelastic and inflexible, for the Puritan requirement of fixed, unyielding, impersonal and universal rules, and for the Pioneer's "insistence upon the exact working out of rules and the devotion to that end of the whole machinery of justice." The father-regarding attitude carried over to the law is a recurrent, ever-present phenomenon. Inevitably, it finds congenial the legal philosophies of the primitive German, the Puritan and the Pioneer, since they all sought in law characteristics essentially similar to those ascribed by children to the father.[10]

Let us now examine somewhat more closely Pound's observations[11] on the influence of the Puritan's legal philosophy in current American jurisprudence.

The Puritan character, says Pound, was curiously inconsistent. The Puritan "rebelled against control of his will by state or magistrate, yet he loved to lay down rules, since he realized the intrinsic sinfulness of human nature." The Puritan's ideal state would have yielded "a permanent deadlock where the individual, instructed by a multitude of rules, but not coerced, had full play for the dictates of his own reason and conscience."

Hence developed contradictory attitudes towards the judge, compounded of respect and jealousy, attitudes which manifest themselves in our administration of justice even today.[12]

[10] The stress on the patriarchal element in Puritan family life and in the Puritan's legal attitudes we shall discuss presently. The early Germanic family was likewise emphatically patriarchal and the point of view of strict Germanic law, to which Pound directs attention as an active element in modern American law, was no doubt immensely influenced by the primitive Germanic familial pattern.

[11] "The Spirit of the Common Law," Chapter II.

[12] "In more than one state codes and Practice Acts aim to *regulate every act of the judge from the time he enters the court room,*" writes Pound. "It is hardly too much to say that the ideal judge is conceived as a pure machine. Being a human machine and in consequence tainted with original sin, *he must be allowed no scope for free action.* Hard and fast rules of evidence and strict review of every detail of practice by a series of reviewing tribunals are nec-

Pound's point seems to be well taken. Certain Puritan traditions are apparently alive in American law today. But Pound fails to consider:

1. What caused the "inconsistency that is part of the Puritan character"?

2. Why is this Puritan "inconsistency" still exhibited in our legal system?

Is it not a partial answer to the first question that the Puritan was, *par excellence,* a father-worshiper? His religious beliefs and ethical code were based upon obedience to and fear of a stern and relentless heavenly Father, the Jehovah of the strictest period of the Old Testament. Naturally enough, for the ideal Puritan pater familias was himself stern and relentless; there was a harsh, authoritative relationship between the father and his children.[13] Where worship of the father was thus overemphasized, we might well expect to find evidence of jealousy surrepti-

---

essary to *keep him in check.* In many states he may not charge the jury in any effective manner; he must rule upon and submit or reject written requests for academically-phrased propositions of abstract law; he must not commit any error which might possibly prejudice a party to the cause,—whether in fact there is prejudice or not. The past two decades have seen a steady movement away from this type of procedure; but in more than one Western community, settled from New England, which preserves the pristine faith, it is dying hard. Dunning has pointed out that in America the Puritan was able to carry into effect what in England could be only abstract opinions. Hence in America, in addition to a ritual of justice belonging to a past age of formalism that put gold lace and red coats on the picket line, we have a *machinery of justice devised to keep down the judicial personality which has made legal procedure in some sort an end in itself."*

[13] Here we may find a partial clue to the genesis of other Puritan legal habits which Pound admirably describes but leaves largely unexplained: such distinctive characteristics of the Puritan element in our law as (a) the opposition to equity and judicial discretion, (b) the overstressed retributive theory of our criminal law with its hatred of "subjective individualization" in punitive justice, and (c) the emphasis on abstract, inflexible and impersonal legal rules— these would be naturally compatible with the Puritan father-worship and the carry-over to the law of resultant childish father-regarding attitudes.

tiously expressed—particularly with reference to father-substitutes, such as the judge who embodies the law.[14]

As for our second question (Why is the duality found in the Puritan's dealings with the law still exhibited in our legal system?), cannot it be fairly conjectured that if the Puritan world-attitude is in some sort a living force in our law today, this is to some extent due to the fact that our contemporary father-regarding attitude is still measurably like the Puritans?

Perhaps the foregoing may help to a reinterpretation of Pound's comments on some of the contradictory conceptions embodied in the United States Constitution. As a result of the Revolution, the people were assumed to have succeeded to unlimited sovereign power. And yet there was a fear and distrust of the rulers who were to be elected to exercise this power. "Hence," says Pound, "by bills of right they sought to impose legal limits upon the action of those who wielded the powers of sovereignty, while adhering to a political theory of illimitable and uncontrollable power in the sovereign itself. It was inevitable that this compromise between inconsistent theories should sooner or later produce a conflict between courts and people."

Pound contents himself with quoting Bryce to the effect that there is a "hearty Puritanism in the view of human nature" pervading the Constitution. Bryce here dwells on the theological convictions of the Puritan; the Constitution was, he writes, the work of men who "believed in original sin, and were resolved to leave open for transgressors no door which they could possibly shut." Might it not also be said that the duality of the Puritan's attitude towards the father was expressing itself in the Constitution as it did in his dealings with the judiciary?

It is interesting, in the light of this discussion, to reflect on contemporary self-delusions concerning our Constitution. We like to think of that instrument as rigid and im-

[14] See Part Three, Chapter I for a discussion of the "subservience of contradiction."

mutable, as insuring permanence and stability in government, as a firm guaranty against easy legislative changes. Pridefully we contrast it with the Constitution of Great Britain, which we think of as "writ in water," the plaything of Parliament. And yet, as Woodrow Wilson put it, we have adopted "a serviceable framework of fiction which enables us easily to preserve the forms without laboriously obeying the spirit of the Constitution." We have secretly amended it, sometimes in drastic fashion, "without constitutionally amending it."

This we have done in part by judicial interpretation. "If one of the framers of the Constitution could be reincarnated and visit us today," wrote Chauncey Depew,[15] "he would find the same great instrument almost unchanged, still the fundamental law of the land, but he would discover that legislation forced by the growth of the country, the rapid development of its resources, the influence of steam and electricity, had compelled the enactment of restrictive laws which he would regard as tyrannical restrictions upon individual liberty, and that those laws had been sustained as constitutional by the interpretations of the Supreme Court. He would discover that these interpretations had so treated the general principles of his Constitution as to make them applicable and serviceable by a process so radical as to seem to him revolutionary."

For while we have wanted to believe that our organic law was undeviating, we have practically insisted on a flexible construction of its words to permit of the legalization of social changes which were never contemplated by our forefathers who drafted and adopted the sacred instrument.

A shrewd English observer[16] has said:

[15] Quoted in Horwill, "The Usages of the American Constitution," 222.

[16] Horwill, loc. cit., 223-4, 241-3. Horwill points out that changes in our Constitution have been made not alone by judicial interpretation but also by "usages" which have nullified or drastically modified the purposes of the framers. For example, our method of electing the President. There is also the method of

"That the interpretation of the text of an authoritative document is a fine art has been illustrated quite as notably in the constructions placed upon the Fundamental Law by the Supreme Court as in those placed upon any theological creed by any ecclesiastical assembly—or, for that matter, by any individual subscriber thereto. No doctrinal confession in the history of the Church has suffered a more startling metamorphosis in meaning, combined with an unimpaired respect for the letter, than the Fundamental Law of the American Constitution. It is not a coach and four but a heavily loaded freight train that has been driven through some of its clauses. . . . The change that has been wrought in the system of his own national government is little realized by the American citizen. Again and again the Fundamental Law has been nullified in practice by judicial interpretation, by sheer neglect to carry out its provisions, and by the accretion of usages which, even if they observe it in the letter, do violence to its intention and spirit. In short, the attempt to contrive what Mr. Walter Lippman happily calls 'an automatic governor' of the political machine has broken down. Yet it is still the orthodox and popular belief that the Fundamental Law of the American Constitution stands out unshaken, like a Rock of Gibraltar in the midst of a changing world, and that nothing short of an earthquake could avail to disturb it. . . . An unchanging and unchangeable scheme of government would be in striking contrast with the rest of the national life, which is not set in moulds but is in a constant state of flux. *One thing, and one only, seems to be beyond the reach of the change, and that is the American citizen's conviction, amounting almost to a superstition, that a system of government devised by the Fathers[17] of the Republic*

"Evasion by Discreet Nomenclature" as where the necessity of procuring the consent of the Senate to the making of a treaty is circumvented by calling the agreement with a foreign nation a "convention."

[17] M. D. Eder suggests that just because Americans have no king they have a popular belief in the "divine right" of the Constitution

with well-nigh superhuman wisdom has been guaranteed to him and his heirs forever by being inscribed in a 'written Constitution.' "

and a popular doctrine that "the work of the framers, the elders, must not be touched." It is not without interest that the men who drafted that instrument of government are often called the "Founding Fathers."

The duality of attitude towards the Constitution has affected the American attitude towards legal problems generally. In other words, the basic legal myth is more disturbing in America than in England. For a somewhat different view of this subject, see Goodhart, "Case Law in England and America," 15 Cornell Law Quarterly, 173, 188.

NOTES ON THE JURY

There are three possible theories of the function of the jury:

There is what may be called the official or naïve theory to the effect that the judge conclusively decides the law, and the jury are confined to finding the facts. This theory is patently not a description of what takes place. Nevertheless, it is frequently repeated to this day.

There is what may be termed the sophisticated theory which runs somewhat as follows: The judge has one function and the jury two. The judge announces authoritatively the pertinent rules of law. The jury (1) ascertain the facts and (2) apply to these facts the rules of law laid down by the judge and (3) thus arrive at their general verdict. The judge, that is, supplies the major premise, consisting of the abstract rules of law; the jury determine the minor premise from the evidence, and then work out the syllogism to its logical conclusion in the verdict which they report to the judge.

In other words, according to this more sophisticated theory, the jury are something more than a mere fact-finding body. The application of the legal rules to the facts involves legal reasoning and the jury, therefore, is in part engaged in playing the rôle of law-finding. It has been said that trials do not primarily concern themselves with determining the truth of propositions of fact so much as with the legal consequences which follow such a determination; it is these consequences which it is the province of the jury to declare. According to the more sophisticated theory, the result announced in the general verdict is a composite one, a blend of fact-finding and legal reasoning. That this blending inherent in the general verdict is a composite one, a compound of fact-finding and legal reasoning, has long been noted. "Ordinarily," said Eyre, C.J., in 1793, "he [the judge] declares to the jury what the law is upon the fact which they find, and then they *compound their verdict* of the law and fact thus ascertained."[1]

Now on the basis of this theory, the system of general verdicts has been severely criticized because it imposes upon the jury an impossible task. It is said that the application of a rule of law to the facts, if it is to be done intelligently, requires an interpretation (and therefore an understanding) of the meaning of the rules of law. But to comprehend the meaning of a rule of law requires special training. It is inconceivable that a body of twelve ordinary men, casually gathered together for a few days, could, merely from listening to the instructions of the judge, gain the knowledge necessary to grasp the true import of the judge's words, since these words have acquired their meaning often as the result of hundreds of years of professional disputation in the law courts. Inevitably, then, the jury cannot be equal to the task imposed upon them. At best, they bunglingly discharge their duty.

Reflection and observation sharpen this criticism since they indicate not only that juries cannot, but that ordinarily they do not, wholly try to discharge this duty. Thus it is said that juries do not find the facts in accordance with the evidence, but distort the facts and find them in such a manner that (by applying the rules of law laid down by the judge to the facts thus found) the jury are able to produce the desired result in favor of one party or the other; "the facts are found in order to reach the result."

But this criticism, while approaching the truth, is still unrealistic. It assumes that what we have called the more

[1] Vaughan, C.J., in Bushell's Case (1670) remarked that the jury in its general verdict of necessity resolves "both law and fact *complicately* and not the fact by itself."

sophisticated theory of the general verdict is correct and
that the jury does, in part at least, fulfill its function. In
other words, it assumes that the jury comprehends and
applies the rules of law as stated in the instructions of the
judge and departs from its function only to the extent of
warping its finding of facts in order to reach a verdict in
accordance with such rules of law: the jury "finds the
facts in such a way as to compel a different result from
that which the legal rule strictly applied would require."

These critics would have us picture the jury thus: The
jury carefully and with keen understanding study the rules
of law as expounded by the judge. They then consider the
testimony. If the rules of law as applied to the jurors' normal inferences from the testimony would lead to a verdict
which they consider unfair, the jurors shrewdly decide to
circumvent the judge. They do so by devising, with consummate skill and cunning, the exact finding of facts
which, when correlated with the judge's statement of the
law, will logically compel the result which they desire to
reach. They then make this finding of fact, apply the
judge's rule of law thereto, and thereby reach their conclusion which is reported to the court in a general verdict for
plaintiff or defendant.

It is assumed, that is, even by some of the more reflective critics of the jury, that the legal formulas set forth in
the instructions of the judge actually control the conduct
of the jury, and that the errors of the jury, if any, result
from unreasonable or deliberately incorrect conclusions
as to the facts.

So much for the sophisticated theory. The realistic
theory[2] (described in Part One, Chapter XVI) tells the

[2] Cf. Sunderland, "Verdicts, General and Special," 29 Yale Law
Journal, 253: "The peculiarity of the general verdict is the merger
into a single indivisible residuum of all matters, however numerous, whether of law or fact. It is a compound made by the jury
which is incapable of being broken up into its constituent parts. No
judicial reagents exist for either a qualitative or quantitative analysis. The law supplies the means for determining neither what facts
were found, nor what principles of law were applied, nor how the

bald truth that the jury determine the law of the particular cases submitted to them.

But this truth many lawyers would deny. Their denial is difficult to maintain in regard to criminal cases, because, when the verdict in a criminal case is one of acquittal, the judge (due to constitutional limitations) has no power to set the verdict aside. Regardless of whether or not the verdict seems to be entirely contrary to the weight of the evidence, when the jury decides in favor of the accused, its decision is final and conclusive.

In some states, it is frankly announced that in criminal cases the jury may decide for itself the rules of law; the jury is there said to be "supreme as to law as well as to fact."[3] In most jurisdictions, however, the courts insist that even in criminal actions the judge alone can decide the law. And here we come upon several subsidiary myths. Judges and text-book writers have been busy deluding themselves with words. "It is true," said Judge Thompson, "the jury may disregard the instructions of the court, and in some cases there may be no remedy; but it is still the *right of the court* to instruct the jury on the law and the *duty of the jury* to obey the instructions.[4] Sometimes there

---

application was made. There are therefore three unknown elements which enter into the general verdict: (a) the facts; (b) the law; (c) the application of the law to the facts. And it is clear that the verdict is liable to three sources of error, corresponding to these three elements. It is also clear that if error does occur in any of these matters it cannot be discovered, for the constituents of the compound cannot be ascertained. . . ."

[3] In some states the statutes expressly so provide.

[4] Mr. Justice Story conceded that the jury's general verdict in both civil and criminal cases "is necessarily compounded of law and fact and includes both. In each they must necessarily determine the law as well as the fact. In each they have the physical power to disregard the law as laid down to them by the court. But, I deny that, in any case, civil or criminal, that they have a *moral right* to decide the law according to their own notions or pleasure. . . . It is the *duty* of the jury to follow the law as it is laid down by the court."

Mr. Justice Harlan admits that "a verdict of guilty or not guilty will determine both (the facts and the law) in the particular case

is a verbal play on the distinction between the jury's "power" and the jury's "right"; the jury has the power but cannot "rightfully exercise it"; or the jury has the "physical power" but not the "moral power"; or, it is said, the jury has no power to "judge the law" but only to "set aside the law in a given instance." Chamberlayne states that most American courts in this connection "very properly distinguish between a *right* and an incorrectible *abuse* of power."

Now, since there is no way of enforcing the jury's so-called duty to obey the court, and no way of correcting the so-called abuse of their power to decide the law for themselves, we must agree with the refreshingly direct views of Judge Sharswood that "this distinction between power and right . . . is very shadowy. He who has the legal power to do anything has the legal right," especially when any so-called "abuse" of that power leads to no punishment and cannot be corrected.[5]

---

at hand." He adds sagaciously, however, that "this falls far short of the contention that the jury, in applying the law and the facts may *rightfully* refuse to act upon the principles of law announced by the court."

[5] Another euphemism, invented by Coke but still popular, is that the jury has the power to decide the law as well as the facts, but this power to decide the law is "only incidental." This locution apparently furnishes great consolations to Coke's successors, combining as it does a true statement of what the jury does, with a qualification which verbally—not actually—diminishes the importance of the jury's power. Chief Justice Shaw reluctantly agrees that a general verdict "does embody and declare the result of both the law and the fact and there is no mode of separating them on the record so as to ascertain whether the jury passed their judgment on the law or only on the evidence. The law authorizes them to adjudicate definitively on the evidence; the law presumes that they acted upon correct rules of law given them by the judge; the verdict, therefore, stands conclusive and unquestionable in point both of law and fact. In a certain limited sense, therefore, it may be said that the jury have the power and a legal right to pass upon both the law and the fact." He goes on to say, however, with obvious satisfaction, "But it would be more accurate to state that it is the right of the jury to return a general verdict; this draws after it as a necessary consequence that they *incidentally* pass upon the law." It

However, in the majority of states, it is still stoutly asserted that the jury can never determine the law. Yet the only practical distinction between the so-called majority and the so-called minority rule in criminal trials is that (1) in the states where the latter obtains, the judge tells the jury in effect that "they can determine for themselves what is the law if they can say, upon their oaths, that they are better judges of law than the court," while (2) where the majority rule obtains, no such explicit invitation is given to the jury. But the results fairly indicate that the silence of the court on this matter in the majority states is of little importance. The jury are not backward in learning the real truth as to their power. Pragmatically, the difference between the two rules is negligible.

Much is made of the fact, however, that in civil (*i.e.* non-criminal) jury trials, the "duty" of the jury to follow the judge's instructions is "enforceable" and therefore real. The judge in such cases possesses the power to grant a new trial. But this judicial power does not transfer the decision of the rights of the parties from the jury to the judge. It merely means that the judge will set the verdict aside if he believes that the jury could not reasonably have made some inference of fact which, coupled with the rules of the law he has announced, would have led to the jury's verdict—if, that is, he is convinced that the jury have completely misapprehended the facts proved or have drawn an inference so wrong as to be perverse. "A sphinx-like puzzle is handed to the court. If the ingenuity of counsel or the judge can guess at a reasonable basis on which it may be sustained, the verdict will be allowed to stand."[6]

In other words, even in civil jury trials the judge has at most a veto based upon a guess, a veto which he is obliged to exercise cautiously. The result of exercising this veto, we repeat, is not to transfer the power of deciding the law

may be pleasant to call this power "incidental"; to the losing litigant it must often seem painfully important.

[6] Chamberlayne, "Evidence," Section 95.

of the case from the jury to the judge; the judge can do no
more than to require that another jury be given the opportunity to decide the law of the case.[7] Nor can this process
of vetoing go on endlessly. "Courts rarely grant a new
trial after two verdicts upon the facts in favor of the same
party," says the United States Supreme Court; it is so
provided by statute in many states. Accordingly, if
three juries arrive at the same conclusion, the third verdict
stands, however erroneous it may be in the eyes of the
judge. It follows that only in a very limited sense has the
judge the power to rectify what he may consider the jury's
errors, even in civil cases.[8]

In 1697 Lord Holt denied that the jury have an "absolute despotick power" to disregard the judge's instructions. And judges and legal writers today still futilely repeat that denial. They continue quaintly and naïvely to
predict dire consequences were the jury to possess the
power to ignore the judge's legal pronouncements. If the
jury possessed such a power, it is said, the jury would be
lawless and a lawless jury might be as dangerous as a
lawless mob.[9]

[7] At best, the granting of a new trial is a cumbersome and wasteful method of mitigating the vices of the general verdict. It leads
to congestion of the court's dockets, to undesirable delay and bur-
densome expense. It has been well said that there is no scourge in
the hands of the strong against the weak like the scourge of new
trials.

[8] Of course, in many cases tried before judge and jury, the judge
"does not let the case go to the jury" but decides it himself.

Also the judge prevents certain evidence from being heard or
seen by the jury and thus, to some extent, affects the result. The
power of the English judge or the Federal judge in this country to
give the jury his own views of the facts has the effect, often, of
persuading the jury to arrive at the general verdict desired by the
judge. But even then the decision of the rights and liabilities of the
parties is for the jury to determine.

[9] "To permit casual bodies of twelve untrained men, selected by
lot from the community, to construe the law, would introduce such
an element of confusion as to what the law is as would amount to
an intolerable abuse and degradation of the administration of justice," says Chamberlayne. "More than this, under such circum-

"The principle of law by which the jury must be governed in finding a verdict," said the United States Supreme Court, "cannot be left to their arbitrary determination. The rights of parties must be decided according to the established law of the land . . . and not according to what the jury in their own opinion suppose the law is, or ought to be. Otherwise, the law would be as fluctuating and uncertain as the diverse opinions of different juries in regard to it." But, as, in practical effect, the rights of the parties are often decided "according to what the jury in their own opinion suppose the law is, or ought to be," the real situation is that the law, where the jury has a hand in it, *is* "as fluctuating and uncertain as the diverse opinions of different juries in regard to it."[10]

---

stances, 'Jurors would become not only judges but legislators as well.' " "If the jury were at liberty to settle the law for themselves," said Mr. Justice Story, "the effect would be, not only that the law itself would be most uncertain, from the different views which juries might take of it, but, in case of error, there would be no remedy or redress of the injured party; for the court would not have the right to review the law as it had been settled by the jury. Indeed, it would be almost impracticable to ascertain what the law, as settled by the jury, actually was."

[10] Inasmuch as a realistic appraisal of the function of the jury discloses that in both civil and criminal cases they do have and exercise the power to decide questions of law as well as questions of fact, it is not without interest to note further what has been said by courts and others, who have erroneously assumed that the jury had no such power, as to the effect of giving "despotick" power to the jury. "If this power be once admitted," said Mr. Justice Chase, "petit jurors will be superior to the national legislature and its laws will be subject to their control. The power to abrogate or to make laws nugatory is equal to the authority of making them. The evident consequences of this right in juries will be, that a law of Congress will be in operation in one state and not in another. . . . It appears to me that the right now claimed has a direct tendency to dissolve the union of the United States, on which, under divine Providence, our political safety, happiness and prosperity depend." Chief Justice Robertson uttered a prediction which may well be said to have been realized: "The circuit judge would be a cypher and a criminal trial before him a farce if he had no right to decide all questions of law which might arise in the progress of the case." Judge Ames of Rhode Island inquired "if the jury can receive the

law of a case on trial in any other mode than from the instructions of the court given in pursuance of parties and counsel, how are their errors of law, with any certainty, to be detected and how with any certainty, therefore, to be corrected."

Worthington, an English writer, states that "Were they [the jury] permitted to decide the law, the principles of justice would be subverted; the law would become as variable as the prejudices, the inclinations and the passions of men." Chief Justice Best considered that "if the jury were to be made judges of the law, as well as of fact, parties would always be liable to suffer from an arbitrary decision." To Mr. Justice Harlan it appeared that, were juries to determine questions of law, "The principal function of the judge would be to preside and keep order while jurymen, untrained in the law, would determine questions affecting life, liberty or property according to such legal principles as in their judgment were applicable to the particular case being tried." Decisions, he believed, would "then depend entirely upon juries uncontrolled by any settled, fixed, legal principle. . . . The courts, although established in order to declare the law, would, for every practical purpose, be eliminated from our system of government as instrumentalities devised for the protection of the state and of individuals in their essential rights. When that occurs our government will cease to be a government of laws and become a government of men."

NOTES ON CODIFICATION

Napoleon made the following penetrating comment on code-making: "I often perceived that over-simplicity was the enemy of precision."[1]

Not all code-makers have been as intelligent. Notably in America, codification has suffered from a failure to distinguish two incompatible aims: (1) the procuring of simplicity and (2) the procuring of precision. These aims are irreconcilable, as Napoleon sensed, because simplicity implicates flexibility, while precision leads in the direction of rigidity and completeness. How the American Codes of Procedure have suffered from the struggle between these two warring aims has been well described by Professor Clark.[2]

Perhaps code systems tend unduly to foster the second aim.[3] "It is a fair question to ask," writes Ehrlich,[4] "whether codification of the law may not be objectionable on this ground alone, *viz.:* that it enforces on human life the will of the State in a thousand instances, although frequently the State is not interested in the least that such should be the case."

[1] Lobingier, "Napoleon and his Code," 32 Harvard Law Review, 129. The reader will gather from Part One, Chapter XVII, that Napoleon did not accomplish the impossible end of complete precision in his code and that the writer's sympathies are in opposition to such an end.

[2] 35 Yale Law Journal, 259; cf. Hepburn, "Development of Code Pleading."

[3] Austin saw that no code could abolish all judicial legislation but, even so, he made the concession grudgingly—thus: "It is impossible to prevent the growth of judiciary law; but it may be kept within narrow limits."

[4] "The Science of Legal Method", 62.

The lawyer-reader will find an apt illustration of this evil of codification in the case of *President etc. of Manhattan Co.* vs. *Morgan,* 242 N. Y. 38, where Judge Cardozo was reluctantly constrained to hold that a codification of the Negotiable Instruments Law had foolishly made invalid important business customs which developed after the date of the codification.

But a code deliberately devised with reference to the desirability of growth and stated in terms of general guiding and flexible principles may some day prove to be the way out of some of the difficulties of legal administration in America.

NOTES ON FICTIONS

In a book with a remarkable history,[1] "The Philosophy of As If," Vaihinger has given the world a brilliant exposition of the function of fictions. Some of his salient points are as follows:

1. "In fictions thought makes deliberate errors." For a fiction is an error, a "more conscious, more practical and more fruitful error." One who employs a fiction makes a statement which deviates from or contradicts reality, but with full awareness of this deviation or contradiction. A fiction is a "conscious mistake" or a "conscious contradiction." A statement made with full consciousness, at the moment of utterance, that it does not correspond to the truth of the matter, is a fiction.

2. The chief characteristics of a fiction are:

a. Its arbitrary deviation from reality.

b. Its tentativeness: It is a point of transition for the mind, a mere temporary halting place for thought.

c. "The express awareness that the fiction is just a fiction, in other words, the consciousness of its fictional nature and the absence of any claim to actuality." Fictions are "assumptions made with a full realization of the impossibility of the thing assumed."

d. The requirement that it be useful. A fiction is a means to an end, it is an expedient. "When there is no expediency the fiction is unscientific." Every fiction must justify itself, must perform a service. The fiction is

[1] It was begun in 1877 but not published until 1911. For the history of this work see Vaihinger's introduction to "The Philosophy of As If" and Havelock Ellis, "The Dance of Life," 86.

a "legitimatized error," *i.e.,* "a fictional conceptual construct that has justified its existence by its success."

One must guard against the vice of assuming that, because a fiction is useful, it therefore has objective validity. "The gulf between reality and fiction must always be stressed"; one must avoid "the fundamental error of converting fictions into reality."

3. The synonyms for fictions are illuminating. Among them are:

Inventions, conceits, imaginary ideas, quasi-ideas, conceptual aids, auxiliary operations, makeshifts, expedients, devices, artifices, artificial concepts, counterfeit ideas, stratagems, dodges, contrivances, byways, approaches, short-cuts, ingenious abbreviations, instrumental ideas, interim concepts, bridges, props, ladders, scaffolding, surrogates, suppositions, substitutes, subjective auxiliary constructs, psychological pulleys, psychical levers, counters, metaphors, paper-money ideas, play-ideas, provisional ideas, heuristic ideas, regulatory ideas, figures of thought, short-hand expressions, means of orientation, modes of speech, modes of reflection.

4. Fictions have been employed effectively in all fields of thought:

We find the "artificial classification" (such as that of Linnaeus in botany); "abstractive or neglective" fictions (such as the economic man or the average man or the absolutely healthy man); Utopias; "symbolic" fictions (society as an organism); mathematical fictions (the circle treated as if it were a polygon or an ellipse; the notions of surface, line, point, absolute motion); juristic fictions;[2] personificatory fictions (*vis dormativa*), etc., etc.

5. Fictions are often derided. This is due to the fact that their detractors confuse fictions with statements intended to conform with reality.

6. Fictions must not be confused with hypotheses:

a. "An hypothesis is directed toward reality, . . . it

[2] His views on juristic fictions are referred to below in this appendix in connection with the discussion of Tourtoulon.

claims or hopes to coincide with perception in the future. . . . It demands verification, *i.e.*, it wants to be proved true, real, and an expression of reality." It is a statement of an assumption which, it is expected, will turn out to correspond with truth.

b. A fiction, on the other hand, "is not concerned to assert a real fact but [to assert] something by means of which reality can be dealt with and grasped."

While the hypothesis is comparable to a discovery, the fiction is comparable to an invention [cf. Addenda to Second Printing].

The hypothesis must be confirmed by *verification*. "To the *verification* of the hypotheses corresponds the *justification* of the fiction. For a fiction that cannot be proved to be useful must be eliminated, no less than an hypothesis that cannot be verified."

At a time when he was still unfamiliar with Vaihinger, Tourtoulon wrote searchingly on the subject of legal fictions.[3] His definition of a fiction is substantially the same as Vaihinger's: "the statement of an erroneous fact with knowledge of its falsity." "It is not a fiction if the fictional idea is not recognized as such." Fictions "cannot falsify a process of reasoning so long as one does not forget what they have in them of the relative, and so long as one can calculate to what extent they represent real, and to what extent imaginary, dispositions." "Judicial fiction is therefore not to be condemned, provided it points out as artificial what is artificial."

Tourtoulon has made a helpful classification[4] of untrue utterances:

a. *The lie* is an affirmation of fact contrary to the truth with the intention of deceiving others.

b. *The myth* is the affirmation of a fact contrary to the truth—though not known to be such—*i.e.* self-deception.

[3] "Philosophy in the Development of Law," 293–6; 383–399. See 644, *et seq.*, for his discussion of Vaihinger.
[4] See above, Part One, Chapter IV.

c. *The fiction* is an untrue assertion which one enunciates without being his own dupe or wishing to dupe others.

Tourtoulon points out that among lawyers fiction-phobia is prevalent. "Certain writers have labored under the strange delusion that the law can be constructed upon objective realities; . . . quite the contrary, juridical theory is all the more objective when it presents itself as fictitious, and all the more delusive when it claims to do without fictions."

Here it is pertinent to revert to Vaihinger and note his excessive laudation of the lawyers with respect to fictional thinking. Jurists, he writes, through their treatment of the fiction of juristic persons have prepared the ground for a general acceptance of the distinction between the fiction and the hypothesis.[5] English law, he states, has especially developed the fictional device.

Lawyers, in this view, appear to be more sophisticated concerning fictions than ordinary men. We have expressed a contrary opinion. To us it has seemed that lawyers have too seldom observed the essential nature of valid fictional thinking. What has misled Vaihinger?

No doubt his superficial acquaintance with law and lawyers caused him to ignore lawyers' deficiencies. He seems to know little of the continued use of so-called legal fictions as semi-myths to conceal the actualities of legal change and adaptation—a misuse of fictions which indicates that liberated fictional thinking is not too evident, as yet, in law.[6] Vaihinger has not been apprised of that fiction-phobia among lawyers of which Tourtoulon speaks. To be sure, that phobia may be the first step in a

[5] Vaihinger comments that the Medieval nominalists might have advanced their thinking had they made the obvious comparison between *fictiones rationis* and *fictiones juris et legis*. They would then have seen that concepts may be fictional and yet highly useful and necessary.

[6] See Part One, Chapter III.

healthy reaction against the misuse of legal fictions, that is, against the use of fictions in law as semi-myths.[7] But such a reaction, when it leads to a war on legitimate fiction, is a vice; the cure for such fiction-phobia is to be found in the next step—the recognition by the legal profession of the correct use of valid fictions and the acknowledgment that all legal rules are relative and instrumental. What Vaihinger observes of thinkers in other fields is no less true—is perhaps the more true—of lawyers: A vast deal of their thought-devices involves conceptual distortion of the truth without awareness of the distortion. Nominalism (the first step towards knowledge of the provisional or relative character of all concepts) has made but little headway in jurisprudence. Conceptualism may perhaps be said to have its chief modern stronghold in the law. Many lawyers are still infected with that scholasticism which converts abstractions into independent entities having an "out-there" character. Vaihinger would doubtless be astonished to discover how greatly the legal profession would be helped by assimilating the following criticism which he makes of the naïve use of "general ideas":

"General judgments, when connected with a general subject, only represent convenient methods of expression. There is no such thing as a general subject in reality. . . . As opposed to particulars, the [concepts or general ideas] have been regarded as the permanent essence, and this permanent essence has been hypostasized into an energetic thing interpreted as the general basis of particular phenomena. . . . General ideas thus come to be regarded as the subjective counterpart of actually existing substances endowed with powers which are interpreted as the forces behind and above individual things, as the sources from which the particular takes its origin. . . .

[7] Bentham's assault on legal fictions is perhaps to be thus explained. See below in this appendix for discussion of Bentham's theory of fictions.

The products of thought are hypostasized and actual reality despised. . . ."[8]

Tourtoulon describes as one of the most important functions of the legal fiction "the desire to efface the reality of an unfortunate event." "The idea of a Roman Citizen taken prisoner by the enemy and led into slavery was too hard on Roman pride. The existence of such a fact was not admitted." Hence, arose the following fiction: "If the citizen died a slave, it was said that he died in war and was killed on the field of battle; if he regained his liberty, he was supposed to have been at home all the time at the head of his family and business." "This mechanism is typical," says Tourtoulon. So that, while fiction is a "subtle instrument of juridical technic, it is also clearly the expression of a desire inherent in human nature, the desire to efface unpleasant realities and evoke imaginary good fortune."

Tourtoulon, as the foregoing shows, is less blind than Vaihinger to the effect of human weaknesses on legal technology. But his suggestion that the desire to mask the unpleasant is an important cause of legal fiction-contriving merits a protest. Tourtoulon first carefully discriminates between fictions and myths, describing how a myth may become a fiction by the dropping out of the element of self-deception. He then blurs his definition when he purports to find that the desire to efface unpleasant realities is an important factor in the making of valid fictions.[9] It

[8] See Part One, Chapters VI and VII.

For a criticism of Vaihinger's nominalism as too extreme see Cohen's article noted below in this appendix.

[9] Not that Tourtoulon is ever unaware of the essential difference between a myth and a fiction. The point is that he fails sufficiently to keep in mind the fact that my myth (i.e., the affirmation I fatuously believe "real") may be your fiction (i.e., something you look upon as an invention everybody knows is not supposed to be true); or that what I now stoutly believe to be "true" may later merge into and become, for me, a fiction—something I know, and think everybody knows, is only a fabrication. The shift may also be the other way—from a fiction into a myth.

would seem fair to say that, in so far as a thought-contrivance effectively serves as such an emotional anodyne, it is not being used as a fiction but as a myth.[10] Vaihinger has been more discriminating in his undeviating contention that a fiction ceases to be a fiction whenever it is not employed with full knowledge of its artificial character.

One of Vaihinger's most striking observations has to do with the relation between dogmas, hypotheses and fictions:

A dogma is an idea which, without hesitation, is regarded as the expression of reality. Where there is some doubt as to the objective validity of an idea, where its objective validity is only tentatively assumed, it is an *hypothesis*. Where an idea is used as a means to aid thinking, but with no belief that it does or may prove to correspond with reality, it is a *fiction*. A given idea may be first expressed as a fiction, later become an hypothesis and later a dogma, or vice versa.

There is a strong tendency to convert fictions and hypotheses into dogmas. (The Social Contract and the Platonic Ideas, for instance, started as fictions and became dogmas.) Why this tendency? Because, says Vaihinger, to entertain ideas of less fixed character than dogmas involves a condition of tension extremely disagreeable to the mind which tries to bring ideas into equilibrium and to establish an unbroken connection between them. "An idea that has once been accepted as objective, has a stable equilibrium, the hypothesis an unstable one. The psyche tends to make every psychical content more stable and to extend this stability. The condition of unstable equilibrium is as uncomfortable physically as it is psychically."

According to Vaihinger, the feeling of discomfort created by mental tension explains the tendency to transform every hypothesis into a dogma. The legitimate way to ac-

---

[10] More justifiably Tourtoulon says that the fiction is the way the jurist has of amusing himself: fiction reduces mental fatigue. He also calls it "the algebra of the law" and notes that it has played a part in law similar to that of metaphor in language.

complish the transformation is by verification. But the feeling of mental discomfort drives men unwarrantably to turn hypotheses into dogmas without such verification.

The condition of mental tension developed by a fiction is, of course, greater than that created by an hypothesis. In the case of a fiction the mind is obliged to regard a subjective idea "as if" it were objective but, at the same time, to remain aware that the idea is actually subjective. The lack of equilibrium is greater than in the case of the hypothesis, the discomfort therefore more severe, and the tendency consequently pronounced to turn the fiction either into an hypothesis and then into a dogma or directly into a dogma.[11]

And here we come upon a contradiction in Vaihinger's terminology—perhaps in his reasoning. Dogma and hypothesis relate to reality, fiction to the unreal, he maintains. But, at another point, we find him maintaining that, in a fundamental sense, all thought is fictional.[12]

"There is no identity of thought and reality, for the 'world' is merely an instrument of thought and, for that reason, the world of ideas is not the ultimate goal of thought. . . . The world of ideas is essentially an expedient of thought, an instrument, for rendering action possibly in the world of reality.

"We must leave behind us the naïve belief that what is thought really exists. . . . Ideas and logical products should be considered no longer as revelations of reality but as purely mechanical instruments, whereby thought may move forward and attain its practical objects. By thus regarding both logical functions and logical products as mere means, the *way is prepared for their interpretations as fictions,* i.e., as constructions of thought, thought-edifices deviating from and even contradicting reality but

---

[11] Vaihinger's views of the nature of this tendency are discussed above in Part One, Chapter XV.
[12] He says, in effect: (1) *Hypotheses* are to be carefully distinguished from *fictions.* (2) All thought-devices, *including hypotheses, are fictions.*

invented and interpolated by this very thinking in order to attain its end more expeditiously."

Tourtoulon correctly states that Vaihinger is carried away by the desire to prove too much. "By trying to show that everything is a mental construction," comments Morris Cohen, in like vein,[13] "the distinction between fact and fiction is obliterated." Cohen finds fault with the Aristotelian classification of all propositions into the *existentially* true and false. There are truths whose validity is non-factual: "The world contains, besides things and their qualities, also relations and processes between them," and "the fruitfulness of science consists precisely in not copying the qualities of things but in grouping and symbolizing those relations or processes which most frequently repeat themselves." We should adopt "the modern relational view of the nature of a proposition—which metaphysically means that not things, but a complex of things-in-relation, is the subject matter of science."

From this point of view, Vaihinger may be at fault in characterizing as fictional "the economic man" or frictionless engines. "They have," says Cohen, "their truth or validity in the realm of the non-factual."

But Cohen concedes that abstractions, in a sense, may usefully be considered, together with metaphors and "ceremonial expressions," under the head of fictions. All propositions, he admits, are more or less metaphorical and conventional, and must be used with proper precautions, "precautions that may all be deduced from the rule that the truth of a proposition holds only in its proper universe of discourse."

Once Cohen makes these concessions, once he admits that metaphor is inherent in much valuable thinking and once he asserts that grave "fallacies result from the inadequate realization of the metaphoric character of many propositions," it is manifest that, in certain broad essen-

[13] "On the Logic of Fiction," The Journal of Philosophy, Vol. XX, 477, 484.

tials, he and Vaihinger are not too far apart.[14] They both stress the usefulness of conceptual short-hand despite the fact that the abbreviation involved in such thought-contrivances does not contain all the truth. Both assert the necessity of using metaphorical devices, while both warn of the harm that may result if the limited character of any analogy goes unrecognized. Cohen, no less than Vaihinger, urges thinking men to be on their guard against accepting unqualified statements of partial truths as final and complete, and to observe carefully the elliptical character of all propositions.

While Vaihinger may err in terming fictional what Cohen would call elliptically stated hypotheses (or truths valid enough but valid only in their proper universes of discourse), we may accept Vaihinger's views (as to the relation of dogma, hypothesis and fiction) in this modified form: Any concept used without awareness of its unexpressed qualifications is a harmful dogma.[15] More than that, the failure to be on the alert for the necessary qualifications of all thought-constructs whatsoever is an index of immaturity.

Tourtoulon, like Cohen, refuses to agree with Vaihinger that it is permissible to contemplate all logical forms as fictional. But he admits freely that "all is uncertainty in this world." He finds grave philosophic insight in a scene from a drama of the poet Mistral, where galley slaves, as they row, believe they see the light of a fairy castle to which they seem quite near. Perhaps, however, the light

[14] See Cohen's Introduction to Tourtoulon's book.
[15] Ellis remarks that if the world had realized with Vaihinger "that axioms are akin to fictions, the doctrine of Einstein, which sweeps away axioms so familiar to us that they seem obvious truths, and substitutes others which seem absurd because they are unfamiliar, might not have been so bewildering." Cf. Bridgman, "The Logic of Modern Physics," 1–2, 24. Bridgman's description of the "operational character of concepts" in modern physics can be immensely helpful as a guide to clear thinking about the fictional aspect of legal rules.

is but a star. They sing: "Castle or no castle, let us row as if it were there."

And Tourtoulon concludes his work with the following brave words:

"The philosophy of chance seems to me the most natural conclusion of a philosophy of legal history. It substitutes the search for probability for the search for certainty. It shows the complexity of causes where others wish to see only a deceptive simplicity. It permits man to utilize, so far as possible, his own ignorance. It inspires a salutary scepticism: not that of negation, but that of prudence, —the kindly, scrupulous, and searching scepticism which might well be the best instrument of progress for humanity."

"Fictions are falsehoods, and the judge who invents a fiction ought to be sent to jail," wrote Bentham. He seems to have considered fictions in law as the entire equivalent of lies and unmitigatedly evil. He apparently made no distinction between (1) legal lies (*i.e.,* misstatements designated to deceive others), (2) legitimate legal fictions (*i.e.,* inaccurate statements made for convenience, with full knowledge of their departure from reality and with the intention that the auditor or reader should be aware of their "untruth"), and (3) legal myths (*i.e.,* erroneous statements uttered without knowledge of their falsity and therefore based on self-delusion). Legal lies, legal fictions and legal myths—he lumped them all together under the name of "legal fictions" and denounced them all as falsehoods, as "the most pernicious form of lying."[16]

That clearer understanding of the validity of legitimate legal fictions which has, since Bentham's day, been brought about by the writings of Vaihinger and Tourtoulon was not, it seems, a part of Bentham's equipment. C. K. Ogden, however, has recently published a previously unprinted manuscript of Bentham on which Ogden bases the conten-

[16] See Part One, Chapter IV, for other colorful denunciations by Bentham of such devices.

tion that Bentham had in his day worked out a theory of fictions which not only anticipated Vaihinger's theory but, in some respects, cut deeper in its analysis.[17]

Now it must be admitted that this recently discovered manuscript discloses surprising subtlety on Bentham's part with respect to fictions generally. Bentham, without doubt, had some discernment of the nature of a valid fiction as an object spoken of, for convenience, as existing, but with full awareness of the fact that it has no existence. Such "fictitious entities," says Bentham in effect, are indispensable and not harmful so long as persons observe their lack of correspondence with reality. He gives as examples the words, "motion, relation, faculty, power."

So far so good. If the Bentham essay, published by Ogden, had made no mention of legal fictions, one might have assumed that Bentham intended to carry over his fiction theory to the field of law and was revising his earlier and more naïve notions of legal fictions. But, alas, Bentham, for all his sophisticated remarks on fictions in general, at the close of this very essay uses the following sentence:

"By the priest and the lawyer, in whatsoever shape fiction has been employed, it has had for its object or effect, or both, to deceive and, by deception, to govern, and by governing to promote the interest, real or supposed, of the party addressing, at the expense of the party addressed."[18]

On the basis, then, of the evidence presented by Ogden, it seems impossible to avoid the conclusion that, when it

[17] See "Psyche" for July, 1928, 4, *et seq.*

[18] His last sentence states that fiction has been, in the minds of all, "the coin of necessity: . . . in that of the priest and the lawyer of mischievous immorality in the shape of mischievous ambition, —and too often both priest and lawyer have framed or made in part that instrument."

Bentham, as above suggested, was inspired by a distaste for the bastard fictions, or semi-myths, he encountered in the law. In repudiating such devices, he went too far and overlooked that use of valid fictions in law which he advocated in other fields.

came to legal thinking, Bentham, unregenerate, retained over-simplified notions of truth, and was still incapable of observing, in legal diction, any distinction between legal lies, fictions and myths—all of which he was determined to wipe out.[19]

[19] Perhaps the explanation of Ogden's over-estimation of Bentham's fiction theory is to be found in Ogden's tendency to over-emphasize word-magic as the basic vice in faulty thinking. (See Part One, Chapter X.) For Bentham's article on fictitious entities centers about the following thesis which is essentially similar to Ogden's: "To language, then—to language alone—it is to that, fictitious entities owe their existence—their impossible, yet indispensable existence."

Referring to this sentence, Ogden says:

"The chief defect of Vaihinger's monumental work was its failure to lay stress on the linguistic factor in the creation of fictions. The next step would have been to rectify this defect, had not that step been taken by Bentham a century ago."

Ogden's satisfaction at finding a century-old confirmation of his own views may explain his neglect of the defects in Bentham's attitude towards legal fictions.

In passing, it is proper to question whether Ogden is correct in his charge that Vaihinger did not stress the linguistic factor. If Ogden means that Vaihinger found causes other than language for fiction-making, his criticism is well founded. But it is not true that Vaihinger left out of account the relation between language and fiction. Thus, in speaking of the hypostatisation of "substance" Vaihinger says, "The uncritical use of language has taken over this method of expression, which dates from the childhood of the human race when everything was personified." And again: "The assumption of a Thing would never have been possible without the assistance of language, which provides us with a word for the Thing and gives the attributes specific names. It is to the word that the illusion of the existence of a Thing possessing attributes attaches itself, and it is the word that enables the mistake to become fixed." See especially p. 176 where he relates the development of the "categories" to the development of language, and suggests that language aids in the relief of mental tension created by the chaos of the environment.

FOR READERS WHO DISLIKE REFERENCES TO "UNCONSCIOUS MENTAL PROCESSES"

For an excellent discussion of the propriety of using such concepts as "unconscious mental processes," or "the unconscious," see Hart, "The Psychology of Insanity," Chapter II, and "Psychopathology." (See pages 392 to 395.) See also Appendix VII hereto on fictions, and Northridge, "Modern Theories of the Unconscious."

However, if the reader, even after consulting those authorities, remains unregenerate, he may be mollified by the following description, in more physiological terms, of the father-substitute notion:

An organism, writes Rignano, has a tendency to maintain its original "stationary" physiological state, a tendency to invariability in its external and internal environment. If such a stationary state is disturbed, the organism strives to restore it. To this physiological striving there may be said to be a corresponding "longing" or "desire" for the original condition of the organism.

If the restoration is balked, the organism tends to pass to a new stationary state consistent with its new external or internal environment: the organism "adapts itself." The new or "adapted" physiological state, if it lasts for a sufficient period, now likewise, if disturbed, tends to restore itself. But there still remain "affective tendencies"—longings and desires for the older physiological state. So that even when circumstances have forced the organism far beyond its original state, there may still exist a condition of nostalgia, of hankering, for this original stationary state.

It also seems to be true that there may be a "substitution of a part for the whole," so that a mere fragment of a given environmental relation or condition, or some factor only partly similar to such a relation, or a means of attaining a given environmental relation, evokes the same longing as that aroused by the entire environmental relation. The attachment for the part may then become stronger than the attachment for the whole, so that this partial relation, or means, finally becomes an habitual environmental relation, and is sought for its own sake, quite apart from the original whole which originally evoked the desire.[1]

The new-born human animal, it seems, strives to return to the undistracted, relatively stationary condition which he enjoys prior to his emergence into the world. He is compelled to accept new and less stable states of equilibrium as he develops. But for the original state of undisturbed uterine security he retains a strong nostalgia.[2] As he grows, this longing is being constantly thwarted, but something of this early security and serenity is procured for him, in part, through his relation to and belief in his father's omnipotence. Wherefore the father comes to be a substitute for the originally desired end. When the implicit belief in the father has to be given up, because of disillusionment as to his perfection, the longing still continues; substitutes for the father (persons or institutions which seem in part to resemble him) now become the objects to which these longings attach themselves.

[1] See Rignano, "The Psychology of Reasoning," Chapter I.
[2] Cf. Bernfeld, "The Psychology of the Infant." See further, page 396, as to this "nostalgia."

APPENDIX IX

REFERENCE NOTES, BY CHAPTERS

PART ONE, CHAPTER I

[1] 12 American Bar Association Journal, 153.

[2] Napoleon later modified these views somewhat; see Part One, Chapter VII.

[3] Frederick Soddy, one of the world's great physicists, winner of the Nobel prize in 1921, views lawyers as "charlatans" who deal in legal necromancy and who aim to preserve legal secrets and "mystify the public" when they should make law "intelligible and predictable." "A clergyman or statesman or doctor are, as such, useful men," said the Marquis of Salisbury. "These professions do good. But the barrister is at best but a tolerated evil. He derives his living from the fact that law is unintelligible."

William Durran has recently written a book, "Bench and Bar," devoted entirely to portraying "the conflict of attitude between barrister and layman." The layman, he finds, "dreads uncertainty in law," whereas the lawyer "naturally loves opportunities for expatiating on the largest possible number of points. . . . It is not the certainty of the law but the uncertainty that pays the lawyer. . . . The multiplication of uncertainties, of lawlessness, and of advocates' incomes keep pace with each other. . . . A gross deception is being practiced upon the man in the street. Nor is it for his good; it is for the good of the profession of lawyers which admittedly prospers by piling one uncertainty on another. . . . A vested interest, far and away the greatest trade union in the world, will fight resolutely and with all the resources of wealth and sophistry in support of guess-work in law. . . . [There is] confusion and uncertainty in the legal standards deliberately engineered and increased by the Bar." Durran writes of "the common law with its evil train of uncertainties . . . uncertainties which pay the lawyer" and sees little likelihood that "those who derive their income from the fact that law is unintelligible will . . . be overcome by a desire to make it intelligible, accessible and inexpensive."

[4] Barry, "The Scientific Habit of Thought," 138; Whitehead, "Science and the Modern World," 166; Whyte, "Archimedes or The Future of Physics," 30–39; Burtt, "The Metaphysical Foundations of Physics"; Eddington, "Space, Time and Gravitation," 198, 201, and "The Nature of the Physical World"; Bridgman, "The Logic of Modern Physics"; Reuff, "From the Physical to the Social Sciences"; Morris Cohen, "The Social Sciences and the Natural Sciences," in "The Social Sciences and Their Interrelations," 437.

See Bridgman, "The New Vision of Science," Harper's Magazine, March, 1929, 443, for a statement of Heisenberg's "Principle of Uncertainty," the essence of which is "that there are certain inherent limitations to the accuracy with which a physical situation can be described," and that the ultimate possibility of exactness of measurements in physics is forever limited. See Eddington's account of the "Principle of Indeterminacy," in "The Nature of the Physical World," 306.

The postulate of complete ultimate scientific certainty may still be useful if accepted on a purely fictional basis. See Appendix III, on "An Unscientific Conception of Science."

[5] In this country, in upper courts alone, approximately five hundred cases are decided each week, of which presumably one-half turn primarily on disputed "law points." If lower court cases are also considered, the number of weekly decisions of this type may safely be numbered in the thousands.

That questions of law and questions of fact are not really separable in many cases, see Part One, Chapters XII, XIII and XIV.

[6] Abbott, "Justice and the Modern Law."

[7] See Part Two, Chapter III, for a discussion of these types of security.

[8] "Methods of Juridical Thinking," printed as Chapter X of "The Science of Legal Method." Although the writer here and later criticizes Wurzel, he must acknowledge his immense debt to Wurzel's stimulating way of formulating many of the problems discussed in this book and particularly those considered in Chapters I and III.

PART ONE, CHAPTER II

[1] Frankwood Williams, quoted in Otto, "Natural Laws and Human Hopes," 55.

The description of the child's development, as traced in Chapter II and thereafter, is more fully treated in the writings of such as Piaget, Flügel, Miller and White. It derives from the Freudian school, who, however, take into account other factors that deserve attention but which here are given no consideration.

In this and succeeding chapters the writer has relied chiefly upon Piaget, an eclectic psychologist, who has done an immense amount of first-hand work with children. See Piaget's "The Language and Thought of the Child," "Judgment and Reasoning in the Child" and "The Child's Conception of the World."

[2] By Floyd Dell. The subject-matter of that book on education is, however, not relevant to our discussion. In "Love in the Machine Age" he considers education from a point of view more germane to this essay.

[3] James' shift of attitude, however, may have been excessively violent. His distaste for all guaranties may not have represented a thoroughly stable reaction. His protests are suspiciously overemphasized. This perhaps explains the contradictory views on religion expressed in his "The Varieties of Religious Experience." A completely adult attitude would not involve undue stress on the value of chance. See Part Three, Chapter I.

[4] See Part One, Chapter XVIII, for a fuller discussion of that theme.

[5] The anthropologist Sapir is suggestive here: "A very interesting problem arises—that of the possible transfer of a psychological attitude or mode of procedure which is proper to one type of social unit to another type of social unit in which the attitude or procedure is not so relevant. Undoubtedly such transfers take place both on primitive and sophisticated levels." The transfer of the child-father attitude to the law-regarding attitude would seem to be an instance of such a transfer.

In some types of social organization—and perhaps in some families in any form of society—the mother may be said to be the arbiter of conduct. However that may be, in our own quasi-patriarchal society that rôle is usually the father's. Accordingly we shall for convenience in this essay refer to the father as if he were the sole wielder of parental disciplinary power.

⁶ See Appendix I on "Other Explanations."

⁷ See Chapter XVIII "The Religious Explanation."

⁸ For a discussion of such survival theories see Part One, Chapter XVIII, "The Religious Explanation" and Appendix IV.

⁹ "As a rule," says Vaihinger in his invaluable book, "The Philosophy of As If," "the reason for the formation of these fictions is to be sought in the highly intricate character of the facts which make theoretical treatment exceedingly difficult owing to their unusual complexity. . . . Since, then, the material is too complicated for thought to be able to break it up into its components and since the causal factors are probably of too complicated a nature for them to be determined directly, thought makes use of an artifice by means of which it provisionally and temporarily neglects a number of characters and selects from them the more important phenomena. . . . Such fictions should be accompanied by the consciousness that they deliberately substitute a fraction of reality for the complete range of causes and effects."

We have worded our analysis as if the drive towards an infantile world, and moreover one component of that drive, were always in operation and always dominating. Of course, such is not the case. Our statement is "fictional" and we would have the reader so recognize. This infantile drive has an important causal relation to the tendency to seek excessive legal certainty. But it is not incessant; it is usually unconscious, and is supported by other human aims and desires. We have singled out this particular drive and treated it as if it were unceasing because it has been too much ignored. The possible value of focussing attention almost exclusively on this ignored element will be discussed in what follows.

PART ONE, CHAPTER III

¹ Little attention has been paid by psychologists to legal rationalization, although Hart states: "The distinction between the real and apparent causes of mental processes is well illus-

trated in the advice given to the newly created judge, 'Give your decision, it will probably be right. But do not give your reasons, they will almost certainly be wrong.' "

PART ONE, CHAPTER IV

[1] "I take judge-made law as one of the realities of life," says Judge Cardozo. And again: "Hardly a rule of today but may be matched by its opposite of yesterday. . . . These changes or most of them have been wrought by judges. The result has been not merely to supplement or modify; it has been to revolutionize and transform."

Professor Jeremiah Smith (See 27 Yale Law Journal, 147, 149) has summarized the various theories as to judicial law-making thus:

(1) That judges cannot "make" law; that they merely discover and apply law which is already existing (Carter; Blackstone);

(2) That judges can and do make new law on subjects not covered by previous decisions, but the judges cannot unmake old law—cannot even change an existing rule of judge-made law (Dicey; Pollock);

(3) That judges can and do make new law; and also can and do unmake old law—i.e. the law previously laid down by themselves or by their judicial predecessors. (Austin; Gray; Holmes; Smith; Cardozo).

These differences of opinion relate to the making of new "rules of law" by judges. That judges make "law" even when they purport to adhere to old rules, see Part One, Chapter XIV and Appendix II.

[2] "What was the law in the time of Richard Coeur de Lion on the liability of a telegraph company to the persons to whom a message was sent?" asks John Chipman Gray, in "The Nature and Sources of Law," Sec. 222.

[3] Zane, 16 Michigan Law Review, 338.

[4] Austin referred to the "childish fiction employed by our judges, that judiciary or common law is not made by them, but is a miraculous something made by nobody, existing, I suppose, from eternity and merely declared from time to time by the judges." Austin's notion that the vagaries of judge-made laws could be largely obliterated by codification is discussed in Part One, Chapter XVII.

[5] Demogue has pointed out that even this belief is illusory. See Part Two, Chapter III.

And cf. Gray, loc. cit., Sections 275, 366, to the effect that it is not what the statute says but what the courts say the statute says, which constitutes the legal effect of the statute. So that, even in the case of statutes, the correct rules must await the *ex post facto* decision of the courts. See Chapter XIII.

[6] "The Nature and Sources of Law," Section 225; see also Austin, "Jurisprudence" (4th Ed.) 674, for an earlier statement of similar character but with a different emphasis due to Austin's vain hopes of "reform" through codification.

[7] Even where they act on the basis of documents prepared by lawyers, they can receive no blanket assurances covering (1) the other "facts" almost sure to be involved in connection with the use of these documents, "facts" which will affect the court's "interpretation" of the documents, or (2) the relative weight which the courts will accord to the documents as against the weight to be accorded such "facts." It is impossible to tell, until some case arises involving these documents, precisely what the court will consider to be the controlling "facts." See Chapter XII.

[8] In any event, since retroactivity and uncertainty are objectively unavoidable, their existence must be candidly recognized by any person who is mature.

[9] See Appendix VII, "Notes on Fictions."

[10] The distinction between lies, myths and fictions is nicely made by Tourtoulon; see Appendix VII, "Notes on Fictions."

[11] Although Gray states that judges want to conceal the truth he gives no adequate explanation of the cause of this desire.

[12] See Appendix VII, "Notes on Fictions," for a discussion of the views of Vaihinger, Tourtoulon, Cohen and Bentham.

[13] Trouble ensues when the "as if" and the "for certain purposes" are neglected. Corporation law is full of such trouble. Much of the confusion in thinking about sovereignty is traceable to a like source.

[14] It is worth noting again that the essence of valid fictional thinking is "the express awareness that the fiction is just a fiction, in other words, the consciousness of its fictional nature and the absence of any claim to actuality." "A fiction is not a fiction if the fictional idea is not recognized as such." A

fiction is "a statement made with full consciousness, at the moment of utterance, that it does not correspond to the truth of a matter." Cf. Appendix VII.

[15] See Appendix VII for a discussion of Bentham's blindspot as to the value of fictions in law as distinguished from other fields of thought.

[16] 21 Harvard Law Review, 129.

[17] He calls them "fictions." But it is plain that he is applauding the semi-myths; it is precisely the mythical (self-deluding) character of these "fictions" which he admires. He would not consider them as useful if they were purely and avowedly fictional.

If Mitchell & Co. were to argue that in the infancy of society legal myths were necessary instruments of progress, their position would be sound. The point is that they urge the continued use of semi-myths today.

PART ONE, CHAPTER V

[1] The case discussed in the text and especially the conversations there quoted are suppositions. But the questions involved are very nearly those involved in *Black & White Taxi & T. Co. v. Brown & Yellow Taxi & T. Co.*, 276 U. S. 518.

[2] This was what three of the justices of the United States Supreme Court (Holmes, Brandeis and Stone) did hold to be the law.

[3] See Part One, Chapter XIII and Appendix II for a further discussion of this subject and of some of the thinkers who have developed legal realism.

PART ONE, CHAPTER VI

[1] Beale concedes that there can be changes in the body of principles. But these changes are, as he describes them, glacial in their velocity. For "the law of a given time must be taken to be the body of general principles which is accepted by the legal profession" so that law "changes with the change of professional opinion about it." In so far, but only in so far, as decisions of judges induce the legal profession to accept a change of opinion about the general principles, are decisions related to changes in the law.

Beale does not indicate how one is to find out when such changes of views about principles have been sufficiently accepted so that they will bring about a change in the law. Take the case of the minimum wage statute; thirty-two judges held such a statute valid and nine held it invalid. The last decision of the United States Supreme Court held it invalid by a vote of five to four. Would Beale say that it was valid, despite that decision?

[2] Like Beale, Blackstone explained how human law comes to deviate from the authentic original: "But in order to apply this to the particular exigencies of each individual, it is still necessary to have recourse to reason: whose office is to *discover what the law of nature directs in every circumstance of life. . . . And if our reason were always clear and perfect . . . the task would be pleasant and easy; we should need no other guide but this.*"

[3] Abbott, "Justice and The Modern Law," 10, 11, 236.

[4] Figgis, "Divine Right of Kings," quoted by Dickinson, "Administrative Justice and the Supremacy of Law," 88.

PART ONE, CHAPTER VII

[1] Swain School Lectures, 121, quoted in "The Meaning of Meaning," Ogden and Richards, (2d ed.) 46.

[2] 28 Columbia Law Review, 1014.

[3] See also the writings of Professors Cook, Bingham and Yntema, referred to in Part One, Chapters XIII and XIV and Appendix II. Thirty years ago Mr. Justice Holmes admonished the bar, "We must think things, not words, or at least we must constantly translate words into the facts for which they stand. . . ." Cf. Llewellyn in 30 Columbia Law Review, 431, and Klaus in 28 Columbia Law Review, 441, 458.

[4] "I cannot help thinking," he wrote, "if there be anything beautiful other than absolute beauty, should there be such, that it can be beautiful only in so far as it partakes of absolute beauty . . . and am assured in my own mind that nothing makes a thing beautiful but the presence and participation of beauty . . . ; I stoutly maintain that by beauty all beautiful things become beautiful. . . . And that by greatness only great things become great and greater greater, and by smallness the less become less. . . ." There is "no way in which anything comes into existing except by participation in its own essence and consequently . . . the only cause of two is the participation in duality. . . ."

Ogden and Richards have fairly described Plato's "real" world as "A Realm of Pure Ideality in which the name-souls dwell, pure, divine, immortal, uniform, indissoluble and unchanged."

[5] Lange, "History of Materialism," I, 75.

[6] Cf. Kallen, "Value and Existence" in "Creative Intelligence," 409.

[7] See the Introduction by Professors Oliphant and Hewitt, to Rueff, "From the Physical to the Social Sciences."

[8] Schiller, "Formal Logic," 46. See Lange, loc. cit., for a description of Aristotle's scientific method: After adducing a few isolated facts he immediately formulated from these facts a "universal" principle to which he then dogmatically adhered as the basis of knowledge about experience. This relative imperviousness to experience led him to the conclusion, for instance, that the left side of the body is colder than the right. In the same way he "proved" that there are a definite number of animal species. The propositions thus contrived he used deductively with logical consistency in such a way as to render accurate observation difficult, if not impossible; with Aristotle it was difficult, but not always impossible; with scholasticism (which copied Aristotle's faults and ignored his virtues) it became virtually impossible.

[9] Which, for the most part, ignored opposing tendencies in Plato and especially in Aristotle. As to Aristotle's virtues as a biologist, see Thompson, "Aristotle" in "The Legacy of Greece," 136.

[10] "The Middle Ages," writes F. C. S. Schiller, "were the ages of faith not in Christianity so much as in Formal Logic."

[11] "Because of its appearance of guaranteeing absolute mechanical exactness, formal logic has always appealed powerfully to lawyers. . . . Since Coke, formal logic has been a chief weapon in the armory of the common law lawyer. . . ." Pound, in 37 Harvard Law Review, 733.

[12] As to other logics, see below, note 14 to Chapter XIII.

PART ONE, CHAPTER VIII

[1] This tendency, to attribute to every name an origin justifying it, has been called the "etymological instinct," an erroneous designation if the label "instinct" is taken literally.

[2] As to which see Schiller, loc. cit., Chapter XXV.

[3] In this sense it may be said that there is a new crop of Platonists annually.

PART ONE, CHAPTER IX

[1] Here is Plato's description of his own childish day-dreaming tendencies: "Yet grant me a little favor; let me feast my mind with the dreams as day-dreamers are in the habit of feasting themselves when they are walking alone; for before they have discovered any means of effecting their wishes—that is a matter which never troubles them—they would rather not tire themselves by thinking about possibilities; but assuming that what they desire is already granted to them, they proceed with their plan, and delight in detailing what they mean to do when their wish has come true—that is a way which they have of not doing much good to a capacity which was never good for much."

[2] The same is true of religion; see Chapter XVIII. Some men "get rid of father" in their religious attitudes, before they have abandoned him in their legal attitudes. And with others vice versa. So, Plato, despite his religious views, seems to have been less of a "Platonist" in respect to law than some modern lawyers: "The difference of men and their actions," he writes, "and the fact that in human affairs nothing ever stands still, do not permit a general and universal rule in anything. No art can lay down a rule which will last forever."

PART ONE, CHAPTER X

[1] Ogden and Richards, "The Meaning of Meaning" (2d ed.); Malinowski, "The Problem of Meaning in Primitive Language"; Ogden, "The Meaning of Psychology."

Ogden & Co. have apparently written little with reference to legal thinking; see, however, Appendix VII for Ogden's discussion of Bentham's views on fictions.

[2] See the article on "Magic" in Encyclopedia Britannica (11th ed.) 308. "For primitive peoples the name is as much a part of the person as a limb; consequently the magical use of names is in some of its aspects assimilable to the processes dependent on the law of sympathy. In some cases the name

must be withheld from anyone who is likely to make a wrong use of it, and in some parts of the world people have secret names which are never used. Elsewhere the name must not be told by the bearer of it; but any other person may communicate it without giving an opening for the magical use of it. Not only human beings but also spirits can be coerced by the use of their names; hence names of the dead are forbidden, lest the mention of them act as an evocation, unintentional though it be. Even among more advanced nations it has been the practice to conceal the real name of supreme gods; we may probably explain this as due to the fear that an enemy might by the use of them turn the gods away from those to whom they originally belonged. For the same reason ancient Rome had a secret name."

[8] "The power of words is the most conservative force in our life. Only yesterday did students of anthropology begin to admit the existence of those ineluctable verbal coils by which so much of our thought is encompassed. The common inherited scheme of conception which is all around us, and comes to us as naturally and unobjectionably as our native air, is none the less imposed upon us, and limits our intellectual movements in countless ways—all the more surely and irresistibly because, being inherent in the very language we must use to express the simplest meaning, it is adopted and assimilated before we can so much as begin to think for ourselves at all." "And from the structure of our language we can hardly even think of escaping. Tens of thousands of years have elapsed since we shed our tails, but we are still communicating with a medium developed to meet the needs of arboreal man. And as the sounds and marks of language bear witness to its primeval origins, so the associations of those sounds and marks, and the habits of thought which have grown up with their use and with the structures imposed on them by our first parents, are found to bear witness to an equally significant continuity."

The primitive man's notion is that "the name of a thing or group of things is its soul; to know their names is to have known their souls."

"We may smile at the linguistic illusions of primitive man, but may we forget that the verbal machinery on which we so readily rely, and with which our metaphysicians still profess to probe the Nature of Existence, was set up by him, and may be responsible for other illusions hardly less gross and not more easily eradicable? . . .

"The persistence of the primitive linguistic outlook not only throughout the whole religious world, but in the work of the profoundest thinkers, is indeed one of the most curious features of modern thought."

[4] On the one hand, words are to be recognized as symbolic aids to thinking (which in turn is to be observed in its true character as a casual relation); on the basis of this recognition there is to be developed a Science of Symbolism which will systematically endeavor to make more effective this symbolic function of words. On the other hand, we shall recognize that words also have an emotive use: to express or excite feelings and attitudes. "The symbolic use of words is *statement;* the recording, the support, the organization and the communication of references. The emotive use of words is a more simple matter, it is the use of words to express or excite feelings and attitudes." When we are using speech symbolically, we must attend to the correctness of the symbols and the truth of the things to which the symbols refer. Not so when we are using words emotively, as in poetry.

One of the grave difficulties to which our word-doctors point is the fact that these two functions of words, the symbolic and emotive, become subtly interwoven. But the new sciences of symbolism will "enable us to differentiate between these two functions; to ask, when a statement is made, 'Is this true or false in the ordinary strict scientific sense?' If this question is relevant, then the use is symbolic; if it is clearly irrelevant, then we may have an emotive utterance."

Both uses of language are legitimate. The point is to take care that they are not confused. It is the confusion of the scientific and the poetic use of words which accounts for Platonizing.

[5] Cf. "The Meaning of Psychology," 158.

Anatole France was less optimistic: "And then, what is thinking? And how do we think? We think with words; that by itself constitutes a sensible basis and brings us back to our natural preconditions. Reflect a little; a metaphysician possesses, to build up his system of the Universe with, only the perfected cries of apes and dogs. What he styles profound speculation and transcendental method is only setting in a row, arbitrarily arranged, the onomatopoetic noises wherewith the brutes expressed hunger and fear and desire in the primeval forests, and to which have gradually become attached meanings that are assumed to be abstract, only because they are less definite. Never fear; this series of petty noises, deadened and enfeebled in the course of ages, that goes to make up a book of philosophy, will not ever teach us so much of the Universe as to permit us to inhabit it no longer. We are all in the dark together; the only difference is, the savant keeps knocking at the walls, while the ignoramus stays quietly in the middle of the room."

[6] See Appendix III.

[7] "No convenient symbolic device is objectionable so long as we know that it is a device and do not suppose it to be an addition to our knowledge." An "essential of all true education" is "to put us on our guard against the pitfalls and illusions due to words." "A false attitude towards language and its functions is one of the main obstacles in the advance of philosophical thought and scientific investigation."

[8] See Part One, Chapter I; Part Three, Chapter I; Appendix II.

[9] It may be that the Ogdenites would say that they are in accord with this so-called revised statement. But their description of the relation between primitive and childish uses of language seems to indicate that the former is the cause of the latter. See, however, "The Meaning of Psychology," 157, 302, 310. Malinowski's article at times seems to suggest a theory of genetics more in accord with the revised statement.

"The child's action on the surrounding world," writes Malinowski, "is done through the parents, on whom the child acts by its appeal, mainly its verbal appeal. When the child clamors for a person, it calls and he appears before it. When it wants food or an object or when it wishes some uncomfortable thing or arrangement to be removed, its only means of action is to clamor, and a very efficient means of action this proves to the child.

"To the child, words are therefore not only means of expression but efficient modes of action. The name of a person uttered aloud in a piteous voice possesses the power of materializing this person. Food has to be called for and it appears—in the majority of cases. Thus infantile experience must leave on the child's mind the deep impression that a name has the power over the person or thing which it signifies.

"We find thus that an arrangement biologically essential to the human race makes the early articulated words sent forth by children produce the very effect which these words *mean*. Words are to a child active forces, they give him an essential hold on reality, they provide him with the only effective means of moving, attracting and repulsing outer things and of producing changes in all that is relevant. This of course is not the statement of a child's conscious views about language, but it is the attitude implied in the child's behavior.

"Following the manner in which speech is used into the latter stage of childhood, we find again that everything reinforces this pragmatic relation to meaning. In all the child's experience, words *mean*, in so far as they act and not in so far as they make the child understand or apperceive. His joy in using words and in expressing himself in frequent repetition, or in playing about with a word, is relevant in so far as it reveals the active nature of early linguistic use. And it would be incorrect to say that such a playful use of words is 'meaningless.' It is certainly deprived of any intellectual purpose, but possesses always an emotional value, and it is one of the child's favorite actions, in which he approaches this or that person or object of his surroundings. When a child greets the approaching person or animal, item of food or toy, with a volley of the repeated name, he establishes a link of liking or disliking between himself and that object. And all the time, up to a fairly advanced age, the name of an object is the first means recurred to, in order to attract, to materialize this thing."

But it is not altogether clear whether Malinowski means that childish uses of language are a direct cause of the prevalent use of word-magic by modern adults or whether he considers that the word habits of children are influenced by an analogue of primitive word habits, while the primitive habits, encased in language itself, are the direct cause of the sway of word-magic among present day grown-ups.

[10] Compare Freud's thesis that sexual habits normal in childhood are perversions in the adult. Consider, too, that a grown-up who has to be fed like a child is pathological.

[11] See Chadwick, "Psyche," April 1928, p. 58, to the effect that for the child one "fundamental idea of language is to gain some wish or to gratify some need. It has yet another

function, to satisfy the infant's emotional requirements and to be a source of pleasure."

Rignano suggests that the metaphysician's use of intellectually contentless terms as a means of emotional satisfaction is "derived from the illusion acquired from childhood that to every term there always corresponds some object."

[12] Of course, it will not do to be dogmatic about childishness being the primary cause of the belief in word-magic in the modern world, for language itself does, no doubt, augment the child's natural tendencies to confuse words and things, etc. But these tendencies seem to have an origin independent of the past history of language.

[13] Schiller, loc. cit. 259; Lange, loc. cit. Book I, 236.

See below, note 4 to Chapter XI. Schiller points out that for all Bacon's jibes at the schoolmen, Bacon's procedure was still primarily verbalistic.

[14] Compare Schiller's comment: "It may be that the sole alternative of a logic which comes to terms with psychology is one which is enslaved in grammar."

[15] It should be noted that language is, of course, a potent factor in keeping alive fatherly authority. For language is *par excellence* the medium by which tradition is handed on from father to son. As soon as the child learns to speak he becomes a victim of the "traditional naming patterns." Cf. Ogden, "Meaning of Psychology," 157, 302, 310. See also Chadwick, "The Child's Early Discrimination Between Sound and Speech," in "Psyche," April 1928, p. 58, as to the enduring emotional effect of the domestic "vibration-patterns"—accounting, in part, for the suspicion felt towards strangers and foreigners whose vibration-patterns are unfamiliar.

PART ONE, CHAPTER XI

[1] "Over against that world of flux, 'Where nothing is, but all things seem,' it is the vocation of Plato," writes Pater, "to set up a standard of unchangeable reality, which in its highest theoretic development becomes the world of eternal and immutable ideas, indefectible outlines of thought, yet also the veritable things of experience; the perfect Justice, e.g. which even if the gods mistake it for perfect injustice, is not moved out of its place; the beauty which is the same yesterday, today

and forever. In such ideas, or ideals, eternal as participating in the essential character of the facts they represent to us, we come in contact, as he supposes, with the insoluble, immovable granite, beneath and amid the wasting torrent of mere phenomena."

Plato blamed the body because it interferes with perfect knowledge of these pure ideas: "The soul is dragged by the body into the region of the changeable, and wanders and is confused; the world spins around her, and she is like a drunkard, when she touches change. The soul is in a state of wisdom when she abandons the body and passes into the region of purity, eternity, immortality and unchangeableness." He depicts the mind of the wise man as "disdaining the littleness and nothingness of human things . . . not condescending to anything which is within reach." That the Socratic-Platonic movement was a reaction from a developing scientific attitude, see Singer in "The Legacy of Greece," 163, 175; Lange, loc. cit., Bk. I, Chap. III.

[2] Lange says of the Platonic "reaction" that it "struggled fanatically to retain a teleology which even in its most brilliant forms conceals flat anthropomorphism, and whose radical extermination is the indispensable condition of all scientific progress."

[3] The quotations from Hammond and Bishop will be found in Dickinson, 29 Columbia Law Review, 141–142.

[4] Something of this sort is perhaps what Harvey (who, ignoring time-honored authority, discovered the circulation of the blood) had in mind when he said of Francis Bacon's "Novum Organum," "He wrote on science like a Lord Chancellor." As a Lord Chancellor, Bacon declared that, "certainty is so essential to law that law cannot even be just without it." His views of scientific procedure were not dissimilar; as C. S. Peirce puts it, Bacon was convinced that "we have only to make some crude experiments, to draw up briefs of the results in certain blank forms, to go through them by rule, checking off everything disproved and setting down the alternatives, and that thus in a few years physical science would be finished up—what an idea!"

Bacon thought nature could be studied by infallible rules, without the aid of hypotheses or scientific imagination. Armed with these rules, any one could, by hard work, make scientific discoveries. He was contemptuous of the great

cientists of his day, Galileo and Gilbert. Mach said of him,
I do not know whether Swift's academy of schemers in
.ogado, in which discoveries and inventions were made by a
ort of verbal game of dice, was intended as a satire on Francis
lacon's method of making discoveries by means of huge
ynoptic tables constructed by scribes. It certainly would not
lave been ill-placed." Bacon himself said, "Our method of
iscovering the sciences is such as to leave little to the acute-
less and strength of wit, and, indeed, rather to level wit and
ntellect."

PART ONE, CHAPTER XII

[1] See Dewey, "Logical Method and the Law," 10 Cornell
.aw Quarterly, 17, 20. It is of interest that the best available
lescription of the logical method employed by judges is from
he pen, not of a lawyer, but of a psychologist.

[2] Cf. Cardozo, "The Nature of The Judicial Process," 170.

[3] "The Role of Penalties in Criminal Law," 27 Yale Law
ournal, 1048.

[4] Even the older psychology would suggest that these
iigeon-holes are insufficient. See, for instance, Spencer's
'Study of Sociology" in which he considers at length the ob-
tacles to dispassionate judgment; he includes impatience, ir-
ational irritation in the presence of unpleasant truths which
ire disappointing cherished hopes, hates, antipathies, awe of
)ower, loyalty to the group. Francis Bacon included in his
dols those of the Cave or Den, that is, errors due to causes
)eculiar to a specific individual.

The "new psychology," Freudian or otherwise, properly
:mphasizes these peculiarly individual factors.

[5] "On the Witness Stand," 13–71.

[6] "Two years ago in Göttingen there was a meeting of a
cientific association, made up of jurists, psychologists, and
)hysicians, all, therefore, men trained in careful observation.
iomewhere in the same street there was that evening a public
estivity of the carnival. Suddenly, in the midst of the scholarly
neeting, the doors open, a clown in highly colored costume
ushes in in mad excitement, and a negro with a revolver in
land follows him. In the middle of the hall first the one, then
he other, shouts wild phrases; then the one falls to the ground,
he other jumps on him; then a shot, and suddenly both are

out of the room. The whole affair took less than twenty seconds. All were completely taken by surprise, and no one, with the exception of the President, had the slightest idea that every word and action had been rehearsed beforehand, or that photographs had been taken of the scene. It seemed most natural that the President should beg the members to write down individually an exact report, inasmuch as he felt sure that the matter would come before the courts. Of the forty reports handed in, there was only one whose omissions were calculated as amounting to less than twenty per cent. of the characteristic acts; fourteen had twenty to forty per cent. of the facts omitted; twelve omitted forty to fifty per cent., and thirteen still more than fifty per cent. But besides the omissions there were only six among the forty which did not contain positively wrong statements; in twenty-four papers up to ten per cent. of the statements were free inventions, and in ten answers—that is, in one-fourth of the paper—more than ten per cent. of the statements were absolutely false, in spite of the fact that they all came from scientifically trained observers. Only four persons, for instance, among forty noticed that the negro had nothing on his head; the others gave him a derby, or a high hat, and so on. In addition to this, a red suit, a brown one, a striped one, a coffee-coloured jacket, shirt sleeves, and similar costumes were invented for him. He wore in reality white trousers and a black jacket with a large red necktie. The scientific commission which reported the details of the inquiry came to the general statement that the majority of the observers omitted or falsified about half of the processes which occurred completely in their field of vision. As was to be expected, the judgment as to the time duration of the act varied between a few seconds and several minutes." "On the Witness Stand," 51.

[7] What, for instance, affects the judge's attention to the testimony? Kimball Young ("Source Book for Social Psychology," 271) enumerates the following features of external stimuli which influence the attention of any observer: Intensity, novelty, configuration, mode of presentation, size, change or monotony, repetition, definiteness. The "internal" stimuli he catalogues as follows: Physiological (hunger, thirst, sex, fatigue, illness, weariness); emotional (fear, rage); old associations (legends, myths, stereotypes); aims (purposes,

ideals); attitudes (likes, dislikes, loves, hatreds, anxieties, avoidances).

What Hans Gross says of the mistakes of witnesses is worth quoting here: "The numberless errors in perceptions derived from the senses, the faults of memory, the far-reaching differences in human beings as regards sex, nature, culture, mood of the moment, health, passionate excitement, environment, all these things have so great an effect that we scarcely ever receive two quite similar accounts of one thing; and between what people really experience and what they confidently assert, we find only error heaped upon error."

[8] See Cardozo, "The Nature of The Judicial Process," 167–177.

[9] "What is Never in the Record But Always in the Case," McEwen, 8 Illinois Law Review, 594.

[10] Everson, "The Human Element in Justice," 10 Journal of Criminal Law and Criminology, 90; see also Haines, "General Observations on the Effect of Personal, Political and Economic Influences in the Decisions of Judges," 17 Illinois Law Review, 98, 105.

[11] "The Psychologic Study of Judicial Opinions," 6 California Law Review, 89.

[12] Loc. cit.

PART ONE, CHAPTER XIII

[1] "Science of Legal Method," LXXV–LXXXII.

[2] Cf. Saleilles, "The Individualization of Punishment," 64–5.

[3] Austin, referring to Bentham's strictures and judge-made law, wrote, "I cannot but think that, instead of blaming judges for having legislated, he should blame them for the timid, narrow, and piecemeal manner in which they have legislated, and for legislating under cover of vague and indeterminate phrases. . . ." "Jurisprudence" (4th Ed.), 224. Cf. Kent, "Commentaries," 477; Cohen, "The Place of Logic in the Law," 29 Harvard Law Review, 622, 634; "The Process of Judicial Legislation," 48 American Law Review, 161, 189–190.

[4] Cf. Wigmore, "The Judicial Function" in "The Science of Legal Method," XXXII to XXXIV; Radin, "Statutory In-

terpretation," 43 Harvard Law Review, 863; Landis, "A Note on 'Statutory Interpretation,' " 43 Harvard Law Review, 886.

[5] Salmond maintains that if a question cannot be brought within the scope of "preëstablished and authoritative principle" it is not a "question of law" but a "question of fact."

In Appendix II will be found a discussion of the similar views of Dickinson who has developed Gray's distinction between law and its sources and who has adhered to the belief that law consists of rules.

[6] This new attitude had at least been intimated by Holmes in "The Common Law" published in 1881. Holmes, like Gray, was a professor in Harvard Law School. Holmes's work was surely known to Gray who, significantly, omits any mention of Holmes's theories in his book (published in 1902) which is devoted to discussions of other men's theories.

For a reference to Continental theories resembling Holmes's, see Appendix II.

[7] "When we say in a particular case that the plaintiff had a right or the defendant was under a duty, and the like, this but means that we have already passed judgment. . . . The process has been concluded in some unknown way; the result is merely being vocalized. . . . As lawyers we constantly delude ourselves and likewise delude others by insisting that those delightful word jousts we call opinions are dependable guides to the workings of the judicial processes. When that stage is reached, the action has already been fought. An opinion is but the smoke which indicates the grade of mental explosive employed. Somewhere behind the curtains of legal expression lie the laboratories of our intellect. They are not legal. They comprise all that we are. Perhaps our judgments on the least item of the day are given shape there in the same way as our most solemn decision in a law suit." Dean Leon Green, 28 Columbia Law Review, 1014.

[8] 33 Yale Law Journal, 457, 475.

[9] Cook's program for scientific training of the lawyer we have discussed above, Part One, Chapter XI.

[10] 13 American Bar Association Journal, 303, 308.

Bingham, whose views are substantially the same as those of Holmes and Cook, objects to the statement that judges "legislate." "Undoubtedly," he says, "judicial decisions make law and their multiplication tends to simplify the prediction of potential adjudications and the definite and certain generalizations of the results; but a court has no legislative power to enact expression which is binding in other litigation. Its essential function is to hear, supervise, and determine particular concrete controversies within its jurisdiction." 11 Michigan Law Review, 112.

For a further discussion of Bingham, see Appendix II.

[11] Cf. "Science and the Law," J. W. Bingham, 25 Green Bag, 62. See also Llewellyn's brilliant article, 30 Columbia Law Review, 431, published while this book is in preparation.

[12] Ex parte Chase, 43 Alabama, 303.

[13] "Judicial Freedom of Decision: Its Principles and Objects," in "Science of Legal Method," 47, 74. See Gmelin, in the same volume, 124–5, 137. As to the Continental theory of "free judicial decision" see Appendix II.

[14] Compare Holmes's famous aphorism, "The life of the law has not been logic; it has been experience." ("The Common Law," 1.) Morris Cohen insists that this epigram must be interpreted in the light of Holmes's "great scientific interests and achievements in the logic of analysis of legal ideas and issues." To Cohen "experience or life without logic is stupid and brutish and supplies no guide for the good or civilized life." (The American Law School Review, Vol. 6, 236; see also "The Place of Logic in the Law," 29 Harvard Law Review, 622.) No doubt Holmes would agree, but would answer that Cohen has misread his aphorism by failing to put the proper stress on the word "life." See Holmes, "Collected Legal Papers," 225, 238, 306. See also Dewey, "Legal Method and the Law," 10 Cornell Law Quarterly, 17, to the effect that Holmes was thinking of logic as equivalent to the syllogism, as he was quite entitled to do in accordance with the orthodox tradition, that from the standpoint of scholastic formal logic, there is an antithesis between experience and logic, between logic and good sense. "There are different logics in use," adds Dewey. "That of the syllogism has exercised the greatest influence on legal decisions. To this logic the strictures of Holmes apply in full force. It purports to be a logic of rigid demonstration, not of search and discovery."

[15] To make this matter clear, note what Pound calls "law" as distinguished from "discretion." "Before the law we have justice without law; and after the law and during the evolution of law we still have it under the name of discretion, or natural justice, or equity and good conscience, as an anti-legal ele-

ment. Without entangling ourselves in the discussion as to the definition of law, we may say that laws are general rules recognized or enforced in the administration of justice."

[16] "The Influence of the Universities on Judicial Decision." Cornell Law Quarterly, I–X.

[17] Hutcheson goes on, "I had been trained to expect inexactitude from juries, but from the judge quite the reverse. I exalted in the law its tendency to formulize. I had a slot machine mind, I searched out categories and concepts and, having found them, worshipped them.

"I paid homage to the law's supposed logical rigidity and exactitude. A logomachist, I believed in and practiced logomancy. I felt a sense of real pain when some legal concept in which I had put my faith as permanent, constructive and all-embracing opened like a broken net, allowing my fish to fall back into the legal sea. Paraphrasing Huxley, I believed that the great tragedy of law was the slaying of a beautiful concept by an ugly fact. Always I looked for perfect formulas, fact-proof, concepts so general, so flexible, that in their terms the jural relations of mankind could be stated, and I rejected most vigorously the suggestion that there was, or should be, anything fortuitous or by chance in the law."

[18] President Hutchins, working with Adler, Michael and Slesinger, has made an admirable beginning in the field of evidence. See 28 Yale Law Journal, 1017; 28 Columbia Law Review, 432; and 41 Harvard Law Review, 860.

[19] The courts and text-books sometimes state rules of thumb for determining whether a witness is biased, mistaken or lying. One judge reports that he always notes if a prisoner has abnormal ears; he also considers that liars have restless hands. A well-known lawyer advises that "the witness who is swearing to a clear-cut lie will, while so doing, throw back his head with an indifferent air and close his eyes or blink; my experience has taught me to believe that that is an almost certain sign of deliberate dishonesty."

Too little has been done as yet to systematize and test out such observations. Even if better systematized and checked up with the observations of psychologists, such guides will be of relatively small value until the judge who is making use of them has carefully checked up on his own biases and prejudices.

PART ONE, CHAPTER XIV

[1] 37 Yale Law Journal, 468, 480.

[2] Oliphant is doubtless right as far as he goes. A given conclusion may be correct although the arguments by which it is justified may be inadequate. It is possible to work out a considerable number of syllogisms in which the same conclusion is derived from varying premises. When a judge attaches an opinion to his decision he may explain that his judgment was derived from a certain rule or principle as its major premise. The decision with respect to the facts of the particular case may be quite satisfactory. It is possible, however, to relate this judgment to a markedly different principle as the major premise.

There are many dark spots in legal history owing to the fact that judges, seduced by the wisdom of a *decision* rendered by a judge in an earlier case, have gone beyond the use of the earlier *decision* as an analogy and have used the *"principle"* to which the judge in his opinion in the earlier case purported to relate his conclusion. Thus seduced, they feel obliged to follow the "principle" announced in the earlier opinion and thence to reason syllogistically, using this "principle" as a major premise.

See Goodhart, 15 Cornell Law Quarterly, 173 at 185, to the effect that Oliphant's suggested return from *stare dictis* to real *stare decisis* resembles Rousseau's demand for a return to a law of nature which never existed. See also Dean Green, 28 Columbia Law Review, 1014 at 1038.

[3] If all judges were completely sophisticated and casuistical, they could usually avoid this problem by deliberately insincere expressions of the reasoning which they employ in their opinions. In other words, in many cases they could mouth the old formulas, even when they knew they were actually reaching conclusions that were at variance with the established doctrines. But professional conscientiousness prevents the deliberate and conscious use of such disingenuous methods.

[4] Dickinson, "Administrative Justice and the Supremacy of Law." Dickinson in this book was struggling away from an obsessive interest in rules, an interest which expresses itself in such of his language as the following: "It is the reason embodied in the purposes of the law and not the arbitrary discre-

tion of the judge that must determine whether or not a particular legal concept controls a case which from some angles fits within it. A concept ought never to be held inapplicable to a case to which it seems to apply unless it ought also to be held inapplicable to all similar cases where its application would similarly defeat the purpose of the law. What is needed is not arbitrary discretion, but a rule for making exceptions, —a rule for breaking a rule—and of such rules the law is of course full." Can there, indeed, be a "rule"—*i.e.* a general abstract formula—for breaking a rule?

There are other passages in which Dickinson approaches the problem of judicial discretion more realistically; his realistic trend finds still more marked expression in his more recent articles in "The Law Behind Law," 29 Columbia Law Review, 114, 284. See comments on Dickinson in Appendix II.

[5] Cf. the writings of Frazer, Leuba, Hart and Piaget.

[6] Cf. Clerk Maxwell's ideal of freedom of will, "whereby, instead of being consciously free and really in subjection to unknown law, it becomes consciously active law, and really free from interference of an unrecognized law." Quoted in Otto, "Natural Laws and Human Hopes," 60.

Compare the following from Wm. Stern (quoted in Gmelin, loc. cit., 106) : "The great forward movements of science are not composed of the sudden emergence of new concepts and ideas out of nothingness, but rather consist in this, that familiar experiences, which hitherto were accepted as matters of course, are subjected to criticism, so that their problematical character is recognized and an endeavor to understand them is put in the place of an acquiescence in what is supposed to be self-evident."

See Appendix III.

PART ONE, CHAPTER XV

[1] See Dewey, "How We Think."

[2] "The Philosophy of As If." See Appendix VII.

[3] "The equilibratory tendency of the psyche" appears to be a fictional idea which Vaihinger appears to use without full recognition of the fiction involved. He seems unwittingly to be converting a "fiction" into a dogma. See Appendix VII.

[4] "The Scientific Habit of Thought," 58, 83.

⁵ Cf. Vaihinger, who in speaking of the "equilibratory tendency of the psyche," says: "The only way to transform an unstable into a stable equilibrium is to support the body in question" and thus explains the drive towards the substitution of dogmas for hypotheses and fictions.

⁶ Barry also says of the conservative habit of thinking that "It is, as a matter of fact, the analogue of our equally unchanging physical habit, which is itself the analogue of mechanical inertia—the phenomenon which serves physical science as the basis of all natural law."

⁷ Cf. Lewis, "The Anatomy of Science," 9: "If we once get rid of the childlike notion that every act is either right or wrong, that every statement is either true or false, that every question can be answered with a 'Yes' or 'No.' . . ." Also on p. 154, after stating that the second law of thermodynamics is now beginning to be questioned as an absolute, he goes on:

"If this discovery comes to us as a great disillusionment, it is only because our minds are tinged from infancy with the hoary superstition of the absolute. We say, 'If this great law is not always true, what becomes of our other exact laws.' But can we have no reverence for any institution without making the childish assumption of its infallibility? Can we not see that exact laws, like all the other ultimates or absolutes, are as fabulous as the crock of gold at the rainbow's end?"

⁸ On this point, Barry vacillates. See especially his last chapter.

⁹ In different terms, Barry says the same. See loc. cit., 83–4; 354–7.

¹⁰ Vaihinger uses the phrase, "the law of persistence of concepts," to describe the fact that while a dogma may lose its prestige among the intelligent, it is often kept alive by them as a fiction for themselves and a myth for the public. "Ideational constructs that once become firmly rooted are retained as fictions rather than discarded." See Part Two, Chapter V.

¹¹ See G. B. Foster, "The Function of Religion in Man's Struggle for Existence," 63–4; G. B. Shaw, "The Quintessence of Ibsenism," (2nd Edition) p. 18–28. For words of caution as to the dangers of confusing science and poetry, see Richards, loc. cit., especially Chapter VI.

Paradoxically, those who outgrow infantile dreaming (*i.e.* give up the hope of too much security) are usually the pliant-minded folk whom we think of as ever-youthful, even if they be old in years.

[12] Graham Wallas, "Our Social Heritage," p. 194, referred to, with approval, by Cardozo, "The Growth of the Law," 89–92; see also Wallas, Chapter II, especially pp. 38, 41, 42–3.

PART ONE, CHAPTER XVI

[1] This is a liberal paraphrase of Dickinson, "Administrative Justice and the Supremacy of Law," 141–2. See note to Part One, Chapter XIV and Appendix II for a discussion of Dickinson's attitude towards rules and principles.

[2] The jury is seldom employed in equity cases.

One of the little-observed aspects of the jury problem is that purely arbitrary factors often determine whether a case is to be tried without a jury. Jones had contracted to sell me a thousand barrels of flour of a certain grade to be delivered on a fixed date. I claim that he delivered the flour two weeks late and that it was not of the agreed quality. Just as I am about to sue Jones, he files a petition in bankruptcy and shows that he has $50,000 worth of assets and $60,000 of debts. If I sue now, a judge without a jury will decide the case, whereas had I sued a week earlier, I could have had a jury trial. Likewise, Jones's death, while solvent, before I sued would deprive me of a jury. There are numerous other situations where accidental circumstances take away the right of resort to the "palladium of our liberties."

[3] The peculiar facts of English and American history are conventionally referred to as explaining our unwise use of the general verdict. But Saleilles ("The Individualization of Punishment") has shown that in French criminal law a like recourse has been had to the general verdict of the jury. In France, also, too great a rigidity of legal formulas and too imperfect adjustability of abstract rules to the facts of each case has led to results similar to those we have experienced. The power of the judge to individualize has been denied and the task of individualization has been handed over to the jury. "All this," says Saleilles, "leads to capricious and variable decisions. Each jury has its own standards of judgment and each juryman individually has his. It is almost a justice of chance, which is the worst and most disconcerting of all." He also

speaks of "the wholly inconsistent verdicts of juries, the injustice of which is well nigh scandalous; for there is no rule, no uniform standard of judgment."

[4] "The record must be absolutely flawless, but such a result is possible only by concealing, not by excluding, mistakes. This is the great technical merit of the general verdict. It covers up all the shortcomings which frail human nature is unable to eliminate from the trial of a case. In the abysmal abstraction of the general verdict concrete details are swallowed up, and the eye of the law, searching anxiously for the realization of logical perfection, is satisfied. In short, the general verdict is valued for what it does, not for what it is. It serves as the great procedural opiate, which draws the curtain upon human errors and soothes us with the assurance that we have attained the unattainable." Sunderland, loc. cit., 282.

For an illustration of the coupling of certainty-hunger and jury-worship see Jackson in 15 Cornell Law Quarterly, 194.

[5] The special verdict, said the court in Pittsburgh R. Co. vs. Spencer, 98 Ind. 186, exhibits "the facts of the case in such a manner that the court can decide according to law, and relieve the jury from the necessity of deciding legal questions on which they may have some doubts." It is clear who the court believed decided the law where the general verdict was used.

See Sunderland, loc. cit., and Wicker, "Special Interrogatories to Juries in Civil Cases," 35 Yale Law Journal, 296. "We come, then," says Sunderland, "to this position, that the general verdict is not a necessary feature of litigation in civil actions at law and that it confers on the jury a vast power to commit error and do mischief by loading it with technical burdens far beyond its ability to perform, by confusing it in aggregating instead of segregating the issues, and by shrouding in secrecy and mystery the actual results of its deliberations."

[6] Part One, Chapter XII.

[7] "The layman chancing to listen to a criminal trial finds himself gasping with astonishment at the deluge of minute facts which pour from the witnesses' mouths in regard to the happenings of some particular day a year or so before," writes Arthur Train. "He knows that it is humanly impossible actually to *remember* any such facts, even had they occurred the day before yesterday. He may ask himself what he did that very morning and be unable to give any satisfactory reply. And yet the jury believes this testimony, and because the witness swears

to it, it goes upon the record as evidence of actual knowledge. In ninety-nine cases out of a hundred counsel's only recourse is to argue to the jury that such a memory is impossible. But in the same proportion of cases the jury will take the oath of the witness against the lawyer's reasoning and their own common sense. This is because of the fictitious value given to the witness's oath by talesmen who attach little significance to their own. 'He *swears* to it,' says the juryman, rubbing his forehead. 'Well, he *must* remember it, or he wouldn't swear to it!' And the witness probably thinks he *does* remember it."

Lord Brougham once observed, "that a single expression, a showy case made out of a single loose phrase, such as 'Go into the room and tell that I have got a man here to bid,' it being untrue that he has any man to bid—I am giving this as a specimen—or such a phrase as 'a set of old fools in the next room,' used by one party to the other, a thing of that sort, as we all know, coming before a jury, has always much greater force than its real value entitles it to, in finally disposing of the whole matter. It is a fault incident to the nature of the investigation, in a limited time, under the heat and pressure of the moment, upon the evidence of the witness and the counsel's comments; it is a defect to which the trial by jury is inevitably subject."

Another judge has commented that "Juries nearly always give more weight to the words of a living witness before them than they do to the writings made even by the same witness at another time."

[8] McEwen continues: "The disposition of the jury to lean upon somebody arises out of their inexperience, timidity and doubt of themselves. If the judge indicates a leaning or belief or disbelief, it is almost sure to carry a leaning and belief to the juror. If one lawyer can demonstrate a position of superiority over the other, and create a belief in his candor and sincerity, his argument in the case or his assertion of a fact will be taken as a basis for a verdict. If a witness, disinterested, at the scene of the crime or of an accident, or the happening of some event, has expressed his opinion at the time of the occurrence, and he appears to be a witness of soundness, it will be taken as the opinion of the jury. The judgment of the bystanders who expressed themselves on the instant approving or condemning, is a powerful force, because the leaning jury say that is the opinion of the man who knows. A juror is apt

to treat all other matter in the case as nothing, for the man who was on the spot, saw the entire transaction, judged it and expressed his opinions, without any motives to misjudge, is the best authority to follow in the view of the jurors. I do not think that I have ever seen it fail—that the judgment of an eye witness, disinterested, expressed at the time, is taken as the judgment of the jury. It might be slight, the words may not be very significant in themselves, may be a policeman's 'I was sorry for him,' may be the passenger on the street car, it may be the motorman, 'What are you trying to do—kill somebody?' It may be the statement 'I was to blame,' or a thousand and one other forms of expression of judgment by the man who ought to know."

[9] "Assuming that each of three witnesses honestly endeavored to disclose the exact facts as he recalled them, which of the three is most likely to have been accurate in his recollection? is the sort of query which triers of facts are constantly obliged to propound to themselves. Can it be reasonably inferred in a given case that a witness would have observed and remembered a fact if it had occurred, so that his testimony that he does not recollect it, assuming him to be honest, justified a finding that the fact did not occur? If a witness testifies positively to a fact and is in no wise contradicted, is the trier of facts at liberty to disbelieve him because it is deemed incredible that the human memory could have retained the fact? Has a witness subjected his entire testimony to grave suspicion by his assertion of extraordinary memory or forgetfulness in some particulars? Does a party's nonproduction of an available witness operate greatly to his prejudice for the reason that the trier of facts can perceive that the absent witness would unquestionably have an accurate memory of the facts; or, on the other hand, weigh lightly against the party because it is evident that the absent witness would not be able to recollect the facts? Such questions as the foregoing, arising on the original trial of cases, on motion for new trial because of a verdict against evidence, and in appellate courts reviewing findings on questions of fact, must be determined by 'the laws which regulate human memory,' and there is reason to believe that judges give more careful consideration to these laws than juries." Moore, loc. cit., 793.

[10] "As to the second element in the general verdict, the *law*, it is a matter upon which the jury is necessarily ignorant. The

jurors are taken from the body of the country, and it is safe
to say that the last man who could be called or allowed to
sit would be a lawyer. They are second hand dealers in law,
and must get it from the judge. They can supply nothing themselves; they are a mere conduit pipe through which the court
supplies the law that goes into the general verdict. But while
the jury can contribute nothing of value so far as the law is
concerned, it has infinite capacity for mischief, for twelve men
can easily misunderstand more law in a minute than the judge
can explain in an hour. Indeed, *can anything be more fatuous
than the expectation that the law which the judge so carefully,
learnedly and laboriously expounds to the laymen in the jury
box will become operative in their minds in its true form?* One
who has never studied a science cannot understand or appreciate its intricacies, and the law is no exception to this rule.
The very theory of the jury and its general verdict is thus
predicated upon a premise which makes practically certain an
imperfect or erroneous view of the principles of law which
are to be compounded into the verdict. The instructions upon
the law given by the court to the jury are an effort to give, in
the space of a few minutes, a legal education to twelve laymen upon the branch of the law involved in the case. Law cannot be taught in any such way. As to this element, accordingly,
the general verdict is almost necessarily a failure." Sunderland, loc. cit., 253.

[11] Primitive magic and folk-lore also use such power words,
say Ogden and Richards: "Almost any European country can
still furnish examples of the tale in which a name (Tom-tit-
Tor, Vargulaska, Rimpelstitken, Finnin, Zi) has to be discovered before some prince can be wedded or some ogre frustrated."

But a large part of the child's magic seems to be indige-
nous. "I feel quite sure," writes Gosse of the "magic" he used
as a child, "that nothing external suggested these ideas of
magic, and I think that they approached the ideas of savages
at a very early stage of development." See Piaget, "The Child's
Conception of the World," Chapter IV and p. 389.

[12] Dean Leon Green has amusingly portrayed the purely
ritualistic meaning of the instructions in negligence cases. See
37 Yale Law Journal, 1028, 1043. The "ordinary prudent
person," "reasonableness," "foreseeability,"—all these he describes as part of the ritual: "How any particular jury arrive

at their judgment is perhaps unknown even to themselves. But a 'scientific' statement of law has very little interest in how they shall treat these terms. The law provides the jury with no table or key by which they can transform these symbols into the terms of human conduct and human qualities. The law recites its ritual and stops. In short, having developed an agency for giving judgment and a ritual for passing the negligence issue to that agency for judgment, the factors which the jury may take into account are of slight, if any, importance, in a scientific statement of the law. Here science is satisfied with ritual. So long as the jury's judgment is not outrageous, it stands."

Green's views on this ritual should be considered in the light of his notions of the law's word-slavery discussed above, Part One, Chapter X.

[13] See articles on "Prayer," "Priests," "Ritual" and "Magic" in the Encyclopedia Britannica (11th Ed.).

PART ONE, CHAPTER XVII

[1] Alvarez, "Methods for Codes," in "Science of Legal Method," 429, 486; see also his articles in Chapters I and V of "The Progress of Continental Law in the Nineteenth Century."

[2] "Codes and Cases," in "Science of Legal Method," 251, 252, 253.

[3] "Dialecticism and Technicality: The Need of Sociological Method," in "Science of Legal Method," 85–6. This code in its first draft was apparently conceived as an exhaustive body of Procrustean rules. This conception was modified in the code as adopted; something of a make-shift compromise was adopted, the judges were, in several instances, given express discretionary power to decide according to the "equities" of the particular case and room was left "for the existence of a general customary law. . . . At the same time, the attempt to include in its provisions all the legal relations of private life fully and with certainty, has by no means been given up." Gény, "Technic of Codes," in "Science of Legal Method," 540–2; 549. Alvarez, loc. cit., 472.

[4] It is proper to note that while this hope was entertained by Napoleon, it did not completely dominate the minds of the

codifiers. Napoleon was greatly irritated at the appearance of the first commentary. "It is true," says Charmont, "that not all of his advisers shared his sentiment; most of them believed that even with codification completed, juridical interpretation was still needful, and that it should be expressed with some degree of liberty. The first commentators upon the Code . . . were of the same mind." The code itself indicated that its provisions were not to be complete but were to be supplemented by reference to other sources, such as natural law, ancient customs, usage and "jurisprudence." See Austin, "Jurisprudence" (4th Ed.), 695; Schuster, loc. cit., 23.

Nevertheless, in the second half of the nineteenth century, the application of the code was controlled by the spirit, which Napoleon had endorsed, of crediting the legislator "with having foreseen and settled all things." Later the more elastic provisions of the code were stressed more and more. See Charmont, loc. cit., 112 et seq.; Gény, "Technic of Codes," in "Science of Legal Method," 498, 529, 537.

[5] See Part One, Chapter XVIII.

[6] Kiss, "Equity and Law," in "Science of Legal Method," 146, 159.

[7] "Nature and Sources of Law," Section 370.

[8] "Analysis of Fundamental Notions," in "Modern French Legal Philosophy," 452.

[9] Charmont, in "Modern French Legal Philosophy," 113, 114.

[10] Charmont, loc. cit., 114.

[11] Stampe quoted in Gmelin, loc. cit., 133; cf. Alvarez, loc. cit.

[12] Gény, loc. cit., 547.

[13] "Jurisprudence" (4th Ed.), 689. Austin acknowledged the necessity of judicial legislation. But this necessity, he thought, was due to incompetence manifested in statutory legislation. If a comprehensive code were adopted "judicial or improper legislation" could be "kept within narrow limits." English law was a "chaos of judiciary law, and of the statute law stuck patch-wise on the judiciary." This chaos "could be superseded by a good code." The complexity and unknowability of the uncodified English common law gave it, he thought, "a disgusting character."

[14] Planial, quoted in Lobingier, loc. cit., 116. Essentially,

this language expresses the belief of Durran from whom we quoted in the notes to Part One, Chapter I.

[15] "Every system of judiciary law" (*i.e.* uncodified law) "has all the evils of a system which is really vague and inconsistent," he wrote. "This arises mainly from two causes: the enormous bulk of the documents in which the law must be sought and the difficulty of extracting the law (supposing the decision known) from the particularly decided cases in which it lies imbedded. By consequence, a system of judiciary law (as every candid man will readily admit) is nearly unknown to the bulk of the community, although they are bound to adjust their conduct to the rules or principles of which it consists. Nay, it is known imperfectly to the mass of lawyers, and even to the most experienced of the legal profession. . . . By the great body of the legal profession (when engaged in advising those who resort to them for counsel) the law (generally speaking) is divined rather than ascertained: And whoever has seen opinions, even of celebrated lawyers, must know that at best they are worded with a discreet and studied ambiguity which, while it saves the credit of the uncertain and perplexed adviser, thickens the doubts of the party who is seeking instruction and guidance."

[16] The strained character of this conception has been frequently demonstrated. See, for instance, the writings of Maine, Gray, Laski, Vinagradoff, Pound, Cardozo and Duguit.

PART ONE, CHAPTER XVIII

[1] A. Eustace Haydon, "The Quest for God," The Journal of Religion, III, 590. Cf. G. B. Foster, "The Function of Religion in Man's Struggle for Existence"; Hoffding, "Philosophy of Religion"; Leuba, "Psychology of Religious Mysticism"; G. Lowes Dickinson, "The Greek View of Life"; Frazer, "The Golden Bough"; Forest Emerson Witcraft, "A Critical Analysis of The Theory that Theism is Essential to Moral Motivation" (an unpublished doctor's thesis); Otto, "Things and Ideals."

[2] Fustel de Coulanges, "Ancient City"; cf. Ludwig Felix, in excerpts quoted in Vol. III, Chap. XIV, of "Evolution of Law" series, compiled by Wigmore and Kocourek; Sir Henry Maine, "Early Law and Custom"; Berolzheimer in "Science of Legal Method," 183; Spencer, "Principles of Sociology."

[3] See translated excerpts from his writings in "Evolution of Law," II, 630.

[4] Kohler, "Philosophy of Law."

[5] Cf. Dewey, in "The Social Sciences and Their Interrelations, 24; Morris Cohen in 6 American Law School Review, 235; Elsie Clews Parsons, "Fear and Conventionality," XI.

[6] "History of Religion," 11–12, 24–5.

[7] Cf. Rignano, "The Psychology of Reasoning," Chapter XII.

[8] Cf. Comte's "Law of the Three States," the Theological, the Metaphysical and the Positive. Using his terms, we would say that most thinking about law has passed from the Theological to the Metaphysical State but has not yet reached the Positive State. Cf. Wurzel, loc. cit., 294.

[9] Cf. Jhering's attitude towards religious and legal security, Part Two, Chapter II.

Note the following lines of Austin who (Cf. Part One, Chapter XVII) saw behind every human law a human sovereign with a command backed by force: "The Divine Laws, or the laws of God, are laws set by God to his human creatures. . . . As distinguished from duties imposed by human laws, duties imposed by the Divine laws may be called *religious duties*. As distinguished from violations of duties imposed by human laws, violations of religious duties are styled *sins*. As distinguished from sanctions annexed to human laws, the sanctions annexed to the Divine laws may be called *religious sanctions*. They consist of the evils, or pains, which we may suffer here or hereafter, by the immediate appointment of God, and as consequences of breaking his commandments."

[10] This essay has to do primarily with law in our civilization. To make the notion outlined in this chapter universally applicable, would require cautious rephrasing so as to include an explanation which would cover polytheistic communities. Suffice it here to say that man "parentalizes" his gods and that, among his gods, are some who take over the disciplinary, rule-making, function of the parents.

PART TWO, CHAPTER I

[1] "Introduction to the Philosophy of Law," pp. 140–3; 36 Harvard Law Review, 825. "Law and Morals" (2d. Ed.), 58, 72.

² "Essays in Psychopathology."

³ 36 Harvard Law Review, 641, 802, 940. Pound was perhaps following "The Individualization of Punishment," 8, 10, where Saleilles characterizes the "classical" theory of criminal law as being "somewhat as if a physician were to maintain that there are only diseases and no patients."

Cf. Aristotle, "Ethics," Book I, Chapter V: "For it appears that a physician does not regard health abstractedly, but regards the health of man or rather perhaps of a particular man, as he gives medicine to individuals."

⁴ See especially his dissenting opinion in Truax vs. Corrigan, 257 U. S. 312, 342–3.

⁵ See Part I, Chapter X, as to Word-Magic, the emotive use of words, the need for word-consciousness and a word-revolution.

⁶ 36 Harvard Law Review, 816, 951; "An Introduction to the Philosophy of Law," 140–1.

⁷ But see Part One, Chapter XIII, on the vagueness of the phrase "intuition."

⁸ "Only an uncritical vagueness will assume that the sole alternative to fixed generality is absence of continuity," says Dewey ("Human Nature and Conduct," 244–5). He finds Bergson's antithesis unreal: "Continuity of growth, not atomism, is thus the alternative to fixity of principles and aims. This is no Bergsonian plea for dividing the universe into two portions, one all of fixed recurrent habits and the other all spontaneity and flux." There is no need to choose between "absolute fixity and absolute looseness."

See Cardozo, "The Nature of the Judicial Process," 145–6; "The Growth of the Law," 137.

⁹ "The Spirit of the Common Law," 171, 172, 173; "Courts and Legislation," in "Science of Legal Method," 202, 206–7, 232, 233. Pound uses the term "fiction" in several senses. When he says that law, at one stage of its development, "grows more or less consciously, but as it were, surreptitiously under the cloak of fictions" he means something between a myth (self-delusion) and a true fiction (artificial distortion of fact used for convenience).

¹⁰ That this is not a fiction but a myth, see Part One, Chapter IV, and Appendix VII.

¹¹ Cf. the discussion of his views on discretion, Part One, Chapter XIII, and in note to Appendix II.

While this book has been in preparation at the printer's there appears a criticism of Pound which, in other terms, directs attention to his inconsistent views and to his lingering devotion to rule-worship. See Llewellyn, 30 Columbia Law Review, 431, 435.

PART TWO, CHAPTER II

[1] See Part One, Chapter XVIII for a discussion of the correlation of father-worship in law and religion.

PART TWO, CHAPTER III

[1] "Analysis of Fundamental Notions" in "Modern French Legal Philosophy," 347.

[2] See Part One, Chapter III.

[3] Part One, Chapter III.

PART TWO, CHAPTER VI

[1] "The Growth of the Law," 70; see also "The Nature of the Judicial Process," 9; 26–30; 161–2.

[2] "The Growth of the Law," 33.

[3] Loc. cit. 66–7.

[4] Loc. cit. 16–7.

[5] "The Nature of the Judicial Process."

[6] "The Paradoxes of Legal Science," 64. See Cardozo's moderate yet effective criticism of Pound's effort to apportion the law between the economic order and the conduct of the individual in "The Growth of the Law," 81–9; see, throughout, "The Nature of the Judicial Process."

[7] "The Paradoxes of Legal Science," 1.

PART THREE, CHAPTER I

[1] Pound, "The Theory of Judicial Decision," 36 Harvard Law Review, 959; cf. Cardozo, "The Growth of the Law," 107, 144.

[2] See Appendix III.

[3] Cf. Miller, "The New Psychology and the Parent."

[4] "The Function of Religion in Man's Struggle for Existence," 126, 133.

[5] "The great thing to remember is that the mind of man cannot be enlightened permanently by merely teaching him to regret some particular set of superstitions. There is an infinite supply of other superstitions always at hand; and the mind that desires such things—that is, the mind that has not trained itself to the hard discipline of reasonableness and honesty, will, as soon as its devils are cast out, proceed to fill itself with their relations." Murray, "Five Stages of the Greek Religion," 162–3.

"We are now awake to the all-important truth that belief in this or that detail of superstition is the result of an irrational state of mind, and flows logically from superstitious premises. We see that it is to begin at the wrong end, to assail the deductions as impossible, instead of sedulously building up a state of mind in which their impossibility would become spontaneously visible." Morley, loc. cit., 151.

[6] "All through the physical world runs that unknown content, which must surely be the stuff of our consciousness," says Eddington (in "Space, Time and Gravitation," 198, 201). "Here is a hint of aspects deep within the world of physics, and yet unattainable by the methods of physics, and, moreover, we have found that where science has progressed the farthest, the mind has but regained from nature that which the mind has put into nature. We have found a strange footprint on the shores of the unknown. We have devised profound theories, one after another, to account for its origin. At last, we have succeeded in reconstructing the creature that made the footprint. And Lo! it is our own." See also "Science, Religion and Reality," 149, 156–7, 217; Richards, "Science and Poetry," 78.

That many of the so-called natural laws are human inventions rather than discoveries, see Karl Pearson, "Grammar of Science," Chapter V; Vaihinger, "Philosophy of As If"; Hobson, "The Domain of Natural Science," quoted in Otto, "Things and Ideals," 214–15: Cf. Bridgman, "The Logic of Modern Physics"; Eddington, "The Nature of the Physical World." See Appendix III.

[7] Stefansson's "Standardization of Error" humorously depicts the layman's resentment at the instability of scientific truth.

See Appendix III for the distinction between science as method and science as results.

[8] Professor Jeremiah Smith says of legal maxims that "they are merely guide posts pointing to the right road, but not the road itself." 9 Harvard Law Review, 13, 23. For a similar point of view in medicine, see the writings of Dr. Crookshank referred to in Part Two, Chapter I.

[9] "Science and the Modern World," 282-3. Whitehead points out the reluctance even among scientists to recognize the implications of the new knowledge. See Appendix III.

See also Whyte, "Archimedes, or the Future of Physics" (especially 30, 52, 80) on the subtle effects in physics of the desire for a static world; Burtt, "The Metaphysical Foundations of Modern Physical Science." As to the popular attitude see Stefansson, loc. cit.

Interestingly enough, Whitehead finds that Roman law had much to do with the (perhaps now obsolescent) static philosophic view in modern physical science. It would be valuable, in this connection, to trace in turn the effect on Roman law of the absolute power of the Roman father, who was considered rather as "a judge than a tyrant, but still a judge, whose authority to enforce his judgment was unchallenged."

PART THREE, CHAPTER II

[1] See note, Part One, Chapter XIII, for Morris Cohen's comment on this aphorism.

[2] "Judges are apt to be naif, simple-minded men, and they need something of Mephistopheles. We too need education in the obvious—to learn to transcend our own convictions and to leave room for much that we hold dear to be done away with short of revolution by the orderly change of law."

[3] Compare the language from Demogue, quoted above, to the effect that European law at times lacks "something of the philosophy of the 'strenuous life,' a philosophy more virile and less afraid of taking chances." The popularizer of the phrase the "strenuous life" was, of course, President Roosevelt, who appointed Holmes to the United States Supreme Court. Frankfurter (loc. cit., 128) quotes Roosevelt as inquiring, prior to the appointment, whether "Holmes was in entire sympathy with our views."

ADDENDA TO SECOND PRINTING

1. Concerning Partial Explanations

As partly explained above (Part One, Chapter XV), tentative thinking is not easy. Wherefore, a deliberately partial explanation—in which a fraction is substituted for the whole with complete awareness of the distortion—is frequently treated by readers as if it were meant to be a complete explanation.

For instance, when Weber called attention to the effect of Calvinistic theology on the rise of modern capitalism, he carefully noted, again and again, that he fully recognized the presence of indispensable economic factors. But most of his critics ignored these cautions and charged him with making the absurd contention that Calvinism was the sole explanation of contemporary capitalism. There are many explanations of such behavior of his critics. In part it would seem to be explicable thus: They were annoyed because Weber was complicating the subject, depriving them of the right to think solely in terms of economics. *So they misread what he wrote and disposed of him by ascribing to him an impossible thesis.*

A writer who presents a partial explanation as if it were complete might be said—if one were to use a partial explanation of his conduct—to be emotionally childish. And, in like manner, the same might be said of the critics who ignore a writer's insistence that his explanation is partial.

2. The "Conceptual" Nature of Psychological
Explanations

The important difference between "hypotheses" and "fictions" (Appendix VII) is often overlooked in thinking about psychology. In variant but related terms this distinction has been admirably phrased by Bernard Hart.[1]

"The behaviour of living organisms has been attacked by several branches of science, each regarding the phenomena from its own standpoint, and interpreting them in terms of its own concepts. Biology, for example, interprets the phenomena in terms of life processes and biological laws; physiology in terms of nervous energy, reflex action, and so forth; chemistry in terms of the interaction of chemical compounds. The essential point which it is desired to emphasize is that there is not one science of living organisms, but a number of different methods of approach, each striving to deal with the phenomena by the aid of its own concepts, and measuring its success solely by the extent to which it achieves the explanation and the control of those phenomena. Psychology has established its claim to rank among these methods of approach, and to attempt an explanation of the phenomena by psychological conceptions, just as chemistry has a right to attempt an explanation by chemical conceptions. Each of these various and more or less independent methods of approach endeavours to attack as much of the field as it can, but it is found that while some of the phenomena are capable of explanation by the concepts of more than one branch of science, some can be more intelligibly and usefully explained by the concepts of one branch rather than by those of another, and some are at present capable of explanation by the concepts of one branch only. When the concepts of one branch are less comprehensive and widely applicable than those of

[1] "Psychopathology."

another, there is always a hope that the former will ulti-
nately be reduced to the latter. For example, we may
reasonably anticipate that the concepts of nervous energy
and reflex action will ultimately be reduced to the concepts of chemistry and physics. But such a reduction is
mostly a goal of the future, and for the present each
branch must be content to explain whatever phenomena
it can in terms of its own concepts. . . .

"There are many phenomena for which at the present
time no other science than psychology can devise a feasible explanation, and many others in which psychological
conceptions are more illuminating and helpful than
physiological. . . . It is not that a psychological explanation is right and a physiological explanation wrong, it is
merely that in certain spheres it is more profitable to
employ a psychological than a physiological conception.
Similarly, if we talk of a disorder as psychogenic it does
not mean that no physiological, chemical, or physical explanation will ultimately be possible, but only that without
existing knowledge a psychological explanation is more
useful. In other words, a psychological conception of a
disorder may enable us to understand and treat our
patients, and if it does so it is sound science and sound
medicine, far sounder than the construction of a quasi-
physiological hypothesis built altogether in the air, without
relation to any observed facts, and with which it is possible
to accomplish nothing. . . .

"The conception of the unconscious has been subjected
to much adverse criticism. It is said that it involves a
contradiction in terms, as consciousness is the essential
character of mental processes, and an unconscious mental
process therefore an absurdity; that the processes in question are not psychological at all, but physiological, and
that they should be conceived not in terms of consciousness, but in terms of brain. These criticisms arise from a
confusion of thought. *The unconscious is not a phenomenal reality, but a concept fashioned in order to explain*

the phenomenal reality. The phenomenal reality, consciousness, obviously forms a disconnected series and, if the psychologist is compelled to take only this into account, he cannot rise beyond the level of a mere description of psychic phenomena. To obtain understanding and continuity it is necessary to go beyond the phenomena and to construct an explanatory concept. The physiologist has of course a perfect right to construct for this purpose a concept in terms of brain, but he cannot deny to the psychologist an equal right to construct a concept in psychological terms. The question is not whether one is correct and the other incorrect, but which one works the best in the present state of our knowledge. So far as the phenomena which Freud seeks to explain are concerned the physiologist cannot yet give an explanation which consists of more than words, and the fact that these words indicate hypothetical material processes rather than hypothetical psychical processes is an inadequate consolation for his entire inability to make any use of the conceptions he fashions. The psychologist is therefore perfectly justified in attempting to find an explanation by the construction of a psychological conception, at any rate until the physiologist can provide one which is practically more useful, and such a conception must involve the assumption of an unconscious in one form or another. If consciousness is defined as the essential attribute of mental processes, then of course the unconscious becomes a contradiction in terms, but as the question is already begged by accepting the definition this is not of much moment. We saw, when discussing Janet's conception of the subconscious, that there is convincing proof that mental processes exist which are not personally conscious, and such processes are unconscious from the standpoint of the personal consciousness. It may be added that, *even if the notion of the unconscious were contradicted by our experience of phenomenal reality this would not necessarily preclude it from ranking as a scientific concept, because a concept is a constructed and not a phenomenal entity. An unconscious mental process, for example, would not be more absurd than a weightless and frictionless ether.* Criticisms directed against the unconscious as a possible conception do not carry much weight, therefore, and we have seen that a conception of this kind is necessary if the psychologist is to be allowed to explain the phenomena of consciousness in psychological terms. . . .

"The unconscious of Freud is a conception of an altogether different kind. Here *we are no longer on the phenomenal plane, we have moved to the conceptual. Unconscious processes are not phenomenal facts, they are concepts, constructions devised to explain certain phenomena; they have not been found, they have been made.* The implicit assumptions underlying Freud's doctrine may be expressed in this way. Certain entities are imagined which may be described as unconscious psychical factors; certain properties are attached to these factors and they are conceived to act and interact according to certain laws. If it is then found that the results deduced from these formulae correspond to the phenomena actually observed in our experience, and that the correspondence is maintained in all the tests and experiments which can be devised, the formulae may be justifiably incorporated into valid scientific theory.

"This train of thought is the analogue of that underlying all the great conceptual constructions of physics and chemistry—the atomic theory, and the theory of the ether and its waves. Here, as in these other instances, its validity must be determined by its ability to satisfy the tests of experiment and experience demanded by the method of science."

The whole field of psychology is still in its early stages. To the nascent science of psychology, Freud and his followers have made invaluable pioneer contributions. Inevitably they have made false steps and have exaggerated the value of some of their suggestions. They have not always been sufficiently aware of the "fictional" nature of their formulations. But in rejecting the exaggerated statements of some psychoanalysts and in denying a papal infallibility to their leader (which he would be the first to disavow), it is unwise not to recognize as vastly illuminating many of their contributions and especially their emphasis on the social significance of the family pattern and its ramifications.

Their concepts are still roughly made and doubtless will be modified markedly as work in psychology progresses. Many of these concepts are at times used too elliptically and, we repeat, with too little acknowledgment of their "as if" nature. Such a phrase as "nostalgia for uterine security" is metaphorical and might well be expanded in the interest of greater adequacy as metaphor or fiction ("as if" or "let's pretend"). Partial expansion, in brief outline, might run something like this: The wise psychologist has heeded the embryologist. He notes that life does not begin with birth. (The lawyers have been wise on that subject for years with their doctrine of *en ventre sa mère*.) Birth does not begin life. Birth is a life-crisis. The child has already been conditioned in the months preceding his emergence into a troubling world from the almost perfect security he has been enjoying *en ventre sa mère*. Rignano has neatly described the tendency of any organism to retain or return to a stationary state. (See Appendix VIII.) There is a considerable amount of evidence that this tendency is operative in the new-born child. The family, to some extent, becomes a substitute for the almost perfect security which existed prior to birth, a refuge from the fears engendered by the distracting environment. The father in that respect plays an important part, etc., etc. There are several major crises in the life of the child. When a child becomes skeptical of his father's omniscience, one such crisis occurs, etc.

There are, of course, many, many other significant

factors in developmental psychology which can, and doubtless will, be employed to explain the legal certainty illusion. We chose to overemphasize one such factor because it had been ignored,—ignored by those interested in legal thinking. We chose it partly because we thought it desirable to call attention to the family relations as the child's pattern of all his future social relations. But we chose it especially because it served easily to illuminate the *emotional blocking* to straight thinking about "law." For that seemed to be the core of the problem of the search for legal certainty.

The peculiar characteristics of legal thinking demand an explanation which explains what it sets out to explain. If you say factor Y explains why the ablest lawyers when thinking about law (as distinguished from the ablest chemists when thinking about chemistry) think thus and so, your solution is inadequate if you do not show why Y is less operative among chemists than among lawyers. So "belated scholasticism" will not serve (see p. 74); or verbomania (p. 94). *For why are these factors relatively stronger in law-thinking than in chemistry-thinking?*

Why is absolutistic thinking so difficult to surmount in cerebration about law? Why is certainty-hunger peculiarly vigorous in lawyerdom? How are you going to make lawyers fiction-conscious, eager to think pragmatically, to use concepts operationally, instrumentally? How get them to see clearly what they are doing?

Bealism is stronger in our profession than Fundamentalism among the clergy. Legal realism is fighting nothing so easy to defeat as mere tradition. It is fighting fear,— fear of a very deep-seated character. There is, we repeat, *a strong emotional element* which fogs the minds of a brilliant profession, makes them use childish thought-ways in meeting adult problems. Our "as if" serves the purpose of revealing that element in several of its manifestations.[2]

[2] It also serves to make somewhat ludicrous a certain kind of pomposity in legal literature.

But, let it be said once more, ours is a *partial explanation*. In Appendix I are listed other explanations,[3] some of which the writer plans to expand in the near future.

3. The Difference between (*a*) What Exists or Can Exist and (*b*) What One Would Like to Have Exist

In this book we have sought to indicate that most specific decisions are not predictable and that there is little likelihood that they ever will be foretellable. The wise reader will not assume that we are therefore arguing that such legal uncertainty is, under all circumstances, desirable. If the writer could make a legal world to suit his wishes, it would contain more definiteness and less vagueness than that in which men now dwell and will probably always inhabit. (If his mere wishes were relevant, he would add that a moderate amount of uncertainty—to allow for growth and the needs of justice in specific cases—would always seem desirable.) But, to repeat, wishes impossible of realization are frivolous. Whatever one may want the legal world to be, it is and will almost surely be uncertain. *And ethical attitudes towards law must conform to possibilities and feasibilities.* "Oughts" must be based upon "ises" and "cans."

And so with respect to judicial discretion and individualization of cases. Judges today, in almost all cases, do exercise discretion and do individualize controversies (*i.e.,* decide with reference to the unique and often unmentioned facts of the particular case). The exercise of those powers is concealed by the traditional manner of writing briefs and judicial opinions. Improvement of the judicial

---

[3] There are doubtless others not there noted.

It should be obvious that, successfully to exploit any partial explanation (or "as if"), it is necessary to "keep a straight face," i.e., to write throughout as if one's "as if" or "let's pretend" were a complete explanation and "objectively true," while warning the reader in advance that the discourse is fictional.

process will be possible only if the unavoidability of discretion and individualization is accepted.

The question is not whether judges should exercise the powers of discretion and individualization. The only question is whether these powers are to be exercised consciously and skilfully.

But when we say that, we are not saying that we believe judges are or can or should be free-willed creatures. Their judgments are and always will be constrained and determined by innumerable factors.[4] Today those factors —economic and many others—are, to an unfortunately large extent, unconscious. Greater awareness of those factors will make it possible for sound intelligence to play a larger part in the process of judging.

That further observation and description of what induces decisions will make future decisions markedly more predictable seems to the writer most improbable. He inclines, tentatively, to the belief that more accurate description of the judicial process will serve to show that efforts to procure such predictability (via anthropology, economics, sociology, statistics, or otherwise) are doomed to failure.

[4] Among those factors are legal "rules." But they play a less important part than is conventionally supposed.

INDEX